General History of Africa · VII

Africa under Colonial Domination 1880–1935

Abridged Edition

The abridged edition of
THE UNESCO GENERAL HISTORY OF AFRICA
is published by the following publishers

In Ghana, Sierra Leone, the Gambia and Cameroon by
Ott–Attafua
P.O. Box 2692
Accra, Ghana
In Kenya by
Heinemann Kenya
P.O. Box 45314
Nairobi, Kenya
In Nigeria by
Heinemann Nigeria
P.O. Box 6205
Ibadan, Nigeria
In Tanzania by
Tanzania Publishing House
P.O. Box 2138
Dar es Salaam, Tanzania
In Uganda by
Uganda Bookshop Publishing
P.O. Box 7145
Kampala, Uganda
In Zambia by
Multimedia
Box 320199
Lusaka, Zambia
In Zimbabwe, Botswana, Swaziland and Malawi by
Baobab Books
P.O. Box 1559
Harare, Zimbabwe
**In the United States of America
and Canada by**
The University of California Press
2120 Berkeley Way
Berkeley, California 94720
**And in Britain, Europe
and the rest of the world by**
James Currey *Publishers*
54B Thornhill Square
Islington, London N1 1 BE
and
UNESCO
7 Place de Fontenoy, 75700, Paris

International Scientific Committee for the Drafting of a General History of Africa (UNESCO)

General History of Africa · VII

Africa under Colonial Domination 1880–1935

EDITOR A. ADU BOAHEN

Abridged Edition

JAMES CURREY · CALIFORNIA · UNESCO

First published 1990 by the
United Nations Educational, Scientific
and Cultural Organization
7 Place de Fontenoy, 75700, Paris

and

James Currey Ltd
54b Thornhill Square, Islington
London N1 1BE

First published 1990
in the United States of America by the
University of California Press
2120 Berkeley Way, Berkeley
California 94720, United States of America

ISBN (Unesco): 92-3-102499-X
    4   5   6   7   8   9   10

British Library Cataloguing in Publication Data
General history of Africa. - Abridged ed.
   7 : Africa under foreign domination, 1880–1935.
   1. Africa, history
   I. Boahen, A. Adu (Albert Adu), *1932-*   II. *Unesco,
   International Scientific Committee for the Drafting of a
   General History of Africa.*
   960

   ISBN 0-85255-097-9

Library of Congress Cataloging-in-Publication Data
Africa under colonial domination, 1880–1935 / editor, A. Adu Boahen. -
- Abridged ed.
      p.   cm. — (General history of Africa : 7)
   At head of title: International Scientific Committee for the Drafting of a
General History of Africa (UNESCO)
   Includes bibliographical references.
   ISBN 0-520-06702-9
   1. Africa—History—1884–1960. I. Boahen, A. Adu. II. Unesco.
International Scientific Committee for the Drafting of a General History of
Africa. III. Series: General history of Africa (Abridged version) ; 7.
DT20.G452   vol. 7
[DT29]
960 s—dc20   89-20397
[960.3'1]   CIP

Typeset in 11pt Bembo by Colset Pte Ltd
Printed in the United States of America

Contents

Preface

AMADOU-MAHTAR M'BOW
Former Director-General of Unesco (1974–1987)

For a long time, all kinds of myths and prejudices concealed the true history of Africa from the world at large. African societies were looked upon as societies that could have no history. In spite of important work done by such pioneers as Leo Frobenius, Maurice Delafosse and Arturo Labriola, as early as the first decades of this century, a great many non-African experts could not rid themselves of certain preconceptions and argued that the lack of written sources and documents made it impossible to engage in any scientific study of such societies.

Although the *Iliad* and *Odyssey* were rightly regarded as essential sources for the history of ancient Greece, African oral tradition, the collective memory of peoples that holds the thread of many events marking their lives, was rejected as worthless. In writing the history of a large part of Africa, the only sources used were from outside the continent, and the final product gave a picture not so much of the paths actually taken by the African peoples as of those that the authors thought they must have taken. Since the European Middle Ages were often used as a yardstick, modes of production, social relations and political institutions were visualized only by reference to the European past.

In fact, there was a refusal to see Africans as the creators of original cultures which flowered and survived over the centuries in patterns of their own making and which historians are unable to grasp unless they forgo their prejudices and rethink their approach.

Furthermore, the continent of Africa was hardly ever looked upon as a historical entity. On the contrary, emphasis was laid on everything likely to lend credence to the idea that a split had existed, from time immemorial, between a 'white Africa' and a 'black Africa', each unaware of the other's existence. The Sahara was often presented as an impenetrable space preventing any intermingling of ethnic groups and peoples or any exchange of goods, beliefs, customs and ideas between the societies that had grown up on either side of the desert. Hermetic frontiers were drawn between the civilizations of Ancient Egypt and Nubia and those of the peoples south of the Sahara.

It is true that the history of Africa north of the Sahara has been more closely linked with that of the Mediterranean basin than has the history of sub-Saharan Africa, but it is now widely recognized that the various civilizations of the African continent, for all their differing languages and cultures, represent, to a greater or lesser degree, the historical offshoots of a set of peoples and societies united by bonds centuries old.

Another phenomenon that did great disservice to the objective study of the African past was the appearance, with the slave trade and colonization, of racial stereotypes that bred contempt and lack of understanding and became so deep-rooted that they distorted even the basic concepts of historiography. From the time when the notions of 'white' and 'black' were used as generic labels by the colonialists, who were regarded as superior, the colonized Africans had to struggle against both economic and psychological enslavement. Africans were identifiable by the colour of their skin, they had become a kind of merchandise, they were earmarked for hard labour and eventually, in the minds of those dominating them, they came to symbolize an imaginary and allegedly inferior *Negro* race. This pattern of spurious identification relegated the history of the African peoples in many minds to the rank of ethno-history, in which appreciation of the historical and cultural facts was bound to be warped.

The situation has changed significantly since the end of the Second World War and in particular since the African countries became independent and began to take an active part in the life of the international community and in the mutual exchanges that are its *raison d'être*. An increasing number of historians have endeavoured to tackle the study of Africa with a more rigorous, objective and open-minded outlook by using – with all due precautions – actual African sources. In exercising their right to take the historical initiative, Africans themselves have felt a deep-seated need to re-establish the historical authenticity of their societies on solid foundations.

In this context, the importance of the eight-volume *General History of Africa*, which Unesco is publishing, speaks for itself.

The experts from many countries working on this project began by laying down the theoretical and methodological basis for the *History*. They have been at pains to call in question the over-simplifications arising from a linear and restrictive conception of world history and to re-establish the true facts wherever necessary and possible. They have endeavoured to highlight the historical data that give a clearer picture of the evolution of the different peoples of Africa in their specific socio-cultural setting.

To tackle this huge task, made all the more complex and difficult by the vast range of sources and the fact that documents were widely scattered, Unesco has had to proceed by stages. The first stage, from 1965 to 1969, was devoted to gathering documentation and planning the work. Operational assignments were conducted in the field and included campaigns to collect oral traditions, the creation of regional documentation centres for oral traditions, the collection of unpublished manuscripts in Arabic and Ajami (African languages written in Arabic script), the compilation of archival inventories and the preparation of a *Guide to the Sources of the History of Africa*, culled from the archives and libraries of the countries of Europe and later published in eleven volumes. In addition, meetings were organized to enable experts from Africa and other continents to discuss questions of methodology and lay down the broad lines for the project after careful examination of the available sources.

The second stage, which lasted from 1969 to 1971, was devoted to shaping the *History* and linking its different parts. The purpose of the international meetings of experts held in Paris in 1969 and Addis Ababa in 1970 was to study and define the problems involved in drafting and publishing the *History*; presentation in eight volumes, the principal edition in English, French and Arabic, translation into African languages such as Kiswahili, Hausa, Fulfulde, Yoruba or Lingala, prospective versions in German, Russian, Portuguese, Spanish and Chinese, as well as abridged editions designed for a wide African and international public.[1]

The third stage has involved actual drafting and publication. This began with the appointment of the 39-member International Scientific Committee, two-thirds African and one-third non-African, which assumes intellectual responsibility for the *History*.

The method used is interdisciplinary and is based on a multi-faceted approach and a wide variety of sources. The first among these is archaeology, which holds many of the keys to the history of African cultures and civilizations. Thanks to archaeology, it is now acknowledged that Africa was very probably the cradle of mankind and the scene – in the neolithic period – of one of the first technological revolutions in history. Archaeology has also shown that Egypt was the setting for one of the most brilliant ancient civilizations of the world. But another very important source is oral tradition, which, after being long despised, has now emerged as an invaluable instrument for discovering the history of Africa, making it possible to follow the movements of its different peoples in both space and time, to understand the African vision of the world from the inside and to grasp the original features of the values on which the cultures and institutions of the continent are based.

We are indebted to the International Scientific Committee in charge of this *General History of Africa*, and to its Rapporteur and the editors and authors of the various volumes and chapters, for having shed a new light on the African past in its authentic and all-encompassing form and for having avoided any dogmatism in the study of essential issues. Among these issues we might cite: the slave trade, that 'endlessly bleeding wound', which was responsible for one of the cruellest mass deportations in the history of mankind, which sapped the African continent of its life-blood while contributing significantly to the economic and commercial expansion of Europe; colonization, with all the effects it had on population, economics, psychology and culture; relations between Africa south of the Sahara and the Arab world; and, finally, the process of decolonization and nation-building which mobilized the intelligence and passion of people still alive and sometimes still active today. All these issues have been broached with a concern for honesty and rigour which is not the least of the *History*'s merits. By taking stock of our knowledge of Africa, putting forward a variety of view-points on African cultures and offering a new reading of history, the *History* has the signal advantage of showing up the light and shade and of openly portraying the differences of opinion that may exist between scholars.

By demonstrating the inadequacy of the methodological approaches which have long been used in research on Africa, this *History* calls for a new and careful study of the twofold problem areas of historiography and cultural identity, which are united by links of reciprocity. Like any historical work of value, the *History* paves the way for a great deal of further research on a variety of topics.

It is for this reason that the International Scientific Committee, in close collaboration

1. At the time of going to press Volumes I and II have been published in Arabic, Chinese, Italian, Korean, Portuguese and Spanish; Volume IV in Arabic, Spanish and Portuguese, and Volume VII in Spanish.

with Unesco, decided to embark on additional studies in an attempt to go deeper into a number of issues that will permit a clearer understanding of certain aspects of the African past. The findings being published in the series 'Unesco Studies and Documents – General History of Africa'[2] will prove a useful supplement to the *History*, as will the works planned on aspects of national or subregional history.

The *General History* sheds light both on the historical unity of Africa and also its relations with the other continents, particularly the Americas and the Caribbean. For a long time, the creative manifestations of the descendants of Africans in the Americas were lumped together by some historians as a heterogeneous collection of *Africanisms*. Needless to say, this is not the attitude of the authors of the *History*, in which the resistance of the slaves shipped to America, the constant and massive participation of the descendants of Africans in the struggles for the initial independence of America and in national liberation movements, are rightly perceived for what they were: vigorous assertions of identity, which helped forge the universal concept of mankind. Although the phenomenon may vary in different places, it is now quite clear that ways of feeling, thinking, dreaming and acting in certain nations of the western hemisphere have been marked by their African heritage. The cultural inheritance of Africa is visible everywhere, from the southern United States to northern Brazil, across the Caribbean and on the Pacific seaboard. In certain places it even underpins the cultural identity of some of the most important elements of the population.

The *History* also clearly brings out Africa's relations with southern Asia across the Indian Ocean and the African contributions to other civilizations through mutual exchanges.

I am convinced that the efforts of the peoples of Africa to conquer or strengthen their independence, secure their development and assert their cultural characteristics must be rooted in historical awareness renewed, keenly felt and taken up by each succeeding generation.

My own background, the experience I gained as a teacher and as chairman, from the early days of independence, of the first commission set up to reform history and geography curricula in some of the countries of West and Central Africa, taught me how necessary it was for the education of young people and for the information of the public at large to have a history book produced by scholars with inside knowledge of the problems and hopes of Africa and with the ability to apprehend the continent in its entirety.

For all these reasons, Unesco's goal will be to ensure that this *General History of Africa* is widely disseminated in a large number of languages and is used as a basis for producing children's books, school textbooks and radio and television programmes. Young people, whether schoolchildren or students, and adults in Africa and elsewhere will thus be able to form a truer picture of the African continent's past and the factors

---

2. The following eleven volumes have already been published in this series: *The peopling of ancient Egypt and the deciphering of Meroitic script; The African slave trade from the fifteenth to the nineteenth century; Historical relations across the Indian Ocean; The historiography of Southern Africa; The decolonization of Africa: Southern Africa and the Horn of Africa; African ethnonyms and toponyms; Historical and socio-cultural relations between black Africa and the Arab world from 1935 to the present; The methodology of contemporary African history; Africa and the Second World War; The educational process and historiography in Africa; Libya Antiqua.*

that explain it, as well as a fairer understanding of its cultural heritage and its contribution to the general progress of mankind. The *History* should thus contribute to improved international co-operation and stronger solidarity among peoples in their aspirations to justice, progress and peace. This is, at least, my most cherished hope.

It remains for me to express my deep gratitude to the members of the International Scientific Committee, the Rapporteur, the different volume editors, the authors and all those who have collaborated in this tremendous undertaking. The work they have accomplished and the contribution they have made plainly go to show how people from different backgrounds, but all imbued with the same spirit of goodwill and enthusiasm in the service of universal truth can, within the international framework provided by Unesco, bring to fruition a project of considerable scientific and cultural import. My thanks also go to the organizations and governments whose generosity has made it possible for Unesco to publish this *History* in different languages and thus ensure that it will have the worldwide impact it deserves and thereby serve the international community as a whole.

Description of the Project

B. A. OGOT[1]
President, International Scientific Committee for the
Drafting of a General History of Africa

The General Conference of Unesco at its 16th Session instructed the Director-General to undertake the drafting of a *General History of Africa*. The enormous task of implementing the project was entrusted to an International Scientific Committee which was established by the Executive Board in 1970. This Committee, under the Statutes adopted by the Executive Board of Unesco in 1971, is composed of thirty-nine members (two-thirds of whom are African and one-third non-African) serving in their personal capacity and appointed by the Director-General of Unesco for the duration of the Committee's mandate.

The first task of the Committee was to define the principal characteristics of the work. These were defined at the first session of the Committee as follows:

(a)   Although aiming at the highest possible scientific level, the history does not seek to be exhaustive and is a work of synthesis avoiding dogmatism. In many respects, it is a statement of problems showing the present state of knowledge and the main trends in research, and it does not hesitate to show divergencies of views where these exist. In this way, it prepares the ground for future work.

(b)   Africa is considered in this work as a totality. The aim is to show the historical relationships between the various parts of the continent, too frequently subdivided in works published to date. Africa's historical connections with the other continents receive due attention, these connections being analysed in terms of mutual exchanges and multilateral influences, bringing out, in its appropriate light, Africa's contribution to the history of mankind.

(c)   The *General History of Africa* is, in particular, a history of ideas and civilizations, societies and institutions. It is based on a wide variety of sources, including oral tradition and art forms.

(d)   The *History* is viewed essentially from the inside. Although a scholarly work, it is also, in large measure, a faithful reflection of the way in which African authors view their own civilization. While prepared in an international framework and drawing to the full on the present stock of scientific knowledge, it should also be a

---

1. During the Sixth Plenary Session of the International Scientific Committee for the Drafting of a General History of Africa (Brazzaville, August 1983), an election of the new Bureau was held and Professor Ogot was replaced by Professor Albert Adu Boahen.

vitally important element in the recognition of the African heritage and should bring out the factors making for unity in the continent. This effort to view things from within is the novel feature of the project and should, in addition to its scientific quality, give it great topical significance. By showing the true face of Africa, the *History* could, in an era absorbed in economic and technical struggles, offer a particular conception of human values.

The Committee has decided to present the work covering over three million years of African history in eight volumes, each containing about eight hundred pages of text with illustrations, photographs, maps and line drawings.

A chief editor, assisted if necessary by one or two assistant editors, is responsible for the preparation of each volume. The editors are elected by the Committee either from among its members or from outside by a two-thirds majority. They are responsible for preparing the volumes in accordance with the decisions and plans adopted by the Committee. On scientific matters, they are accountable to the Committee or, between two sessions of the Committee, to its Bureau for the contents of the volumes, the final version of the texts, the illustrations and, in general, for all scientific and technical aspects of the *History*. The Bureau ultimately approves the final manuscript. When it considers the manuscript ready for publication, it transmits it to the Director-General of Unesco. Thus the Committee, or the Bureau between committee sessions, remains fully in charge of the project.

Each volume consists of some thirty chapters. Each chapter is the work of a principal author assisted, if necessary, by one or two collaborators. The authors are selected by the Committee on the basis of their *curricula vitae*. Preference is given to African authors, provided they have requisite qualifications. Special effort is also made to ensure, as far as possible, that all regions of the continent, as well as other regions having historical or cultural ties with Africa, are equitably represented among the authors.

When the editor of a volume has approved texts of chapters, they are then sent to all members of the Committee for criticism. In addition, the text of the volume editor is submitted for examination to a Reading Committee, set up within the International Scientific Committee on the basis of the members' fields of competence. The Reading Committee analyses the chapters from the standpoint of both substance and form. The Bureau then gives final approval to the manuscripts.

Such a seemingly long and involved procedure has proved necessary, since it provides the best possible guarantee of the scientific objectivity of the *General History of Africa*. There have, in fact, been instances when the Bureau has rejected manuscripts or insisted on major revisions or even reassigned the drafting of a chapter to another author. Occasionally, specialists in a particular period of history or in a particular question are consulted to put the finishing touches to a volume.

The work will be published first in a hard-cover edition in English, French and Arabic, and later in paperback editions in the same languages. An abridged version in English and French will serve as a basis for translation into African languages. The Committee has chosen Kiswahili and Hausa as the first African languages into which the work will be translated.

Also, every effort will be made to ensure publication of the *General History of Africa* in other languages of wide international currency such as Chinese, Portuguese, Russian, German, Italian, Spanish, Japanese, etc.

It is thus evident that this is a gigantic task which constitutes an immense challenge to African historians and to the scholarly community at large, as well as to Unesco under whose auspices the work is being done. For the writing of a continental history of Africa, covering the last three million years, using the highest canons of scholarship and involving, as it must do, scholars drawn from diverse countries, cultures, ideologies and historical traditions, is surely a complex undertaking. It constitutes a continental, international and interdisciplinary project of great proportions.

In conclusion, I would like to underline the significance of this work for Africa and for the world. At a time when the peoples of Africa are striving towards unity and greater co-operation in shaping their individual destinies, a proper understanding of Africa's past, with an awareness of common ties among Africans and between Africa and other continents, should not only be a major contribution towards mutual under-standing among the people of the earth, but also a source of knowledge of a cultural heritage that belongs to all mankind.

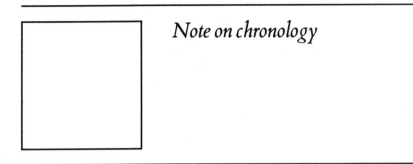

Note on chronology

It has been agreed to adopt the following method for writing dates. With regard to prehistory, dates may be written in two different ways.

One way is by reference to the present era, that is, dates BP (before present), the reference year being + 1950; all dates are negative in relation to + 1950.

The other way is by reference to the beginning of the Christian era. Dates are represented in relation to the Christian era by a simple + or − sign before the date. When referring to centuries, the terms BC and AD are replaced by 'before the Christian era' and 'of the Christian era'.

Some examples are as follows:

(i)   2300 BP   = − 350
(ii)   2900 BC   = − 2900
        AD 1800   = + 1800
(iii)   5th century BC = 5th century before the Christian era
        3rd century AD = 3rd century of the Christian era.

Members of the International Scientific Committee for the Drafting of a General History of Africa

The dates cited below refer to dates of membership.

Professor J. F. A. Ajayi
(Nigeria), from 1971
Editor Volume VI

Professor F. A. Albuquerque Mourao
(Brazil), from 1975

Professor A. Adu Boahen
(Ghana), from 1971
Editor Volume VII

H. E. Boubou Hama
(Niger), 1971–8 (resigned in 1978);
deceased 1982

Dr (Mrs) Mutumba M. Bull
(Zambia), from 1971

Professor D. Chanaiwa
(Zimbabwe), from 1975

Professor P. D. Curtin
(USA), from 1975

Professor J. Devisse
(France), from 1971

Professor M. Difuila
(Angola), from 1978

The late Professor Cheikh Anta Diop
(Senegal), 1971–86; deceased 1986

Professor H. Djait
(Tunisia), from 1975

Professor J. D. Fage
(UK), 1971–81 (resigned)

H. E. M. El Fasi
(Morocco), from 1971
Editor Volume III

Professor J. L. Franco
(Cuba), from 1971; deceased 1989

The late Mr M. H. I. Galaal
(Somalia), 1971–81; deceased 1981

Professor Dr V. L. Grottanelli
(Italy), from 1971

Professor E. Haberland
(Federal Republic of Germany),
from 1971

Dr Aklilu Habte
(Ethiopia), from 1971

H. E. A. Hampate Ba
(Mali), 1971–8 (resigned)

Dr I. S. El-Hareir
(Libya), from 1978

Dr I. Hrbek
(Czechoslovakia), from 1971
Assistant Editor Volume III

Dr (Mrs) A. Jones
(Liberia), from 1971

The late Abbé Alexis Kagame
(Rwanda), 1971–81; deceased 1981

Professor I. M. Kimambo
(Tanzania), from 1971

Professor J. Ki-Zerbo
(Burkina Faso) from 1971
Editor Volume I

Mr D. Laya
(Niger), from 1979

Dr A. Letnev
(USSR), from 1971

Dr G. Mokhtar
(Egypt), from 1971
Editor Volume II

Professor P. Mutibwa
(Uganda), from 1975

Professor D. T. Niane
(Senegal), from 1971
Editor Volume IV

Professor L. D. Ngcongco
(Botswana), from 1971

Professor T. Obenga
(People's Republic of the Congo),
from 1975

Professor B. A. Ogot
(Kenya), from 1971
Editor Volume V

Professor C. Ravoajanahary
(Madagascar), from 1971

The late Professor W. Rodney
(Guyana), 1979–80; deceased 1980

The late Professor M. Shibeika
(Sudan), 1971–80; deceased 1980

Professor Y. A. Talib
(Singapore), from 1975

The late Professor A. Teixeira da Mota
(Portugal), 1978–82; deceased 1982

Mgr T. Tshibangu
(Zaïre), from 1971

Professor J. Vansina
(Belgium), from 1971

The late Rt. Hon. Dr E. Williams
(Trinidad and Tobago), 1976–8; resigned
1978; deceased 1980

Professor A. A. Mazrui
(Kenya)
Editor Volume VIII,
not a member of the Committee

Professor C. Wondji
(Côte d'Ivoire)
Assistant Editor Volume VIII,
not a member of the Committee

*Secretariat of the International
Scientific Committee*
A. Gatera,
Division of Cultural Studies
and Policies
I, rue Miollis, 75015 Paris

Biographies
of the authors who contributed
to the main edition

*The abridged version was prepared from the texts
of the main version written
by the following authors*

CHAPTER 1   A. Adu Boahen (Ghana); specialist in West African colonial history; author of numerous publications and articles on African history; Professor and Head of the Department of History, University of Ghana.

CHAPTER 2   G. N. Uzoigwe (Nigeria); specialist in East African history, with emphasis on the former Bunyoro kingdom in Uganda; author of several works and articles on African history; Professor of History, the University of Michigan, Ann Arbor.

CHAPTER 3   T. O. Ranger (UK); specialist in African resistance and nationalist movements; author and editor of numerous works and articles in this field; former Professor of History of the Universities of Dar es Salaam and UCLA; Professor of Modern History, University of Manchester.

CHAPTER 4   H. A. Ibrahim (Sudan); specialist in the nineteenth- and twentieth-century history of Egypt and the Sudan; published several studies; Lecturer in History, the University of Khartoum.

Abbas I. Ali (Sudan); specialist in the nineteenth-century history of the Sudan and East African history; author of works and articles in these fields; former Head of the Department of History, the University of Khartoum; deceased.

CHAPTER 5   A. Laroui (Morocco); specialist in the history of the Maghrib; author of works and articles on the nineteenth-century history of North Africa; Professor of Modern and Contemporary History at the University of Rabat, Morocco.

CHAPTER 6   M. Gueye (Senegal); specialist in nineteenth- and twentieth-century West African history; author of several works on the slave trade and French colonization; Lecturer in History at the Faculté des Lettres, the University of Dakar, Senegal.

A. Adu Boahen.

CHAPTER 7   H. A. Mwanzi (Kenya); specialist in East African history; author of several works and articles, mainly on the Kipsigi of Kenya; Senior Lecturer in History, the University of Nairobi.

CHAPTER 8   A. Isaacman (USA); specialist in African history; author of several works and articles; Professor of History, the University of Minnesota.

J. Vansina (Belgium); specialist in African history; author of numerous works and articles on pre-colonial history of Africa; Professor of History, the University of Wisconsin, Madison.

CHAPTER 9   D. Chanaiwa (Zimbabwe); specialist in the eighteenth- and nineteenth-century history of Southern Africa; author of numerous works and articles on the history of Southern Africa; formerly Professor of History, California State University, Northridge; Director, Department of Employment and Employment Development, Harare.

CHAPTER 10   M. Esoavelomandroso (Madagascar); specialist in the eighteenth- and nineteenth-century history of Madagascar; Professor of History, Faculté des Lettres, the University of Antananarivo.

CHAPTER 11   M. B. Akpan (Nigeria); specialist in West African economic history; author of several works and articles on West African history; Senior Lecturer, the University of Calabar, Nigeria.

A. B. Jones (Liberia); historian and specialist in nineteenth-century West Africa; former Ambassador and Permanent Delegate of Liberia to the United Nations.

R. Pankhurst (UK), specialist in Ethiopian history; author of numerous works and articles on the history of Ethiopia; former Director of the Institute of Ethiopian Studies, the University of Addis Ababa.

CHAPTER 12   M. Crowder (UK); specialist in West African history; author of numerous works and articles on West African history; held professorship at various universities; editor of *History Today*; deceased.

CHAPTER 13   R. F. Betts (USA); specialist in nineteenth- and twentieth-century European colonialism in Africa; author of several works and articles on African history; Professor of History at the University of Kentucky.

A. I. Asiwaju (Nigeria); specialist in West African history; author of different works and articles on this region; Professor of History at the University of Lagos.

CHAPTER 14   W. Rodney (Guyana); specialist in West African economic history; author of several works and articles on West African slave trade; former Professor of History at the University of Dar es Salaam, Tanzania and the West Indies; deceased.

CHAPTER 15   C. Coquery-Vidrovitch (France); specialist in socio-economic history of Africa; has published several works and articles on the subject; at present Professor of History, Université de Paris VII.

CHAPTER 16   M. H. Y. Kaniki (Tanzania); specialist in West African economic history; has published several works and articles on the subject; formerly Associate Professor of History, University of Dar es Salaam; currently Professor of History, the University of Zambia, Lusaka.

CHAPTER 17   A. Kassab (Tunisia); specialist in economic geography; has published several studies related to this field; Chief Editor of *La Revue Tunisienne de Géographie*.

A. A. Abdussalam (Libya); specialist in Libyan economic history; author of several works on this subject; Assistant Professor of Economics, the University of Garyounis, Benghazi, Libya.

F. S. Abusedra (Egypt); specialist in economic history; Assistant Professor of Economics, the University of Garyounis, Benghazi, Libya.

CHAPTER 18   J. C. Caldwell (Australia); specialist in demography; author of several works on population in tropical Africa; Professor of Demography and Head of the Department of Demography, Research School of Social Sciences, Australian National University.

CHAPTER 19   A. E. Afigbo (Nigeria), specialist in West African history; author of several works and scientific articles on Nigerian history; former Director of the Institute of African Studies, the University of Nigeria (Nsukka).

CHAPTER 20   K. Asare Opoku (Ghana), specialist in African religions; author of several books and articles on various aspects of African religions; Senior Research Fellow in Religion and Ethics, Institute of African Studies, the University of Ghana.

CHAPTER 21   W. Soyinka (Nigeria); specialist in African drama, literature and philosophy; author of numerous works in this area; former Professor at the University of Legon, Ghana and currently Professor of Drama at the University of Ife; Nobel prize for literature.

CHAPTER 22   B. O. Oloruntimehin (Nigeria); specialist in former French West Africa since the nineteenth century; published a number of books and several articles related to this area; Professor of History, the University of Ife.

CHAPTER 23   H. A. Ibrahim.

CHAPTER 24   J. Berque (France); specialist in social history of contemporary Islam; author of several works on Egyptian and Maghrib history; formerly Professor at the Collège de France.

CHAPTER 25   A. Adu Boahen.

CHAPTER 26   E. S. Atieno-Odhiambo (Kenya); specialist in political history of East Africa; author of several works and articles on the rise of nationalism in East and Central Africa; Senior Lecturer in History, the University of Nairobi, Kenya.

CHAPTER 27   A. B. Davidson (USSR); specialist in African history; published a number of works on Africa; Professor at the Institute of General History, USSR Academy of Sciences, Moscow.

R. Pélissier (France); specialist in resistance movements in nineteenth- and twentieth-century African history; author of several works and articles; Researcher.

A. Isaacman.

CHAPTER 28   M. B. Akpan, A.B. Jones and R. Pankhurst.

CHAPTER 29   R. D. Ralston (USA); specialist in nineteenth- and twentieth-century African history; author of several articles on relationship between Africa and the New World; Assistant Professor of History, Afro-American Studies Department, the University of Wisconsin, Madison.

F. A. Alburquerque Mourão (Brazil); specialist in African history; author of several works and

	articles on Afro-Brazilian history; Professor of History and Director of the Centro de Estudos Africanos, the University of São Paulo, Brazil.
CHAPTER 30	A. Adu Boahen.
Editorial Assistant	Y. Kwarteng (Ghana); specialist in journalism and communication; his MA thesis is on 'The development of journalism in West Africa since 1957'.

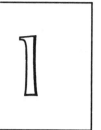

Africa
and the colonial challenge

Never in the history of Africa did so many changes occur and with such speed as they did between 1880 and 1935. As late as 1880, only very limited areas of Africa had come under the direct rule of Europeans and African rulers and lineage heads were in control of their independence and sovereignty (see 1.1). But by 1914, with the sole exception of Ethiopia and Liberia, the whole of Africa had been partitioned and occupied by the imperial powers of France, Britain, Germany, Portugal, Belgium, Spain and Italy and colonialism had been installed. In other words, then, during the period of 1880 to 1935, Africa did face a very serious challenge, the challenge of colonialism.

The state of African preparedness

What was the attitude of the Africans themselves to this establishment of colonialism, involving as it did such a fundamental change in the nature of the relationships that had existed between them and the Europeans over the preceding three hundred years? The answer is quite clear and unequivocal: an overwhelming majority of African authorities and leaders were vehemently opposed to this change and expressed their determination to maintain the status quo and, above all, to retain their sovereignty and independence. This answer can be documented from the very words of the contemporary African leaders themselves.

In 1891, when the British offered protection to Prempeh I of Asante in the Gold Coast (now Republic of Ghana), he replied:

> The suggestion that Asante in its present state should come and enjoy the protection of Her Majesty the Queen and Empress of India I may say is a matter of very serious consideration, and which I am happy to say we have arrived at this conclusion, that my kingdom of Asante will never commit itself to any such policy. Asante must remain as of old at the same time to remain friendly with all white men.

In 1895, Wobogo, the Moro Naba or King of the Mosi (in modern Burkina Faso) told the French Captain Destenave:

> I know the whites wish to kill me in order to take my country, and yet you claim that they will help me to organize my country. But I find my country good just as it is. I have no need of them. I know what is necessary for me and what I want: I have my own merchants: also, consider yourself fortunate that I do not order your head to be cut off. Go away now, and above all, never come back.

1

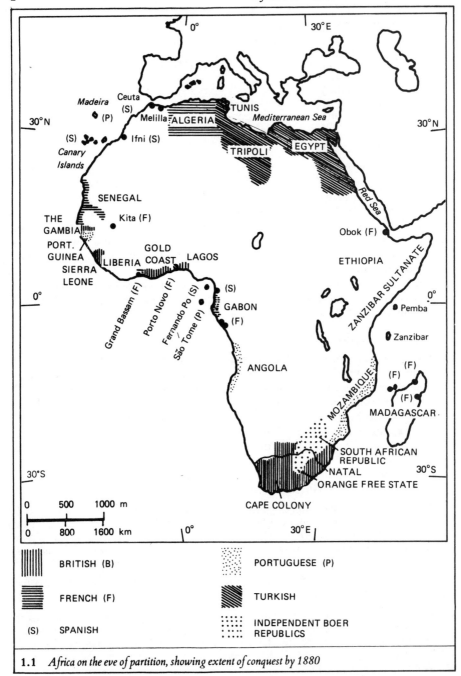

1.1   *Africa on the eve of partition, showing extent of conquest by 1880*

When the Italians launched their campaign against Ethiopia with the connivance of Britain and France, Menelik, the Emperor, issued a mobilization proclamation in September 1895 in which he stated:

> Enemies have now come upon us to ruin our country and to change our religion . . . Our enemies have begun the affair by advancing and digging into the country like moles. With the help of God I will not deliver up my country to them . . . Today, you who are strong, give me of your strength, and you who are weak, help me by prayer.

Similar sentiments were expressed by Lat Dior, the Damel of Cayor (in modern Senegal) in 1883, by King Machemba of the Yao in modern mainland Tanzania in 1890, and by Hendrik Witbooi, a king in South-West Africa.

These are the very words of the men who were facing the colonial challenge and they do prove beyond any doubt the strength of their determination to oppose the Europeans and to defend their sovereignty, religion and traditional way of life.

It is equally clear from all these quotations that these rulers were confident of their preparedness to face the European invaders, as well might they have been. First, they were fully confident that their magic, their ancestors and certainly their gods or god would come to their aid, and many of them on the eve of the actual physical confrontation resorted either to prayers or sacrifices or to herbs and incantations. As will be seen in many of the following chapters, religion was indeed one of the weapons used against colonialism. Moreover, many African rulers had been able to build empires of varying sizes only a couple of decades back, and some were still in the process of expanding or reviving their kingdoms. Many of them had been able to defend their sovereignty with the support of their people using traditional weapons and tactics. Some of them, like Samori Ture of the Mande empire in West Africa and Menelik of Ethiopia, had even been able to modernize their armies. From all this, the African rulers saw no reason why they could not maintain their sovereignty at that time. Furthermore, some thought they could stave off the invaders through diplomacy.

However, many African rulers did in fact welcome the new changes that were steadily being introduced from the third decade of the nineteenth century since these changes had hitherto posed no threat to their sovereignty and independence. In West Africa, for instance, thanks to the activities of the missionaries, Fourah Bay College had been founded as early as 1826, while elementary schools and a secondary school each in the Gold Coast and Nigeria had been established by the 1870s. Indeed, a call for the establishment of a university in West Africa by the Carribean-born pan-Africanist, Edward Wilmot Blyden, had already gone out. As early as 1887, some wealthy Africans had even begun to send their children to Europe for further education and professional training and some of them had returned home as fully qualified barristers and doctors.

Above all, following the abolition of the hideous and inhuman traffic in slaves, the Africans had been able to change over to an economy based on the exportation of cash crops – palm oil in Nigeria, groundnuts in Senegal and The Gambia, all before 1880 – and cocoa had just been reintroduced into the Gold Coast by Tetteh Quashie from Fernando Po in 1879. And all this had occurred without the establishment of any direct European rule except in small pockets on the coast. Indeed, the relatively small group of West Africans who had benefited from European-style education were, by

1880, doing extremely well. They were dominating the few civil service posts; on the coast, some of them were running their own import–export businesses and were monopolizing the internal distribution of imported goods. It was in East Africa that European influences were still minimal, although, after the epoch-making journeys of Livingstone and Stanley and the subsequent propaganda by missionary societies, it was only a matter of time before churches and schools, and with them roads and railways, would make their appearance.

As far as Africans were concerned, then, they did not see any need for any radical change in their centuries-old relations with Europe, and they were confident that, if the Europeans wanted to force any changes on them and push their way inland, they would be able to stop them as they had been able to do for the last two or three hundred years. Hence the note of confidence, if not of defiance, that rings through the words quoted above.

But what the Africans did not realize was that by 1880, thanks to the spread of the industrial revolution in Europe, and the subsequent technological progress signified by the steamship, the railway, the telegraph and, above all, the first machine gun – the Maxim gun – the Europeans whom they were about to face now had new political objectives and economic needs and a relatively advanced technology. That is, they did not know that the old era of free trade and informal political control had given way to, to borrow Basil Davidson's words, 'the era of the new imperialism and rival capitalist monopolies' and therefore that it was not only trade that the Europeans now wanted but also direct political control. Secondly, the African leaders were not aware of the fact that the guns that they had used hitherto and stockpiled, the muzzle-loading muskets – the French captured 21 365 muskets from the Baule of Côte d'Ivoire after the suppression of their revolt in 1911 – were totally outmoded and no match for those of the Europeans, the breech-loading rifles, which had about ten times the rate of fire at six times the charge, and the new ultra-rapid-fire Maxims. The English poet Hilaire Belloc summed up the situation aptly:

> Whatever happens we have got
> The Maxim gun and they have not.

It is here that African rulers miscalculated, and in many cases with tragic consequences. As will be seen later, all the chiefs quoted above, except one, were defeated and lost their sovereignty. Moreover, Lat Dior was killed, Prempeh, Behanzin and Cetshwayo of the Zulu were exiled and Lobengula of the Ndebele died in flight. Only Menelik, as will be seen in a later chapter, defeated the Italian invaders and thereby maintained his sovereignty and independence.

The structure of Volume VII

It is evident, then, that relations between Africans and Europeans did undergo a revolutionary change and Africa was faced with a serious colonial challenge between 1880 and 1935. What, then, were the origins of this phenomenal challenge, the challenge of colonialism? Or, put differently, how and why did the three-centuries-old relations between Africa and Europe undergo such drastic and fundamental change during this period? How was the colonial system established in Africa and what measures, political, economic, psychological and ideological, were adopted to buttress the system? How prepared was Africa to face and how did she face this challenge and with what success? Which of the new changes were accepted and which were rejected? What of the old was retained and what was destroyed? What adaptations and accommodations were made? What were the effects of all this on Africa, its peoples and their political, social and economic structures and institutions? Finally, what is the significance of colonialism for Africa and her history? These are the questions that this volume will attempt to answer.

For the purpose of answering these questions, and explaining African initiatives and responses in the face of the colonial challenge, this volume has been divided, apart from the first two chapters, into three main sections. Each section is preceded by a chapter (3, 13, 22) in which the theme of the section is surveyed in a general way and from a continental perspective, and the subsequent chapters are dealt with on a regional basis. The introductory section, comprising this and the next chapter, discusses African attitudes and preparedness on the eve of this fundamental change in the relations between Africa and the Europeans, and the reasons for the partition, conquest and occupation of Africa by the European imperial powers.

The second section deals with a theme that had, until the 1960s, either been grossly misrepresented or entirely ignored by the colonial school of African historiography, namely, African initiatives and reactions in the face of the conquest and occupation of Africa. To the members of this school, such as H. H. Johnston, Sir Alan Burns and, more recently, Margery Perham, Lewis H. Gann and Peter Duignan, Africans in fact welcomed the establishment of colonial rule since not only did it save them from anarchy and internecine warfare but it also brought them some concrete benefits. Thus Margery Perham:

> most of the tribes quickly accepted European rule as part of an irresistible order, one which brought many benefits, above all peace, and exciting novelties, railways and roads, lamps, bicycles, ploughs, new foods and crops, and all that could be acquired and experienced in town and city. For the ruling classes, traditional or created, it brought a new strength and security of status and new forms of wealth and power. For many years after annexation, though there was much bewilderment, revolts were very few, and there does not *appear* to have been much sense of indignity at being ruled.

Such ideas are also reflected in the use of such Eurocentric terms as 'pacification', *Pax Britannica* and *Pax Gallica*, used rather ironically to describe what amounted to the conquest and occupation of Africa between 1890 and 1914.

It is to correct this wrong interpretation of the colonial school and to redress the balance and highlight the African perspective that we have devoted as many as seven chapters to this theme of African initiatives and reactions.

It will be seen from these chapters that the view that Africans received the invading soldiers with elation and quickly accepted colonial rule is not borne out by the available evidence. In fact, African reactions were the very reverse. It is quite evident that Africans were faced with only two options, either to readily surrender their sovereignty and independence, or to defend them at all costs. It is most significant that the great majority of them, as will be amply demonstrated in this volume, irrespective of the political and the socio-economic structures of their states and in the face of all the odds against them, did decide to defend their sovereignty and independence. John D. Hargreaves poses this interesting question:

> [Given this] range of possible attitudes on the part of the European invaders, a number of options might be open to African rulers. Among the short-term advantages obtainable from treaties or from collaboration with Europeans were not merely access to fire-arms and consumer goods, but opportunities to enlist powerful allies in external or internal disputes. Why then did so many African states reject such opportunities, choosing to resist the Europeans in battle?

This may sound enigmatic, but only so to somebody looking at the whole issue from the Eurocentric point of view. To the African, the issue at stake was not short-term or long-term advantages but rather the fundamental question of his land and his sovereignty, and it is precisely because of this that virtually all African polities, centralized and non-centralized alike, sooner or later chose to maintain or defend or try to regain their sovereignty. To them, there could be no compromise on that, and indeed many of the leaders of these states chose to die on the battlefield, go into voluntary flight or face exile rather than surrender their sovereignty without a struggle.

A great majority of African rulers, then, did opt for the defence of their sovereignty and independence. It is in the strategies and the tactics that they adopted to achieve this universal objective that they differed. Most African rulers chose the strategy of confrontation, using either diplomatic or military weapons or both. As will be seen below, Samori Ture and Kabarega of Bunyoro resorted to both weapons while Prempeh I and Mwanga of Buganda relied on diplomacy. Others, such as Tofa of Porto Novo (in what is now Benin), chose the strategy of alliance or co-operation, *not* of collaboration.

This question of strategy should be highlighted here because it has been grossly misunderstood hitherto and this has led to the classification of some of the African rulers as collaborators and their action as that of collaboration. We are opposed to the use of this term collaboration not only because it is inaccurate but also because it is derogatory and Eurocentric. As we have seen above, the fundamental issue at stake between the 1880s and the 1900s, as far as the African rulers were concerned, was that of sovereignty, and, on this, it was quite clear that nobody was prepared to compromise. Those African rulers who have been mistakenly termed collaborators were those who thought that the best way of safeguarding their sovereignty or even regaining the sovereignty that they might have lost to some African power previous to the arrival of the Europeans was *not* to collaborate but rather to *ally* with the European invaders.

However, whatever strategy the Africans adopted, all of them – with the sole exception of the Liberians and Ethiopians – failed, for reasons that will be discussed below, to maintain their sovereignty, and by the beginning of the First World War, the cut-off date for the first section of this volume, Africa had been subjected to colonial rule. How and why the Liberians and Ethiopians managed to survive in the face of this colonial onslaught is treated in Chapter 11.

What, then, did these colonial powers do with their new colonies in the political, social and economic fields after the interlude of the First World War? It is this question which is answered in the second section of this volume. Here, since the various political mechanisms devised for the administration of their colonies, and the ideologies behind them, are well covered in many of the existing works surveying colonialism in Africa, only a single chapter has been devoted to this theme. Instead, much more attention is given to the economic and social aspects of the colonial system and its impact on Africa so as to redress the balance. It will be seen from these chapters that the period after the First World War and up to 1935, the period which has been described by some recent historians as the high noon of colonialism, did see the building of an infrastructure of roads and railways and the introduction of some social changes, such as primary and secondary schools. However, the colonial rulers had one principal end in view, namely, the ruthless exploitation of the resources of Africa for the sole benefit of the colonial powers and their mercantile, mining and financial companies in the metropolitan countries. One of the chapters in this section to which particular attention should be drawn is the one dealing with the demographic aspects of colonial rule, a theme which is not normally found in existing surveys of colonialism in Africa.

What were African initiatives and reactions in the face of this consolidation of colonialism and the exploitation of their continent? This is the question which is answered in the third section of this volume and a great deal of attention is paid to this question in conformity with the philosophy underlying this work, that is, to view the story from an African standpoint and to highlight African initiatives and reactions. African attitudes in this period were certainly not characterized by indifference or passivity or ready acceptance. If the period has been described as the classic era of colonialism, it is also the classic era of the strategy of resistance or protest in Africa. As will be shown, both in the general survey and in the subsequent regional surveys, Africans did resort to a number of devices and measures – and indeed a whole variety of these were devised – to resist colonialism.

It should be emphasized that the objectives at this time were, with the exception of those of the North African leaders, not to overthrow the colonial system but rather to seek its amelioration and an accommodation within it. The main objectives were to render the colonial system less oppressive and less dehumanizing and to make it beneficial to the Africans as well as the Europeans. African leaders sought the correction of such specific measures and abuses as forced labour, high taxation, compulsory cultivation of crops, land alienation, pass laws, low prices of agricultural products and high prices of imported goods and racial discrimination and segregation, and to improve inadequate social facilities such as hospitals, pipe-borne water and schools.

These grievances against the colonial system were felt, it should be emphasized, among all classes of society, the educated as well as the illiterate and the urban as well as the rural dwellers, and generated a common consciousness among them as Africans and black men as opposed to their oppressors, the colonial rulers and the white men. It is during this period that we see the strengthening of African political nationalism, which had its beginnings immediately after the completion of the establishment of the colonial system in the 1910s.

The articulation of this feeling and the leadership of the movement, which during the period up to the 1910s was the responsibility of the traditional authorities and developed within the framework of the pre-colonial political structures, was now assumed by the new educated elite groups or members of the new middle class. Those new leaders were, rather paradoxically, the products of the very colonial system itself, created and sustained through the schools and the administrative, mining, financial and commercial institutions that it introduced. It is the concentration of the leadership of the nationalist and anti-colonialist activities in the hands of the educated Africans who lived mainly in the new urban centres which has led to the incorrect identification of African nationalism in the inter-war period exclusively with that class and its characterization as primarily an urban phenomenon.

Numerous groups and associations were formed for the articulation of these nationalist aspirations. As is evident in the chapters in this section, the strategies and tactics that were devised during this period in order to give expression to these aspirations were equally diverse. As B. O. Oloruntimehin and E. S. Atieno-Odhiambo (Chapters 22 and 26 below) have shown, these groups included youth associations, ethnic associations, old boys' associations, political parties, political movements of both a territorial and inter-territorial nature and inside as well as outside the continent, trade unions, literary clubs, civil servants' clubs, improvement associations and various religious sects or movements. Some of these had been formed in the period before the First World War but there is no doubt that they proliferated during the period under review, as the chapters show.

The weapons or tactics adopted during the period, unlike those of the pre-First World War period when rebellions and so-called riots were more prevalent, were petitions and delegations to the metropolitan and local governments, strikes, boycotts and, above all, the press and international congresses. The inter-war period was certainly the heyday of journalism in Africa in general and in West Africa in particular while pan-African congresses also became a typical feature of the anti-colonial movement. These congresses were calculated to give nationalist and anti-colonial movements in Africa an international flavour; they hoped to draw the attention of the metropolitan powers to events in the colonies, and it was for this reason that the pan-African congresses organized by the American black, Dr W. E. B. Du Bois, were held in Paris, London, Brussels and even Lisbon. This theme is taken up in greater detail in Chapter 29, which deals with the interactions between the blacks of Africa and the blacks of the diaspora in the Americas during the entire period under review.

However, despite the diversity of associations and the complexity of the tactics they developed, with the sole exception of Egypt, very little real impact had been made on the colonial system by the early 1930s. And when, in 1935, the imperial forces of Fascist Italy under Mussolini seized and occupied Ethiopia, one of the two remaining bastions of hope and the main symbol of Africa's future revival and regaining of sovereignty, it looked as if the continent of Africa was doomed to be for ever under the yoke of colonialism. But this was not to be. The resilience of African peoples, the occupation of Ethiopia itself, the intensification of African nationalism and anti-colonialist sentiment after the Second World War, coupled with the emergence of new mass political parties and a new radical leadership dedicated not to the amelioration but rather to the complete uprooting of colonialism – all these factors combined, as Volume VIII of this work will show, to bring about the liquidation of colonial domination from the continent at a rate as quick, and within about the same twenty-year period, as it took to establish it. However, between 1880 and 1935, colonialism appeared to be firmly imprinted on Africa. What marks, then, did it leave on Africa? This is the question that is answered in the last chapter of the volume.

2

European partition and conquest of Africa: an overview

Introduction: a generation of war and revolutionary change

The generation following 1880 witnessed one of the most significant historical movements of modern times. During this period, Africa, a continent of over 28 million square kilometres, was partitioned, conquered and occupied effectively by the industrialized nations of Europe. What is most remarkable about our period is the co-ordinated manner, speed and comparative ease – from the European point of view – with which this was accomplished. Nothing like it had happened before. What gave rise to such a phenomenon? In other words, why was Africa partitioned politically and systematically occupied in the period that it was? And why were Africans unable to keep their adversaries at bay?

The partition of Africa and the new imperialism: a review

Various theories regarding this crucial movement in African history have been advanced which may be conveniently categorized as economic, psychological, diplomatic and the African dimension.

The economic theory

The popularity of this theory has changed, like fashion, with the times. Before communism became a threat to the capitalist system of the West, no one seriously questioned the economic basis of imperial expansion. Its theoretical roots can be traced back to 1900 when the German Social Democrats placed the subject of *Weltpolitik*, that is, the policy of imperial expansion on a global scale, on the agenda of their annual party congress held at Mainz. It was here that Rosa Luxemburg first pointed out that imperialism was the final stage of capitalism. It was here also that George Ledebour noted that 'the central point of the *Weltpolitik*' was 'an upsurge of all capitalism towards a policy of plunder, which takes European and American capitalism into all parts of the world'. The classic and clearest statement of this theory, however, was provided by John Atkinson Hobson (1858–1940). He argued that over-production, surplus capital, and under-consumption in industrialized nations led them 'to place larger and larger portions of their economic resources outside the area of their present political domain, and to stimulate a policy of political expansion so as to take in new areas'.

Borrowing freely from the central arguments of the German Social Democrats as well as from those of Hobson, V. I. Lenin emphasized that the new imperialism was characterized by the transition of capitalism from a 'pre-monopolist' orientation 'in which free competition was predominant . . . to the stage of monopoly capitalism to finance capital' which '*is connected* with the intensification of the struggle for the partition of the world'. Just as competitive capitalism thrived on the export of commodities, so monopoly capitalism thrived on the export of capital derived from the huge profits amassed by the banks and industry. This development, according to Lenin, was the highest stage of capitalism. Following Luxemburg, and in opposition to Hobson, Lenin believed that capitalism was doomed to self-destruction because it would lead to war between the capitalists and the exploited nations, which the former would inevitably lose.

War, then, is the inevitable consequence of imperialism, and this would cause the violent death of capitalism. This rousing propaganda has been accepted by Marxist scholars and 'Third World' nationalists and radicals, as a matter of course. And, in alliance with radical western scholars, they portray imperialism and colonialism as the outcome of ruthless economic exploitation.

Although Hobson and Lenin were not particularly concerned with Africa, it is obvious that their analyses have fundamental implications for its partition. Consequently, a large army of non-Marxist scholars has, more or less, demolished the Marxist economic imperialism theory as it relates to Africa. But it is now clear from more serious investigations of African history in this period that imperialism was essentially economic in its fundamental impulses.

The psychological theories

These theories constitute what may be described as the non-human impulses towards imperial expansion and are usually classified as *social Darwinism*, *evangelical Christianity* and *social atavism*.

Social Darwinism
The appearance in November 1859 of Charles Darwin's *The Origin of Species by Means of Natural Selection or the Preservation of Favoured Races in the Struggle for Life* seemed to some to provide scientific backing for the belief in the superiority of the European race, a theme that has figured continuously, in various guises, in European writing since the seventeenth century. The later Darwinians, therefore, were elated to be able to justify the conquest of what they called 'subject races' or 'backward races' by the 'master race' as the inevitable process of 'natural selection' by which the stronger dominates the weaker in the struggle for economic existence. They preached, therefore, that might was right. The partition of Africa was consequently seen by them as part of this inevitable and natural process. The fact remains, however, that social Darwinism, applied to the conquest of Africa, was more a rationalization after the event than its cause.

Evangelical Christianity
Another theory that has been advanced for the partition of Africa has been evangelical Christianity. It has been argued that the partition of Africa was due, in no small measure, to a 'broader missionary' and humanitarian impulse which aimed at the westernization of African peoples. It has, indeed, been asserted specifically that it was the missionaries who prepared the ground for the imposition of colonialism on East and Central Africa as well as in Madagascar. Although it is true that missionaries did not resist the conquest of Africa, and that they did, in some areas, actively pursue that conquest, the missionary factor cannot be sustained as a general theory of imperialism because of its limited application.

Social atavism
It was Joseph Schumpeter who first explained the new imperialism in sociological terms. To him, imperialism was not the result of economic pressures, but rather of the natural desire of man to dominate his fellow man for the sake of dominating him, arising out man's universal thirst for power and domination. He argues even further that capitalism is, by its nature, 'anti-imperialistic' and benign. However, this theory is totally unconvincing.

It seems from the above that while the psychological theories may have an element of truth in them as an explanation of the partition, they do not explain why the partition occurred when it did. They do suggest, however, why it was possible and considered desirable.

The diplomatic theories

These constitute the purely political, and perhaps the most popular, explanations of the partition. But, in an interesting way, they provide specific and concrete backing for the psychological theories. These diplomatic theories are divided into three main categories, those of *national prestige*, *balance of power* and *global strategy*.

National prestige
The greatest exponent of this theory is Carlton Hayes. In a perceptive passage he contends:

> France sought compensation for European loss in overseas gain. England would offset her European isolation by enlarging and glorifying the British empire. Russia, halted in the Balkans, would turn anew to Asia, and Germany and Italy would show the world that the prestige they had won by might inside Europe they were entitled to enhance by imperial exploits outside.

Hayes concludes therefore that 'the new imperialism' was basically 'a nationalistic phenomenon' and not an economic one and that the new imperialists were after national prestige.

Balance of power

F. H. Hinsley, on the other hand, emphasizes Europe's need for peace and stability at home as the primary cause of the partition. According to him, the decisive date for the shift towards an extra-European age – an age of imperialism – was 1878. From that year, at the Congress of Berlin, Russian and British rivalries in the Balkans and the Ottoman Empire brought the nations of Europe to the very verge of war. European statesmen averted this crisis in power politics and drew back. Power politics from that point on to the Bosnian crisis of 1908 were removed from Europe and played out in Africa and Asia. When conflicting interests in Africa threatened to destroy European peace, the European powers had no choice but to carve up Africa in order to preserve the European diplomatic balance that had stabilized itself by the 1880s.

Global strategy

There is a third school, which maintains that the European interest in Africa which gave rise to the Scramble was a matter of global strategy, not economics. The foremost exponents of this view, Ronald Robinson and John Gallagher, who stress the strategic importance of Africa to India for Britain, blame the partition of Africa on the 'proto-nationalist' movements in Africa which threatened the global strategic interests of European nations. These 'romantic, reactionary struggles' compelled reluctant European statesmen, hitherto content to exercise informal control and moral suasion in Africa, to partition and conquer the continent. Africa was occupied, therefore, not because of what it could offer materially to the Europeans – for it was economically worthless – but because it was threatening European interests elsewhere.

Convincing as most of these diplomatic theories are, they do not refute the economic and some of the psychological theories but rather complement them. Hayes, for example, has documented in detail the tariff war which took place between the European nations during the crucial period of the partition. He even concedes that 'What actually started the economic push into the "Dark Continent" and the sun-baked islands of the Pacific was not so much an overproduction of factory goods in Europe as an under-supply of raw materials' and that therefore 'to prevent too much of the world from being . . . monopolized by France, Germany, Italy, or any other protectionist power, Great Britain moved mightily to gather the lion's share into her own free-trade empire'. In other words, neo-mercantilism, once established, had very important consequences for the emergence of imperial rivalries. And yet, on the very next page, Hayes sets out to argue confidently, as we have seen, against the economic underpinnings of the new imperialism. With respect to the global strategy thesis, informed reactions have been largely negative. Its attraction, however, for non-Africanist historians – or for the lay reader – has been simply overwhelming. Yet we know that this thesis is too neat and too circumstantial to be acceptable. It has been tested in West, Central, Southern and East Africa and found wanting. And, with respect to Egypt and North Africa, it has been shown that there were strong reasons unconnected with Britain's Indian imperial strategy necessitating a British presence.

The African dimension theory

There is yet another explanation of the partition drama, which is becoming increasingly popular since the work of Dike and more recently Hopkins. This explanation, unlike the previous ones, is African-orientated. Hopkins's conclusion is worth quoting:

> At one extreme it is possible to conceive of areas where the transition from the slave trade was made successfully, where incomes were maintained, and where internal tensions were controlled. In these cases an explanation of partition will need to emphasise external pressures, such as mercantile demands and Anglo-French rivalries. At the other extreme, it is possible to envisage cases where the indigenous rulers adopted reactionary attitudes, where attempts were made to maintain incomes by predatory means, and where internal conflicts were pronounced. In these cases an explanation of imperialism will need to place more weight on disintegrative forces on the African side of the frontier, though without neglecting external factors.

The most recent proponent, G. N. Uzoigwe, agrees with most of the views of members of this school. Like them, he explains the partition in both African and European terms, and therefore sees the African dimension theory as supplementing the Eurocentric theories already discussed. He sees the partition and conquest as the logical consequence of European nibbling at Africa which started well before the nineteenth century; but he accepts that the essentially economic impulse that necessitated that nibbling changed drastically during the last quarter of the nineteenth century; that the change was caused by the transition from slave to legitimate trade and the subsequent decline in both the export and the import trade during that period, and that it was this economic change in Africa and the consequent African resistance to increasing European influence that precipitated the actual military conquest. It would appear, indeed, that the African dimension theory provides a better rounded, more historically focused theory of the partition than any of the purely Eurocentric theories.

The beginnings of the Scramble

Although, by the end of the third quarter of the nineteenth century, the European powers of France, Britain, Portugal and Germany had acquired commercial interests and were exercising considerable influence in different parts of Africa, their direct political control there was extremely limited. Both Germany and, especially, Britain were able to wield all the influence they wanted, and no statesmen in their right senses would have freely elected to incur the costs and to court the unforeseen contingencies of formal annexation when they could derive the same advantages from informal control.

But this attitude began to change as a result of three major events which occurred between 1876 and 1880. The first was the new interest which the Duke of Brabant, crowned a constitutional king (Leopold I) of the Belgians in 1865, proclaimed in Africa. This was signified by the so-called Brussels Geographical Conference which he convened in 1876 and which resulted in the setting up of the African International Association and the employment of H. M. Stanley in 1879 to explore the Congos in the name of the Association.

The second significant series of events was the activities of Portugal from 1876 onwards. Piqued by the fact that it was invited to the Brussels conference only as an afterthought, Portugal sent out a flurry of expeditions which by 1880 had resulted in the annexation to the Portuguese crown of the practically independent estates of the Afro-Portuguese rulers in Mozambique. So far as the Portuguese and King Leopold were concerned, then, the Scramble was under way by 1876.

The third and final trigger which helped to set the partition in motion was undoubtedly the expansionist mood which characterized French colonial policy between 1879 and 1880. This was signified by her participation with Britain in the dual control of Egypt (1879), the beginning of the push eastwards in the Western Sudan in 1879, the dispatch of Savorgnan de Brazza into the Congo and the ratification of his treaties with Chief Makoko of the Bateke, and the revival of French colonial initiative in both Tunisia and Madagascar.

These moves on the part of these powers between 1876 and 1880 gave a clear indication that they were all now committed to colonial expansion and the establishment of formal control in Africa, and it was this that finally compelled both Britain and Germany to abandon their preference for informal control and influence in favour of a formal policy leading to their annexations in Southern, East and West Africa from the end of 1883 onwards.

It seems evident from the above, then, that it was not the British occupation of Egypt in 1882 that triggered off the Scramble, as has been argued by Robinson and Gallagher, but rather the events of the period 1876 to 1880 in different parts of Africa.

The Berlin conference, 1884–5

The idea of an international conference to settle the territorial disputes arising from European activities in the Congo region, first suggested by Portugal, was later taken up by Bismarck, who, after sounding the opinions of the other powers, was encouraged to bring it about. The conference was held at Berlin between 15 November 1884 and 26 February 1885. The news that such a conference was to be held increased the intensity of the Scramble.

It was not, ostensibly, the initial intention of the conference to attempt a general partition of Africa. It nevertheless ended up disposing of territory, passing resolutions dealing with the free navigation of the Niger, the Benue and their affluents; and laying down 'the rules to be observed in future with regard to the occupation of territory on the coasts of Africa'. According to Article 34 of the Berlin Act, the document signed by the participants in the conference, any European nation which, in the future, took possession of an African coast or declared a 'protectorate' there, had to notify such action to the signatory powers of the Berlin Act in order to have its claims ratified. This was the so-called doctrine of *spheres of influence*. Article 35 stipulated that an occupier of any such coastal possessions had also to demonstrate that it possessed sufficient 'authority' there 'to protect existing rights, and, as the case may be, freedom of trade and of transit under the conditions agreed upon'. This was the so-called doctrine of *effective occupation* that was to make the conquest of Africa such a murderous business. It should be emphasized that this conference did not begin the partition of Africa but merely laid down a few rules to govern a process already in motion.

Treaty-making 1885-1902

Prior to the Berlin Act, European powers had acquired spheres of influence in Africa in a variety of ways – through settlement, exploration, establishment of commercial posts, missionary settlements and occupation of strategic areas, and by making treaties with African rulers. Following the conference, influence by means of treaty became the most important method of effecting the paper partition of the continent. These treaties took two forms – those between Africans and Europeans, and bilateral agreements between the Europeans themselves. The African–European treaties were basically of two kinds. Firstly, there were the slave trade and the commercial treaties, friction arising from which had led to European political interference in African affairs. Secondly, there were the political treaties by which African rulers either purportedly surrendered sovereignty in return for protection or undertook not to enter into treaty obligations with other European nations. Typical examples of the latter treaties were those concluded between the Imperial British East Africa Company (IBEAC) and Kabaka Mwanga II of Buganda in December 1890 and March 1892.

The bilateral European partition treaties

While the treaties between the Africans and Europeans defined the latter's sphere of influence, the bilateral treaties, conventions and agreements between the Europeans practically concluded the paper partition of Africa by the end of the century. The Anglo-Germany delimitation treaty of 1 November 1886, for example, is particularly significant. It placed Zanzibar and most of its dependencies within Britain's sphere of influence; on the other hand, it assured Germany's political influence in East Africa, thus officially breaking Britain's monopoly there.

The Anglo-German Treaties of 1890 and 1893 and the Anglo-Italian Treaty of 1891, taken together, recognized the Upper Nile as falling within the British sphere of influence. To the south, the Franco-Portuguese Treaty (1886), the German-Portuguese Treaty (1886) and the Anglo-Portuguese Treaty (1891) recognized Portugal's influence in Angola and Mozambique as well as delimiting the British sphere in Central Africa. The Anglo–Congo Free State Treaty (1894) settled the limits of the Congo Free State. In West Africa, the most important arrangements were the Say–Barruwa Agreement (1890) and the Niger Convention (1898), by which Britain and France concluded the partition of that region. Finally, the Anglo-French Convention of 21 March 1899 settled the Egyptian question while the Peace of Vereeniging (1902) – which ended the Anglo-Boer war – confirmed, temporarily at any rate, British supremacy in South Africa.

Military conquest, 1885-1902

The paper partition of Africa was followed by military conquest and occupation in conformity with the doctrine of effective occupation. For whatever reason, the French were the most active in the pursuit of this policy of military conquest. Advancing from the upper to the lower Niger, they promptly defeated the Damel of Cayor, Lat Dior, who fought to the death in 1886; they beat Mamadou Lamine at the battle of Touba-

Kouta (1887), thus ending the Soninke empire he had founded in Senegambia; they succeeded in breaking the prolonged and celebrated resistance of the great Samori Ture when they finally captured him (1898) and exiled him to Gabon (1900); and by a series of victories – Koundian (1889), Segu (1890) and Youri (1891) – Major Louis Archinard brought to an end the Segu Tukuloor empire while the Battle at Kusseri (1900) destroyed Rabih's empire and led to the conquest of Chad. Elsewhere in West Africa, the French conquered the Côte d'Ivoire and the future French Guinea, where they set up colonies in 1893. And between 1890 and 1894 the conquest and occupation of the Kingdom of Dahomey was accomplished. By the late 1890s, the French had completed the conquest of Gabon, consolidated their position in North Africa, and completed the conquest of Madagascar (exiling Queen Ranavalona III and Prime Minister Rainilaiarivony to Algeria).

Britain's military imperialism was equally spectacular and bloody; African response, as will be seen in the following chapters, was also resolute and often prolonged. Operating from its coastal possessions on the Gold Coast (now Ghana) and in Nigeria, Britain effectively halted French expansion towards the lower Niger and into the Asante hinterland. The last Kumasi expedition (1900) was followed in 1901 by the annexation of Asante, and Nana Prempeh was exiled to the Seychelles. The Northern Territories to the north of Asante were also formally annexed in 1901, having been occupied between 1896 and 1898. From the Lagos colony, Britain launched its conquest of Nigeria. By 1893 most of Yorubaland had been proclaimed a protectorate; the conquest of Itsekiriland was accomplished in 1894. With one excuse or another, both Brass and Benin were conquered by the end of the century. By 1900, British supremacy in southern Nigeria was more or less assured. The effective occupation of Igboland and some other areas of the eastern hinterland, however, was not accomplished until the first two decades of this century. To the north, British conquest was accomplished from Nupe, where, by 1895, George Goldie's Royal Niger Company exercised influence from Lokoja to the sea. Ilorin was occupied in 1897; and the establishment of the West African Frontier Force in 1898 enabled Lugard to conquer the Sokoto sultanate by 1902.

In North Africa, Britain, already in a commanding position in Egypt, waited until 1896, when the reconquest of the Sudan was authorized. This was achieved in 1898 with savage and unnecessary bloodshed. Over 20 000 Sudanese, including their leader, Khalifa 'Abdallāh, died in battle.

Following the formal declaration of a protectorate over Zanzibar in November 1890, Britain used it as a base for the conquest of the rest of British East Africa. The major prize sought by Britain in this region was Uganda; the centre of operations was Buganda. The battle of Mengo (1892) led eventually to the formal declaration of the Uganda Protectorate (1894) and the rest of Uganda had been conquered by 1899 with the capture of King Kabarega and King Mwanga and their exile to the Seychelles in 1899. In Kenya, however, it took Britain some ten years before it established effective rule among the Nandi.

In Central and Southern Africa, Cecil Rhodes's British South Africa Company (BSAC) undertook the occupation of Mashonaland without Lobengula's sanction. In 1893 the king was forced to flee from his capital, and he died the following year. His kingdom was not conquered finally, however, until the bloody suppression of the

Ndebele–Mashona revolt of 1896–7. The conquest of what is now Zambia was less eventful and was completed in 1901.

The other European powers found effective occupation equally arduous. The Germans, for example, were able to establish their rule effectively in South-West Africa by the end of the century, primarily because of the more than one hundred years of hostility that had prevented the Nama and the Herero from working together. In Togoland, the Germans allied themselves with the small kingdoms of the Kotokoli and the Chakossi to facilitate the crushing of the resistance of the non-centralized Konkomba (1897–8) and Kabre (1890). In the Cameroon, the German commander, Major Hans Dominik, encountered the greatest difficulty in the north; but by 1902 he had managed to subdue the Fula principalities. The conquest of German East Africa, however, proved to be the fiercest and most prolonged of all these wars of effective occupation. It lasted from 1888 to 1907.

Portugal's military occupation of its territories, which started in the 1880s, was not completed until well into the twentieth century. For the proud but poor Portuguese, it was a particularly arduous enterprise but it nevertheless led eventually to the consolidation of Portuguese authority in Mozambique, Angola and Guinea (now Guinea-Bissau). The Congo Free State, too, faced very grave problems before it was able to accomplish a military occupation of its sphere of influence.

Italy fared worst in its wars of effective occupation. In 1883 it had managed to occupy a part of Eritrea. It also obtained the eastern coast of Somalia during the first partition of the Omani empire in 1886. But Italy's attempt to occupy Ethiopia ended in the ignominious defeat at Adowa (1896). It managed, nevertheless, to retain its portion of Eritrea and Somalia. In North Africa, it was not until 1911 that Italy was able to occupy the coastal areas of Cyrenaica and Tripolitania (now the Socialist People's Libyan Arab Jamahiriya). Morocco managed to preserve its independence until Spain and France ended it in 1912. By 1914, therefore, only Liberia and Ethiopia remained – at least nominally – independent.

Why were European powers able to conquer Africa?

European powers were able to conquer Africa with such relative ease because in virtually every respect the dice were so heavily loaded in their favour. In the first place, by 1880, thanks to the activities of European explorers and missionaries, Europeans knew far more about Africa and its interior – its physical appearance, terrain, economy and other resources and the strength and weakness of its states and societies – than Africans did about Europe.

Secondly, owing to the revolutionary changes in medical technology and in particular the discovery of the prophylactic use of quinine against malaria, Europeans became far less fearful of Africa than they had been before the middle of the nineteenth century.

Thirdly, as a result of the uneven nature of the trade between Europe and Africa up to the 1870s, and even after, as well as the increasing pace of the industrial revolution, the material and financial resources available to Europe were overwhelming in comparison with those of Africa. Thus, while European powers could afford to spend millions of

2.1–2.6 *Weapons used by Africans and their European opponents during the wars between 1880 and 1935*

2.1 *The Asante War of 1896 (Gold Coast): throwing axes and knives (Photo, National Army Museum, London)*

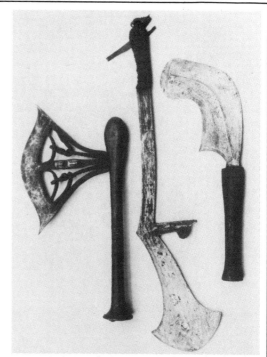

2.2 *Kavirondo warriors (Kenya) with spears and shields (Royal Commonwealth Society)*

2.3 *A nineteenth-century Yoruba (Nigeria) oba (king) with his generals armed with outmoded flintlock Dane guns (Longman)*

2.4 *Soldiers of the King's African Rifles with a Maxim gun (Imperial War Museum)*

2.5   *A Gatling gun (BBC Hulton Picture Library)*

2.6   *Aeroplanes used in the colonial wars of the 1920s (Harlingue-Viollet)*

pounds on overseas campaigns, African states were unable to sustain any protracted military invasion.

Fourthly, while the period after the Russo-Turkish war of 1877–8 was marked, according to J. Holland Rose, by 'a state of political equilibrium which made for peace and stagnation in Europe', the same period in Africa was marked by inter-state and intra-state conflict and rivalry – the Mande against the Tukuloor, the Asante against the Fante, the Baganda against the Banyoro, etc. Thus, while Europe could focus her attention militarily almost exclusively on her imperial activities overseas without any distraction at home, African states and countries had their attention divided. Moreover, not only did Europe enjoy peace at home, but the European powers involved in the partition displayed a remarkable spirit of solidarity which not only eliminated wars among them but also prevented the African rulers and communities from effectively playing one European power against the other. The African powers, on the other hand, never displayed any such solidarity, unity or co-operation and were therefore bound to be defeated.

The final and easily the most decisive factor was, of course, the overwhelming military and technological superiority that Europe enjoyed over Africa. While Europe was using professional and well-drilled armies, very few African states had established standing armies and fewer still had professional armies. Most African states recruited and mobilized individuals on an *ad hoc* basis for either defence or offence. Besides, in addition to their own armies, the European powers could always, as A. Isaacman and J. Vansina have contended, rely on African mercenaries and levies which gave them the numerical superiority they needed. Above all, by the terms of the Brussels Convention of 1890, the imperial powers agreed not to sell arms to Africans. This meant that most African armies were armed with their traditional weapons of bows, arrows, spears, etc., or completely outmoded, old and often unserviceable guns, mainly flint-locks or muzzle-loading muskets, and had no heavy artillery or naval power whatsoever. The European armies, on the other hand, were armed with the most up-to-date heavy artillery, and guns such as the repeater rifle and above all the Gatling and the Maxim guns. They also used the heavy artillery of naval forces. As Laroui has pointed out, even motor vehicles and aeroplanes were used in the later campaigns (see 2.6).

In view of these economic, political and above all military and technological advantages enjoyed by European powers over their African counterparts, the contest was a most uneven one and it is not at all surprising that the former could vanquish the latter with such relative ease. Indeed, for Europe, the timing of the conquest could not have been better; for Africa it could not have been worse.

The map of Africa after partition and occupation

The new geopolitical map of Africa that evolved after about a generation of systematic boundary-making and military occupation was quite different from what it had been in 1879 (see 2.7). The European powers had partitioned the continent into some forty political units. The new boundaries have been regarded by some scholars as unacceptable because they were deemed to be arbitrary and haphazard and to have distorted the national pre-European political order. Others, such as Joseph

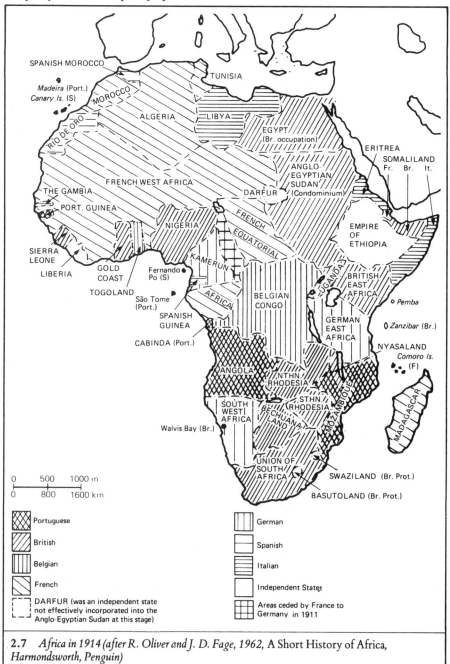

SPANISH MOROCCO

Madeira (Port.)
Canary Is. (S)

MOROCCO

TUNISIA

ALGERIA

RIO DE ORO

LIBYA

EGYPT
(Br. occupation)

ERITREA
SOMALILAND
Fr. Br. It.

ANGLO-
EGYPTIAN
SUDAN
(Condominium)

FRENCH WEST AFRICA

DARFUR

THE GAMBIA
PORT. GUINEA

NIGERIA

FRENCH

EQUATORIAL

EMPIRE
OF
ETHIOPIA

SIERRA
LEONE

LIBERIA

GOLD
COAST

TOGOLAND

Fernando
Po (S)

KAMERUN

AFRICA

UGANDA

BRITISH
EAST
AFRICA

o Pemba

São Tome
(Port.)

SPANISH
GUINEA

CABINDA (Port.)

BELGIAN
CONGO

GERMAN
EAST
AFRICA

0 Zanzibar (Br.)

NYASALAND

Comoro Is.
(F)

ANGOLA

NTHN.
RHODESIA

STHN.
RHODESIA

MOZAMBIQUE

MADAGASCAR

SOUTH
WEST
AFRICA

Walvis Bay (Br.)

BECHUANA-
LAND

UNION OF
SOUTH
AFRICA

SWAZILAND (Br. Prot.)

BASUTOLAND (Br. Prot.)

| 0 | 500 | 1000 m |
| 0 | 800 | 1600 km |

Portuguese

British

Belgian

French

DARFUR (was an independent state
not effectively incorporated into the
Anglo-Egyptian Sudan at this stage)

German

Spanish

Italian

Independent States

Areas ceded by France to
Germany in 1911

2.7 *Africa in 1914 (after R. Oliver and J. D. Fage, 1962,* A Short History of Africa, *Harmondsworth, Penguin)*

Anene and Saadia Touval, have regarded them as making more sense than they did by 1879.

There is some truth in both points of view. Some 30% of the total length of the borders were drawn as straight lines, and these and others often cut right across ethnic and linguistic boundaries. On the other hand, the remaining borders did follow natural boundaries and cannot therefore be considered to be as arbitrary or as ill-considered as the criticisms would suggest. Moreover, African political units, evolving as a result, for example, of the Oyo – Dahomey conflict, the Fulbe (Fulani) *djihāds*, or the Mfecane in Southern Africa during the second half of the nineteenth century, had very fluid boundaries and there is no doubt that the partition solidified these boundaries. On balance, then, although the map of Africa in 1914 (see 2.7), compared with what it was in 1879, may have looked very confusing, the delimitation had nevertheless been a remarkably efficient job, thanks to the new advances in cartography.

By 1902 the conquest of Africa was all but concluded. It had been a particularly bloody business. The devastating power of the Maxim gun and the superiority of European technology must have been a sobering experience for the Africans. But, though the conquest of Africa by Europe was accomplished with such relative ease, the occupation and the establishment of European administration in Africa – as the following chapters will demonstrate – were not.

African initiatives and resistance in the face of partition and conquest

The process of European conquest and occupation of tropical Africa between 1880 and 1900 could clearly not be reversed but it could certainly be resisted. It was irreversible because, as pointed out in Chapter 2, for the first time the whites had a decisive advantage in weapons, and for the first time the railway, the cable and the steamship provided them with some solution to the problem of communication within Africa and between Africa and Europe. It was resistible because of the size of Africa; because of the strengths of its peoples; and because in the event Europe did not send out many men or apply much technology. However, the Europeans were 'bound to win in the end', and after they had won they tidied up the untidy process. Books were written about what was called 'pacification'; the impression was given that most Africans had thankfully accepted the so-called *pax colonica*; and the facts of African resistance were glossed over. But the victory of the Europeans does not mean that African resistance was unimportant at the time or undeserving of study now. And in fact it has been studied a good deal in the last twenty years.

Most of this research of the last two decades has been sober, detailed and scholarly, not avoiding the ambiguities of many of the resistances. But most of it has been based upon, or used to demonstrate, three dogmatic assumptions, which are still essentially true, even though each has been modified by recent research and analysis. It has been argued, first, that the fact of African resistance is significant because it proves that Africans did not acquiesce placidly in the European partition and occupation. It has been argued, secondly, that this resistance was neither despairing nor irrational, but that it was often powered by rational and innovative ideologies. It has been argued, thirdly, that these resistances were not futile; that they had significant consequences in their time and still are of some interest today. These three arguments are worth restating here, together with the modifications proposed to them.

The generality of resistance

In 1965 the Soviet historian, A. B. Davidson, called upon scholars to refute the long cherished European view that Africans regarded 'the coming of the colonialists as good fortune; as deliverance from fratricidal wars, from the tyranny of neighbouring peoples, from epidemics and periodic starvations'; in which peoples who did not resist were described as 'peace-loving' and those who did resist were described as 'blood-thirsty'. Davidson remarked that 'protectors of colonial rule refused to consider rebellion a regular phenomenon.' They explained it in terms of 'primitive and irrational' responses, or in terms of the agitation of the 'blood-thirsty' minority. 'They rejected the only correct explanation which regards rebellions as just wars for liberation, which is why they were supported by the overwhelming majority of Africans.' Finally, he emphasized that 'many rebellions are not yet known . . . Often we do not have concrete information about those rebellions that are considered an established fact'.

Since Davidson wrote, the job of 'discovering' resistances has gone on apace. Historians have begun to classify revolts more rigorously, distinguishing 'social banditry' from 'peasant rebellion', and guerilla warfare from the clash of armies. In some cases, episodes described by the colonialists as rebellions have been shown to have been forced upon the people by white ignorance and fear. In many more cases, considerable and significant resistances have been made fully known for the first time. Detailed studies for most of the major uprisings are now available and in some cases a vigorous argument about how best to explain and interpret them has been taking place. From all this, it is quite clear that Davidson was right to think that resistance was a 'regular phenomenon'.

It is clear also that the old attempts to distinguish naturally warlike from naturally peaceful African societies are irrelevant. Research has shown that there were no so-called warlike, raiding states and so-called peaceful, trading and cultivating ones, since virtually all states had some crucial interests or values which they were prepared to defend, if necessary by armed resistance. The view that only large-scale African polities resisted while small-scale societies could neither resist nor exploit colonial rule has also been conclusively disproved. Shula Marks has shown in her study of Khoisan resistance in South Africa that non-centralized peoples are just as capable of putting up a determined fight against white advance as centralized ones. John Thornton has contrasted the resistance potential of states and of stateless societies much to the advantage of the latter.

In short, virtually every sort of African society resisted, and there was resistance in virtually every region of European advance. We can now accept this as a fact which no longer needs elaboration. What we need to do now is to move from cataloguing to interpretation, from merely demonstrating resistance to assessing and explaining its degrees of intensity.

The ideology of resistance

Colonial apologists stressed the irrationality and desperation of armed resistance. They claimed that it was often the result of 'superstition' and that peoples otherwise content to accept colonial rule had been worked upon by 'witch-doctors'. Many European critics of colonialism, sympathetic to African protest, nevertheless also accepted that Africans had little in their 'traditional' patterns of thought which helped them to come to an effective or practical response to attacks on their way of life. The ideologies of revolt were thought of as 'the magic of despair', bound to fail and incapable of pointing to the future. In such a view the resistances, however heroic, were tragic dead-ends.

Over the last two decades or so, historians of resistance have sought to challenge this sort of interpretation. They have done this in two ways, by showing that African resistance had its underlying ideology and by 'modifying' religious ideologies.

The chief secular ideology which has been proposed is the concept of 'sovereignty'. Jacob Ajayi has written that

> the most fundamental aspect of the European impact was the loss of sovereignty . . . Once people lose their sovereignty, and they are exposed to another culture, they lose at least a little of their self-confidence and self-respect; they lose their right of self-steering, their freedom of choice as to what to change in their own culture or what to copy or reject from the other culture.

A similar point is made with more emphasis by Walter Rodney:

> The decisiveness of the short period of colonialism . . . springs mainly from the fact that Africa lost power . . . The power to act independently is the guarantee to participate actively and *consciously* in history. To be colonized is to be removed from history . . . Overnight, African political states lost their power, independence and meaning'.

The idea of sovereignty clearly did provide an ideology for resistance. Nevertheless, important modifications must be made. Rulers were not always very clearly 'guardians of the sovereignty of the people'. In nineteenth-century Africa – in the west, east and south – new states had arisen. Such states often resisted the direct extension of European power but their resistance was undermined by the disaffection of many of their subjects. Such were the states of Samori Ture and Shehu Ahmadu and the 'secondary states' of the Zambezi valley.

States such as these may be contrasted with longer-established polities in which the rulers had achieved 'legitimacy'. But even here it would be over-romantic to suppose that all ancient ruling families enjoyed popular trust and support. The ruling groups among some long-established peoples exercised their power in an arbitrary manner, with the result that they could not count on popular support in a confrontation with the whites. This partly accounts for the ineffectiveness of resistance in Northern Rhodesia, where the Bemba chiefs faced what Henry S. Meebelo has called 'a popular revulsion against the ruling class', and where the aristocracy of Barotseland feared a slave uprising if they attempted to oppose the extension of British influence.

Even where a long-established polity enjoyed a leadership with recognized legitimacy and was able to mobilize the majority of its population into resistance, recent historians have been inclined to criticize the narrow, parochial and traditional nature of their concept of sovereignty. Such historians have emphasized instead the significance of those resistances in which the idea of sovereignty was redefined. Thus Allen Isaacman argues that, unlike previous resistances 'which were designed to regain the independence of a historical polity or a group of related peoples', the 1917 revolt in the Zambezi valley 'sought to liberate all the peoples of the Zambezi from colonial oppression', appealing especially to the oppressed peasantry of whatever ethnicity. This shift in objective represented 'a new level of political consciousness in which the Portuguese were perceived for the first time as the common oppressor'.

The role of religious ideas

Meanwhile historians have been re-examining the role of religious ideas in the resistances. What they have found is very different both from the 'fanatical witch-doctors' of colonial reports and from 'the magic of despair'. They have found, to begin with, that religious teachings and symbols often bore very directly on the question of sovereignty and legitimacy. Rulers were legitimized through ritual recognition, and when a ruler and his people determined to defend their sovereignty they naturally drew heavily on religious symbols and ideas. It was out of crises of legitimacy of this sort that the great movements which attempted to redefine sovereignty often emerged. Such movements almost invariably had the advantage of spiritual leaders, preaching the message of wider unity. Sometimes this sort of development took place in the context of Islam, sometimes it happened because of the influence of Christian ideas, and very often it happened in the context of African religion. This happened in Southern Rhodesia, where the risings of 1896 were inspired and co-ordinated by religious leaders. Isaacman argues that the 1917 rising in the Zambezi valley was given moral fervour by the teachings of the spirit medium, Mbuya, who did not call for the restoration of her own Barue state but preached instead the gospel of the brotherhood and oppression of all Africans.

The prophetic teaching which underlay some of the great resistances is slowly being rescued from the garbled accounts of their opponents. Gilbert Gwassa's account of the development and character of Kinjikitile's Maji Maji ideology is a classic example of this sort of rescue work. Another striking reconstruction has been made by Mongameli Mabona for the teachings of the great militant Xhosa prophet, Makana, in which he has shown that they were not a bunch of 'incompatible or unrelated religious concepts' but rather 'a skilfully tailored pattern of Khoisan, Xhosa and Christian elements', put together with very great creative imagination. In some ways Makana's teaching was an African version of the Protestant Christian ideology of sovereignty. He appealed for pan-Xhosa unity and for confidence in their moral universe. Dali'dephu, the great ancestor of the Xhosa, would sweep the whites away; the Xhosa dead would return; a new era would begin.

So far from being desperate nonsense, prophetic messages of this kind were a systematic attempt to widen and redefine the idea of deity and its relation to the moral order, and involved wide-ranging changes in Xhosa internal assumptions and relationships as well as providing the 'bedrock of ideology for resistance'. Peter Rigby has argued strongly that African prophetism was not merely the result of exogenous forces of disruption during the colonial period or of the breakdown of African religions but rather of the viability and adaptability of African religions. With this view of African religious systems regularly able to throw up prophetic leadership out of their own tensions and potentialities, and of prophetic leaders able to create new syntheses which simultaneously strengthened the old and allowed for the new, we have moved a long way from the idea of prophetic ideologies of resistance as 'the magic of despair'.

Valuable as all this work has been, the emphasis upon religious ideology in resistance has been challenged from two sides. On the one hand some scholars argue that the role of religion in resistance has been overstated; on the other hand some scholars argue that the role of resistance in religion has been exaggerated.

Thus colonial writers spoke of the female leader of the rising of the Giriama in the coastal hinterland of Kenya as a 'witch'; more recent historians have reinterpreted her as a 'prophetess'. But Cynthia Brantley Smith, in her admirable and exhaustive account of the Giriama, establishes that she was no sort of religious leader: merely a respected and assertive woman. This is a case in which a retranslation of colonialist terms like 'witch' and 'witch-doctor' is not enough to correct the distortion of official accounts. It has been suggested by two researchers on Ndebele and Shona history, David Beach and Julian Cobbing, that the same is true of Ranger's account of the 1896 risings in Southern Rhodesia, that the spirit mediums were of much more restricted influence than he allowed and that the priests of Mwari participated in the risings hardly at all.

All this is relevant to the argument over the centrality of protest to prophetic movements. A prophet emerges in response to a popular sense that there is need for new and radical action, but such a popular sense need not arise only because of external threat. A prophet can be thrown up because of deep anxiety over internal tensions or transformations, or even because of a general desire to accelerate the pace of change and to seize on new opportunities. Thus a prophetic leader often directs his teaching to the internal morality of African societies – sometimes leading a protest movement against internal authoritarianism, sometimes 'protesting' more against the facts of human nature. It emerges clearly from the work that is now being done on the remarkable number of prophetic leaders in nineteenth-century Africa that many of them were not concerned with resistance to the whites, or even directly with the whites at all.

Even those prophetic leaders who were primarily concerned to define the relations of their people to the Europeans were by no means unanimous in recommending rejection or resistance. As Mabona remarks, Xhosa prophetism produced both an 'ideology for resistance' and an ideology 'for a process of controlled accommodation'. The prophet of resistance was Makana; the prophet of 'controlled accommodation' was Ntsikana.

Though no other case presents us with so dramatic and direct a prophetic clash as the debate between Makana and Ntsikana, the same range of prophetic possibilities comes out clearly even in areas of very determined resistance, like the areas in which Maji Maji took place, or the Shona areas of Southern Rhodesia (now Zimbabwe). After the defeat of Maji Maji the cluster of symbols and claims to spiritual power which Kinjikitile had made use of was drawn upon by a succession of prophetic figures who were concerned with the internal purification of African societies, and who led what has been called 'witchcraft eradication movements'.

As for the Shona, Elleck Mashingaidze has written a fascinating paper on the sequence of prophetic advice given to the Shona people of the Mazoe valley area. The most influential mediums first advised the people to listen carefully to missionary teaching; then advised them to take part in the risings and drive out the whites; and then advised them once more to send their children to mission schools to gain what they could of white 'wisdom'. Mashingaidze does not see this as a sequence of confusion or betrayal, but rather as a reminder that there was still room for accepting or rejecting certain aspects of the new order by using traditional religion. Indeed, Professor B. A. Ogot has taken issue with those who interpret Kenyan prophetic movements as essentially anti-colonial. He writes of one such prophet, Simeo Ondeto, that he was indeed 'revolutionary' but that his revolution was in the moral rather than the political sphere and was to take place within the individual. The essence of prophetic movements, writes Ogot, is that they are 'transforming spiritual and social agencies creating new communities capable of facing the challenges of the modern world'. The great prophetic ideologies of resistance thus fall into place as part of a larger attempt to redefine the moral basis of society.

The consequences and relevance of African resistance

Up to about twenty years ago it was generally accepted that resistances led nowhere. Since then it has been strongly argued that resistances looked in all kinds of ways to the future. In so far as they were concerned with sovereignty they can be seen as anticipating the recovery of sovereignty and the triumphs of African nationalism; in so far as they possessed prophetic ideologies they can be seen as contributing to new communities of concept. Some of them resulted in improving the position of the peoples who had revolted. Others threw up an alternative leadership to the officially recognized chiefs. Ranger has argued that the resistances were 'connected' to mass nationalism by virtue of having been movements of mass commitment; by means of a continuity of atmosphere and symbol which ran through other mass movements in the intermediary period; and finally by reason of the explicit inspiration which the nationalist movements drew from the memory of the heroic past.

These arguments have been developed by other writers and the contemporary relevance of the resistances became an axiom of nationalist and guerilla theorists. Thus Walter Rodney, at the end of his examination of the Ovimbundu resistance to the Portuguese, wrote:

> Angolan freedom fighters themselves affirm a connexion between their wars of national liberation and previous resistances, and that (on their authority) the mass of the people are said to recall positively the spirit of such events as the Bailundu war. Idle academicians are in no position to challenge this.

Academicians – whether idle or not – *have* challenged the postulated connection between the resistances and the subsequent freedom struggle. Such challenges have come both from 'right' and from the 'left'. Writing from a position somewhere on the 'right', Henri Brunschwig has denied that there is any clear line of descent from the resistances to modern nationalist movements. Writing from the 'left', a number of other historians, such as Steinhart, have challenged the postulated link between resistance and nationalism on the grounds that this is an intellectual device to allow the ruling, and sometimes selfish, minorities of the new states to claim revolutionary legitimacy.

A later full-length study of resistance – Isaacman's book on African revolt in the Zambezi valley – implicitly seeks to deal with both Brunschwig's and Steinhart's objections. Isaacman deals with Brunschwig by placing his emphasis not on the 'parochialisms' of ethnic revolts but on the redefinitions of sovereignty which he claims to have taken place in the 1917 rising. He deals with Steinhart by linking up this sort of enlarged resistance not with an elite nationalism but with the radical liberation movement, FRELIMO.

The periodization of resistance: the economic interpretation

Besides the political and religious interpretations of resistance, there has been an economic one too. Perhaps the most radical reinterpretation is that of Samir Amin. Amin argues that the really crucial West African resistances to Europe came in the late seventeenth and eighteenth centuries, during the period of the European-controlled Atlantic slave trade and when Islam provided the ideology for resistance, and he dismisses the resistances of the Scramble period itself as the half-hearted, rearguard actions of an already compromised ruling class. In Amin's eyes what was essentially at stake in the confrontation between Africa and Europe was not formal political control but Europe's attempts at economic manipulation. The truly significant African resistance was directed against such economic manipulation.

If Amin argues that the really important resistances came before the Scramble, other historians employing the economic perspective seem to be arguing that the really important resistances to formal colonial rule came only in the twentieth century. Certainly there was plenty of economic resistance during the Scramble. In particular, the Europeans broke away from their old alliance with African traders and middlemen and used force to set up a monopoly of commerce. The result was fierce resistance on the part of African traders – whether it was led by chief Nana Olomu of Itsekiri in the Niger delta (Nigeria) or by the African and Swahili chiefs who had dominated the slave trade in northern Mozambique, or by the great trader, Rumaliza, who fought against both the Belgians and the Germans in East Africa.

Immanuel Wallerstein has seen this war of the traders as one of the decisive events of early colonialism. He has argued that, from 1879, the old partnership between Africa and European traders began to crumble, that by 1900, with the imposition of colonial rule, it had ceased to exist, and that the 'most immediate effect of colonial rule was its impact on African traders . . . by the end of World War I the radical decline of the relative importance of the African, as well as of the Arab, trading class had become an accomplished fact'.

But in general recent historians have been unsympathetic to trader resistance. Hopkins warns us not to imagine that Niger delta traders like Nana Olomu were forerunners of nationalism or spokesmen for popular grievances, pointing out that their 'vision of social justice did not include the emancipation of [their] own slaves'. Nancy Hafkin stresses the purely selfish interests of the resistant chiefs of northern Mozambique: 'In no sense' she concludes, 'was their resistance popular or progressive'.

The capacity of the great traders to resist, like that of the rulers of the secondary states, was undercut because they had generated too many African grievances. When the British Imperial East Africa Company wanted to break the power of Arab, Swahili and African traders it was able to build a new trade route inland from Malindi, 'supported by stockades built by communities of slaves who had run away from their Arab masters on the coastal plantations'. The 'important entrepreneurs' of the Lagos hinterland found it hard to offer effective resistance to the advance of the British because of the unrest of their large labour force, consisting mainly of slaves and serfs. The conditions of international trade, which had brought about the rise of powerful African traders, had also ensured that their success would have to be bought at the price of much internal tension and resentment.

There were exceptions to this situation of tension between the powerful traders and the general populace. Thus in the Bailundu kingdom in Angola, in which everyone engaged in commerce and therefore became prosperous from the 1870s until the drop of rubber prices in 1899–1902 and the intrusion of white traders, no such tension existed. In the opinion of the 1973 study of the Bailundu war of 1902, resentment at this European trade aggression had a great deal to do with the massive popular uprising which broke out against the Portuguese.

But in general historians of resistance who work from the economic perspective associate mass revolt not with resentment at the European attack on trade, but with the more slowly developing realization on the part of African populations that the whites were determined to obtain cheap labour. Many Africans might at first welcome the Europeans as protectors against over-demanding chiefs, or rapacious Swahili traders, or slave-masters. But they very soon discovered that European demands upon them were equally, if not more, intolerable. At first many African slave-owners, chiefs and traders might respond to the Europeans with fear and hatred, but many of them found that in the long run the interest of black and white holders of power often coincided. In this way a profound transformation of the pattern of resistance took place.

Just as the first Scramble for territory and sovereignty was resisted so was this second Scramble for labour. It was resisted in arms, and much of the support given to the great revolts of the early twentieth century which tried to redefine sovereignty came from men who hated forced labour. It was also resisted by desertion and strikes, by refusal to work underground and by compound riots. In the work of scholars like Charles van Onselen a new dimension for studies of resistance has emerged – no longer the dimension of 'Zambian resistance' or of 'Bemba resistance' but the dimension of resistance along the whole early colonial inter-territorial network of labour migration.

Conclusion

It can be seen, then, that the historiography of resistance is a lively and argumentative one. Yet the modifications and new perspectives enlarge rather than refute the three basic propositions that are being discussed. The 'regularity' and 'generality' of resistance emerge yet more clearly when the earlier indirect resistances to European economic aggression are added to our catalogue of armed opposition and revolt during the Scramble. Exploration of the ideological basis of resistance gains a new richness when the first manifestations of 'consciousness' on the part of workers or peasants to the idea of sovereignty and to the search for a new moral order are added. And the exploration of the links between resistance and the present situation of Africa gains a new tone from the idea of economic resistance.

African initiatives and resistance in North-East Africa

Nowhere in Africa were African initiatives and resistance to European partition and occupation of Africa as determined and protracted as in the modern states of Egypt, Sudan and Somalia. These reactions started in 1881 with the military uprising in Egypt and continued in some parts of the area till as late as the 1920s. Never in the history of Africa did a people put up such a strong fight in defence of their freedom, their sovereignty, and above all their culture and religion. In this chapter, a survey of these initiatives and reactions will be attempted, beginning first with those in Egypt, then Sudan and finally Somaliland (see 4.1).

Egypt

In February 1881 the Egyptian army entered politics for the first time in the modern history of Egypt by launching a revolution against European imperialism and Khedive Tawfik under the leadership of Colonel Ahmad 'Urabi. The causes of this revolution are complex and had very far-reaching consequences. The first of the former was undoubtedly the financial maladministration of both Khedive Isma'il (1863–79) and his successor Khedive Tawfik (1879–92). The huge loans that Khedive Isma'il borrowed from Europe had, by 1880, placed Egypt on the verge of bankruptcy. While half of Egypt's revenue had been strictly allocated to the service of these debts, heavy taxes were imposed on the Egyptian people and the *fellahin* majority who could not afford to pay them were mercilessly flogged. This economic hardship and humiliation created widespread discontent and bitter opposition to Khedive Tawfik and his corrupt government.

Another cause of anger was the complete domination of the country by European powers and resident foreigners. The European powers who had granted loans to Egypt took control of the country's finances and government, and it soon became virtually impossible for any Egyptian government to initiate any administrative or economic reform without the prior and unanimous approval of fourteen European powers. While Egyptians were suffering all this misery, foreigners living in the country were enriching themselves, often through corrupt and immoral means, at the expense of the masses. They were not even subject to the law of the land but had their own courts. There is no doubt that the desire to end this humiliating and oppressive

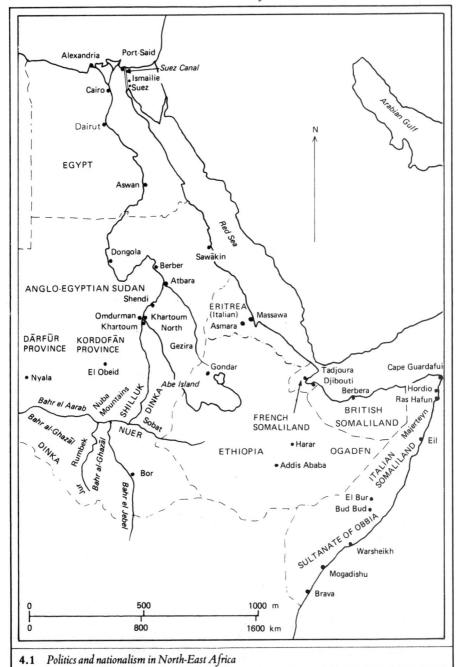

4.1 *Politics and nationalism in North-East Africa*

foreign domination was indeed a major reason for the outbreak of the 'Urabist revolution.

A third reason was the diffusion of liberal political ideas among Egyptians as a result of the spread of education and the development of the press in the course of the nineteenth century. This led to the emergence and development of a constitutional movement in the country from the 1860s, particularly among the western-educated Egyptians, who opposed European control and Khedival absolutism. Led by Muhammad Sharif Pasha, these constitutional nationalists pressed for the enactment of a liberal constitution and the formation of a representative government.

The most important immediate factor in the outbreak of the revolution was, however, the discontent and frustration of the Egyptian army. While the soldiers received very low salaries – 20 piastres a month – Egyptian army officers were not allowed promotion to higher ranks in the army. These were, in fact, exclusively monopolized by the foreign Turco-Circassian aristocratic army officers, who despised and ill-treated their Egyptian subordinates. It was to end this inferior status and to achieve the country's nationalist demands that the Egyptian army launched a revolution early in February 1881 against European colonialism and Khedive Tawfik.

The leader of the revolution, Colonel Ahmad 'Urabi (1839–1911), was an attractive person with a strong *fellah* origin (4.2). Though 'simple and lacking in subtlety and political refinement', 'Urabi was a courageous man and a forceful speaker. These qualities of leadership soon made 'Urabi the undisputed leader of the revolution, and he was instrumental in the formation of *al-Hizb al-Watani* (the Nationalist Party). Its members were a mixture of men of *fellah* origin and some of the Egyptian notables, who were all united in their discontent with the autocracy of Tawfik's rule.

In its initial stages the revolution achieved a remarkable degree of success. 'Uthman Rifki, the notorious Circassian Minister of War and the brain behind the discriminatory policy in the army, was sacked and was replaced by the distinguished poet and revolutionary politician – Mahmud Sami al-Barudi. Subsequently a fully-fledged 'Urabist Cabinet was formed in which Ahmad 'Urabi himself became the Minister of War. Tawfik was so scared that he ordered the formation of a People's Assembly and, on 7 February 1882, enacted a relatively liberal constitution. While making these concessions, the Khedive was conspiring behind the scenes with the European powers and other foreign interests to crush the revolution. To provide a pretext for foreign intervention, some Egyptian historians maintain, the Khedive and the British organized the Alexandria massacre of 12 June 1882, in which many foreigners were killed and a great deal of property was damaged. Whether this accusation is true or not is irrelevant as the Khedive had in fact invited the British to interfere and they enthusiastically and quickly responded by bombarding Alexandria on 11 July 1882. The Egyptian army and people put up a gallant resistance against the invaders, but they were defeated by superior arms. About two thousand Egyptians were killed in this battle.

Following this defeat, 'Urabi declared a *djihad* against the British in a proclamation that was distributed to the Egyptian people. Fighting around Kafr al-Dawar, where the Egyptian army had retreated, broke out several times during August 1882. The Egyptian masses readily sent financial support to their army and thousands of young people offered to join as conscripts. Nevertheless, all the odds were against the Egyptian

4.2 Colonel Aḥmad ʿUrābī ('Arabi Pasha'), 1839–1911 (Mary Evans Picture Library)

resistance movement. 'Urābī could not muster more than 16 000 trained troops, and even this small number was dispersed around Kafr al-Dawār, Dimyāṭ (Damietta) and the Suez Canal area. Moreover, the Egyptian army lacked training, modern arms and ammunition, and efficient means of transport. It was not surprising, then, that a modern British army of 20 000 men under the command of Sir Garnet Wolseley defeated the Egyptians at the battle of al-Tal al-Kabīr on 13 September 1882, and occupied the country. This occupation was to last for seventy-two years.

The failure of the 'Urabist revolution to rid the country of European influence and to end the arbitrary rule of the Turks in Egypt can easily be explained. Although supported by the bulk of the Egyptian people, the revolution did not have sufficient time to mobilize this support. Moreover, a serious rift soon occurred in the united nationalist front as a result of a growing conflict between the military party and the constitutional nationalists. While the latter opposed on principle the involvement of the army in politics, the former insisted that their control of the government would be the best safeguard for the revolution. The revolution, furthermore, suffered from internal intrigues from the Khedive and his Circassian supporters who betrayed the revolution and aided the British occupation.

'Urābī himself made a number of mistakes. His reluctance to depose the Khedive at the beginning of the revolution on the grounds that this would invite foreign intervention and cause chaos inside the country gave Tawfīk valuable time in which to intrigue and conspire against the revolution. Another fatal mistake was 'Urābī's refusal to listen to the advice of some of his military advisers to block the Suez Canal. This he did in the unfounded hope that France would not allow Britain to use the Canal to invade Egypt. Ultimately, however, the 'Urabist revolution was defeated by British military superiority.

Egyptian initiatives and reaction to British conquest, 1882–1914

The military defeat of the 'Urabist revolution broke the national spirit and created an atmosphere of despair and disillusionment. There was therefore no effective resistance during the first decade of the occupation (1882–92) within Egypt itself. The most important nationalist voices during this decade were those of the nationalists in exile. It was from 1893 onwards that internal resistance began and this was inspired and led by none other than the new Khedive, 'Abbās Ḥilmī ('Abbās II, 1892–1914). This ambitious young Khedive encouraged the development of a nationalist movement demanding immediate evacuation of the British. His financial assistance to the press, which enabled the movement to become articulate, was of particular importance. He soon became a very real challenge to the autocratic rule of Lord Cromer, British Agent and Consul-General from 1883 to 1907, and succeeded in forcing the pro-British prime minister to resign on 15 January 1893. Although he was unable after that to act so openly owing to British pressure, Ḥilmī nevertheless attracted some dedicated recruits who were willing to carry on the struggle against the British occupation. They were a group of young intellectuals, who were familiar with the ideas of the French revolution and with modern social and political theories.

The most vehement opponents of British rule at that time were Muṣṭafā Kāmil, a charismatic leader and eloquent orator, and his Nationalist Party. Kāmil had at first concentrated his efforts on winning European support for the cause of Egypt's independence. With generous funds supplied by the Khedive, Kāmil toured European capitals during the period 1895–8, where he addressed meetings, gave interviews to newspapers, and wrote articles and pamphlets. These activities aroused a great deal of interest in Europe, but failed to win any practical support for the Egyptian cause. With her own colonies in North Africa, France could not be won over by Kāmil's arguments in favour of self-rule. Nor was she ready to go to war with England over Egypt, as the Fashoda incident had shown in 1898.

The most urgent tasks facing the young nationalists were to disprove Cromer's biased claim that the Egyptians were incapable of ruling themselves on civilized principles, to convince the Egyptians themselves that they formed a nation capable and indeed deserving of self-rule, and to develop national education in order to strengthen patriotic sentiment. Kāmil was preoccupied with these tasks from 1898 onwards. Until 1906 his views were expressed in numerous speeches and articles in the newspapers of the day, particularly in *al-Liwā* (The Flag), which he founded in 1900. Kāmil's political activities began to bear fruit as he was able to organize a strike of law students in February 1906.

The Dinshāway incident of May 1906 profoundly boosted Kāmil's campaign in Egypt. Briefly, a group of British officers came to Dinshāway village on a pigeon-shooting trip, which the villagers objected to since pigeons were their means of livelihood. A clash followed in which one of the British officers was fatally wounded. The British authorities over-reacted to this incident and passed very severe sentences on the villagers. Four were hanged in public, and the whole village of Dinshāway was forced to watch the executions. The incident certainly caused an upsurge of Egyptian nationalism and awakened people's feelings against the occupation. For the first time since 1882, the British became aware of the insecurity of their position in Egypt. It was this which forced the British to reconsider their oppressive policy and to declare their intention of preparing the country for self-government. Cromer retired in 1907 and was succeeded by Eldon Gorst. The retirement of Cromer was a great triumph for Kāmil and his Nationalist Party, the formation of which was now publicly announced in 1907.

After the premature death of Kāmil in February 1908, Muḥammad Farīd succeeded him as president of the Nationalist Party. Farīd continued to write and address public meetings demanding the evacuation of British troops. His nationalist activities earned him six months' imprisonment in 1911, after which he went into exile.

By 1907 some prominent Egyptian intellectuals had come to believe that Britain was too strong to be expelled from Egypt by revolutionary action. Moreover, they felt that there were real signs of a change in British policy after the Dinshāway incident. Consequently they saw no harm in co-operating with the British in Egypt in order to get from them what could be got until independence could be achieved. This group formed a new political party called the *Umma* Party (the People's Party) in October 1907. Led by the prominent journalist and educationalist, Ahmad Lufṭi al-Sayyid, the party urged the Egyptians to modernize their Islamic tradition by adopting such European ideas and institutions as they considered necessary for progress. The party emphasized above all the need for education as an essential means for training capable administrators and attaining national independence. But the *Umma* Party was not very popular among the Egyptian nationalist because of its co-operation with the British authorities, while its secular liberalism alienated a great number of Egyptians because of their instinctive adherence to their Islamic tradition.

Before the First World War the Egyptian nationalist movement was thus a disunited and a predominantly elitist movement unable to command a popular following. Consequently it was too weak to wrest any significant concessions from the British. The nationalists had to wait until 1919 before coming out in open revolt against the British occupation.

The Sudan

The Mahdist revolution

From 1821 the Sudan was governed by the Ottoman government of Egypt and by 1880 the people of the Sudan – like the people of Egypt – were also fighting to rid themselves of an alien ruling aristocracy. The themes of the *djihād* and Islamic resistance to alien rule, propagated by 'Urābi in Egypt, were also evident in the militant revolutionary movement under the leadership of Muhammad Ahmad al-Mahdī in the Sudan. His movement, the *Mahdiyya*, was essentially a *djihād* and as such claimed the support of all Muslims. Its fundamental objective, as stated repeatedly in the Mahdī's letters and proclamations, was to revive and return to the pure and primitive faith of Islam, 'purged of heresies and accretions', and to spread it to the whole world, by force if deemed necessary.

Besides religion, there were other reasons for the outbreak of the revolution, all arising from the faults of the corrupt Turco-Egyptian administration. The violence that accompanied the original conquest in 1820–1 had created a strong desire for revenge, while the heavy taxes that the Turks imposed and levied by force led to widespread discontent. The attempts of the government to suppress the slave trade had, furthermore, alienated some northern Sudanese as they struck at an important source of wealth and the basis of the domestic and agrarian economy of the country.

The leader of the Mahdist revolution, Muhammad Ahmad Ibn 'Abdallāh, was a pious man whose ideal was the Prophet Muhammad himself (see 4.3). The first armed conflict between the Mahdī and the Turco-Egyptian government lasted from 1881 till 1885. The government had at first underestimated the Mahdī and dismissed him as a mere *darwish* (a mendicant) – as evidenced by the weak and disorganized expedition that was sent to deal with him in Abā Island. A brief skirmish followed in which the *Ansār* (followers of the Mahdī) achieved a quick and easy victory, and the administration was thrown into utter confusion.

After this encounter, the Mahdī decided to 'emigrate' from Abā to Djabal Kādir in the Nuba Mountains. Apart from being another parallel with the life of the Prophet, the most important significance of this *Hidjra* was that it moved the revolution from the riverain regions to the western Sudan, a development that had far-reaching consequences for the movement. From then on, the westerners became its key administrators and military commanders while the riverain people gradually faded into the background.

4.3 *Muhammad Aḥmad Ibn ʿAbdallāh, the Mahdī (1844–85) (BBC Hulton Picture Library)*

Another turning-point in the history of the Mahdist revolution was the battle at Shaykān on 5 November 1883. Bent on crushing the Mahdī, Khedive Tawfīk and his government organized an expedition that was composed of the remnants of 'Urābī's soldiers and commanded by a British army officer, Hicks Pasha. The *Ansār* completely annihilated their enemy in the Shaykān forest in the neigbourhood of al-'Obeid. This victory was a great boost for the Mahdī and his revolution. While many Sudanese joined the revolution, delegates from some Muslim countries came to congratulate the Mahdī on his victory against the 'infidels'. Another consequence of the victory was the total collapse of the Turco-Egyptian administration in the western Sudan and the establishment of Mahdist rule in the provinces of Kordofān, Dārfūr and Bahr al-Ghazāl.

British policy towards the Sudan question underwent a significant change after the battle at Shaykān. While previously maintaining that it was an exclusively Egyptian concern, the British government now felt that its imperial interests necessitated Egypt's immediate withdrawal from the Sudan. Hence it ordered the Egyptian government to abandon the Sudan and sent General Charles Gordon to see that this was done. Meanwhile, the Mahdī advanced towards Khartoum and placed General Gordon in a very critical situation. After a long siege, the Mahdist forces attacked the town, killed Gordon on 26 January 1885, and thereby ended the corrupt Turco-Egyptian rule in the Sudan.

During its first four years (1881–5), the Mahdiyya developed from a movement of religious protest into a powerful and militant state that dominated the Sudan for fourteen years. Its administrative, financial and judicial institutions and its legislation were based strictly on the dual foundations of the Kur'ān and the Sunna.

The relations of the Mahdist state with the outside world were strictly governed by the *djihād*. Both the Mahdī and his Khalīfa, 'Abdullāh Ibn Al-Sayyid Muhammad, had written letters of warning (*indhārāt*) – virtually ultimatums – to some leaders of the world, such as the Khedive of Egypt, the Ottoman emperor and the emperor of Ethiopia, to accept the Mahdī's mission or be faced with an immediate *djihād* if they did not respond positively.

While the Mahdī did not live long enough to pursue such a policy – he died in June 1885 – the *djihād* became the cornerstone of the foreign policy of his successor, Khalīfa 'Abdullāh. In spite of the tremendous administrative and economic problems facing him, Khalīfa 'Abdullāh continued the *djihād* on two fronts: against Egypt and Ethiopia. Under the leadership of 'Abd al-Rahmān al-Nudjūmī, the Mahdist forces invaded Egypt, but they were defeated at the battle of Tushki in 1889. The Mahdists' advance on the eastern front was also checked and the *Ansār* lost Tokar and Kassala respectively in 1891 and 1894. The insistence of the Khalīfa that the emperor of Ethiopia should accept and believe in Mahdism and Islam frustrated the attempts of the latter to conclude an alliance between the Sudan and Ethiopia against European imperialism. This failure led to a long military confrontation that weakened both states and made them an easier prey for European imperialism.

By March 1896 British imperial interests had dictated the invasion of the Sudan and an Anglo-Egyptian force was formed for this purpose under the command of General Kitchener. During the first phase of this invasion – March to September – the enemy forces occupied the whole of Dongola province without encountering any serious resistance from the Sudanese people, partly because of their technical superiority and partly because they took the Khalifa by surprise.

While Kitchener was advancing southwards, the Khalifa ordered total mobilization. Commanded by Emir Mahmūd Ahmad, the *Ansār* tried to repel the enemy attack at the battle of Atbara on 8 April 1898. Three thousand Sudanese were killed, and over 4000 were wounded. Mahmūd himself was captured and put in prison at Rosetta in Egypt, where he died in 1906. The Khalifa himself met the enemy in the vicinity of his capital, Omdurman, where the Sudanese fought with magnificent courage at the battle of Karari on 2 September 1898. Once again, they were defeated by superior armaments. Nearly 11 000 Sudanese were killed and about 16 000 wounded. From there, the Khalifa withdrew to the east of Kordofān and continued to be a problem for the new administration for a whole year. He was, however, finally defeated at the battle of Umm Diwaykrāt on 24 November 1899. After the battle, the Khalifa was found dead upon his sheepskin prayer-rug, all the other Mahdist generals and leaders having been either killed or imprisoned. This marked the collapse of the Mahdist state although the Mahdiyya as a religious and political sentiment never died.

The Mahdist risings

Although the British colonial administration had outlawed the Mahdist sect, a sizeable section of the Sudanese community remained Mahdist at heart. The majority expressed their resentment of British rule quietly by continuing to read the *rātib* (the Mahdi's prayer-book) and to practise other Mahdist rituals. But a dedicated Mahdist minority repeatedly tried to topple the 'infidel' rule by force. Hardly a year passed between 1900 and 1914 without a Mahdist rising in the northern Sudan. Such uprisings occurred in February 1900, in 1902–3 and in 1904. But the most important of them was organized and led in 1908 by a distinguished Mahdist, 'Abd al-Kādir Muhammad Imām, usually called Wad Habūba. He preached Mahdism in the Djazira and defied the government from his camp in Tukūr village near Kamlin. A government force sent against him was disastrously defeated and Wad Habūba went on to launch a surprise attack in May on the enemy at the village of Katfiya. The Mahdists fought bravely, but within a few days the backbone of the revolt had been broken. In the manner of the Mahdi, however, Wad Habūba had 'emigrated', presumably to find asylum in Omdurman. But he was arrested *en route* and publicly hanged on 17 May 1908, while many of his followers were sentenced to death or to long terms of imprisonment.

Though uncoordinated and unable to command any large following, these numerous messianic risings provided an element of continuity with the era of the Mahdist state, and proved that Mahdism was still alive as a vital religious and political force in the Sudan. The risings had, furthermore, demonstrated that the mood of resistance to colonial rule remained entrenched in the hearts of many northern Sudanese.

Protest movements in the Nuba mountains and the southern Sudan

The resistance of the Sudanese people in the Nuba mountains and southern Sudan to European partition and occupation was no less determined and protracted. In spite of the ruthlessness of the colonial forces, various Nuba communities actively opposed

British domination. While Ahmad al-Nu'mān, *mek* of Kitra, declared his open hostility, in 1906 the population of Talodi launched an uprising in which a number of government officials and soldiers were slaughtered. A more serious revolt was that of *mek* Fakī 'Alī of the Miri hills. 'Alī harassed government forces for two years, but he was arrested in 1916 and imprisoned in Wādī Halfa.

In the southern region of the Sudan, resistance was led and sustained by the Nuer people living in the lands adjoining the river Sobat and the White Nile. Under the previous administrations, the Nuer were accustomed to managing their own affairs, since these administrations did not exercise effective control over them. But now the Nuer refused to recognize the supremacy of the new government and continued to show hostility towards it. Two of their leaders, Dengkur and Diu, were particularly active in this respect. Though these two influential leaders died in 1906 and 1907 respectively, Nuer activism never died, and in 1914 another Nuer leader, Dowl Diu, attacked a government post. In spite of the numerous indiscriminate punitive measures, the Nuer resistance continued to gain momentum until it broke out in the popular and widespread Nuer revolt of 1927.

The Azande under the leadership of Yambio, their chief, were determined not to allow any foreign troops to enter their land. They faced the danger of invasion from both the Belgians and the Condominium government. Yambio seemed to have feared Belgian invasion more than the British. He therefore thought that the best policy open to him was to neutralize the British with signs of friendship and thereby gain a free hand to deal with the imminent Belgian danger. He invited the British to establish a trading post in his kingdom. The invitation was made in the belief that the British would not be able to come, but that if they did he would fight them.

But the British accepted the invitation and in January 1903 a patrol left Wau for Yambio's territory. While on the march it was attacked by the Azande. The patrol escaped to Rumbek. In January 1904 the government in Khartoum sent another patrol, which was also attacked by the Azande and ultimately forced to retreat to Tonj.

While the Belgians were preparing an attack on Yambio's territory, the latter mobilized a force of 10 000 Azande and launched a daring attack on the Belgian post at Mayawa. The Azande courageously harassed the intruders, but they could not stand up to the Belgian rifle fire with spears alone. This battle seriously weakened Zande military power and morale. With his military power shattered, Yambio had to meet a government expeditionary force in January 1905. He was ultimately defeated and imprisoned, and died soon afterwards, on 10 February 1905. His people, however, continued the struggle. In 1908 some of Yambio's warriors attempted to stir up a rising while others fought the British during the First World War.

Somaliland

The Somali reaction to partition 1884–97

From the middle of the nineteenth century, the Somali peninsula was rapidly drawn into the theatre of European colonial competition between Italy, Britain and France. Because of their interests in India and other parts of Asia, Britain and France had established themselves by the early 1880s on the Somali coast. They were joined by Italy and each of them extended its influence into the interior. In 1885 the French declared a protectorate over their sphere of influence. They were followed by the British in 1887, and then by the Italians, who declared a protectorate over the towns of Brava, Merca, Mogadishu and Warsheikh and subsequently Obbia and the Midjurteyn Somali in the north. Ethiopia had also expanded into Somali-inhabited territories, and had managed to establish its administrative control in the Houd and Ogaden. The partition of Somaliland was formally virtually completed by 1897.

The Somali chiefs and sultans never willingly gave up their sovereignty and, in fact, provided the leadership for some of the most numerous and protracted local risings against European imperialism during the era of partition. Being aware of the rivalry between European powers in the field of colonial expansion, the Somali chiefs tried to play them off one against the other by concluding treaties with one or the other. The Somali chiefs, for example, signed many treaties with the British. Ultimately, these treaties failed in their objective since the European powers came to settle their imperial disputes peacefully.

Besides this diplomatic effort, some of the Somali clans took up arms to try to maintain their sovereignty. The British had to send four expeditions: in 1886 and 1890 against the Isa, in 1893 against the Habar Gerhajis and in 1895 against the Habar Awal. The Italians also suffered heavy losses of life. In 1887 a party of Italians was massacred at Harar, and in 1896 a party of fourteen Italians was killed by the Bimal people. The frequent clashes between the Ethiopian forces and the Somali clans did not permit the former to complete their occupation of the Ogaden or to extend their authority far beyond the scattered military posts established throughout the region.

The Somali fight for freedom 1897–1914

Somali resistance reached its highest point with the declaration of *djihād* against European imperialism by Sayyid Muḥammad 'Abdille Ḥassan. He was born in 1864 and after studying at the major centres of Islam in eastern Africa, Harar and Mogadishu and possibly the Mahdist strongholds in Kordofan, he set out on a pilgrimage to Mecca in 1895, and spent a year in Arabia, also visiting Hidjāz and Palestine. While in Mecca, he studied under Shaykh Muḥammad Sālih, and joined his sect, the Sālihiyya order. Possibly these extensive travels and periods abroad in different parts of the Muslim world brought the Sayyid into contact with the then current ideas of Islamic revivalism, while he was also, like many other religious leaders, inspired by the brilliant career of the Mahdī. On his return home, he settled for a time in Berbera where he preached to his countrymen, urging them to return to the strict path of Muslim devotion and reject Christian colonization and western education.

Through his personal charisma and brilliant leadership, and in particular through the numerous poems that he composed, many of which are still well known throughout Somalia, al-Sayyid 'successfully rallied a host of contentious clansmen behind the twin banners of Islam and homeland' and created a standing army which was estimated at 12 000 men.

Al-Sayyid started his *djihād* at Berbera where, between 1895 and 1897, he tried to arouse the people against the imperialists. But his first revolutionary action was the occupation of Burao in the centre of British Somaliland in August 1899. The British were so harassed by this that between 1900 and 1904 they sent four expeditions to repel al-Sayyid's attacks. Though the British were helped in these operations by the Italians, al-Sayyid's exceptional military skills and his successful use of cavalry and guerrilla tactics won his warriors a number of victories. One of these was at Gamburu hill in April 1903, in which nine British officers were killed.

By the end of 1904, however, the Sayyid's force had been greatly weakened. He, therefore, withdrew to the Italian Midjurteyn Protectorate, where, on 5 March 1905, he signed the Treaty of Illig with the Italians, in which he dictated his own terms. By 1908 al-Sayyid had mobilized his forces for a new round of fighting that forced the British to withdraw from the interior in November 1909 and to concentrate on the coast. But al-Sayyid threatened to attack the coastal towns as well. In August 1913 he gained a major victory by annihilating the newly established camel constabulary. This disaster forced the British to continue to fight al-Sayyid until his death in November 1920.

Although this Somali *djihād* ultimately failed to rid the country of alien rule, it encouraged a strong nationalist feeling. The Somali people had come to see themselves as a single whole fighting against foreign incursions. Besides that Sayyid Muhammad's struggle left in the Somali national consciousness an ideal of patriotism which could never be effaced, and which was to inspire later generations of his countrymen.

Conclusion

Perhaps no part of Africa resisted European conquest and occupation in the period 1880–1914 so forcefully as the north-eastern part of the continent. This is shown by the thousands of Egyptians, Sudanese and Somali who lost their lives in the battles and skirmishes fought between them and European forces. The strength of this resistance was due to the fact that, besides the patriotic sentiment which inspired it, there was an even more fundamental sentiment at work, namely an intense religious faith. The peoples of Egypt, the Sudan and Somaliland were not fighting in defence of home alone, but also in defence of religion. The Muslims there, like their fellow adherents in the rest of the Islamic world, were conscious of the social and religious disruption that would be caused by alien encroachment on hitherto Muslim territories. It was also against the spirit of Islam that a Muslim population should accept a position of political subordination to a Christian power. The revolutionary movements of 'Urābi, the Mahdī and Sayyid Muhammad should therefore be understood in the context of the numerous reforming movements that spread in and profoundly affected the Muslim world during the eighteenth and nineteenth centuries.

African initiatives and resistance in North Africa and the Sahara

The European conquest and occupation of the North African states (see 5.1) of Morocco, Algeria, Tunisia and Tripoli (Libya) took place at different times. While Algeria was conquered by the French as early as 1830 and the area around Melilla in Morocco by Spain in 1860, it was not until 1881 that Tunisia was conquered by France, while Libya and Morocco were not conquered and occupied by Italy and France respectively until as late as between 1911 and 1934. However, as far as African initiatives and reactions were concerned, they are all virtually the same throughout the period. They took the form, in part, of diplomatic manoeuvres but mainly of armed resistance in defence of their sovereignty and independence.

Tunisia

No sooner had the French conquered Tunisia and forced the Bey to sign a treaty putting him under a French protectorate on 12 May 1881 than the inhabitants of the Sahel and of the religious capital Kayrawān revolted. The French had to launch a second expedition but this was strongly resisted in the mountainous areas of the north-west, the centre and the south. Safākus and Kābis had to be bombarded by naval units while Kayrawān withstood a long siege in the autumn of 1881. Even after all this resistance had been overcome, the southern territories of Tunisia near Tripolitania remained an insecure area for a long time.

Morocco

The Moroccan government had for centuries been resisting the Spaniards who had established themselves at Ceuta and Melilla. It always forbade the inhabitants to have anything to do with them, and it was to break this blockade that Spain launched the 1859–60 war that was so disastrous for Morocco. She was forced to pay a heavy fine, to agree to the enlargement of the fortified part of Melilla and to cede a port on the Atlantic coast as a refuge for fishermen from the Canary Islands. With the acquisition of the bay of Rio de Oro, whose occupation was notified to the signatories to the Berlin Act on 26 December 1884, Spain by the end of the century had three bridgeheads on the North African coast.

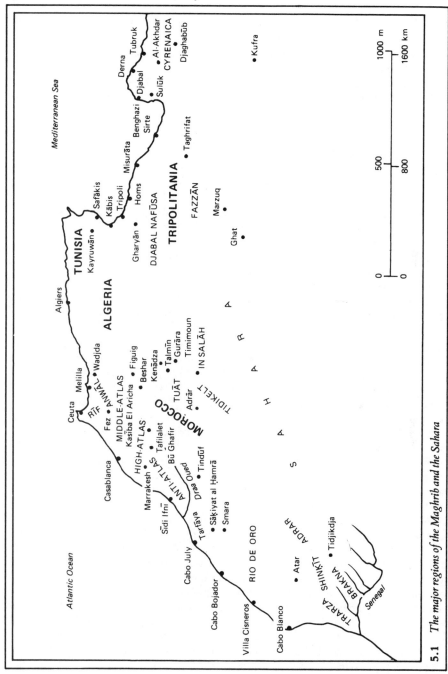

5.1 *The major regions of the Maghrib and the Sahara*

In 1880 and 1881, when the Madrid Conference on the protection of individuals in Morocco met in two sessions, the *Makhzen* made a last attempt to get its independence and sovereignty over a clearly defined territory accepted at the international level. Despite English support, the attempt failed in the face of the selfish alliance of France, Spain and Italy. France raised the Tuwāt problem but, with English support, the Sultan of Morocco rejected the French demands and at the same time strengthened his administrative and political presence in Tuwāt.

In December 1899, however, on the pretext of scientific exploration, a strong French expedition was despatched to In Salāh and demanded immediate surrender. The local chief appointed by the Sultan of Morocco, assisted by the soldiers of the *Makhzen* and the *sharifs* of In Salāh, resisted fiercely. After bloody battles, such as that of In Ghār on 27 December 1899, where the outcome was not in doubt given the disparity between the two sides, the whole oasis region was conquered; the last battle took place at Talmin in March 1901. England and Germany advised the young Sultan 'Abd al-'Azīz to accept the *fait accompli*; and this he did, signing under duress the draft treaty of 20 April 1902. In return for this major concession, however, he tried to have the line of demarcation in the south and east between Morocco and the French possessions clearly defined; but to no effect, for France preferred the vagueness which offered her the prospect of further conquests.

The loss of Tuwāt was one of the main reasons for the break-up of the Sultan's authority, which got worse and worse until 1911. The *Makhzen* knew that France planned to encircle Morocco in order to isolate and subjugate it; it also knew that England no longer opposed French designs. The domestic reforms it had introduced to strengthen the army and administration had not had the desired results. From Germany, it no longer expected anything but diplomatic help; and Germany did indeed uphold Moroccan independence until November 1911, when she signed an agreement with France giving the latter a free hand in Morocco in exchange for compensations in equatorial Africa.

After 1905 France decided to precipitate matters and occupy the so-called *bilād al-sibā*. These were poor, underpopulated desert areas which the Sultan for this reason left to be administered by local chiefs, though without giving up his sovereign rights. He was regularly kept informed of colonial intrigues, and when the French threat took definite shape he sent a duly authorized representative to direct the resistance. This is what happened in the Kenādza area and at Shinkīt.

Having always refused to define the frontier with Morocco beyond Figuig, France pursued a policy of slowly nibbling away at territory. Working their way up the valley of the Sawra, her forces gradually occupied the territory between Wādi Gīr and Wādi Zūsfānā, on the pretext of ending lawlessness and insecurity and allowing frontier trade to expand. The French government also suggested to the *Makhzen* that it should share customs receipts with it, and this was accepted in March 1910.

Further south, France had imposed her protectorate on the emirs of the Trarza and the Brakna. Then, in 1905, a specialist in marabout affairs Xavier Coppolani, came from Algeria to introduce the policy of 'peaceful penetration', which took the form of making direct contact with the chiefs and leaders of religious brotherhoods with a view to winning them over to French influence. He found himself up against a worthy opponent in <u>Shaykh</u> Ma' al-Aynayn, who, for more than thirty years, had given the impression of being the Sultan of Morocco's representative. Mulāy 'Abd al-'Aziz was informed, and sent his uncle Mulāy Idris, who galvanized the resistance forces. Meanwhile, Coppolani's camp at Tidjikdja was attacked in April 1905 and the apostle of peaceful penetration was killed. Taking advantage of the internal crisis in Morocco, France demanded the recall of Mulāy Idris, and obtained it in January 1907; but resistance continued none the less. A strong expedition led by Colonel Gouraud moved northwards; it suffered a serious reverse at al-Moynām on 16 June 1908, but succeeded in entering Atar on 9 January 1909. <u>Shaykh</u> Ma' al-Aynayn withdrew with his followers into the Sākiyat al-Ḥamrā', whence his forces continued to harass the French and the Spaniards until 1933.

During the same period, Spain followed France's example. When France occupied <u>Shinkīt</u>, Spain moved out of her settlement on the bay of Rio de Oro and in 1906 organized the Saharan intervention force which penetrated 30 km inland. In the north, the Spaniards waited until the French entered Wadjda in 1907 before mounting a 45 000-strong expedition which, in September 1909, set out to conquer the Rīf. In response, the local population, inspired by <u>Shaykh</u> Ameziyān's call to *djihād*, mounted a fierce resistance which died out only in 1926.

Even more determined was the resistance in the areas of the Atlas and the Sahara. Until 1931, huge parts of these areas existed outside any colonial control. In that year, however, a change took place in French colonial policy. Worried by the fact that Germany was rebuilding her strength, the French Minister of War, Messimy, set the year 1935 as the terminal year for conquest and occupation. All necessary means were given to the army in Africa and arrangements were made to co-ordinate operations with the Spaniards; the advent of a republic in Madrid made this co-ordination easy. Thus every spring an expedition was mounted to put down one of the 'dissident spots'.

Yet, despite that, final conquest was nowhere easy. The Middle Atlas was reduced in two campaigns, in 1931 and 1932; from 12 July to 16 September of the latter year the bloody battle of Tazīkzaūt took place. The French army surrounded 3000 families who had been retreating before the colonial advance since 1922. The battle lasted from 22 August to 11 September. Neither massive bombardment nor blockade could break the resistance led by al-Wakki Amhouch and his brothers. The shelters had to be cleared by grenades. After the battle, they counted 500 killed among the Moroccans. In 1933 it was the turn of the Djabal Saghrū, where the battle of Bū <u>Gh</u>āfir (13 February to 25 March) was equally bloody. In 1934 the last resistance fighters were surrounded in the Anti-Atlas, after which the French entered Tindūf, in March. The Spaniards captured Sīdī Ifni a week later, on 6 April 1934.

Libya

But probably nowhere was the African–European confrontation as protracted, bloody and brutal as in Libya. In October 1911, Italy suddenly invaded Libya, then under the rule of the Ottomans, and easily captured the towns of Tripoli, Benghazi, Homs and Tubruk. However, when the Italians ventured outside the city limits, they faced fierce resistance. A series of battles took place on the outskirts of the cities, among which was al-Hāni on 23 October 1911, outside Tripoli. The Italians suffered a humiliating defeat and committed great atrocities against the population of the city of Tripoli. Outside Benghazi, the Italians fought three major battles at Djulianā, al-Kuwayfiya and al-Hawwāri, on 28 November 1911. They were defeated and forced to retreat to Benghazi. At al-Khums the Italians and the Turkish–Arab forces fought desperately for the control of the strategic point of al-Markib from 23 October 1911 until 2 May 1912 before the Italians succeeded in driving the defenders out.

In Derna, the small Turkish force withdrew to the mountains overlooking the town and with the help of the indigenous population, clashed with the Italians. The resistance in Derna was buttressed by the arrival of a group of Turkish officers under the command of Anwar Pasha (Enver), and Mustafā Kamal (later Atatürk). With the help of Ahmad al-Sharīf, the spiritual leader of the Sanūsiyya, Anwar and his group mobilized the Arabs of the hinterland and succeeded in recruiting a formidable army.

Anwar led this army in two battles against the Italians, at al-Karkaf and Sīdī ‘Abdallāh on 8 October 1912 and 3 March 1912. At Tubruk the Arabs met the Italians in two major encounters: al-Nādūra on 3 March 1912, and al-Mudawwar on 17 July 1912, in which the Italian commander, General Salsa, was killed. It is difficult to cover all the battles fought against the Italians in Libya in a survey history; however, it is sufficient to say that, in and around every city, town and valley, there was an encounter against the Italians. It was because of this fierce resistance that the Italians gained little more than the five towns in the first six months of the war.

By the end of 1911, many Italians had begun to show signs of disappointment about the duration of the war in Libya. In order to pressure Turkey into withdrawing from Libya, the Italian government attacked the Dodecanese Islands and the Dardanelles. Italy's new action in the heart of the Turkish land threatened world peace and the revival of the ‘Eastern Question’, an issue no European power wanted raised because of its complications. The major European powers therefore put pressure on Turkey and Italy to come to a peaceful agreement and succeeded in inducing, if not forcing, Turkey to sign the Lausanne Agreement with Italy on 18 October 1912. According to this treaty, Turkey – to save her face before the Islamic world – granted independence to the Libyan people, and, in return, Italy promised to withdraw from Turkish waters.

The reaction of the Libyans to the peace treaty – on which they were not consulted – was divided. Some wanted to negotiate with the Italians, while others wanted to fight to the end. The people of Cyrenaica under the spiritual leader, Ahmad al-Sharif, belonged to the latter camp.

Seizing the opportunity of the Turkish withdrawal from Libya, the Italians launched an attack on Ahmad al-Sharīf's forces south of Derna, but suffered a stunning defeat at the battle of Yawm al-Djumā‘ on 16 May 1913. This battle was of great significance because it was the first large-scale encounter between the Arabs and the Italians after the Turkish withdrawal. Citing the decree issued by the Turkish Sultan which granted the Libyans independence, Ahmad al-Sharīf declared the formation of a government called ‘al-Hukūma al-Sanūsiyya’, the Sanūsi government. Thus, on the eve of the First World War, the Libyans had successfully resisted the Italians and were in control of large areas of their country.

After the war, however, the Italians resumed their offensive in Libya and launched a number of invasions for a 'reconquista' in 1922. A large army under the command of General Graziani marched on Gharyān, capital of Tripolitania, which was captured on 7 November 1922. Another attacked Misurātā and took it on 20 February 1923. The central committee of the United Republic set up in January 1922, torn by disputes among its members as well as civil war between Misurātā and Warfallāh on the one hand, and civil strife between the Arabs and the Berbers of the Western Mountains on the other, could not mobilize sufficient force to stop the Italians. Consequently, the central committee collapsed and its members fled the country to Egypt, the Sudan and Tunisia.

To worsen the situation even further, on 21 December 1922, Emir Idrīs al-Sanūsī, the Union's spiritual leader and supreme commander, went into voluntary exile to Egypt. His unexplained and sudden departure, which is being debated among historians, completely demoralized the people and caused many of the warriors either to leave the country or to surrender to the Italians. However, before leaving, al-Sanūsī appointed his brother al-Riḍā as his deputy, and 'Umar al-Mukhtār (see 5.2) as commander of the national forces in the Green Mountains, and it was under al-Mukhtar's leadership and because of the efficient guerilla warfare that he developed that the resistance continued until 1931. He divided his forces into three major mobile companies (*adwār*) and camped in the mountainous area south of al-Mardj at Djardās. The series of attacks launched against him in the summer of 1923 were all repelled. Another army sent against his camp in March was routed.

It was Tripolitania that fell first. By June 1924, all arable land was occupied. But, aware of their weakness as long as they did not control the desert, the Italians began a long campaign to control the desert and finally Fezzān. This was not marked by success despite the use of aerial bombing and poison gas. Several Italian advances were stopped. As late as 1928 the Libyans blocked the main Italian force at Faghrift south of Surt. But, by the end of 1929 and the beginning of 1930, Fezzān was finally occupied and the Libyan resistance in the west and south collapsed.

Meanwhile, the resistance in Cyrenaica continued and succeeded in inflicting heavy defeats on the Italians. When the Fascists failed to suppress the revolution of 'Umar al-Mukhtār in Cyrenaica through direct military attack, they resorted to some measures unprecedented in the history of colonial wars in Africa. They first erected a 300 km-long wire fence along the Tripoli–Egyptian border to prevent any aid coming from Egypt. Secondly, continually reinforced, they occupied the oases of Djalo, Djaghabūb and Kufra to encircle and isolate the warriors in Cyrenaica. Finally, they evacuated all the rural population of Cyrenaica to the desert of Sirt where they kept them in fenced concentration camps. This measure was meant to deprive al-Mukhtār's forces of any local assistance. Other mass prisons and concentration camps were established at al-Makrūn, Sulūk, al-Aghayla and al-Barayka. Conditions in these camps were so bad that it is believed that more than 100 000 people died of starvation and diseases, not to mention their animals which were confiscated. In al-Barayka prison camp alone, there were 80 000 persons of whom 30 000 are said to have died between 1930 and 1932, according to the Italians' own statistics.

Despite these extreme measures, the revolt continued and hit-and-run tactics were resorted to. The Italians again offered to negotiate with al-Mukhtār. A series of

5.2 '*Umar al-Mukhtār (b. c. 1862), a leader of Sanusi resistance to Italian colonization until his execution in 1931 (Garyounis University, Benghazi, Central Library)*

meetings were held between the two sides. Among them was the one held near al-Mardj on 19 July 1929, attended by Governor Badoglio. At this meeting, the Italians offered to bribe al-Mukhtār, who turned down the offer and insisted on liberating his country. Later, when al-Mukhtār discovered that the Italians were trying to apply the policy of 'divide and rule' among his followers, he broke off the talks with the Italians and resumed his tactics of guerilla warfare, which included skirmishes, raids, ambushes, surprise attacks and incursions spread all over the country. In the last twenty-one months before his capture, he fought 227 battles with the Italians, as Graziani himself admitted. In September 1931, however, al-Mukhtār was captured and taken to Benghazi. He was then court-martialled and executed before thousands of Libyans at the town of Suluk on 16 September 1931.

After the capture of al-Mukhtār, his followers elected Yūsuf Abū Rāhil, his deputy, as commander. He continued the struggle for six months and then decided to suspend operations and withdraw to Egypt. He was killed in his attempt to cross the Libya–Egyptian border. On 24 January 1932, Badoglio announced the conquest and occupation of Libya and one of the longest resistances to European imperialism thus came to its more or less inevitable end.

The failure of African initiatives and resistance

In spite of the strong determination of the people of the Maghrib to maintain their sovereignty and way of life, and despite the protracted nature of the resistance, the whole of the Maghrib had fallen to the imperial powers of France, Spain and Italy by 1935. The final question to be considered then is why the Maghribians failed.

Contrary to what might be supposed, the demographic, physical and economic circumstances were for most of the time against the North African resistance fighters.

We now know that the population of North Africa was overestimated in the nineteenth century. Men old enough to carry arms were limited in number and also available only for a very short period because of the requirements of farming and stock-rearing; and this left the initiative in the hands of the enemy. Tidikelt was conquered by a column of 1000 men, having a population not exceeding 20 000. At Tīt on 7 May 1902, when the Tawārik of the Ahaggar were defeated, they numbered 300 as against 130; but that was the most they could muster, and the loss of 93 dead was a blow from which they did not easily recover. The highland areas, supposedly overpopulated, were little better off; in every decisive engagement the assailants had the advantage of numbers. The people of the Rif were attacked by 300 000 French soldiers (not counting the Spaniards) – i.e. the equivalent of the whole population of northern Morocco. At the height of the resistance in the Middle Atlas, a total number of 10 000, including women and children, had to face an army of 80 000 men. In the Djabal Saghrū 7000 fighting soldiers were assailed by 34 000 men equipped with the latest weapons. Admittedly not all the colonial troops were fighters; but it is undeniable that, in terms of sheer numbers, the advantage always lay with the colonial army, which set out to strike 'the natives with terror and despondency'.

Much is often made of the indigenous fighters' mobility and knowledge of the terrain; but these were tactical advantages that counted for less and less as the war went on. The exploit at Tidjikdja in June 1905, in which Xavier Coppolani was killed and which delayed the conquest of the Adrār until 1909; the battle of Kasība, from 8 to 10 June 1913, in which the French lost 100 dead and 140 wounded; the even bloodier one at al-Harī on 13 November 1914, when they left behind 510 dead and 176 wounded; the battle of Anwāl, from 22 to 26 July 1921, in which the Spaniards lost 15 000 dead, 700 prisoners, 20 000 rifles, 400 machine guns and 150 field guns; all these heroic feats of arms (showing admirable knowledge of the terrain and decisively influenced by mobility and ruthlessness in battle) stopped the colonial advance for a few years but did not help to regain lost territory. Neither the desert dwellers not the highlanders could take much time off from their orchard farming and stock-rearing; and this allowed the invader to launch real economic warfare against them. During the Adrār campaign in 1909 the French soldiers occupied the oases at the time of the date harvest and waited for the men to be compelled by hunger to come and surrender (admittedly not for long). In areas where seasonal migration with stock took place, they closed off the winter pastures and relied on cold and hunger to bring the inhabitants to terms. When operations began, a total blockade was imposed, as against the Zayyān in 1917–18 and the people of the Rīf in 1925–6. In 1928–9 the Italians, as has been pointed out above, deported the people of Cyrenaica to the north and concentrated them in camps surrounded by barbed wire. One consequence of the nagging hunger created by such policies, harder on the livestock than the people, was that the colonial army found volunteers immediately after the end of the operations.

The resistance fighters' great asset, mobility, soon became only relative. From 1901 onwards the French army took up racing camels, to such good effect that the conquest of the Sahara has been described as due to Sha'amba camel-riders. The railway also preceded conquest almost everywhere: it reached 'Ayn Sifrā in 1887, Bishār in 1905 and Zīz in 1930. In 1915 motor vehicles were tried for the first time, and Epinat lorries drove up and down the roads of the Atlas in anticipation of the 1931–3 campaigns. Lastly, aircraft were used from 1920 onwards, for aerial photography in preparation for the campaigns and to demoralize the inhabitants during operations.

This brings us to the problem of weapons, which, not being produced locally, had to be taken from the enemy. France had always made an international issue out of arms smuggling to the Maghrib, accusing Germany and Turkey of being suppliers, and Spain and even England of tolerating arms traffic on the coasts of the Rīf and the Atlantic coast in the case of Morocco and via the Libyan oases for Tunisia and the central Sahara. It is true that this traffic had always existed; but nevertheless the fact remains that the French authorities themselves admitted that they found hardly any German weapons in the Middle Atlas or Anti-Atlas. As each large clan grouping was forced to surrender, it passed its rifles on to its neighbours who were still free; so that it was at the end of operations in March 1934 that the French recovered the largest numbers of rifles, namely 25 000. We must remember that these weapons were often useless because of lack of ammunition, and above all that they were of doubtful effectiveness against the aircraft, long-range heavy artillery and armour with which the invading armies were equipped after the First World War. It was this that made the French generals say that the 1931–4 campaigns were 'real manoeuvres with a live enemy'.

African initiatives and resistance in West Africa, 1880–1914

During the period 1880 to 1914, the whole of West Africa, with the sole exception of Liberia (see Chapter 2), was brought under colonial rule. This phenomenon, which meant essentially the loss of African sovereignty as well as land, was accomplished in two phases. The first phase lasted from 1880 to the early 1900s, and the second from the early 1900s to the outbreak of the First World War in 1914. Each of these phases saw different European activities, which produced different initiatives and reactions on the part of the Africans.

The first phase saw the use of either diplomacy or military invasion, or of both, by the Europeans. This was the classic era of treaty-making in practically every nook and corner of West Africa followed in most cases by military invasions, conquests and occupation by armies of varying sizes and discipline. Never in the known history of the continent has so much military action been seen and so many invasions and campaigns launched against African states and communities (see 6.1).

During this first phase, practically all Africans had the same objectives, that of defending their sovereignty and traditional way of life. It is the methods adopted that varied. Three options were open to the Africans, that of confrontation, that of alliance and that of acquiescence or submission. The strategy of confrontation involved open warfare, sieges, guerrilla tactics and scorched-earth policies as well as diplomacy. As will be seen below, all three options were resorted to.

Conquest and reaction in French West Africa, 1880–1900

It is quite clear from the available evidence that the French – from 1880 onwards – adopted a policy of occupying the whole region from the Senegal first to the Niger and then to Chad and linking these areas with their posts on the Guinea coast in Côte d'Ivoire and Dahomey, and its execution was entrusted to officers of the Marine Corps. In their occupation of West Africa, therefore, the French resorted almost exclusively to the method of military conquest rather than the conclusion of treaties of protectorate as the British did. In terms of African reactions, all the options open to them were resorted to, namely, submission, alliance and confrontation. However, as will be seen below, far more of the rulers opted for the strategy of armed confrontation than those of submission and alliance while opposition here was far more protracted than anywhere else

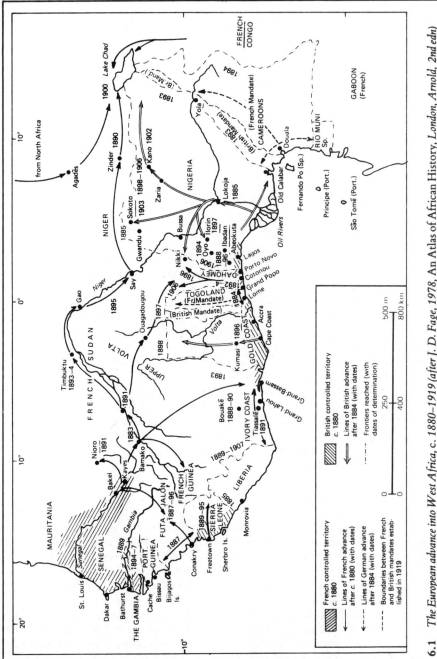

6.1   *The European advance into West Africa, c. 1880–1919 (after J. D. Fage, 1978, An Atlas of African History, London, Arnold, 2nd edn)*

in West Africa for two main reasons. The first, as pointed out already, was that the French used the method of military conquest almost exclusively, which consequently evoked militant reaction. The second was that the people were far more Islamized than those of the other areas of West Africa, and, as Michael Crowder has pointed out, since 'for Muslim societies of West Africa the imposition of white rule meant submission to the infidel which was intolerable to any good Muslim', they tended to resist the Europeans with added determination and tenacity often lacking among non-Muslims. Let us illustrate these general conclusions by a study of the events in Senegambia, in the Tukuloor and Mande empires and finally in Dahomey.

Senegambia

In Senegal, where the French had been extending their influence mainly by conquest since 1854, one of their greatest opponents was Lat Dior Diop, the Damel of Cayor. Having fought the French since 1861, Lat Dior was particularly determined to prevent the construction of the railway through his kingdoms. On 17 November 1882 he sent a letter to Governor Servatius forbidding him to begin construction even in the suburbs of the territory that was an integral part of Cayor. 'As long as I live, be well assured', he wrote, 'I shall oppose with all my might the construction of this railway.'

Bent on the construction of the railway, the French launched an invasion of Cayor in December 1882. From his past experiences, Lat Dior Diop knew that he had little chance of defeating them in conventional warfare. He therefore withdrew at Wendling's approach and went to settle in Jolof. It was not until 1886 that Cayor was conquered and effectively occupied and a decree was passed expelling Lat Dior from Cayor. When he was notified of this measure, Lat Dior went into a towering rage. He mobilized the 300 partisans who had remained faithful but released from oath all those who were not resolved to die with him, and took to the field against the French and their allies, his former subjects. Lat Dior was firmly resolved to sell his life dearly. On 27 October 1886, at about 11 a.m., he surprised the French and their allies at the well of Dekhle and inflicted heavy losses on them. He fell there, as did his two sons and eighty of his partisans. The death of Lat Dior naturally spelled the end of Cayor's independence and facilitated French seizure of the rest of the country.

Tukuloor empire

In the Tukuloor empire (see 6.2), Ahmadu, who succeeded his father, al-Hadj'Umar, the founder of the empire, was, like most African rulers, determined to ensure the survival of his state and maintain its independence and sovereignty. To achieve these objectives, he chose the strategies of alliance and militant confrontation. However, unlike most of the rulers of the region, he relied more on the former than on the latter, mainly because he needed arms and financial resources to consolidate his own position on the throne, both of which necessitated friendly relations with the French. Right from his accession, therefore, he agreed to negotiate with them. The negotiations took place between him and Lieutenant Mage, the representative of the French. Both agreed that, in return for the supply of cannon and the recognition of his authority, Ahmadu was to allow French traders to trade in his empire.

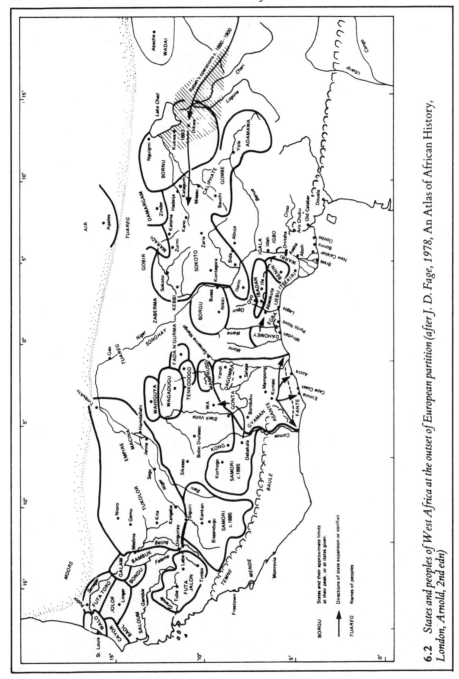

6.2   *States and peoples of West Africa at the outset of European partition (after J. D. Fage, 1978, An Atlas of African History, London, Arnold, 2nd edn)*

Though this treaty was not ratified by the French administration nor did Ahmadu receive any cannon, and though the French continued to assist the rebels and in 1878 even attacked Sabusire, the Tukuloor fortress in Kuasso, Ahmadu continued his friendly attitude towards the French. This served him well for it enabled him to quell the rebellions of his brothers in 1874, and those in the Bambara territories of Segu and Kaarta by the late 1870s. The French, who were preparing to conquer the area between the Senegal and the Niger, also needed the co-operation of Ahmadu. It is not surprising, then, that both of them resumed negotiations in 1880, which led to the treaty of Mango. Under the terms of this treaty, Ahmadu undertook to allow the French to build and maintain trade routes through his empire and granted them permission to build and sail steamboats on the Niger. In return, the French recognized the sovereign existence of his empire, agreed to grant him free access to Futa, and promised not to invade his territory or build any fortifications in it. Above all, the French agreed to give in payment four field guns and 1000 rifles, and to pay a yearly rent of 200 rifles, 200 barrels of gunpowder, 200 artillery shells and 50 000 flints.

This treaty was obviously a great diplomatic victory for Ahmadu and, had the French ratified it and sincerely implemented its terms, Ahmadu's empire would have survived. But of course even Gallieni himself had no intention of implementing the treaty and in any case his government did not ratify it. Under the new Upper Senegal military command headed by Lt.-Colonel Borgnis-Desbordes, the French began their invasion of the empire in 1881 and by February 1883 they had occupied Bamako on the Niger without any opposition. However, primarily because Ahmadu did not still feel secure at home, as is shown by his attack on Nioro, the capital of Kaarta, then ruled by his brother Moutaga, he agreed to conclude another treaty with the French, the Treaty of Gori, on 12 May 1887. Under its terms, Ahmadu agreed to place his empire under the nominal protection of the French while the French in turn pledged not to invade his territories and to remove the ban that they had placed on the purchase of arms by Ahmadu.

However, by 1888, the French had suppressed Lamine's rebellion and, as will be seen later, concluded another treaty with Samori and therefore did not need an alliance with Ahmadu any longer. This, together with the aggressiveness of the French military command, led to the assumption of the offensive against Ahmadu signified by their attack on the Tukuloor fortress of Kundian in February 1889. This was so solidly built that it took an intensive bombardment of eight hours' duration by Archinard's 80-mm mountain guns to break through the walls. The Tukuloor, who had held fast under this deluge, put up fierce resistance to the French, meeting their bombardment with continued musket fire followed by a house-to-house fight. Many of them perished with their weapons in their hands.

Ahmadu, at grips with his internal difficulties, thereupon transferred the struggle to the religious plane. He appealed to all the Muslims of the empire to take up arms in defence of the faith. Letters requesting help were dispatched to Jolof, Mauritania and Futa. These steps failed to produce satisfactory results, and Archinard, after careful preparation and the acquisition of adequate arms including 'two 95 mm field-guns with 100 of the latest melinite shells', seized the capital of the empire in April 1890. From there, he marched against the fortress of Wesebugu, defended by the Bambara loyal to

Ahmadu. All of them were slain in battle though not without inflicting heavy losses on their assailants. Faced with the stubborn resistance of the Tukuloor garrisons, Archinard called a halt and requested Ahmadu to capitulate and abdicate.

It was not until this point that Ahmadu abandoned his weapon of diplomacy in favour of a military one. In June 1890, his soldiers attacked the railway at Talaari and engaged the French in numerous skirmishes between Kayes and Bafulabe. In one of them, the French lost forty-three killed and wounded out of a force of 125. In September, taking advantage of the isolation of Koniakary by flood, Ahmadu's soldiers attempted but failed to reconquer it. They put up a spirited defence at Nioro when it was attacked by the French in December 1890 but they were routed by the French using their 80-mm and 95-mm guns, and on 1 January 1891 Archinard entered Nioro. After the failure of his attempt to retake Nioro, during which the Sultan lost more than 3000 killed or taken prisoner, he first retreated to Macina, which he left after the hard-fought battle of Kori-Kori, and then went into exile. Even in exile in Hausa territory, he maintained an attitude of 'uncompromising independence' toward the French.

Samori and the French

Unlike Ahmadu, Samori Ture (See 6.3) chose the strategy of confrontation, not of alliance, though he used the weapons of both diplomacy and warfare but with the emphasis on the latter. By 1881, Samori had already created a large empire in the southern part of the Sudanese savannah. The conquest of the area had enabled Samori to build a powerful professional, well-trained and disciplined army, relatively well equipped with modern European arms such as Gras rifles and Kropatscheks, which were Gras repeater rifles. This army was divided into two wings, the infantry wing (the *sofa*), which by 1887 numbered between 30 000 and 35 000 men, and the cavalry wing numbering no more than 3000 by 1887. From 1888, he added to his stock some of the new quick-firing rifles and by 1893 he had about 6000 of them. However, he never acquired any artillery, which was a great handicap in his campaigns against the French. He paid for these guns with money obtained from the sale of ivory and gold mined from the old medieval goldfields of Bure in the south and from the exchange of slaves for horses in the Sahel and Mosi regions.

It is evident, then, that Samori was virtually at the height of his power when he first came into contact with the French in 1882. In February of that year, he was ordered by the French to withdraw from Kenyeran, an important market centre barring Samori's way to the Mande areas. As one would expect, Samori refused. This led to a surprise attack on his army by Borgnis-Desbordes, who was, however, forced to beat a hasty retreat. Samori's brother, Keme-Brema, attacked the French at Wenyako near Bamako in April. Though he won the battle on 2 April, he was defeated on 12 April by a much smaller French army. Samori thereupon tried to avoid conflict with the French and directed his action towards Kenedugu.

In 1885, when Combes occupied Bure, the gold of which was important to the economy of Samori's empire, Samori resolved to expel the French from the area by force. Three armies, his own and those of Keme and Masara-Mamadi, were charged with this operation. By a vast pincer movement, Bure was easily recaptured and the

6.3 *Samori Ture (c. 1830–1900) after his capture by the forces of Captain Gouraud (right) in September 1898 (Harlingue-Viollet)*

French were forced to decamp for fear of being encircled. Samori thereupon decided to cultivate his relations with the British in Sierra Leone with a view to winning the respect of the French. After having occupied Falaba in 1884, he dispatched emissaries to Freetown to propose to the governor that he place his entire country under the protection of the British government.

When that move failed, Samori turned to the French and signed a treaty with them on 28 March 1886. He agreed to withdraw his troops to the right bank of the Niger, but maintained his rights over Bure and the Mande of Kangaba. In another treaty with the French on 25 March 1887, which amended that of the previous year, Samori ceded the left bank of the river to the French and even agreed to place his country under French protection.

Samori had perhaps signed the second document in the hope that the French would help him against Tieba, the *Faama* of Sikasso, whom he attacked in April 1887 with a 12 000-strong army, while the French had signed it because they needed to prevent any alliance between Samori and Mamadou Lamine, whom they were then fighting. When he saw that instead of behaving as allies and assisting him, the French were rather encouraging dissidence and rebellion in the areas recently subdued and were attempting to prevent him from obtaining supplies of weapons from Sierra Leone, Samori began to prepare to take up arms against the French. He organized the army and concluded a treaty with the British in Sierra Leone in May 1890 which enabled him to buy modern weapons for the next three years in increasing quantities.

The major confrontation between the French and Samori, however, did not take place until 1892. Bent on defeating Samori, Humbert launched an attack on the central part of the empire in January 1892 with 1300 select riflemen and 3000 porters. Samori took personal command of his carefully chosen army of 2500 men to meet Humbert. Though these men, 'fighting like demons, clung fiercely to every defensive point on the way', to quote Yves Person's words, they were defeated and Humbert succeeded in capturing Bisandugu, Sanankoro and Kerwane. It is important to note, however that Humbert himself admitted that the results were very meagre in comparison to the heavy losses that he had sustained.

In the light of this heavy defeat, two options were open to Samori: either to surrender or to withdraw. He ruled out the former and decided to abandon his homeland and move to the east to create a new empire out of the reach of the Europeans. Still continuing his scorched-earth policy, he began his move eastwards towards the Bandama and Comoe rivers. At the beginning of 1895, he encountered and beat back a French column coming from the Baule country under the command of Monteil, and between July 1895 and January 1896 went on to conquer the Abron (Gyaman) kingdom and the western part of Gonja. By that time, he had succeeded in creating a new empire in the hinterland of the Côte d'Ivoire and Asante (see Fig. 6.2). In March 1897, his son Sarankenyi-Mori met and defeated a British column under the command of Henderson near Wa while Samori himself attacked and destroyed Kong in May 1897 and pushed on to Bobo, where he encountered a French column under the command of Caudrelier.

Caught between the French and the British and having vainly attempted to sow discord between the British and the French by returning to the latter the territory of Bouna coveted by the former, Samori decided to return to his Toma allies in Liberia. On the way, he was captured in a surprise attack at Guelemou by Gouraud on 29 September 1898 and deported to Gabon, where he died in 1900. His capture brought to an end what a recent scholar has described as 'the longest series of campaigns against a single enemy in the history of French Sudanese conquest'.

Dahomey

Behanzin, the king of Dahomey (Abomey), like Samori, chose the strategy of confrontation in defence of the sovereignty of his state. Direct conflict occurred during the last decade of the nineteenth century when France declared a protectorate over Porto Novo, a vassal of Abomey (see Fig. 6.1), and occupied Cotonou in February 1890. Prince Kondo, who had begun his reign in December 1889 under the name of Behanzin, reacted by mobilizing his troops and attacking Cotonou. He also took some economic measures against the French, which included the destruction of palm trees around Porto Novo. According to him, those economic counter-measures quickly induced the French to sue for peace. On 3 October, Father Dorgère presented himself in Abomey with proposals for peace. In return for the recognition of Cotonou as a French possession and the right of the French to levy custom duties and station a garrison of troops there, the French were to pay Behanzin an annuity of 20 000 francs. The king accepted these terms and the treaty was signed on 3 October 1890.

The French, however, were bent on conquering Dahomey and obtained the necessary excuse when the Resident of Porto Novo, who was making a trip up the Weme River in the gunboat *Topaz*, was fired upon on 27 March 1892 by some Fon soldiers. Colonel Dodds, a Senegalese mulatto, was placed in charge of this mission. He arrived at Cotonou in May 1892 and began his march to Abomey in October. The Fon united all the three divisions of their army of about 12 000 strong and moved it against the invading French army. However, all the efforts of the Fon soldiers, using their traditional methods of surprise dawn attacks, unexpected strikes, defensive stands, harrying invading forces and other guerrilla tactics, failed to halt the French and they suffered heavy casualties. The losses of the Fon were estimated at 2000 dead (including virtually all the Amazons, those dreaded female warriors), and 3000 wounded while French losses were only 10 officers and 67 men.

With the disintegration of the Fon army, the only solution, needless to say, was peace. Dodds then camped at Cana, accepted the proposals of Behanzin, but demanded payment of a heavy war indemnity and the surrender of all weapons. Such conditions were obviously unacceptable to the very dignity of the Fon people. In November 1892, Dodds, continuing his advance, entered Abomey, which Behanzin had set on fire before heading to the northern part of his kingdom where he settled and succeeded in regrouping 2000 men who carried out numerous raids in the areas held by the French. In April 1893, the notables made new proposals for peace. They were prepared to cede the southern part of the kingdom to France but could not accept the deposition of Behanzin. The French therefore launched another expeditionary force in September under the command of Dodds, now a general, which succeeded in conquering northern Dahomey. Goutchilli was appointed and crowned king on 15 January 1894 and Behanzin was arrested following a betrayal on 29 January 1894.

Conquest and reaction in British West Africa, 1880–1900

While the French resorted mainly to warfare in their occupation of French West Africa during the period 1880 to 1900, the British, by contrast, used a combination of peaceful diplomacy and warfare. Using the former approach, they concluded a number of treaties of protection with African states as they did in the northern parts of Sierra Leone, in the northern parts of the Gold Coast (now Ghana) and in some parts of Yorubaland. In other places, as in Asante, Ijebu in Yorubaland, in the Niger Delta areas and especially in northern Nigeria, however, the British by and large used force. In reacting to the British, the peoples of the area in question, like those in French West Africa, resorted to all the options open to them, those of confrontation, alliance and submission or a combination of any of these options. Let us analyse what happened in Asante, Southern Nigeria and Northern Nigeria as cases in point.

Asante (Gold Coast)

Nowhere in West Africa had there been a longer tradition of confrontation between Africans and Europeans than in the Gold Coast between the Asante and the British. This started in the 1760s and culminated in a military engagement in 1824 in which the Asante defeated the British forces and their allies and killed their commander, Sir Charles MacCarthy, the then governor of the Gold Coast. Two years later, the British avenged this defeat at the battle of Dodowa. In 1850 and 1863, war was narrowly averted but, between 1869 and 1872, the Asante attacked and occupied virtually all the southern and coastal states of the Gold Coast. To beat back the Asante, the British government launched one of the best organized campaigns of the period under the command of one of the most famous British officers of the day, General Garnet Wolseley. Armed with the latest weapons, this army succeeded in pushing the Asante army across the Pra river and entered and sacked Kumasi in February 1874 after a very fierce last-ditch stand by the Asante army at Amoafo near Bekwai.

This decisive defeat of the Asante by the British in 1874 had very far-reaching consequences and was to influence, to a great extent, the reactions of the Asante during the period 1880–1900. The first obvious effect was the disintegration of the Asante empire. By the Treaty of Fomena, Asante recognized the independence of all the vassal states south of the Pra. Taking advantage of the weakening of the military power of Asante, the vassal states to the north of the Volta river also broke away. Even the core of the empire that remained began to break up. Anxious to see that the Asante empire was never revived, the British instigated some of the member states of the Asante Union to assert their independence, and Dwaben, Kokofu, Bekwai and Nsuta began to defy the Asantehene. Above all, the Asantehene was deposed partly as a result of the outcome of the 1874 war. On the death of his successor only seven years later, a civil war broke out over the succession and it was not until 1888 that Prempeh I emerged as the new Asantehene.

Fortunately, Prempeh proved equal to the crisis with which he was confronted. Within three years of his succession, he was able to reunite the member states of the Asante Union (or Confederacy). Alarmed partly by this revival of Asante and partly by the possibility of either the French or the Germans taking over Asante, the British offered to place Asante under their protection. When Prempeh firmly but politely rejected this offer, the British again proposed to station a British resident at Kumasi in return for the payment of annual stipends to the Asantehene and his other leading kings. Again, he turned down this proposal and instead dispatched a high-powered mission to the Queen of England 'to lay before Your Majesty certain divers matters affecting the good estate of our kingdom'. This diplomatic mission left for England on 3 April 1895. Not only did the British government refuse to see the Asante mission but, while it was still there, they instructed the governor on the coast to issue an ultimatum to the Asantehene to receive a British resident and pay the war indemnity of 50 000 ounces of gold imposed on Asante in 1874. Of course, the Asantehene refused to comply with these requests, all the more so since he was awaiting the outcome of the mission to London.

Using this as an excuse, the British launched a full-scale expedition against Asante under the command of Sir Francis Scott. This expedition entered Kumasi in January 1896 without firing a shot since Prempeh and his advisers had decided not to fight the British but to accept British protection. In spite of this, Prempeh, his mother, who was also then the Queen, his brother, and some of the war chiefs were arrested and deported, first to Sierra Leone and thence to the Seychelles Islands in 1900 (see 6.4).

Southern Nigeria

The agencies and methods that the British adopted to bring the whole of modern Nigeria under their control varied, as did the initiatives and reactions on the part of the Nigerians. Yorubaland was won by the missionaries and the consuls; and Northern Nigeria by both the National African Company (from 1886 the Royal Niger Company) and the British government. The main weapons used by the British were diplomacy and conquest. Nigerian reactions therefore varied from open military confrontation to temporary alliances and submission.

Mainly as a result of the activities of the missionaries, British influence and trade had penetrated from Lagos, occupied in 1851, to most parts of Yorubaland and a number of anti-slave trade, trade and protection treaties had been concluded between the British and many Yoruba rulers by 1884. In 1886, the British administration was also able to convince Ibadan and the Ekitiparapo (comprising the Ekiti, Ijesha and Egba), who had been at war since 1879, to sign a peace treaty. The only state in Yorubaland that had effectively resisted the missionaries, the British traders and the Lagos administration until the 1880s was Ijebu. Bent on occupying Yorubaland from the early 1890s, the British decided to teach Ijebu a lesson and at the same time demonstrate to the remaining Yoruba states the futility of opposing them. Using an alleged insult to Governor Denton in 1892 as a pretext, the British launched a well-prepared expedition of about 1000 men armed with rifles, machine guns and a Maxim gun. The Ijebu courageously raised an army of between 7000 and 10 000 men. However, in spite of this huge numerical superiority, the Ijebu were routed by the invaders. It would appear that all the remaining Yoruba states learnt this lesson very well and it is not surprising that between 1893 and 1899 Abeokuta, Ibadan, Ekiti-Ijesa and Oyo readily agreed to negotiate treaties and accepted British residents. It was merely to ensure the total

6.4 *Nana Prempeh I of Asante (c. 1873–1931) during his exile in the Seychelles, c. 1908. Seated on his right is Nana Yaa Asantewaa, Queen of Edweso and leader of the 1900 Asante rebellion, and, on his left, his mother and father (Susan Hopson)*

submission of the Alafin that the British bombarded Oyo in 1895. Abeokuta remained nominally independent until 1914.

While the Yoruba, by and large, chose the strategy of submission, the rulers of the kingdom of Benin and some of the rulers of the states of the Niger Delta chose that of confrontation. Though Benin had signed a treaty of protection with the British in 1892, she none the less guarded her sovereignty with determination. This, of course, would not be tolerated in that age, and, using the killing of the British acting consul-general and five other Englishmen on their way to Benin as an excuse, the British launched a punitive expedition of 1500 men against Benin in 1897. The Oba himself would have liked to submit but a majority of his chiefs raised an army to beat back the invasion. They were, however, defeated and the capital was looted of its precious art treasures and then burnt.

In the Niger Delta, as in many others areas of Nigeria, the British had signed treaties of protection with most of the chiefs by 1884. However, while some, like the kings of Calabar and Bonny, had allowed missionaries to operate in their states, others had not. Moreover, all of them were insisting on their sovereign rights to regulate trade and to levy duties on British traders. This, the new British consuls, such as Hewett and Johnston, would not tolerate. A typical example of the rulers who stood up to the British consuls and missionaries was Jaja of Opobo. He insisted on payment of duties by British traders and ordered a complete stoppage of trade on the river until one British firm agreed to pay duties. The consul, Johnston, ordered him to stop levying duties on English traders. But, instead of doing so, Jaja dispatched a mission to the Foreign Office to protest against the order. When Jaja still refused to comply in spite of Johnston's threats to bombard his town with British gunboats, Johnston enticed Jaja on board a ship in 1887 under a promise of safe-conduct but arrested him and sent him to Accra, where he was tried and deported to the West Indies. Stunned by this treatment of one of the most powerful and wealthy rulers of the Delta states and divided internally, the other Delta states – Old Calabar, New Calabar, Brass and Bonny – surrendered and accepted governing councils imposed on them by Johnston.

Another ruler who defied the British was Nana, the governor of the river in the Itsekiri kingdom. Like Jaja, he insisted on controlling the trade on the Benin river and therefore the British raised an army to seize his capital. The first attempt in April 1894 was repulsed but the second, in September, succeeded. Nana escaped to Lagos, where he surrendered himself to the British governor, who promptly tried him and deported him to the Gold Coast.

Conquest and reaction in Northern Nigeria

If the conquest and occupation of Southern Nigeria was the work of the British government with the assistance of the traders and the missionaries, that of Northern Nigeria was accomplished by the National African Company (from 1886 the Royal Niger Company – RNC) and the British government, and the main means used, like that of the French in the Western Sudan, was military conquest. This had been preceded by a series of treaties between the rulers of Northern Nigeria and the RNC. These treaties were calculated to secure the area for the British rather than the French or the Germans, who were advancing from the west and east respectively.

Following the establishment of the principle of effective occupation at the Berlin Conference and to forestall the French and the Germans, the RNC felt compelled to move in. The doors to the north lay through Ilorin and Nupe, both of which were determined to maintain their independence and sovereignty. Nupe was therefore invaded in 1897. The Etsu of Nupe and his huge army, estimated at 25 000–30 000 of cavalry and infantrymen and armed mainly with the traditional weapons of bows, arrows, spears and swords, put up a spirited fight. Nevertheless, the RNC came out victorious in the end, deposed the Etsu and installed a more pliable one. A similar invasion was launched against Ilorin in the same year. After meeting another spirited defence, the RNC brought Ilorin into subjection.

Surprisingly, other rulers of the north were not intimidated by these victories. On the contrary, apart from that of Zaria, all the other emirs, spurred on by their implacable hatred for the infidel, were determined to die rather than surrender their land and faith. The British therefore had to launch a series of campaigns – against Kontagora in 1900, Adamawa in 1901, Bauchi in 1902, and Kano, Sokoto and Burwuri in 1903. The rulers of all these emirates rose to the occasion but they had no effective answer to their enemies' Maxim guns, rifles and muzzle-loading 7-pounder cannon and therefore suffered defeat.

African reactions and responses in West Africa, 1900–14

As is evident from the above, by 1900, all the efforts of the West Africans to maintain their sovereignty had been unsuccessful and the period from 1900 to the outbreak of the First World War saw the introduction of various kinds of machinery for the administration and, above all, for the exploitation of the newly acquired estates. District commissioners and travelling commissioners were appointed, new courts were established, new codes and new laws were introduced, chiefs were confirmed or deposed and new ones appointed, direct and indirect taxation was introduced, and forced labour was demanded for the construction of roads and railways. All these measures naturally generated various reactions.

During this second phase, while there were differences in the objectives in view, the strategy adopted for the attainment of these objectives by West Africans was the same. The main objectives were three: to regain their independence and sovereignty, which implied expelling the colonial rulers altogether; to seek to correct or redress certain specific abuses or oppressive aspects of the colonial system; or to seek accommodation within it. The strategy that was adopted during this phase was neither submission nor alliance but resistance, and this took many forms: revolts or rebellions, migrations, strikes, boycotts, petitions, delegations and finally ideological protest.

The most popular weapon used by West Africans during this period was rebellion or revolt. Notable among rebellions were that led by Mamadou Lamine in Senegal between 1885 and 1887; those led by Fode Silla, the marabout king of Kombo, and Fode Kabba, the Muslim ruler of Niamina and the Casamance districts, in The Gambia between 1898 and 1901; the Hut Tax rebellion of 1898 in Sierra Leone led by Bai Bureh;

the Asante rebellion of 1900 in the Gold Coast led by Yaa Asantewaa, the Queen of Edweso; the Ekumeku rebellion of 1898–1900 and the Aro rising between 1898 and 1902 in Eastern Nigeria; the rebellions of the Bariba of Borgu and the Somba of Atacora in Dahomey between 1913 and 1914; the Mosi rebellions in Koudougou and Fada N'Gurma in Upper Volta (now Burkina Faso) from 1908 to 1914; those of the Lobi and the Dyula in French Sudan between 1908 and 1909; the uprising in Porto Novo in Dahomey; the revolts of the Baule, Akouse, Sassandra and Guro in Côte d'Ivoire between 1900 and 1914; and the numerous uprisings in several parts of Guinea between 1908 and 1914. It is interesting to note that these rebellions increased in intensity during the First World War.

A typical example of the rebellions that took place during the period under review was the Hut Tax rebellion of 1898. It was the reaction of the Temne and the Mende of Sierra Leone to the consolidation of British rule over them by the appointment of district commissioners, the expansion of the frontier police, the abolition of the slave trade and slavery, the implementation of the Protectorate Ordinance of 1896, which empowered the government to dispose of waste land, and, finally, the imposition of a tax of 5s. a year on all two-roomed houses and 10s. on all larger houses in the Protectorate. All the Temne chiefs unanimously decided not to pay the tax and rose up in rebellion under the leadership of one of them, Bai Bureh. They were joined by the Mende people, thereby involving almost three-quarters of the Protectorate. The rebel forces attacked and looted trading stations and killed British officials and troops and all those suspected of assisting the colonial government. By May 1898, the rebel armies were within about 40 km of Freetown and two companies of troops had to be hastily brought in from Lagos to defend the town.

What was the true nature of this revolt? The British governor of Sierra Leone, who was stunned by the rebellion, attributed not only that rebellion but the general resistance to colonial rule that was raging at the time to 'the growing political consciousness of the African, and his increasing sense of his worth and autonomy'. Cardew's analysis cannot be faulted and is equally true of most of the rebellions and guerilla wars that occurred in West Africa between the late 1890s and 1914.

Mass migration

Besides revolts and rebellions, one widespread method of resistance was migration in protest against the harshness of colonial rule. This was particularly common in the French colonies where, unable to resort to armed revolt owing to the stationing of military control units in the annexed sector, the Africans resorted to fleeing, in order to elude the measures that they found so oppressive and humiliating. Thus, between 1882 and 1889, the Fulbe population of the suburbs of Saint-Louis dropped from 30 000 to only 10 000. In 1916 and 1917 more than 12 000 people left the Côte-d'Ivoire for the Gold Coast. Large numbers also left Senegal for The Gambia, Upper Volta for the Gold Coast and Dahomey for Nigeria during the period. It should be pointed out that these rebellions and protest migrations were resorted to, by and large, by the rural folk and in the inland parts of those colonies, whose direct contact with the Europeans dated only from the 1880s and 1890s. In the coastal areas and new urban centres where the educated elite lived and where a working class was emerging, less violent options were resorted to. These included strikes, boycotts, ideological protest, the use of newspapers and, above all, the dispatch of petitions and delegations to the local as well as the metropolitan colonial governments by various societies and movements.

Strikes

Strikes as a weapon of protest became more common after the First World War, but there were a few in the period before. A strike by railway workers on the Dakar – Saint-Louis line occurred as early as 1890; in 1891 there was the strike of Dahomey women who were employed in the Cameroons; labourers went on strike for higher pay in Lagos in 1897; in 1918–19 there was a strike of the Cotonou and Grand Popo paddlers in Dahomey; and in 1919 there occurred the first strike of dockers at the Conakry port in Guinea.

Ideological protest

Ideological protest against colonial rule was particularly strong in French West Africa, where the concept of *négritude* was evolved in reaction to the French policy of assimilation. This concept, as Crowder has pointed out, 'either partially or totally rejected the cultural aspects of European domination and asserted that, contrary to the views propounded by European colonialists, Africa had a history and culture of its own'. Ideological protest was seen not only in the cultural field but also in the religious field: among Christians, Muslims and Traditionalists. Thus, as Oloruntimehin has shown, the Lobi and the Bambara of French Sudan banded together against the spread of French culture as well as the Christian and Muslim religions. The adherents of the Islamic religion, especially in the Western Sudan belt, also revived Mahdism or founded movements, such as the Mouridiyya led by Shaykh Ahmadu Bamba and the Hamalliyya led by Shaykh Hamallah, to protest against the French presence. The African Christians, especially in the British West African colonies, also rebelled against the European domination of the churches and the imposition of European culture and liturgy. This resulted in the breakaway of these members to form their own messianic or millenarian or Ethiopian churches with distinctively African liturgies and doctrines. Such, for example, was the Native Baptist Church, the first African church formed in Nigeria in April 1888.

Elite associations

Many clubs and associations were also formed by the educated Africans, mainly in the urban centres, as vehicles for protest against the abuse and iniquities of the colonial system during this period. These associations used newspapers, plays, tracts and pamphlets as their main weapons. Examples of such bodies which acted as 'watch dogs of colonial rule' were the Aborigines' Rights Protection Society (ARPS) formed in the Gold Coast in 1897, the Young Senegalese Club founded in 1910, and the People's Union and the Anti-Slavery and Aborigines' Protection Society formed in Nigeria in 1908 and 1912 respectively. The ARPS was easily the most active. It was formed to protest against the Land Bill of 1896, which was to give control of all so-called waste or unoccupied lands to the government. As a result of a delegation it dispatched to London in 1898 which met the Secretary of State for Colonies, this obnoxious bill was withdrawn. From then on, the ARPS sent a series of petitions to the local administration as well as the Colonial Office protesting against various projected Bills. It sent two further delegations to England, one in 1906 to demand the repeal of the 1894 Towns Ordinance and the second in 1911 to oppose the Forestry Bill of 1910. In French West Africa, the Young Senegalese Club also actively campaigned for equal rights.

It should be evident from this discussion that the people of West Africa devised all kinds of strategies and tactics, first, to oppose the establishment of the colonial system and, second, after the failure of their early efforts, to resist certain specific measures and institutions of the system. These various strategies and measures proved on the whole unsuccessful, and by the end of the period under review, colonialism had become firmly entrenched in the whole of West Africa.

African initiatives and resistance in East Africa, 1880–1914

In East Africa, as in other parts of Africa, African initiatives and resistance to European conquest and occupation were determined by the structure of each society at the time.

In the 1890s, the period that preceded European occupation of East Africa, the societies of the region had achieved differing stages of social organization. Some, such as the Baganda and the Banyoro in Uganda, the Banyambo in Tanganyika (now Tanzania) and the Wanga in Kenya, had achieved a high degree of centralized government. In such societies, response to foreign penetration tended to be dictated by the king or the leadership as a whole. Other societies, such as the Nyamwezi in Tanganyika or the Nandi in Kenya were in the process of forming centralized governments. However, the vast majority of societies in this region did not have centralized governments. But lack of central governments does not imply lack of government, a mistake which some foreigners commenting on African societies have made in the past.

Again, various societies had different levels of contact with Europeans or Arabs, the two external forces impinging on East Africa at this time. On the whole, coastal areas had had a longer contact with Europeans and Arabs than the interior areas. Of the interior peoples, three or four groups – the Akamba and Wanga of Kenya, the Nyamwezi of Tanganyika and the Baganda of Uganda – had had longer contact, through the caravan trade, with the Arabs than the rest. The degree of exposure to these outside influences determined the type and extent of resistance put up by the various societies.

Apart from these human influences, there were ecological changes taking place in East Africa in the 1890s, which also affected response to foreign penetration. The whole region underwent ecological stress resulting in drought with consequent famines. Rinderpest epidemics also occurred. Some societies were affected by these natural calamities more deeply than others. Pastoral societies, such as the Maasai of Kenya, seem to have been hit worst of all. A number of Maasai families, including the Waiyaki and Njonjo, took refuge among the neighbouring Gikuyu, where they were to play a different role, both in relation to their response to colonial advance and in relation to the colonial system that was consequently set up, as well as to the post-colonial society. Others took refuge among the Nandi. Still others were to offer their services as soldiers, first to King Mumia of Wanga among the Abaluyia as mercenaries, and, second, to British imperial agents as part of the expeditionary force that was used to conquer the country that is now called Kenya. The Maasai example serves to illustrate the kind of dislocation that had taken place among the economies of various societies in this general area. Thus, colonialism came to an area already suffering from an economic crisis with all its attendant effects.

The European Scramble for East Africa and the patterns of African resistance

The colonialist Scramble for East Africa involved three competing powers: the Sultanate of Zanzibar, Germany and Britain. The first on the scene were the Arabs who operated from Zanzibar. Their interests both on the coast and in the interior were largely commercial, revolving around the trade in slaves and ivory. Before the 1880s and 1890s, these Arab and Swahili traders were content to operate from the coast. But, during the closing decades of the last century, Arab interests in the interior of East Africa began to be threatened by German and British interests that had been steadily penetrating the area. In the face of this, the Arabs attempted to take political control of some areas in order to protect their commercial concessions. Thus, they set up a colony at Ujiji on the shores of Lake Tanganyika, and, in Buganda, they staged a coup at the expense of the Christians after co-operating with them to remove Mwanga from the throne. The Europeans in the interior included traders and missionaries, all of whom wanted the occupation of East Africa by their home governments in order to provide them with security as well as a free hand to carry out their enterprises without hindrance.

The methods of European advance varied from place to place. But, on the whole, they were characterized by the use of force combined, where possible, with diplomatic alliances with one group against another. Force took the form of invasions, which were often also looting exercises. To facilitate advance inland, railways were constructed. The Uganda railway, linking the interior of Uganda and Kenya with the coast, reached the Lake Victoria basin in 1901. The Germans likewise started the construction of railways and road networks. The first railway was started on the coast at Tanga after 1891 and reached the foothills of the Usambara mountains in 1905.

The response in Kenya

African response to all this was, as already indicated, both military and diplomatic, though at times there was withdrawal or non-co-operation or passivity. The Nandi in Kenya, for instance, resisted militarily the construction of the railway through their territory. Of all the peoples of Kenya, they put up the strongest and longest military resistance to British imperialism; it began in the 1890s and did not end until their leader was murdered by the British commanders in 1905, on his way to the negotiations which had been treacherously arranged. That event weakened Nandi resistance and eventually led to the British occupation of their territory.

That the Nandi resisted the British so long was due to the nature of their society. Nandi society was divided into territorial units called *pororiat*. Warriors from each unit were responsible for the defence of the territory. For this reason, the warriors slept in a common hut. This was the nearest thing to a standing army. These territorial armies came together under the leadership of an *orgoiyot*, or traditional leader. It was he who decided when the army would go on a raid. The armies were linked to him through a personal representative who sat at each territorial council. Because territory rather than clan was the centre of Nandi social life, this meant that clan rivalry was absent. The result was a cohesive society, and it was this cohesion that gave the society military superiority over its neighbours.

This contrasts with the response of some other communities in Kenya. In central Kenya, for instance, each leader or group or clan reacted separately to this foreign intrusion. A typical example was the reaction of Waiyaki among the Gikuyu. His parents were originally Maasai who, because of the upheavals that took place in Maasailand in the nineteenth century, had moved to settle in southern Gikuyuland. Here, Waiyaki had gained influence partly because of his contact with caravan traders. At first he sought the friendship of the Imperial British East African Company (IBEAC), who wrongly regarded him as the paramount chief of all the Gikuyu. He ensured the safe passage of Count Teleki's expedition through southern Gikuyu and entered into a blood-brotherhood treaty with Frederick Lugard, who was then the company's agent. The blood-brotherhood ceremony was the highest expression of trust among the Gikuyu. After this treaty, Waiyaki allowed Lugard to build a fort on his land. But, when later Waiyaki's requests for such things as firearms were turned down by the IBEAC, the agents of British imperialism, he turned against them and stormed the company's station at Dagoretti. Subsequently, he again changed his tactics and made an alliance with the foreigners in a diplomatic effort to safeguard his position, but he was deported. Waiyaki's behaviour illustrates the point, sometimes missed, that no one was a resister or a so-called collaborator all his life. People changed their tactics in accordance with the prevailing situation and probably as their understanding of the forces surrounding them deepened.

Lenana of the Maasai similarly allied himself with the British, by contrast with another section of the Maasai who were opposed to a foreign presence in their area. Often those who made an alliance with the British were rewarded with posts such as chiefships in the colonial system. So Lenana, like many others, was made a paramount chief of the Maasai in Kenya.

On the coast, the Mazrui family resisted the take-over by the IBEAC. This resistance was led by Mbaruk bin Rashid, who organized hit-and-run warfare against the superior weapons of the British forces. It took reinforcements of Indian troops brought in by the British to defeat him. He fled Tanganyika, only to fall into the hands of the Germans.

Further inland, the Akamba did not like the British interference in their affairs. The founding of Machakos station by the IBEAC in 1889 led to hostilities between the Company and the local community. Company agents looted the surrounding areas of food and property – mainly goats and cattle. They also interfered with religious shrines which people regarded as sacred. In response to this, the local population under Msiba Mwea organized a boycott of the IBEAC station in 1890, refusing to sell it food. Peace only prevailed when Lugard arrived to make a peace treaty which involved the signing of a 'blood-brotherhood' accord with the local population.

In northern Kenya, in the hinterland of Kisimayu, the Ogaden Somali, the Mazrui family and the Akamba resisted British intrusion. Again it took Indian reinforcements to defeat them in 1899. The Taita, who had refused to provide porters and who had resisted caravan traders' interference in their country, were besieged in 1897 by IBEAC troops under the command of Captain Nelson. They put up a stiff resistance and Captain Nelson himself and eleven of his men were wounded by Taita poisoned arrows before they were defeated.

Elsewhere, in western Kenya, among the Abaluyia, the pattern of response was the same, involving military encounter as well as diplomatic alliance. King Mumia of the Wanga was particularly skilful at the use of diplomacy. He saw the British as an ally whom he could use to extend his influence over the whole of western Kenya by helping him to defeat his neighbouring adversaries such as the Iteso and the Luo with whom he had been at loggerheads for quite some time. Likewise, the British saw in Mumia a willing agent to help them to extend their control over the whole area. Indeed, the British occupation of western Kenya was accomplished largely through his help.

The response in Tanganyika

The pattern of response in Tanganyika was similar to that obtaining in Kenya as described above, that is, it involved the use of force as well as diplomatic alliances. The Mbunga clashed with German forces in 1891 and 1893, while the hinterland of Kilwa had its armed resistance organized behind Hasan bin Omari. The Makonde defied German penetration till 1899. The Hehe, under their leader Mkwawa, clashed with German forces in 1891, killing about 290. The Germans set out to avenge this loss. In 1894, they stormed the Hehe region and captured its capital, but Mkwawa escaped. After being hunted for four years by his enemies, he committed suicide in order to avoid capture.

The coastal people of Tanganyika organized their resistance around the person and leadership of Abushiri. He was born in 1845 of an Arab father and an Oromo mother. He was a descendant of one of the first Arab settlers on the coast, a member of a group who had come to regard themselves as local people. Like many others, he opposed the influence of the Sultanate of Zanzibar on the coast and even advocated independence. As a young man, he had organized expeditions into the interior to trade in ivory. From the profits made, he bought himself a farm and planted sugar cane. He was also engaged in a campaign against the Nyamwezi. This had enabled him to assemble warriors who were later to be used against the Germans. Under his leadership, the coastal people fired on a German warship at Tanga in September 1888 and then gave the Germans two days to leave the coast. They later attacked Kilwa and killed two Germans. Describing this as 'the Arab revolt', the Germans sent out Hermann von Wissmann to suppress it. He reached Zanzibar in April 1889, attacked Abushiri in his fortress near Bagamoyo and drove him out. Abushiri escaped northwards to Uzigua, where he was betrayed and handed over to the Germans, who hanged him at Pangani on 15 December 1889. The coastal resistance finally collapsed when Kilwa was bombarded and taken by the Germans in May 1890.

Besides those who took to arms in Tanganyika in an effort to defend their independence, there were others who chose the weapon of diplomacy. The Marealle and the Kibanga near the Tanganyikan mountains of Kilimanjaro and Usambara were, to name but two examples, among those who allied with the Germans in order to defeat their enemies. These people, like the Wanga in Kenya, believed that they were using the Germans even though in the process they were made use of much more by the Germans than perhaps they realized.

The response in Uganda

A similar pattern of response to British colonialism took place in Uganda. The period between 1891 and 1899 saw a clash between the forces of Kabarega, the King of Bunyoro, and those of Lugard and other British agents. After some clashes in which Kabarega's forces were defeated, he turned to diplomacy. Twice he attempted to come to terms with Lugard, but the latter would not countenance these gestures. Eventually, Kabarega resorted to guerilla warfare, probably the first of its kind in East Africa. He withdrew from Bunyoro to the Lango country in the north, from where he harassed British forces time and again. His hideout was, however, stormed in 1899 and he was captured and exiled, first to Kisimayu and thence to the Seychelles Islands, where he died in 1923.

When Mwanga, the Kabaka of Buganda, ascended the throne in 1894, he was suspicious of Europeans, mostly missionaries at that time, so he sought to restrict his people's interactions with them. Those among the Baganda who had embraced the Christian faith and who would not obey his orders were put to death as traitors: Mwanga was violently resisting attempts by British agents to take over his country, even though disguised as missionaries. But his diplomatic ability also became apparent in the way he handled various, often warring, religious sects. At one time, he would play the two Christian sects, Catholics and Protestants, against Muslims when he thought the latter were becoming too powerful and therefore threatening his control of the country. At another time, he would ally with Muslims against Catholics or Protestants or both, depending on whom he thought dangerous to his rule. When necessary, Mwanga resorted to a revival of some old tradition in an attempt to drive out all foreigners, as happened in 1888. On this occasion, he intended to entice all foreigners and their Baganda followers to the traditional naval parade on an island on Lake Victoria with the intention of leaving them there to starve to death. However, the plan was leaked to the foreigners, who then staged a coup, deposed Mwanga and put his brother on the throne as a kind of puppet ruler. Later, however, in 1889, Mwanga managed to regain his throne but was deposed; so he joined Kabarega in Lango where both of them were captured (see 7.1) and exiled to Kisimayu, where he died in 1903.

There were, however, others among the Baganda who allied themselves firmly with British imperialism. It was Baganda agents, especially after the 1900 Agreement, who were responsible for spreading British colonialism to the rest of the country. Notable among them was Kakunguru, a Muganda general, who largely spearheaded the spread of British control to eastern and northern Uganda. It was he, for instance, who captured Kabarega when the British decided to storm his hide-out in Lango country. The 1900 Agreement made the Baganda partners with the British in the advance of British imperialism in the area. Hatred for colonialism consequently came to be directed at the Baganda rather than at the colonial masters themselves, and many of the political

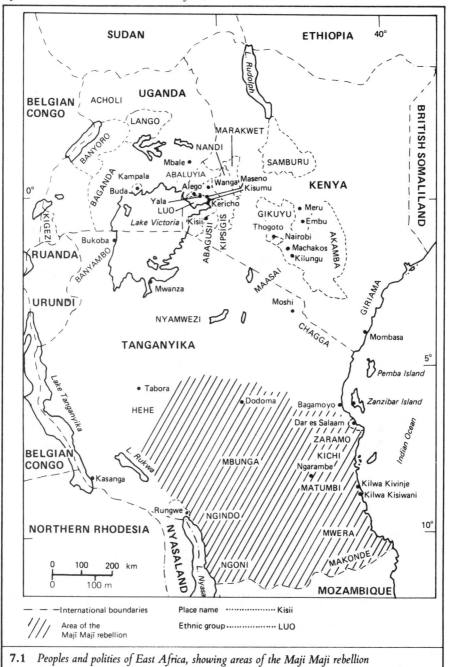

7.1 *Peoples and polities of East Africa, showing areas of the Maji Maji rebellion*

problems that later plagued Uganda stem from this early partnership between the British and the Baganda.

East Africa under colonial domination

Having thus suppressed all opposition and resistance by the East Africans and having established firm control over their spheres of influence, the colonial powers set out to transform the region both politically and, even more importantly, economically. The aim was to turn East African economies towards export by making the area dependent on economic arrangements in Europe. In this regard, it was to be a source of raw materials rather than an area for industrialization. One of the first colonial activities was, as already indicated, to build railway lines, both in Tanganyika to the Usambara and Kilimanjaro areas and in Kenya to link the coast with the Lake Victoria basin.

Ukambani was the first area in Kenya to be occupied by white settlers in the late 1890s. But, of all the peoples of Kenya, the Maasai lost more land to white settlement than any other community. Twice land was taken from them, first in 1904, when they were removed to a reserve in Laikipia, and then in 1911, when they were again removed to give room to white settlement. On both occasions, the Maasai were said by the colonial government to have entered into an agreement to surrender their land. However, on the last occasion, the Masai challenged the decision in a British court, which, not surprisingly, ruled against them. At the same time, white settlement was also taking place in Tanganyika. By 1905, there were 284 white settlers there, mainly in the Usambara and Kilimanjaro areas.

From the beginning, settlers sought to dominate these colonies. In Kenya, for instance, they had by 1902 formed a Planters and Farmers Association to press for their demand to have the highlands of Kenya reserved for them. Though Indians had been used to construct the Uganda railway, they were excluded from this area. Eliot, who was the governor then, agreed with this demand and confined Indian settlement to land immediately along the railway. The policy of excluding Indians from the highlands was eventually adopted by every protectorate commissioner and colonial governor after Eliot. The response of the Indians was to form their own association to press for a share of the highlands. In 1907, they presented their case to the Secretary of State for the Colonies, Winston Churchill, when he visited East Africa. However, the conflict between these two groups was not resolved until the 1920s. By the beginning of the First World War, cash crops and the plantation economy in Kenya were firmly in the hands of white settlers, who excluded both Africans and Indians from participation. This state of affairs influenced the African response to the white presence in Kenya.

The position in Tanganyika and Uganda was different. In Tanganyika, beginning in the southern part of the country, Africans were encouraged, first by missionaries and then by colonial officials, to take to peasant production of cash crops, basically cotton and coffee. In addition, collective farms for cotton were introduced. By 1908, Africans were exporting two-thirds of Tanganyika's cotton exports while, by 1912, the African contribution accounted for over 70%. During the same period, African coffee production around the Kilimanjaro area had caught up with that of the settlers. The extent to which changes had taken place in Tanganyika can be seen in the amount of wage labour employed. It has been estimated that, by 1931, the African wage-earning population in Tanganyika was 172 000, or about one-fifth of the able-bodied male population at the time.

Probably the most far-reaching economic reorganization, in comparison with Kenya and Tanganyika, took place in Uganda. The 1900 Agreement distributed land in Buganda in an attempt to create a landed class that would be loyal to the colonial system. This land distribution led to the development of different class and property relations, since landlords and tenants came into existence. In addition, it was understood that Uganda was to be a country where African agricultural production would predominate. This was one of the factors that acted as a barrier to large-scale white settlement, such as took place in Kenya and Tanganyika. Unlike in Kenya, but as was more the case in Tanganyika, efforts were made by the colonial regime to place the export-oriented economy into the hands of the indigenous people. The peasant production of cash crops was to become the mainstay of the economy of Uganda. What started in Buganda was eventually extended to other parts of the colony, notably in the west where the climate, as in Buganda, was favourable. By 1907, cotton produced in this manner accounted for 35% of all exports from Uganda. Generally speaking, cash transactions were well entrenched in Uganda, as in the rest of East Africa, on the eve of the First World War. Peasants sold their produce to Asian and European traders. A monetary economy had set in and the grounds for further incorporation into the capitalist system had been laid.

The demands of the system brought Africans face to face with what had happened and was happening among them. These included introduction of a hut tax, labour requirements, loss of further land, lack of political freedom and corrosion of their culture. Taxes were introduced not so much as, or not entirely as, a means of raising revenue, but as a way of forcing Africans away from their homes into the labour market and into the monetary economy. Labour was required for settler farms and for public works such as road construction. The conditions under which Africans worked were often harsh. There were other influences introduced by more subtle agents of imperialism, such as missionaries and traders.

Anti-colonial movements in East Africa to 1914

In these early days of colonialism, each locality responded differently, except in a few cases where there was co-ordinated action over a wider area. In Kenya, as elsewhere in East Africa, the early responses by such people as the Mazruis and the Nandi, were meant to protect their independence against foreign threats. The subsequent responses in the interior of the country were meant to rid people of oppression and colonial domination. Although this was not a period of nationalist struggle in the modern sense, there are signs of the beginnings of it. Among the Luo in western Kenya, protest against mission domination led to the establishment of an independent Church in 1910 under John Owalo. Then in 1913 came the Mumbo cult, a movement which was against white domination but which used religion as an ideology. From Luoland, it spread to the Gusii, thus showing that it had the potential of spreading to other parts of Kenya. The reaction of the colonial regime was to suppress this movement, as indeed they suppressed every movement that challenged their domination.

A similar movement to the one described above was taking place among the Akamba in eastern Kenya. Here, it was meant to protest against the way in which settlers in Ukambani were treating their African labour force. Again, religion was used. It started in 1911 when a certain woman by the name of Siotume was said to be possessed with a spirit. However, the movement was soon taken over by a young man named Kiamba, who turned it into a political protest against colonialism in Kenya. He formed some kind of police force to help him carry out his threat. He was, however arrested and banished.

On the whole, early anti-colonial movements in Kenya, in the period before the First World War, took place in the west and the east of the country. The Giriama on the coast, who had been resisting the British since the late nineteenth century, took the opportunity offered by the war to revolt against colonial rule in 1914. The British reaction was to burn down houses and confiscate property. The Giriama, like the Mazruis and others, resorted to a form of guerilla warfare, but were eventually defeated.

Uganda was calmer than Kenya. But, in 1911, the Acholi in northern Uganda revolted against British colonial rule. It was a reaction against labour recruitment as well as against an effort to disarm them. One of the chief concerns of colonialism was to make sure that the colonized were rendered helpless in the face of cruel exploitation. For this reason, it was important that they did not possess firearms; hence the campaign to collect arms and to disarm the colonized population. The Acholi refused to surrender their guns voluntarily. However, they lost the fight in the ensuing contest.

The most serious challenge to colonial rule in East Africa during this period – the Maji Maji uprising – occurred in Tanganyika and it was one in which both religion and magic were resorted to (see 7.2). Forced labour, taxation, harassment and harsh conditions of work all combined to cause the Maji Maji uprising. However, the immediate cause was the introduction of a communal cotton scheme. People were required to work on this scheme for twenty-eight days in a year. But the proceeds did not go to the workers. They were paid such low sums that some refused to take them. This African response was not against growing cotton as such, which they had willingly started growing as a cash crop. It was a reaction against this scheme, which exploited their labour and threatened the African economy by forcing them to leave their own farms to work on public ones.

To unite the people of Tanganyika in their challenge to the Germans, the leader of the movement, the prophet, Kinjikitile Ngwale made use of their religious beliefs. He taught them that the unity and freedom of all Africans was a fundamental principle and therefore that they were to unite and fight for their freedom against the Germans in a war which had been ordained by God, and that they would be assisted by their ancestors, who would return to life. The movement, which lasted from July 1905 to August 1907, spread over an area of 26 000 sq km in the southern third of Tanganyika.

The war broke out in the last week of July 1905 and the first victims were the founder himself and his assistant, who were hanged on 4 August 1905. His brother picked up his mantle and assumed the title of 'Nyamguni', one of the three divinities in the area, and continued to administer the 'maji' but it was ineffective. The ancestors did not return as promised and the movement was brutally suppressed by the German colonial authorities.

7.2　*Mwanga (c. 1866–1903), ex-King of Buganda, and Kabarega (c. 1850–1923), ex-King of Bunyoro, on their way to exile (Royal Commonwealth Society)*

The Maji Maji uprising was the first large-scale movement of resistance to colonial rule in East Africa. In the words of John Iliffe it was 'a final attempt by Tanganyika's old societies to destroy the colonial order by force', and it was truly a mass movement of peasants against colonial exploitation. It shook the German regime in Tanganyika; their response was not just the suppression of the movement but also the abandonment of the communal cotton scheme. There were also some reforms in the colonial structure, especially with regard to the recruitment and use of labour, which were designed to make colonialism acceptable to Africans. But the rebellion failed and this failure did indeed make 'the passing of the old societies inevitable'.

On the whole, between 1890 and 1914 dramatic changes took place in East Africa. Colonialism was imposed on the people, violently in most cases even if the violence was sometimes disguised in the form of law. African responses to the initial impact combined military confrontation with diplomatic efforts in a vain attempt to preserve their independence. Where Africans did not engage in military or diplomatic activity, they acquiesced or remained indifferent, except where direct demands were made on them. The establishment of colonialism meant the reorganization of the political and economic life of the people. Taxes were introduced. Forced labour and general deprivation of political rights were practised. Some Africans responded to these changes violently. Others acquiesced. In Tanganyika and Uganda, some Africans had moved to peasant production of cash crops, particularly cotton and coffee. In Kenya, Africans were denied the production of cash crops. The economy there was settler-based. Various African responses to this position have been outlined. More were to follow in the period after the First World War.

African initiatives and resistance in Central Africa, 1880–1914

In Central Africa, African initiatives and resistance to European conquest and occupation took several forms between 1880 and 1914. Central Africa is defined as the area included in the states of the Belgian Congo (now Zaire), Northern Rhodesia (now Zambia), Nyasaland (now Malawi), Angola and Mozambique. Like most regions of Africa on the eve of the Scramble, this zone was occupied by a host of peoples organized either in state or centralized political systems or in small-scale political units. Among the first category were the Lunda and Luba kingdoms of the Belgian Congo, the Humbe and Chokwe states of Angola, the Mozambican kingdom of the Mwenemutapa, the Undi kingdom in Nyasaland, and the numerous states founded by the Nguni and the Kololo in the Zambezi–Limpopo basins. Among the latter were the Yao and lakeside Tonga of Nyasaland, the Bisa and Lala of Northern Rhodesia, the Sena and Chopi of Mozambique, the Kisama and Loango of Angola, and the Loga and Bowa of the Belgian Congo (see 8.1). Despite these political divisions and the ethnic and regional differences and internal conflicts between the emerging competing classes, confrontation and resistance remained the dominant reaction to European imperialist conquest and occupation.

Rather than merely describing the anti-colonial activity from country to country, the patterns of opposition which characterized the region as a whole will be our focus. By analysing African reactions in terms of the goals of the participants, three broad categories can be identified:

(1) opposition or confrontation which attempted to maintain the sovereignty of the indigenous societies;
(2) localized resistance which sought to check specific abuses imposed by the colonial regime;
(3) rebellions which aimed to destroy the alien system which had generated these abuses.

The struggle to maintain independence: the era of confrontation and alliance

The strategies of confrontation adopted by the Central Africans shared a common objective – to drive out the Europeans and protect their homelands, way of life and

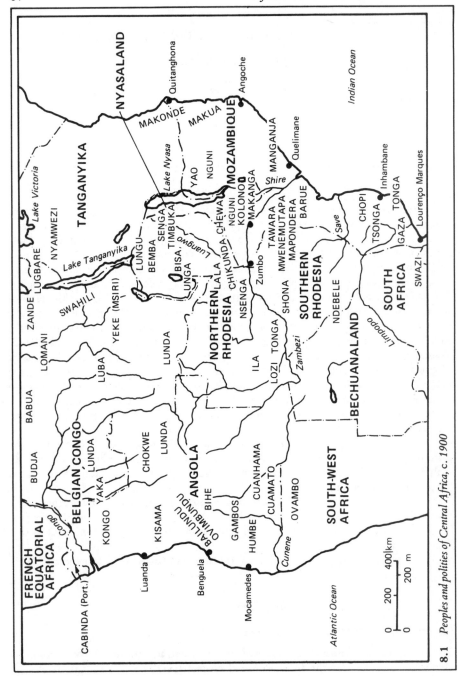

8.1 *Peoples and polities of Central Africa, c. 1900*

means of livelihood. In Nyasaland, for example, the Nguni of Gomani attacked missionary stations in 1896, in part to protest against the weakening effect of Christianity, while in Mozambique the Barue frustrated Lisbon's efforts to incorporate them into its informal empire by using the Catholic Church to convert the royal family. During the last two decades of the century, the Yao, Makua, Yeke, Chikunda, Ovimbundu and Chokwe, among others, forcefully resisted the attempts by the Europeans to abolish the slave trade and end their middleman role. Simultaneously, many peasants and agriculturalists fought to maintain control over the means of production and prevent the seizure of their land, cattle, labour and women.

African leaders recognized the necessity of neutralizing the European arms advantage if they were to survive. Many societies already participating in international trade benefited from access to the weapons market and had acquired vast arsenals in exchange for captives. The Chokwe, Ovimbundu and Chikundu were so successful that their forces were often better armed than the respective Congo Free State and Portuguese troops who sought to conquer them. Other Central African peoples, previously not involved in extensive commercial ventures, increased their exports to obtain modern guns and ammunition. During the last quarter of the century, for example, the Ovambo, the Shangaan and even several conservative Nguni offshoots acquired modern rifles in anticipation of a clash with the Europeans.

A number of African societies also expanded their ability to defend themselves through internal military changes. The Barue developed munitions plants which produced powder, rifles and even components for their artillery. New and expansive defensive structures such as the fortified town of Jumbe of Kota and the *aringas* of the Zambezi and Luangwa valleys were built to withstand European siege. Other Africans, among them the Makua, the Lunda and the diverse bands who operated in the Gambo region of southern Angola, developed guerilla tactics that thwarted the first imperialist advances.

Despite the common commitment of some of the Africans to prevent foreign rule and to acquire modern weapons, the immediate tactics they employed varied substantially. In several cases African states reacted violently to the first European encroachments despite the overwhelming military advantage which the enemy enjoyed. Thus, the Chewa leader Mwase Kasungu led his people in a futile effort against the British, ultimately committing suicide in 1896 rather than capitulating. At about the same time, the Bihe of Angola ambushed a colonial force seeking to establish 'interior posts which would cut through their homelands.

Other African leaders sought to avoid initial confrontations in the hope that they could either strengthen their military capacity or negotiate a 'just' treaty in which the sovereignty of their state would be recognized. For almost a decade Gungunyane negotiated with both the British and the Portuguese and was prepared to make a variety of concessions short of renouncing Shangaan independence (see 8.2). The Barue royal family pursued a similar policy, seeking to enlist the support of Karl Peters, a German adventurer, while sporadic Bemba resistance at the end of the century occurred only after fifteen years of diplomatic manoeuvring with Great Britain. This strategy, however, invariably led to confrontation in view of the principle of effective occupation laid down by the Congress of Berlin.

8.2 *Gungunyane and his warriors (J. R. Baptista, Caminho de terro da Beira a Manica, 1892)*

Many Central African societies that were unable to offer effective opposition or that failed to comprehend the implications of colonial rule submitted peacefully in the first instance but soon after rose up in an effort to regain their independence. This pattern of delayed confrontation regularly occurred in the Congo, where the indigenous population initially considered the agents of the Congo Free State as trading partners and allies against the alien slavers. Only when Free State officials sought to impose taxes and conscript labour did the local societies recognize that they had inadvertently yielded their autonomy. During the period between 1885 and 1905 more than a dozen nominally 'subjugated' groups revolted in the lower and central Congo.

In addition to the variety of initial reactions, the resisters differed in their preparedness to seek co-operation and alliances. At one extreme were a number of societies, both large and small, that confronted the invaders without any effort to create broader alliances. In Angola, the Bihe, Humbe and Gangwela initially fought the aliens without the assistance of their neighbours who shared a common hatred of the Portuguese. Even the related Nguni states were unable or unwilling to co-operate in the face of British expansion in Nyasaland. In the 1890s the Maseko, Gomani and Mpeseni individually fought the undermanned British colonial force and were overwhelmed, enabling Great Britain to establish the Nyasaland colony.

Other African polities sought to overcome their limited military capacity by organizing broad-based multi-ethnic and anti-colonial alliances. The powerful Gaza ruler Gungunyane, for example, appealed to the Swazi to join the struggle against the Portuguese, while the Barue created a wide network which included Tonga, Tawara and a variety of Shona peoples living in Southern Rhodesia (now Zimbabwe). As in the case of the Barue, such temporary unions occurred most often where economic, kinship or religious alliances had previously existed. Occasionally, historic rivals cast aside their mutual hatred in an effort to survive. This explains the alliance of the central Lunda and Chokwe against the Congo Free State's forces despite a mutual enmity which dated back over a generation.

Because the resistance movements did not achieve their ultimate political goals, there has been a tendency to minimize or ignore their immediate military accomplishments and to brand them all as failures. While many African polities were defeated quickly, an equally large number contained the initial European incursions and inflicted heavy losses on the enemy. In southern Angola, the Humbe and Cuamato repulsed several Portuguese attacks and in the battle of 1904 killed more than 300 of the 500-man contingent. The Chikunda states repeatedly defeated Lisbon's disorganized army during the last decade of the nineteenth century while, to the north in Nyasaland, the Yao kept the British colonial army at bay for almost five years. Perhaps most successful were the Swahili–Makua alliance, which remained outside the sphere of Portuguese rule until 1910, and the Cuamato and Cuanhama, who were not finally defeated until 1915.

Despite these hard-won successes, all wars of independence in Central Africa ultimately failed. A combination of several factors, most of which occurred before the Scramble, help to explain the failure of the Africans to halt European advances. These include the conquest origin of many of the most powerful states and internal divisions among the ruling stratum or class and, occasionally, between it and its subject population. Their net effect was to limit the likelihood of large-scale, broad-based and co-ordinated anti-colonial efforts necessary to counteract the Europeans' distinct advantage in firepower and military technology. African rivalries, moreover, facilitated a strategy of divide and rule which Harry Johnston and other colonial officials employed with great skill. The Inhambane Tonga and the Sena helped the Portuguese against their respective Shangaan and Barue overlords, while in the Congo a number of subject people co-operated with the Belgians to free themselves from Yeke and Arab rule or from the slave raiders. In addition, several African leaders recognized that alliances with the Europeans could help them to expand their own states. Such a consideration, for example, motivated Tippu Tib and the sons of Msiri to aid the Congo Free State.

Without African allies and mercenaries, it would not have been possible for the Europeans to impose their rule at such minimal cost in manpower. More than 90% of the Portuguese armies which finally 'conquered' the Zambezi valley in 1902, for example, were African levies. Although not as extreme, a similar pattern existed in Angola.

Early localized resistance against colonial rule and capitalism

Unlike pre-colonial resistance, the major aim of which was to maintain independence, resistance by peasants and workers during the early twentieth century was directly motivated by the efforts of the colonial regimes to strengthen their rule and impose capitalist relationships designed to exploit the human and natural resources of Central Africa. Although a detailed examination and comparison of the Portuguese, British and Belgian colonial systems falls outside the scope of this study, it is useful to examine their inherent abuses, which generated recurring patterns of localized resistance.

The most immediate concern of the colonial officials was to establish an administrative system to control the activities of the subject peoples. Towards this end, they removed a substantial number of uncooperative 'traditional' rulers, thereby violating the religious and cultural sanctity of kingship. To reinforce their tenuous rule, they created African police and mercenary forces – the Force Publique of the Congo, the Guerras Pretas of Angola, the Sepais of Mozambique, and the British Native Police of Northern Rhodesia and Nyasaland – to oversee the activities of 'colonial chiefs' and to intimidate the local population.

To provide a pool of cheap labour for government projects and European capitalist interests, the colonial powers resorted to forced labour practices coupled with repressive taxation. In the Congo, Africans were compelled to collect rubber and to work on the railways and in the mines, while in Mozambique a variety of multi-national concessionary companies benefited from forced labour. Other Mozambicans were exported to Southern Rhodesia, South Africa and São Tome. On the cocoa plantations in São Tome, they were joined by thousands of Angolans. The peasants who remained at home were not exempted from conscription. Many members of the rural population were required by law to provide several weeks of free labour on public works or face immediate imprisonment. They were also subject to the capricious demands of local officials and were often compelled to sell their produce at reduced prices.

These abuses generated recurring protests by peasants and workers aimed at ameliorating specific grievances rather than eliminating the repressive system which created them. Because of its sporadic nature, much of this local opposition has been ignored by contemporaries and historians alike. Nevertheless, 'day-to-day resistance', withdrawal, 'social banditry' and peasant revolts constituted an important chapter in the anti-colonial legacy of Central Africa.

Like the slaves in the American South, many African peasants secretly retaliated against the repressive system. Because both groups lacked any significant power, they avoided direct confrontation. Instead, they expressed their hostility through tax evasion, work slowdowns and secret destruction of property. Tax evasion occurred with great frequency throughout all of Central Africa. Just before the arrival of the tax collector, all or part of a village would flee into an inaccessible region until the state official departed. In Northern Rhodesia, the Gwemba Tonga were notoriously successful evaders, as were their Bisa and Unga neighbours, who fled into the Bagwelu swamps. This practice was also very common in Mozambique.

The peasants also developed a number of techniques to avoid or minimize the discomforts of forced labour. In the most extreme situations, as in the case of the Namwhana and Lungu of Northern Rhodesia, they took up arms and drove the recruiters off their land. Labour grievances also precipitated the 1893–4 Manjanga insurrection in the lower Congo and countless uprisings in the rubber-collecting areas. Other less dangerous tactics included feigned illness, work slowdowns, strikes and fleeing. In the Abercorn District of Northern Rhodesia colonial officials repeatedly complained that the African 'loafed and systematically had to be driven'. Ultimately, the workers ceased their labour entirely until they were guaranteed a salary. Other disgruntled workers sabotaged agricultural equipment, burned warehouses and robbed stores belonging to the concessionary companies and local traders, and destroyed transportation and communication lines.

Flight across international borders was yet another common expression of discontent. Although no accurate assessment can be made of such flights, they appear to have been rather large in scale. Official British records indicate that more than 50 000 Africans living in the Zambezi valley fled into Southern Rhodesia and Nyasaland between 1895 and 1907 in the misguided hope that British colonialism would be more humane (see Fig. 8.1). In Nyasaland large numbers of lakeside Tonga and Tumbuka migrated from the Rukuru watershed to outside the sphere of British control to avoid paying taxes.

Creation of refugee communities in desolate areas constituted another form of the withdrawal strategy. Rather than crossing international boundaries, the peasants, many of whom had refused to satisfy their 'legal' responsibilities, created autonomous enclaves. This phenomenon occurred with some regularity among Bemba dissidents who fled into the interior. A similar pattern occurred in the Gambo region of southern Angola, which became a hide-out for outlaws and the disenchanted, in the rugged Gaerezi mountains separating Mozambique from Southern Rhodesia, and in the forest and mountainous areas of the Congo.

Other fugitive communities, not content just to remain outside the sphere of European control, adopted an aggressive posture towards the colonial regimes. They attacked specific symbols of rural oppression – the plantations, labour recruiters, tax collectors and African police – in an effort to protect their villages and kinship groups from continued harassment and exploitation. Like the 'social bandits' of Sicily or north-eastern Brazil, analysed by Eric Hobsbawm, these communities were led by individuals who were not regarded as criminals by their own society although they had violated the laws of the colonial regime. The best known of 'social bandit' leaders was Mapondera, who successfully battled Southern Rhodesian and Portuguese colonial forces from 1892 to 1903 while protecting the local peasantry from tax collectors, labour recruiters, exploitative company officials and abusive administrators. Mapondera and his band of followers repeatedly attacked the warehouses of the Companhia de Zambésia and the shops of rural merchants, both of which were symbols of economic exploitation. The rebels were able to survive against overwhelming odds because they received the constant support of the rural population, which regularly provided them with food, ammunition and strategic information. A number of other 'social bandits' operated in Mozambique, including Mapondera's successor, Dambakushamba, Moave and Samakungu, as well as in the Huila highlands of southern Angola. This suggests that this form of resistance was not uncommon and needs to be explored for other parts of Central Africa as well.

On occasion, the African levies recruited to quash local dissidents themselves revolted to protest against the colonial abuses from which they were not entirely immune. Low wages, harsh punishment and the capricious actions of their European officers generally precipitated the insurrections. The most famous mutinies occurred in the Congo Free State, where the entire Luluaborg garrison revolted in 1895. Led by dissident non-commissioned officers, the soldiers killed the commandant of the post because of his abusive rule. For more than six months the rebels controlled most of Kasai province but they were ultimately defeated by loyalist troops. Two years later the bulk of the field army revolted.

During the early colonial period, there were also numerous peasant revolts, which tended to be relatively localized and of short duration. Rarely did the peasants seek to solidify their initial gains or to shift their goals from an attack on the symbols of their oppression to an attack on the colonial system as a whole. As a rule, increased or more strictly enforced taxation and labour demands precipitated the uprisings. In the Zambezi valley between 1890 and 1905 at least sixteen different uprisings occurred. Most of these revolts were directed against the Companhia de Mozambique and the Companhia de Zambésia, to which Lisbon ceded most of central Mozambique. During this period there were also several small-scale uprisings in Angola. Peasant revolts among the Ila, Gwemba Tonga and Western Lunda during the first decade of this century concerned British officials in Northern Rhodesia, while in the Congo conservative estimates place the number of localized rural uprisings at more than ten per year.

Where Africans either were unable effectively to express their hostility to colonialism or resented the discrimination within the European-dominated Protestant churches, they often formed independent or separatist churches to remedy their grievances. A proliferation of these independent religious bodies occurred in Nyasaland and Northern Rhodesia during the first decade of the twentieth century. Perhaps the most famous was the Ethiopian Church founded by Willie Mokalapa. Mokalapa and his disciples repeatedly protested against discrimination by European missionaries and the existence of a promotion bar which limited the upward mobility of skilled Africans. Their long-term goal was to demonstrate that Africans could direct their own religious and secular activities independently of the Europeans. Other church groups such as the Watch-tower movement in Northern Rhodesia and the AME (African Methodist Episcopal Church) in Mozambique pursued similar programmes.

In addition to this localized resistance in the rural areas, reformist agitation was beginning to take place in the urban centres, where educated Africans and mulattoes quickly learned that their training and the doctrines of equality preached by the mission-aries did not preclude social, economic and political discrimination. The mulatto intel-lectuals of Angola, such as José de Fontes Pereira, were among the first to express their frustration and hostility. Having adopted Portuguese culture *in toto*, they were dismayed at the growing racism that accompanied the influx of European immigrants at the end of the nineteenth century. In an effort to protect their privileged status, they published long editorials and essays bemoaning their declining position, while simulta-neously urging Lisbon to guarantee their rights and to end the flagrant exploitation of the Africans. These expressions of discontent proved futile and in 1906 they organized the first mulatto association to lobby for their rights. Four years later, a union of mulatto intellectuals throughout the Portuguese colonies was formed. At about the same time a small number of reformist intellectual organizations emerged in Mozambique. Among the most important was the Associação African, which pub-lished the newspaper *Brado Africano*, Mozambique's first protest journal.

At about the same period, in neighbouring Nyasaland and Northern Rhodesia, civil servants, teachers and other African professionals were organizing associations to pro-tect their relatively privileged class position and to agitate for reforms within the existing colonial order. Between 1912 and 1918 a number of such organizations, including the North Nyasa Native Association and the West Nyasa Association, were founded. These groups were to become a prominent force in Central African politics in the inter-war period.

Colonial insurrections to 1918

Colonial insurrections differ from localized forms of resistance in terms of both their scale and their goals. Unlike the sporadic protests, which tended to be separate and uncoordinated, the rebellions were based on mass mobilization and involved many ethnic groups. The increased involvement of an oppressed peasantry, at least in some of the uprisings, suggests that class considerations were also becoming an important factor. Inextricably related to this broader base of support were a redefinition and expansion of the goals. Protests against a particular set of grievances were rejected in favour of a strategy designed to destroy the repressive system which had generated them.

From 1885, when the first areas of Central Africa were conquered, until 1918, there were more than twenty insurrections. None of the five colonies – Angola, Mozambique, Nyasaland, Northern Rhodesia and the Congo – were spared, although most of them occurred in the Portuguese colonies and the Congo, where the combina-tion of extremely oppressive rule and a weak administrative and military structure precipitated recurring revolutionary activity.

These insurrections, although differing in detail, all faced similar organizational problems which, in turn, generated common characteristics and made it difficult for them to succeed. Among the fundamental problems which had to be resolved were: finding a leader with the prestige, commitment and expertise to mobilize and direct a mass movement; determining the principles around which to organize a broad anti-colonial movement; and locating a source of arms and munitions.

The initial unsuccessful struggles to remain independent had resulted in the death of many of the most respected and militant leaders, such as the Chewa leader Mwase Kasungu and the Yeke ruler Msiri, or in their exile, like Gungunyane and the royal family of the Barue. But some of these royal families remained and provided the leadership. Examples are the exiled Mwenemutapa ruler, Chioco, who organized the rebellion of 1897, the Dembo ruler, Cazuangonongo, who led the rebellion in 1908, and the Lunda king, Mushidi, who organized the major rebellion which lasted from 1905 to 1909. This prominent role played by a number of royal families in the insurrections challenges the generally held assumption that the earlier defeats had undercut the position of the indigenous authorities.

Besides these royal families, commoners also emerged to mobilize mass support. Gungunyane's principal lieutenant and war leader, Maguiguana, organized the Shangaan insurrection of 1897. Kandolo, a disaffected sergeant in the Force Publique, led a military revolt in 1897. Cult priests and spirit mediums also provided leadership, which was a logical extension of their historic role as spiritual guardians of the homelands. In 1909 the Tonga priest Maluma called for the immediate expulsion of the colonial overlords in Nyasaland and subsequently led the Tonga into battle. Similarly, the Mbona cult priests played an important leadership role in the Massingire rebellion of 1884, while the cult priestess Maria Nkoie instigated the Ikaya rebellion in the Congo, which lasted for five years, until 1921. Nowhere was religious leadership so significant as in the Zambezi valley, where Shona spirit mediums were behind the abortive rebellions of 1897, 1901 and 1904.

Alienated African converts to Christianity also led some of the anti-colonial movements. The most famous of these early leaders were Kamwana and John Chilembwe, both of Nyasaland. The former, a member of the Watchtower, prophesied that a new order of divinely sanctioned African states would begin in 1914 and appealed to his 10 000 followers to avoid any violent resistance to the British till then. Chilembwe, on the other hand, expecting a divinely inspired African state there and then, led his followers in an abortive and perhaps symbolic insurrection in 1915.

Like Chilembwe, almost all the leaders recognized the need to create alliances which transcended their local base of support. The unsuccessful wars of opposition had demonstrated that individual states lacked the requisite resources to prevent European penetration. Efforts to build broad-based revolutionary movements followed three general patterns. The first was an attempt to reactivate historical links with culturally related peoples in order to recruit entire polities into the camp of the insurgents. Thus, Ovambo chieftaincies joined with Cuamato groups in the rebellion of 1907. The rebels also sought to secure the assistance of powerful groups which, by virtue of their relative distance or past differences, had not previously been considered allies. The Bailundu gained the support of a number of former subject people, including the Kasongi,

Civanda and Ngalanga, while in Mozambique the Sena, who fought on the side of the Portuguese in the 1901 Barue war, supported the Barue sixteen years later as part of a pan-Zambezian movement to destroy the repressive colonial system. Finally, the leaders directed economic appeals specifically at alienated peasants and rural workers who individually opposed the continued demands of the colonial authorities and their capitalist allies. Instead, the rebels urged the economically oppressed to join the insurrection in order to eliminate both the abusive taxation and labour practices and the system which had produced them. The Kamwana movement in Nyasaland was initially based on the support of the lakeside Tonga but rapidly grew to include alienated Nguni, Senga and Tumbuka peasants. Similarly, Chilembwe's appeal to the rural masses lacked ethnic overtones, addressing instead the need to end exploitation and create a divinely sanctioned African nation.

The question of arms acquisition need not be examined at length. It suffices to say that the rebels obtained modern weapons through surreptitious trade agreements with European, Asian and African merchants, raids on European stockades, acquisitions from defecting African police and mercenaries, alliances with neighbouring peoples who were still independent and, in some cases, construction of arms and munitions plants. While some of the rebels, such as the Barue and Cuamato, were able to build up relatively large arsenals, the insurgents rarely possessed the firepower that earlier resisters had amassed.

Given the extremely unfavourable balance of military power and the expanded size of the African police and mercenary forces, it is little wonder that the insurrections all ultimately failed. Nevertheless, a number of them scored significant though short-term successes, challenging the commonly held belief in African docility. The Bailundu, for example, drove the Portuguese off the Ovimbundu highlands in 1904. Three years later the Portuguese suffered a similar defeat at the hands of the Cuamato in southern Angola. Perhaps the greatest military accomplishment was achieved by the Barue and their allies who during the 1917 rebellion liberated the entire Zambezi valley for a fleeting moment.

Conclusion

This study has examined the early forms of African initiatives and resistance in the face of European rule. Throughout the essay we have attempted to document the frequency and vigour of this anti-colonial activity. The desire of most Africans to be free was matched by the ambitions of a smaller group of mercenaries and allies without whom it would have been impossible for the Europeans to have imposed their rule so thoroughly. Thus, there existed both a tradition of confrontation and resistance and a tradition of co-operation. Although the political context changed, the struggle between these two competing forces was to remain a vital factor in Central and Southern Africa during the struggle for independence in the 1960s and 1970s.

African initiatives and resistance in Southern Africa

Southern Africa on the eve of colonial rule

As in other parts of the continent African responses to European colonization of Southern Africa in the nineteenth century were shaped by the major prevailing historical forces. In this case, these forces were expansionist settler colonialism, missionary Christianity and education, and, finally, the Zulu revolution and its by-products – the *Mfecane* and the Nguni migrations.

European settlers in southern Africa, unlike their counterparts in the rest of Africa, were from the beginning interested in establishing permanent homes in their new environment, with its appealing temperate climate, fertile agricultural land, cheap African labour and abundance of minerals. Thus, by the time of the Berlin Conference (1884–5), the Scramble between the British and the Afrikaners for white Southern African territories had been going on for over seventy years and four settler colonies had already been established. These were the Cape Colony and Natal, with their predominantly English-speaking white population of over 185 000 and 20 000, respectively, and the South African Republic and Orange Free State, each with over 50 000 Afrikaans-speaking whites. In these colonies, vast majorities of indigenous Africans were dominated by white minorities.

Under the Sand River Convention (1852), the British and Afrikaners had agreed not to sell firearms to the Africans throughout Southern Africa. Thus, by the time the European nations adopted the Brussels General Act of 1890, forbidding the sale of firearms to Africans, whites in Southern Africa had for some time been implementing a systematic policy of disarming the Africans. Additionally, the Afrikaners, the English colonists and the British government maintained a common racial attitude despite their political and economic differences. They felt it was in their common interest to conquer, rule and exploit the Africans. All this considerably conditioned African initiatives and reactions and limited the options open to them.

The Zulu revolution and its aftermath

Added to this were the epoch-making events which had occurred throughout Southern Africa during the early nineteenth century. These included the Zulu revolution, and the *Mfecane* in South Africa; the Nguni migrations of the Ndebele into Southern Rhodesia (now Zimbabwe), the Kololo into Northern Rhodesia (now Zambia) and the Nguni into Nyasaland (now Malawi) and Tanganyika (now Tanzania); the Bemba activities in northern Zambia; the Yao–Swahili alliance; and the slave trade in Malawi. Some of these events spread with explosive speed and caused sudden changes in the political, economic, social and military systems of numerous African societies throughout Southern Africa. This was a period of nation-building and political expansion which saw the strongest and most centralized states establish domains or spheres of influence over the weaker and less united ones.

Though creative, these far-reaching changes caused immeasurable destruction to human and natural resources. Natural disasters such as drought, epidemics and famine also often accompanied the violence and increased the extent of the ensuing destruction. This continuing incidence of conflict and disasters created a perpetual sense of insecurity and despair among the small, unaggressive tributary communities, many of whom were forced to adapt to living in caves or crude hilltop dwellings to avoid attacks by raiders. There arose ruling aristocracies, class distinctions and taxation without political representation or consultation. As a result, there were soon the rulers and the ruled, the oppressors and the underdogs, and the haves and the have-nots.

The missionary factor

Both missionary Christianity and education were also important factors which determined the course and nature of African responses to colonial conquest. The missionaries had created an African class of evangelists, teachers, journalists, businessmen, lawyers and clerks, most of whom accepted the supposed cultural inferiority of the Africans, accepted settler colonialism as a fact of life and admired the white man for his power, wealth and technology. Examples of these individuals were: Tiyo Soga (1829–71), the first African missionary to be ordained by the United Presbyterian Church in Britain and founder of the Mgwali mission, where he preached to both Africans and Europeans; John Langalibalele Dube, a Methodist minister, ardent follower of Booker T. Washington, founder-president of the Zulu Christian Industrial School and the Natal Bantu Business League and the first president of the African National Congress; John Tengo Jabavu (1859–1921), a devout Methodist, founder-editor of the English/Xhosa weekly *Imvo Zabantsundu*; and Walter Rubusana, a Congregationalist minister and the only African ever elected to the Cape Provincial Council.

Ideologically, these mission-educated Africans shared the common brotherhood and non-racialism of the missionaries and of the Aborigines' Protection Society. They were committed to constitutionalism, gradualism and cultural assimilation, as advocated by a few white liberals among the settlers. But they were also disciples of Booker T. Washington's doctrine of black economic self-determination and of his conservative politics of accommodation.

Like the missionaries, they categorized the African masses as 'benighted people' and 'noble savages' and then assumed the responsibility of reforming traditional Africa by introducing such aspects of western civilization as Christianity, education, capitalism and industrialization. They generally acquiesced in colonial expansion and conquest, partly because, like the missionaries, they associated colonialism with Christianity and 'civilization', and partly because they respected the 'overwhelming superiority' of European weapons and warfare. They therefore condemned and did not join African resistance to colonialism, a resistance which they equated with heathenism and backwardness.

Models of African initiatives and reactions

The above-mentioned factors significantly affected the nature and intensity of African responses to the encroaching European imperialism and colonization. Generally, there were three distinct models of initiatives and responses: (1) that of violent confrontation, as exhibited by the Zulu, Ndebele, Changanana, Bemba, Yao and Nguni, and the Mangwende, Makoni and Mutasa paramountcies; (2) that of protectorate or wardship, chosen by the Sotho, Swazi, Ngwato, Tswana and Lozi, all independent, non-tributary states who sought protection from the British against the Zulu, Ndebele, Bemba, Nguni and Boers; and (3) that of alliance, adopted by the numerous small tributaries, raid victims and refugees such as the Khoi-Khoi, Xhosa, Pondo, Thembu, Nfengu and Hlubi in South Africa; the Bisa, Lungu, Iwa and Senga in Northern Rhodesia; and the Cewa, Njanja, Nkonde and Tonga in Nyasaland, in the hope of securing 'protection, peace and security'.

The Zulu, Ndebele, Bemba and Yao: the politics of confrontation

Violent confrontation, conquest and destruction were virtually inevitable for the Zulu, Ndebele, Bemba and Yao because they and the European colonizers sought to rule the same territories and the same peoples. As a group, they occupied or dominated the most densely populated, fertile and mineral-rich lands of Southern Africa. Their interests made it impossible for them to compromise or coexist with the Europeans. Only the superior power would survive.

The Zulu were the most powerful African nation south of the Limpopo, the Ndebele between the Limpopo and the Zambezi, the Bemba in Northern Rhodesia and the Yao in southern and northern Nyasaland. Up to the early 1870s, they had been able to maintain their sovereignty, independence and security. They had also successfully resisted the intrusion of the European missionaries, traders, concessionaries and labour recruiters, who had by then reached the conclusion that the conquest and dismantling of these resistant African states were essential. The Boers and the Portuguese were particularly uncompromising in their conduct of external affairs, pursuing a policy of raid and conquest.

The Zulu

The Zulu under Cetshwayo therefore decided on the strategy of confrontation, using first the tactics of diplomacy and later those of armed resistance. In accordance with this strategy, Cetshwayo at first continued the isolationist, pacifist foreign policies of his predecessor Mpande. His old enemies being the Transvaal Boers, he maintained an effective alliance with the English colonists of Natal and developed friendly relations with Theophilus Shepstone, the famous Secretary for Native Affairs in Natal. But, when the British annexed the Transvaal in 1877 and made Shepstone the Administrator, Cetshwayo's alliance system quickly collapsed. Shepstone then supported the Boers, who had crossed the Buffalo River into Zululand, had pegged out farms and were claiming land titles.

Cetshwayo appealed to Sir Henry Bulwer, the Lieutenant-Governor of Natal, to settle the Zulu–Boer border dispute. Sir Henry appointed a boundary commission, which reviewed the dispute, declared that the Boers' claims were illegal and recommended that they return to the Transvaal side of the river. However, determined to dismantle the Zulu nation in order to achieve a federation of the settler colonies, the new British High Commissioner for South Africa, Sir Henry Bartle Frere, concealed the report and recommendations of the commission and took advantage of the crossing of the Buffalo river by a Zulu party to bring back the wives of Chief Sirayo, to order Cetshwayo to surrender the members of the party for trial. He followed this up with an ultimatum on 11 December 1878. Among its demands were the delivery of the accused along with 500 head of cattle, the disbanding of the Zulu army within thirty days, the admission of missionaries and the stationing of a British Resident in Zululand. Frere knew that no independent and self-respecting ruler would comply with such extreme demands.

Then, on 11 January 1879, under the command of Lord Chelmsford, a British army of over 7000 soldiers with some 1000 white volunteers and 7000 African auxiliaries invaded Zululand from three points. On 22 January the Zulu army staged its memorable opposition at the battle of Isandhlawana, when it killed 1600 of the invaders and turned back the assault. But on 4 July the British forces returned and overran the Zulu nation. Cetshwayo was banished to Cape Town, and Zululand was divided into thirteen separate chiefdoms, which were placed under the supervision of puppet chiefs. These chiefs included Cetshwayo's rival, Zibhebhu, his cousin, Hamu, who had deserted to join the British forces during the war, and John Dunn, a white man.

The degree of rivalry among the chiefs was so great, however, and the threat of anarchy increasing so rapidly that Cetshwayo had to be brought back, though Zibhebhu was allowed to keep his chiefdom. But soon civil war broke out between the forces of Cetshwayo and Zibhebhu. Cetshwayo died in flight at the height of the battle in 1884. The diminished Zulu nation was then placed under the leadership of Dinizulu, Cetshwayo's 15-year-old son, whose power and authority were dependent on white support. The Zulu had at last succumbed to British control.

The Ndebele

From 1870 to 1890 Lobengula (see 9.1), like Cetshwayo of the Zulu, consistently and successfully pursued a well-formulated diplomatic strategy to protect the vital interests of the Ndebele nation. He restricted immigration and informed alien whites that he was not interested in opening his country to them for mining or hunting. Added to this, he had developed several tactics, such as constantly moving from one town to another, pitting one European nation, company or individual against another, and postponing decisions to frustrate impatient and panicky concessionaires. As a longer-range strategy,

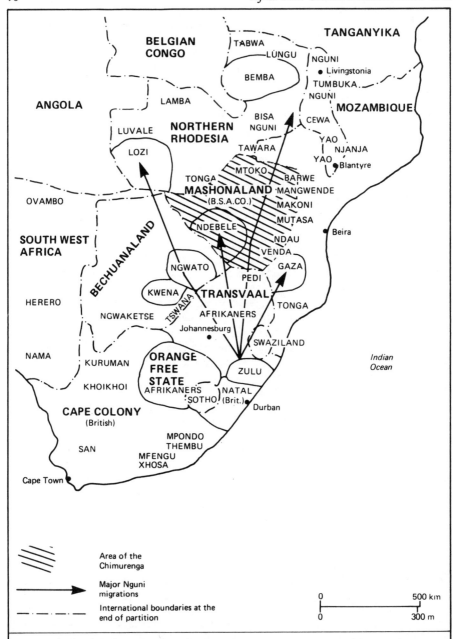

9.1 *Peoples and polities of Southern Africa, showing the Nguni migrations and the area of the Chimurenga*

he sought either military alliance or protectorate status with the British government to counter the Germans, Portuguese and Afrikaners and so prevent uncontrolled South African colonial expansion.

These forms of diplomatic resistance apparently worked effectively until 1888, when the South African financier, Cecil John Rhodes, persuaded Sir Hercules Robinson, the High Commissioner, and Sir Sidney Shippard, the Deputy Commissioner for Bechuanaland, to enlist the help of the Reverend John Smith Moffat. Moffat had left Matabeleland in 1865 after totally failing to convert the Ndebele. He had ultimately become Shippard's assistant commissioner. Moffat was eager to effect the colonization of the Ndebele to vindicate himself for his past failure. Also, he resented Mzilikazi, Lobengula and the Ndebele rulers generally for their successful resistance to Christianity.

Moffat therefore chose to support Rhodes and the Chartered Company. Posing at first as a spiritual adviser who was not interested in gold, game or conquests, he advised Lobengula to 'ally' with the British, rather than with the Afrikaners, Portuguese or Germans, and persuaded him to sign what has since become known as 'the Moffat treaty' on 11 February 1888. Under its terms, Lobengula promised to refrain from entering into any correspondence or treaty with any foreign state or power with a view to selling, alienating or ceding the whole or any part of the land he controlled, without the previous knowledge and sanction of Her Majesty's High Commissioner for South Africa. With this treaty in force, the British occupation of Rhodesia began. Moffat had put both Matabeleland and Mashonaland squarely under the British sphere of influence. Soon, hordes of British concessionaires and syndicates descended on Lobengula seeking mineral and land rights in Matabeleland and Mashonaland.

Noting this, Rhodes dispatched Rudd, Thompson and Maguire to seek a monopolistic agreement with Lobengula, which would be used to apply for a royal charter to shut out other British concessionaires and syndicates. This agreement, which came to be known as the Rudd Concession, was primarily obtained by the conspiratorial deception of Lobengula through a conspiracy of both British imperial officials and missionaries, especially Moffat.

The Rudd Concession consisted of two distinct and interrelated parts: the written part, which was both important and advantageous to the concessionaires; and the verbal, which was advantageous to Lobengula. Under the written agreement – that is, the original draft of the proposals presented to Lobengula – the king granted to the concessionaires complete and exclusive domain over all the metal and mineral resources in his kingdoms, principalities and dominions, together with full power to do all they deemed necessary to procure these resources. Lobengula further agreed not to grant concessions of land or mining rights to any other persons or interests without the prior consent and concurrence of the grantees. In return, the concessionaires agreed to pay Lobengula and his heirs £100 sterling per month in perpetuity. They also agreed to give him 1000 Martini-Henry breech-loading rifles and 100 000 rounds of suitable ball cartridges. The concessionaires also agreed 'to deliver on the Zambezi River a steamboat with guns suitable for defensive purposes upon the said river'.

During the course of the negotiations, however, the king verbally set forth certain conditions which he apparently regarded prima facie as being thereafter an integral part of the agreement. According to Helm, Lobengula thus stipulated and the conces-sionaires consented that: (1) the grantees would bring no more than ten white men at a time to perform mining work in his territories; (2) the miners would not dig in or near the towns; (3) the whites would 'abide by the laws of his country and in fact be as his people'; and (4) the miners would fight in defence of the country under Ndebele command, if needed. Unfortunately, these verbal conditions were not written into the final agreement, and thus, under European contractual law, were not enforceable parts of the agreement.

From disappointed rival concessionaires and especially from two literate Africans, John Kumalo and John Makunga, who sympathetically interpreted the concession, Lobengula and his *indunas* (councillors) learned that they had been cheated; that the concession had already been published in European newspapers and that Rhodes had already formed the company to occupy both Matabeleland and Moshonaland. Shock, fear and confusion took over the Ndebele nation as the people became aware of the full meaning and consequences of the concession. Several of the *indunas* and warriors were furious, and Lobengula was terribly embarrassed and fearful of losing power.

He published notice of repudiation of the concession in the *Bechuanaland News* of February 1889. On his orders, the pro-British *induna*, Lotshe, was killed by the Mbesu regiment, together with his wives, children and livestock. Through letters and a delegation, he also appealed to Queen Victoria to repudiate the treaty or to declare a protectorate over Matabeleland and Mashonaland. In January 1889 he sent an official delegation to London consisting of *indunas* Motshede and Babiyance, who had an audience with Queen Victoria and some leading members of the Aborigines' Protection Society. The *indunas* returned with royal greetings but no repudiation. Rhodes obtained his monopolist royal charter to colonize the area. In early 1890 his pioneers marched from South Africa, through Matabeleland into Mashonaland and hoisted the Union Jack at Salisbury on 12 September 1890.

Lobengula, like Cetshwayo, tried to prevent war by appealing to Jameson, Rhodes and the British government. But by then he had no white or African friends anywhere. The total force that invaded Matabeleland consisted of 1200 white soldiers from Mashonaland and South Africa – including 200 imperial troops of the Bechuanaland Border Police. Then there were 1000 African auxiliaries made up of Shona, Mfengu, Khoi-Khoi, Coloureds and 600 mounted Ngwato under the command of Kgama.

Rather than throw his estimated 20 000 soldiers into suicidal armed resistance against the well-armed settlers and their African auxiliaries, Lobengula and his people evacuated Matabeleland and fled northwards towards Northern Rhodesia. Like Cetshwayo, Lobengula died in flight, either of smallpox or of a heart attack. Now leaderless, the Ndebele nation fell apart. One by one Ndebele *indunas* came to surrender to Jameson at the *indaba* (meeting) tree. The settlers immediately went about staking their new farms and minerals claims. By the end of 1895, the Company had instituted an African administration modelled on those of the Cape Colony and Natal, including the hut tax, reservations and passes, for the purpose of dispossessing the Africans of their land, livestock and minerals, as well as forcing them to work for the whites.

The Ngwato, Lozi, Sotho, Tswana and Swazi initiatives and reactions: the model of protectorate or wardship

Unlike the Zulu and the Ndebele, the Ngwato, Lozi, Sotho, Tswana and Swazi, chose the strategy of protectorate or wardship, using the humanitarian-imperialist mission-aries of the 'government from London' school as their main agents. The choice made by the rulers of these people is not surprising. One dominant characteristic of the pro-missionary rulers, namely, Kgama of the Tswana, Moshoeshoe of the Sotho, Lewanika of the Barotse and Ngwane of the Swazi, was their general political and military weak-ness. Their kingships had grown largely out of *coups d'état*. For example, in 1875, Kgama drove out Sekgoma, his father, and Kgamane, his brother, and named himself king. Kgamane fled with his followers and established his kingdom on the Transvaal side of the Limpopo river. The loyalist and conservative segments of the Ngwato, how-ever, still remained loyal to the deposed Sekgoma. Lewanika, on the other hand, was deposed in 1884 and forced into exile at Kgama's capital. He returned in 1885 and ousted the usurper, Tatila Akufuna. Thus, these pro-missionary kings had insecure positions and were constantly faced with the imminent dangers of civil wars and unrest.

Added to this, their states had barely survived the Zulu revolution and the Nguni subjection. The Sotho and Swazi continued to be perennial targets of Zulu raids, while the Ngwato, Tswana, Kwena and Lozi suffered the raids and invasions of the Ndebele. They were also the victims of land-hungry, often trigger-happy, Boer 'filibusters', who launched commando raids on their villages, capturing livestock and seizing captive labourers, making frequent 'treaties of friendship' with neighbouring sub-chiefs and then claiming land rights and spheres of influence. Through such infringements, the Zulu, Ndebele, and Boers became their inveterate enemies.

Much as these kings may have abhorred the principles of westernization and colo-nialism, they none the less were in desperate need of foreign support to assure their survival. Thus, they ultimately adopted missionary alliance and British (metropolitan) protection as essential instruments of policy. For the same reason, they turned to the missionaries for advice and spiritual guidance in matters relating to Europeans, and attempted to manipulate them to enhance their shaky internal situations. Coillard, Mackenzie and Casalis were the closest European friends, confidants and foreign minis-ters, of Lewanika, Kgama and Moshoeshoe, respectively.

Out of necessity, these kings accepted Christianity and protectorate status. Kgama and Lewanika became practising Christians and, like most converted doctrinaires, they occasionally proved to be even more devout than the missionaries. They not only abandoned their ancestral traditions, beliefs and rituals, but also used their political offices to impose the tenets of western 'Christian' civilization on their people. They strictly banned the public use of alcoholic beverages and imposed stringent liquor laws that included a ban on the brewing of African beer. The more they alienated their people by the enforcement of such measures, the more they were forced to rely on missionaries.

The humanitarian missionaries, for their part, were all too ready to come to the assistance of these rulers. They were not opposed to colonialism as such but rather to uncontrolled expansion by the white colonists of South Africa, especially the Boers and Rhodes, and to the accompanying instances of frontier violence and exploitation which disrupted their earnest and successful work. At the same time, they also emphasized the need for imperial responsibility (paternal guardianship) over the Africans. They sought to smooth cultural contact between the colonizer and the colonized and to 'protect and civilize' the African in an effort to make him a more useful member of the new colonial community. Through letters, delegations and personal appearances, they lobbied relentlessly with the High Commissioner, the Colonial Office and humanitarian groups in England to achieve this protection.

It was as a result of the combination of these missionary pressures and lobbies and the petitions and delegations of the African rulers to the 'Great Queen of the English people' such as those by Kgama in 1876, the delegation of Kgama and Sebele to England accompanied by Rev. W. C. Willoughby in 1895, and that of the queen regent of Swaziland and her council to England in 1894 that Nyasaland, Bechuanaland and Swaziland became British protectorates between 1883 and 1903. Thus, by refusing to preserve their culture and allying with the humanitarian and anti-Boer, anti-Zulu and anti-Ndebele missionaries, these kings were able to maintain their independent existence up to the eve of the Scramble and subsequently won imperial protection at the expense of local settler colonialism.

The Hlubi, Mpondomise, Bhaca, Senga, Njanja, Shona, Tonga, Tawara, etc., initiatives and reactions: the model of alliance

Internally, each of these groups lacked the political unity and military strength to withstand the increasing threat of white colonialism. They were also without diplomatic and military alliances with their neighbours. Instead, they frequently raided, fought and generally distrusted each other. Their compositions ranged from autonomous chieftaincies to bands of nomadic refugees, captive slaves, and wards of either the colonialists or missionaries. Most were tributaries or raid victims of the Zulu, Ndebele, Bemba, Yao or Nguni.

While some of these small groups, like the Barwe, Mangwende, Makoni and Mutasa paramountcies, chose armed resistance against the threat of colonialism as did the Xhosa, many others such as the Hlubi, Mpondomise, Bhaca, Senga and Njanja allied themselves with the whites in the often misguided hope of thereby assuring their protection and security. On the whole, these small societies were accustomed to the diplomatic practice of switching allegiances and gravitating towards the stronger prevailing power, or of pretending to be non-aligned while manipulating the dominant powers to their own advantage. The Shona, Tonga, Tawara, Venda and Ndau had frequently employed these strategies throughout the eighteenth and nineteenth centuries, during the rivalry between the Changamire and Mwenemutapa dynasties, while the Sotho, Mpondo, Mfengu, Thembu and Tonga had utilized similar strategies to exploit the rivalry between the Mtetwa and Ndwande confederacies. Thus, many of these peoples readily aligned themselves with the British against the Zulu, Ndebele, Bemba, Nguni and Yao. Added to this, several of the small groups, such as the Mfengu, Thembu, Njanja, Cewa and Tawara, had for some time existed under strong military influence. As a result, they had among their people significant segments of Christianized, sometimes educated, Africans who not only rejected the traditional culture but also challenged the traditional leadership, to the advantage of the colonizer.

Thus, by offering alliance, protection and/or liberation, the British were easily able to divide and conquer them. They then established permanent white settlement in these areas.

African initiatives and reactions, 1895–1914

By the late 1890s practically all the peoples of Southern Africa had been either fully or partly colonized and were everywhere being subjected to various forms of pressures, economic, political and religious.

Before long, the hut tax, forced labour, severe suppression of traditional beliefs and customs and, especially, land alienation were introduced. This foreign interference intensified in proportion to the settlers' increasing need for cheap indigenous labour to work on the farms and in the mines, and for the hut tax to meet at least part of the administrative expenses. Africans were compelled to vacate their homelands to make room for white settlers and to serve as army 'volunteers'. In Rhodesia (Northern and Southern) and Nyasaland, the Chartered Company administrators simply transplanted the 'Native Laws' of South Africa. In Rhodesia, where white settlement was the heaviest, the administration tolerated no obstacles to its economic ventures, even if these obstacles were Shona lives and rights. It readily seized Shona lands, livestock, crops and stores of food and subjected the Shona to forced labour to serve the interests of the settlers, who had been drawn to Mashonaland with promises of a better, easier and richer way of life. Above all, the colonial justice introduced was characterized by arbitrariness and irregularities. Coupled with all this was a succession of natural disasters, including epidemics of smallpox and rinderpest, drought and even a plague of locusts.

The Africans did not of course watch these events unconcerned. In this atmosphere of colonialism, landlessness, oppression and westernization, most of them came to believe, like the Xhosa, that the white man was the cause of all their troubles. Resentment against alien rule produced a growing attitude of resistance towards whites and a strong sense of unity among political leaders, followers, priests and even formerly hostile groups. Examples of such responses aimed at overthrowing the oppressive colonial system were the Ndebele–Shona *Chimurenga* of 1896–7, the Herero revolt of 1904 and the Bambata or Zulu rebellion of 1906.

The Ndebele–Shona *Chimurenga*

The *Chimurenga*, as the Shona termed their form of armed resistance, began in March 1896 in Matabeleland and June 1896 in Mashonaland. The first casualty was an African policeman employed by the British South Africa Company, killed on 20 March. The first attack upon Europeans occurred in the town of Essexvale on 22 March, when seven whites and two Africans were killed. The *Chimurenga* then swiftly spread throughout Matabeleland and Mashonaland (see 9.2). Within a week, 130 whites had been killed in Matabeleland. Africans were armed with Martin-Henry rifles, Lee Metfords, elephant

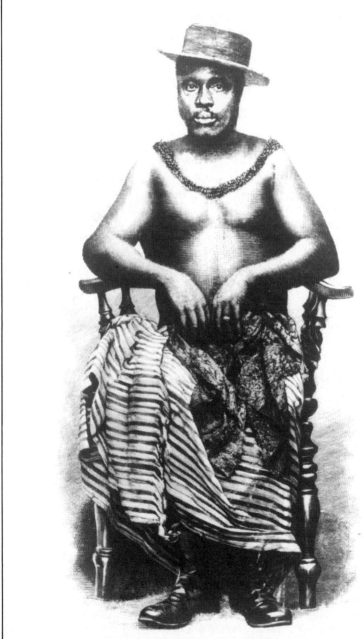

9.2   *Lobengula (c. 1836–94), King of the Ndebele, 1870–94 (Longman)*

guns, muskets and blunderbusses, as well as with the traditional spears, axes, knobkerries and bows and arrows.

The Company hurriedly mobilized the Europeans into the Matabeleland Relief Force, which consisted of imperial troops and the Rhodesia Horse Volunteers (settlers), as well as Africans. At its peak the force consisted of 2000 Europeans. 250 Ngwato sent by Kgama, 200 'Colonial [South African] Natives', and about 150 Rhodesian Africans, under the supreme command of Sir Frederick Carrington, a veteran of the Xhosa–settler wars. Essentially, the *Chimurenga* was conducted as guerilla warfare. The troopers relied on the siege and dynamite. They also destroyed crops and appropriated African cattle, goats, sheep, fowl and grain to starve the resisters and to enrich themselves.

In Matabeleland, the *Chimurenga* lasted from March to December 1896, and, because of the Company's fear that a prolonged *Chimurenga* or a military stalemate would cause bankruptcy and/or force the British imperial government to turn the colony into a protectorate, Rhodes finally chose to negotiate. What followed was a series of peace talks between Rhodes and the Ndebele *indunas* that lasted from August 1897 to 5 January 1898, when Rhodes included six of the *Chimurenga* chiefs (*indunas* Dhliso, Somabulana, Mlugulu, Sikombo, Khomo and Nyamanda) among the ten Company appointees. He assigned them land for settlement, donated 2 300 000 kg of grain, and promised to redress their grievances against the Company.

With peace in Matabeleland, the Company then concentrated upon the Shona *Chimurenga*, which had been raging simultaneously since June 1896 and continued intermittently to 1903. The leading centres of the *Chimurenga* were the paramountcies of Mashayamombe, Makoni and Mangwende in Mashonaland, but several smaller paramountcies such as Nyandora, Seke, Whata and Chiota, either took the initiative for a *Chimurenga* themselves or allied with others.

The *Chimurenga*, like the Xhosa cattle-killing episode, has been labelled by Eurocentric historians as atavistic and millenarian because of the important role of the traditional prophets and priests, known as the *svikiro*. The leading *svikiro* were Mukwati in Matabeleland, Kagubi in western Mashonaland and Nehanda (a female *svikiro*) in central and northern Mashonaland, together with a host of local junior prophets. The *svikiro* told the Ndebele and Shona that the white man had brought all their sufferings, namely forced labour, the hut tax and flogging, as well as the natural disasters of locusts, rinderpest and drought. They convinced many Africans that the Shona God, Mwari (Mlimo in Sindebele), having been moved by the suffering of his people, had decreed that the white men were to be driven out of the country; and that the Africans had nothing to fear because Mwari, being on their side, would turn the white man's bullets into harmless water. Generally speaking, many Africans believed that the *svikiro* were announcing Mwari's commandments and that failure to obey would bring more sufferings to the paramountcies and personal misfortunes to individuals.

The *svikiro* were primarily revolutionary prophets who expressed the real causes of the *Chimurenga* and the general consensus of the people without which they would have had relatively little credibility and influence. Furthermore, as the custodians of Shona traditions and acknowledged authorities on many aspects of Shona life, they feared that their role was being usurped by the European missionaries. More importantly, the apparently leading role of the *svikiro* was a function of the politico-military division of the Ndebele and, especially, the Shona people. The *svikiro* were the only authorities whose influence extended across paramountcies. The spiritual provinces of Mukwati, Nehanda and Kagubi covered more than one paramountcy. Unlike the paramount chiefs, the *svikiro* had an elaborate but secret network of communication through which they exchanged numerous messages and co-ordinated their efforts adeptly.

Kagubi and Nehanda were most influential over the young and militant princes of the paramountcies, such as Muchemwa of Mangwende, Mhiripiri of Makoni and Panashe of Nyandoro. But Kagubi was captured in October and Nehanda in December 1897. On 2 March 1898, they were charged with murder and condemned to death by hanging.

Without a highly centralized politico-military machinery, without guns and ammunition, and, more significantly, without the *svikiro*, Shona paramountcies were defeated one by one in 1897. On 4 September, Makoni was handcuffed, blindfolded and shot. Similarly, Mashayamombe, who had nearly paralysed communications between Salisbury and Bulawayo, was defeated and killed on 25 July. Between July and September, the settlers successfully carried out sieges against the paramountcies in central Mashonaland. Mangwende was conquered in September but his militant son, Muchemwa, together with a few councillors, continued the resistance until 1903 when the *Chimurenga* was finally contained.

The toll of the *Chimurenga* has been estimated at 450 dead and 188 wounded Europeans, and 8000 African deaths. Of the 450 Europeans, 372 were resident settlers, representing one-tenth of the white population in the colony. The remainder were imperial troopers and mercenaries.

The Herero

In 1904, the Herero, feeling the cumulative and bitter effects of colonial rule in South West Africa, took advantage of the withdrawal of German troops from Hereroland to put down an uprising among the Bondelswarts, and revolted in January 1904, killing 100 Germans, destroying several farms and capturing cattle. Theodor Leutwein, the German commander, was replaced by General von Trotha, who decided upon total military victory and complete destruction of the Herero people by ruthless tactics and massacres. Between 75% and 80% of an estimated Herero population of 60 000–80 000 were slaughtered; 14 000 were put in prison camps; and 2000 fled to South Africa.

Samuel Maherero and 1000 followers fled across the Kalahari desert to Bechuanaland. Just after this Herero uprising Hendrik Witbooi of the Nama also rebelled and this rebellion lasted even after Witbooi's death until 1907. All land and livestock were confiscated, and the Africans were forbidden to form ethnic organizations and practice traditional ceremonies. They had no means of existence other than employment by white settlers. Their own gods and priests having been defeated and thereby proved inferior, they submitted to Christianity in mass conversions. Then, in 1915, British South African troops occupied South West Africa and kept it under martial law until 1921. By that date, 10 673 white South Africans had joined those German settlers who had not been repatriated to Germany. The Africans were allowed to resume subsistence-level agriculture in barren reserves and therefore forced to depend on migrant employment.

Conclusion

By the first decade of the twentieth century, there were practically no indigenous sovereign states in Southern Africa. The vast majority of the Africans had by then entered the third level of resistance characterized by the struggle to obtain a favourable *modus vivendi* under colonial rule, economy and culture. In reality it was a different form of response from the strategies against colonial conquest and occupation, and it belongs to a different chapter in African history. For, by then, both the political and religious leadership of the traditional societies had been conquered, colonized and humiliated. The traditional kings had been supplanted by an alien Secretary for Native Affairs such as Theophilus Shepstone in Natal, or the so- called 'Native Commissioners' and 'Native Departments' elsewhere. The African masses were primarily recognized as the 'black problem' and were, as Jabavu described them, 'landless, voteless, helots, pariahs, social outcasts in their fatherland with no future in any path of life'. Furthermore, these were the first Africans to face the crisis in identity created by new artificial colonial boundaries which partitioned cultural-linguistic-historical groups, by cultural shock in mining and farming compounds, in the homes of the whites, and in Christian churches and schools throughout the settler-dominated world. But, despite their fate, the Africans left a legacy of resistance to colonial rule, of cross-ethnic allegiances and of cultural, historical, racial and nationalist consciousness that was inherited by later generations of freedom fighters throughout Southern Africa.

Madagascar
from 1880 to 1939

Madagascar, that great island off the east coast of Africa, did not escape the colonialist imperialism of Europe of the last two decades of the nineteenth century. The French conquered and occupied the island after two wars – from 1883 to 1885 and from 1894 to 1895. Like most Africans, the Malagasy rose up and reorganized themselves, first to oppose the conquest and occupation, then to combat the abuses of the colonial regime, and subsequently to recover independence for their country.

In February 1822, the king of the Merina kingdom, Radama I, who had been recognized as the 'King of Madagascar' by the Anglo-Merina Treaty of October 1817, proclaimed his sovereignty over the entire island. This was recognized by the French rather belatedly in 1862, although they reserved their specific claims to their former trading posts and establishments and to the Sakalava and Antakarana protectorates. To ensure the independence of the island, Rainilaiarivony, who became prime minister in 1864, set about modernizing the country and turning it into a 'civilised state'. Thus he freed slaves in 1877, modernized the legal system in 1878 and promulgated a new constitution in 1881.

In spite of these efforts at modernization, under the joint pressure of the French parliamentarians of the island of Réunion, who wanted more space to solve the problem of over-population of their island, the right-wing Catholic lobby, and finally the colonial faction, who wanted to eliminate British economic and religious influence, the French invaded Madagascar in May 1883, bombarded the ports in the north-west and east of the island and occupied Tamatave. The first Franco-Merina war continued desultorily until it was ended by a treaty between the two powers in December 1885. Far from ensuring peace, the treaty strained relations further, since the French interpreted its vague terms to mean that Madagascar had become a French protectorate, while the Malagasy government, under Queen Ranavalona (see 10.1) and the prime minister, Rainilaiarivony, denied this.

Thus, a state of tension came to exist between the prime minister and successive French residents-general as misunderstandings continued to multiply. Without waiting for the outcome of the endless negotiations on the demarcation of the French zone around Diego Suarez, the French navy occupied a broad strip of land to the south of the port. A second conflict, over the 'exequatur' ('a written official recognition and authorization of a consular officer issued by the government to which he is accredited'),

10.1 *Ranavalona III, Queen of Madagascar 1883–97, in full court dress (Harlingue-Viollet)*

dominated the history of Malagasy–French relations from 1885 to 1895. The resident-general demanded that he be granted the 'exequatur' in order to prove that Madagascar was a protectorate, but Rainilaiarivony refused to grant it so as to assert the kingdom's independence. Until the signature of the Anglo-French agreement of 1890, whereby the French recognized the British protectorate over Zanzibar in exchange for Britain accepting the French protectorate over Madagascar, the prime minister stuck to the stand he had taken.

These diplomatic difficulties were worsened by the economic problems which the kingdom experienced. In order to settle the indemnity due to France, the Malagasy government contracted a loan with the Comptoir National d'Escompte de Paris (CNEP), the guarantee for which consisted of the customs receipts of the island's six main ports: Tamatave, Majunga, Fenerive, Vohemar, Vatomandry and Mananjary. Agents – who were appointed by the French bank but paid by the royal authorities – supervised the tax collection, which deprived the Malagasy state of a substantial source of revenue.

This need for funds, and the pressure exerted by Le Myre de Vilers, the first French resident-general in Tananarive, compelled the prime minister to grant vast concessions to the Europeans, both for the mining of copper in the Betsileo and gold in the Boina and for timber exploitation. The Suberbie gold-deposit concession in the Maevatanana region, notorious for its use of forced labour in the mines, brought in very little income to the government. On the other hand, it contributed to the weakening of authority on account of the number of workers who fled and swelled the ranks of the *fahavalo* or irregulars, thereby creating an atmosphere of insecurity in the north-west of the island.

The proceeds of the customs duties were not sufficient to cover the six-monthly payments due to the CNEP since the concessions granted to foreigners had not produced the results expected. Thus, in order to raise revenue, the royal government increased the number of taxes and stepped up forced labour. Some people refused to perform the tasks required of them under the *fanompoana* or forced labour system, while others took to banditry, and the gangs of plunderers were bold enough to attack the holy city of Ambohimanga in 1888 and even the capital in 1890.

These disturbances, which threatened the interests of the privileged classes and the expatriates, alarmed the resident-general and revealed a grave crisis of authority in the 'kingdom of Madagascar'. The French parliament made the most of this situation and dispatched Le Myre de Vilers, who had been resident-general from 1886 to 1889, with a plan for setting up a real protectorate. When Rainilaiarivony rejected this plan, the French parliament voted by a large majority to go to war, and the invasion of the island was launched in 1894 under the command of General Duchesne. The French army put the Queen's regular troops to flight before taking Tananarive on 30 September 1895.

That Madagascar should have been conquered and occupied so easily by the French should not surprise us. On the eve of the French conquest, the 'kingdom of Madagascar' was sapped by serious internal tensions. At the official level at least, the baptism of Queen Ranavalona II marked the beginning of the decline in ancestor worship, the disappearance of the royal and even local *sampy* or shrines which formed the political and religious foundations of traditional Imerina, and the rise of a Christian-ized elite. Political, economic and religious affairs were all intertwined. The supporters of the Église du Palais (the Palace Church) not only handled the affairs of state, such as censuses, education and recruitment for the army and forced labour, but also took advantage of their positions and the economic system to enrich themselves through trade and moneylending. Guardians of *sampy* and local dignitaries who had been deprived of their traditional powers and privileges opposed the island's leaders by taking flight or by refusing to build churches or setting fire to them.

Moreover, the Christianized Merina were by no means unanimous in their support for the official Church. Those who were not integrated into the Church and who practised a sort of popular Christianity, drawing its inspiration from the Bible and from local history and folklore, formed an educated elite which could lay claim to political leadership. They engaged in trade and made a practice of preaching their ideas on market days. Other Christians reacted against the overbearing tutelage of the official Church by turning to Catholicism or placing themselves under the protection of a dignitary. Others struggled for religious independence, like the dissidents of Ambatonakanga who, in 1893, created their own church which they named *Tranozozoro*, the house or church of reeds. This dissident movement took shape in the very heart of the capital, which was a stronghold of Christianity, and bore witness to the sense of unease felt by some of the faithful.

The officer merchants recovered their losses by exploiting the forced labour system to the full, by investing in land and by engaging in moneylending. Opposing these magnates of the capital and devotees of the Palace Church were the host of small farmers and day-labourers who were in debt to them and on whom the *fanompoana* bore down most heavily.

All this greatly weakened the social fabric and the machinery of government and revealed the existence of a deep-seated crisis within the 'kingdom of Madagascar', which was thus incapable of resisting the French expedition.

Besides, there was a failure of leadership. The ageing and dictatorial Rainilaiarivony had become unpopular. Faced with having to put down a whole series of plots involving his close associates, and even his own children, he could not have complete confidence in the leading dignitaries of the regime, who coveted his high office and hoped one day to replace him. Nor was the royal army in any position to resist the invaders. It had become disorganized by the increasing number of desertions and was demoralized by rampant corruption and greed. Neither the soldiers nor their officers had received any proper military training, and there were dissension and strife in the army. Furthermore, Rainilaiarivony had succeeded in humbling the *Mainty* and excluding the *Andriana*, who had formed the backbone of the armies of the eighteenth and early nineteenth centuries, but had failed to build a large, well-trained army properly commanded by men who were loyal to him and intent on preserving their country's independence. A country so demoralized and divided against itself could not stand, and Madagascar did not.

The Menalamba movements in Imerina

The capture of Tananarive, which spelt the downfall of the urban Christian world, sparked off the mobilization of the rural areas in defence of the ancestral heritage. The uprising at Amboanana, which broke out in November 1895 on the day of the

Fandroana, the queen's birthday and a public holiday, marked the beginning of the population's opposition to the French conquest. This large-scale rebellion was known as _Menalamba_ (or the 'Red Plaids'), because the rebels 'coloured their garments with the red soil of the country in order that they might not easily be recognized at a distance'. The insurgents seized Aribonimano, killed the governor and an English missionary and his family, and demanded the abolition of Christian worship, schools, military service, and forced labour. In March 1896, other movements broke out in the north and south of Imerina, with demands for a return to the ancient beliefs and a purge of the governing class and with the aim of compelling the French to withdraw.

The _Menalamba_ took over the weapons of the soldiers who had deserted from the _foloalindahy_ or purchased them from Indian or Creole traders, which suggests that communication with the coast was relatively easy. They were organized after the manner of the royal troops, complete with a table of honours and a division into regiments. They attacked the representatives of the oligarchy, whom they regarded as holding power illegally and being responsible for the defeat, as well as foreign missionaries and Malagasy evangelists, who were regarded as enemies of traditional beliefs. They accordingly set about burning down churches and schools and restoring the ancestral religion to a place of honour.

However, some of the actions of the _Menalamba_ alienated part of the population. Their strategy included attacks on market-places in a bid to cause panic, to undermine an institution that was a symbol of the exploitation by the oligarchy and to replenish their supplies. These assaults on markets and the raids they made to seize the crops of villages which had not come over to their side made it easier to sow confusion in the minds of the sedentary population, who failed to distinguish between the _Menalamba_ and the _jirika_, or plunderers and brigands. The colonizers and their local allies took advantage of this confusion to isolate the insurgents.

Popular resistance in Imerina failed because of the severity of the repressive measures taken, but above all because of the lack of co-ordination between the different movements and the failure to join up with the insurrections which broke out in the other regions of Madagascar.

Popular opposition in the regions subject to the royal authority

In some regions, the population's reaction to the French conquest stemmed from the influence wielded by the _Menalamba_. In 1896, in the Mampikony region in the north-west, Rainitavy, a former Merina governor, recruited and armed a motley crowd of Merina deserters and Sakalava herdsmen to organize the _Menalamba_ of Rabozaka. The uprising was the only _Menalamba_ movement in which commercial considerations played a fundamental part: the aim was to take control of regional trade, of which the Indians and Creoles had a virtual monopoly.

In the provinces that were most firmly controlled and hence most heavily exploited, the fall of Tananarive in September 1895 was the signal for attacks on the Manamboninahitra, who were chiefly officer merchants, and on Merina immigrants and foreigners. In the eastern province, for example, the revolt of the 'Vorimo', a clan living on the lower Mangoro, triggered off a series of uprisings which created a climate of insecurity in the region throughout 1896. In the first instance, these revolts were directed exclusively against the Merina oligarchy. However, the very harsh measures which detachments of the army of occupation took to put down the revolts alienated the Betsimisaraka against the French as well. From then on the insurgents stepped up their offensive, and attacked the French as well as the Merina. The movement did not start to die down until December 1896, and disappeared altogether with the introduction of the measures taken by General Galliéni to replace the representatives of the oligarchy by local chiefs.

The resistance of the independent peoples

At the outset, the French thought that by capturing Tananarive they had gained control over the entire island. However, after putting down the *Menalamba* movements and thereby having effectively occupied Imerina, they discovered that they also had to conquer the independent regions. The peoples who had not been subject to the royal authority took up arms and repelled the French attempts at penetration.

In the Ambongo – an example of a region whose principal feature was its political division into a host of small units – the French employed several stratagems to gain control. While seeking to reach an understanding with the main chiefs or kings both on the seaboard and in the interior, from 1897 onwards they established military posts in the large villages so as to keep order in the region. Nevertheless, early in 1899, disturbances stemming from the same determination to reject colonial domination broke out under the leadership of the main chiefs. However, since the bands of resisters were isolated from one another and were therefore incapable of uniting in the face of the common enemy, they were defeated by the French.

The conquest of Menabe, a large and well-organized kingdom, began in 1897. King Toera and his principal chiefs had wanted to surrender but Major Gérard, who was in charge of the operation, preferred to capture the capital rather than accept their submission and to 'massacre all the Sakalava who could not escape, including King Toera'. This cruel act precipitated a well-organized resistance movement, led by Ingereza, the brother and successor of Toera, which spread throughout the Menabe and lasted until 1902. The peoples of Antandroy and Mahafale in the south also opposed French attempts at penetration and only submitted in 1904.

As a result of his policy of gradual annexation, Galliéni was able to claim in 1904 or thereabouts that the conquest, occupation and unification of the island were complete.

A country united by its submission to France and its opposition to colonial domination

Malagasy reactions to the conquest and colonial penetration which had come to an end in 1904 had all come to nothing. Officially, the military operations were over and the different administrative, economic and cultural systems of colonization were then set up by Galliéni to allow France to establish its ascendancy once and for all and to 'civilize' and 'assimilate' the Malagasy. Yet that same year of 1904 saw the beginning of a new period that was to be marked by the struggle of the Malagasy people against colonial oppression and exploitation and the attempt to destroy their national personality and to change their way of life.

From the administrative standpoint, the colonial venture dismantled the long-established political framework. In Imerina, Galliéni abolished the monarchy on 28 February 1897 and the privileges of the aristocracy on 17 April. Elsewhere, however, he did not abolish the different dynasties, at least not *de jure*. On the contrary, he started by attempting, as the Minister had instructed him to do, to end Merina hegemony and to embark on the *politique des races* which had earlier been tried out in the Soudan (French West Africa) and Indochina. Former rulers or their sons were accordingly brought into the administration as 'native governors' while 'internal protectorates' were created among the extensive kingdoms in the west and south-west. This system did not prove satisfactory, however, and from 1905 onwards the number of Merina assistants was increased to a disproportionate degree, since the Merina were regarded as being more suitable material for 'progress and adaptation' than the other peoples. Galliéni also brought French settlers (*colons*) and Asian immigrant workers into the new colony, which greatly alienated the indigenous people. Finally, Galliéni extended the *fokonolona*, which were village communities considered as having collective responsibility for their affairs, to cover the entire island and reintroduced the royal *fanompoana* or forced labour.

The territorial unification of Madagascar was completed with three measures. The first was the standardization of the administration (between 1927 and 1933, three attempts were made to define the boundaries of administrative districts). The second was the widespread introduction of administrative *fokonolona* as the medium for the exercise of authority. The third was the setting up of a restrictive body of law with the institution, in 1901, of the 'native code', forming the basis for dispensing administrative justice in which the judiciary and the executive were merged.

For the Malagasy, colonization also meant the economic exploitation of the island by the expatriate minority. Very early on, this so-called 'development' of the colony came up against the problem of labour. Galliéni reintroduced the Merina royal *fanompoana* and decided to extend it to the whole of the island in 1896 and 1897, thereby compelling every able-bodied Malagasy male between the ages of 16 and 60 to provide fifty days of unpaid labour a year. The Office Central du Travail was established in 1900 and was charged with the task of facilitating the recruitment of workers for private firms. Faced with the resistance of the Malagasy to any form of recruitment, the administration took over and, in 1926, established the Service de la Main d'Oeuvre pour les Travaux d'Intérêt Général (SMOTIG), which required conscripts not actually called up for military service to work for three years – subsequently reduced to two years – on the colony's construction sites. The SMOTIG, which was regarded by the Malagasy as 'slavery in disguise', was deeply resented not only by the people who were commandeered but also by the workers who lost their jobs as a result.

The colonial oppression was further aggravated by the forcible takeover of land, which was then distributed to settlers. Under a decree promulgated in 1926, the state was declared owner of 'all vacant and ownerless land not developed, enclosed or granted by way of a concession as of the date of promulgation of the decree'.

The first reactions in opposition to the colonial system

These economic and political changes drastically affected the social structures, caused the breakup of a number of clans, and destroyed ancestral values and practices. In Imerina, the vastly increased number of schools and the wholesale recruitment of junior civil servants gave rise to dismay, both in the ranks of the former oligarchy, which had been deprived of its power by the conquest, and among the new elite trained in the colonial schools, who felt that they were being denied positions of responsibility by the colonial system. Thus, colonial oppression affected all the different levels of Malagasy society, and it provoked different reactions.

The first of these reactions was the insurrection which broke out in November 1904 in the province of Farafangana and which spread very quickly westwards, as a result of the traditional contacts that had existed in historical times between the eastern peoples' and the Bara (see 10.2). The insurgents – led by chiefs belonging both to the Bara clans and to the south-eastern clans, or by dissident militiamen like Corporal Kotavy – attacked military posts at Amparihy, Begogo and Esira, and concessions, including the *Emeraude*, where they killed the owner, Lieutenant Conchon. Locally recruited infantrymen deserted their posts at Tsivory and Bekitro, or joined the rebellion, as in the case of Antanimora.

The second important reaction was the *Sadiavahe* movement (1915–17). This was an armed peasant uprising which first began in the south-west on the left bank of the river Menarandra in early February 1915 and spread very quickly to the districts of Ampanihy and Tsihombe. The *Sadiavahe* stole cattle, attacked villages, cut telegraph wires, and withdrew into hiding-places well away from the posts controlled by the administration. They formed bands, ranging in number from ten to forty members at most, which were extremely mobile. Among the reasons why entire villages gave open or clandestine support to the *Sadiavahe* were the acute poverty of the population as a result of the very infrequent but violent rainfall, the imposition of a cattle tax, and the far-reaching effects of the First World War, which had led to the mobilization of people and to food shortages.

Another very widespread form of anti-colonial response was passive resistance: a refusal to comply with orders; the rejection of everything that was regarded as a sign of 'civilization' but was closely bound up with colonization and the foreign presence; keeping children away from school, which was looked upon in some circles as merely being a form of 'colonial forced labour'; and abandonment of the villages created along the roads in the south in an attempt to keep the population together. These refusals to co-operate did not seem dangerous to the colonizers.

Then there were the activities of the secret society known as *Vy Vato Sakelika* (VVS) or 'strong and hard like stone and iron' (see 10.1). The VVS was created in July 1913 in Tananarive by seven students from the capital's medical school, which was the

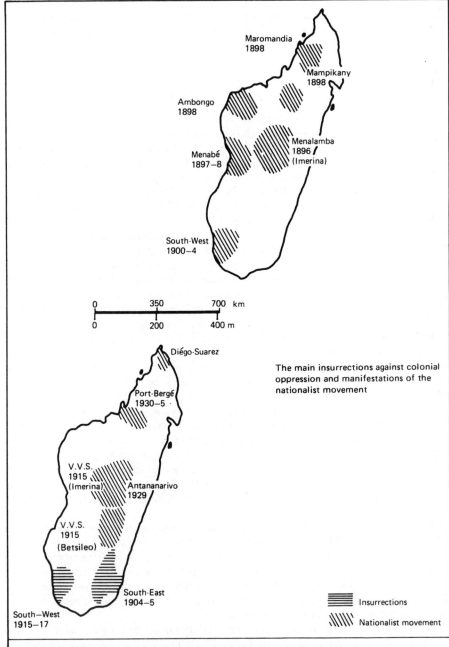

10.2   *Resistance, insurrection and nationalism in Madagascar, 1896–1935*

only institution providing tuition for the highest degree then open to Malagasy nationals. This was just after the publication of a series of articles written by the Protestant minister Ravelojaona under the title of 'Japan and the Japanese'. These articles called on the Malagasy to model themselves on Japan, where modernism and tradition had been so skilfully blended. The students were joined by clerks and office workers and primary-school teachers. Although the VVS was a clandestine organization, it expressed its opinions openly in the press by calling on the Malagasy to sacrifice themselves for their homeland so that its people could advance and live in freedom and dignity. As the bearer of a national message, this secret society was an intolerable challenge to the administration, especially in wartime. The French adopted very harsh measures to suppress the movement. These included hard labour, deportation to the camp at Nosy Lava, banning of the newspaper whose editors were implicated in the affair, and dismissal from the civil service. The harshness of all these measures shows how conscious the colonizers had become of the nascent nationalism within the elite and how much they feared its consequences. The outcome of the repression was that the Malagasy were prompted to abandon their clandestine activities and, from then onwards, to switch openly to channelling their political demands through press campaigns, the establishment of trade unions, and so on.

Struggles to recover dignity

The decade following the First World War was an important period because of the growing awareness displayed throughout the country and the formation and consolidation of a national movement. The beginning of this decisive turning-point in Malagasy history can be dated from the return of the ex-servicemen to Madagascar. Basking in glory, these war veterans, who were convinced that they had served France in the same way as any Frenchman, demanded the same rights as those the French enjoyed, and they were supported in this by a large number of their compatriots. Under the leadership of Ralaimongo, therefore, they embarked on a long-drawn-out struggle to obtain French citizenship.

Ralaimongo (1884–1942), who had been successively a Protestant primary-school teacher, a clerk, a student in Paris, an ex-serviceman and a socialist, was the true founder of the national movement. When he returned to Madagascar in 1922, he settled in Diego Suarez, which was an ideal environment for spreading propaganda because of the presence of the workers at the naval arsenal and the complexity of the land-tenure problems in the Mahavavy plain and the Antalaha region. Until May 1929, it was Diego Suarez rather than Tananarive that was the focal point of the national movement, which, besides agitating for equal rights, denounced the intolerable abuses of the colonial system. The movement was warmly supported by the business community, who showed more drive than the members of the civil service, who were afraid of administrative sanctions. The movement was, in fact, financed by traders, especially those in the capital.

The Ralaimongo group – which was strengthened by the support of Ravoahangy, a former member of the VVS, Emmanuel Razafindrakoto, Abraham Razafy, secretary of the Tananarive branch of the French SFIO trade union, and Jules Ranaivo – was joined by several left-wing Europeans, including Albertini, a lawyer, Dussac, Planque and Vittori. In an endeavour to present and defend their demands, from 1927 onwards they published two newspapers – *L'Opinion* in Diego Suarez and *L'Aurore Malgache* in Tananarive – which had to contend with all sorts of petty harassment by the administration. At the political level, the group demanded 'the management of the overall interests of the country by a Council-General with extended powers', the abolition of the Government-General and the representation of Madagascar in the French government.

In parallel with the action of the Ralaimongo group, religious agitation flared up again in the *Tranzozoro* cult. Renewed controversy between the Malagasy congregation and the European Protestant ministers only ended in 1929, when judgement was given by the Conseil du Contentieux recognizing the *Tranzozoro* as an indigenous mission. From then onwards, the sect agitated for self-government under cover of a movement preaching religious autonomy, whose leaders were followers of Ralaimongo and Dussac.

Having organized, with Ralaimongo and Ravoahangy, the 'Pétition des Indigènes de Madagascar' demanding French citizenship, the abolition of the 'native' regime and the application of the social and cultural benefits introduced under the Third Republic, Dussac arrived in Tananarive in May 1929 to explain the petition's aims. A conference, which was planned for 19 May but which 'Malagasy subjects' were barred from attending, turned into a vast procession in the streets of the capital, in which thousands of demonstrators chanted rebellious slogans such as 'Long live freedom and the right of assembly!' and 'Down with the "native" regime!' This first mass demonstration marked a decisive stage in the growth of the nationalist movement.

The events of 19 May 1929 represented both the culmination of the struggle for equality and the starting-point of the demands for independence. They also marked the beginning of real political militancy, in the shape of propaganda campaigns, the creation of political cells and parties, and the emergence of a broad-based and varied press. Ralaimongo, who had been exiled to Port Bergé, encouraged the peasants to engage in the type of resistance practised by Gandhi. In 1931, he openly mooted the idea of independence in response to a speech by Paul Reynaud, the Minister of the Colonies, which rejected the case for wholesale naturalization. In *L'Opinion* of 20 July 1934, Ravoahangy evoked 'the natural and inalienable right to form a free and independent nation'. From 1935 onwards, other newspapers that were openly nationalistic in outlook began to appear. Both *Ny Fierenena malagasy* ('The Malagasy Nation') and *Ny Rariny* ('Justice') constantly urged that Madagascar must become free. The movement was losing momentum, however, for a number of reasons. First, the business community, which had been hard-hit by the economic crisis of the 1930s, withdrew its support. Secondly, civil servants, afraid of compromising themselves and of losing their jobs, also backed out. Thirdly, the Protestant ministers, embarrassed at the political turn taken by developments, retreated into their churches. Finally, the Malagasy middle class steadily adopted a wait-and-see attitude and preferred the direct and personal benefits accruing from French citizenship. It would take the Popular Front to give the movement fresh impetus.

Conclusion

The armed, but scattered and uncoordinated, resistance of the people of Madagascar to the French conquest did not prevent the colonial system from being established. But the logic of colonialism and the traumatic shock suffered by the Malagasy, threatened as they were with the loss of their identity, prompted them to adopt several measures in a bid to recover their dignity. The struggles against colonial oppression fostered the birth and vigorous growth of the national movement. However, by 1935 too many regional, religious and social dissensions had weakened the nationalist movement and had left the position of the administration apparently unshakeable.

Liberia and Ethiopia, 1880–1914: the survival of two African states

Like other African states, the states of Liberia and Ethiopia had also to face the challenge of European colonial imperialism and were subjected to varying degrees of European imperialist pressures and aggression during the last two decades of the nineteenth century. However, unlike the others, these two states were able to face up to this challenge and to maintain their independence and sovereign existence. The interesting questions that this chapter addresses itself to, then, are why both states escaped European colonial rule and what major political, economic and social changes occurred in them during the period of the Scramble.

European aggression on Liberian and Ethiopian territory, 1880–1914

Both Liberia and Ethiopia enjoyed more or less amicable relations with the European powers up to 1879. During the period of the Scramble from the 1880s onwards, however, these relations began to change.

Liberia

European imperialism in Liberia during the period under review occurred in three main forms: (1) expropriation of Liberian territory by European powers; (2) gross interference in Liberia's internal affairs by them; and (3) control of Liberia's economy by European merchants, financiers, concessionaires and entrepreneurs who enjoyed the confidence and patronage of these powers.

Heeding invitations by the Vai of north-western Liberia and by Sierra Leone and British merchants stationed on the Vai Coast, and mindful of Sierra Leone's commerce and revenue, Britain intervened from 1860 allegedly to protect the Vai and the merchants from Liberian impositions. After fruitless, intermittent discussions between British, Liberian and Vai representatives, Britain annexed most of the Vai chiefdoms to Sierra Leone in March 1882, although the Vai chiefs never desired British rule but rather British intervention. Liberians, stunned by the British action but helpless, issued an emotional 'Memorandum and Protest' against the action, copies of which were sent to all nations with which Liberia had treaty relations, imploring them to aid Liberia and to mediate 'to arrest a course of events which threaten her destruction'. Liberia's appeal, however, fell mostly on deaf or unsympathetic ears. In November 1885 Liberia therefore signed an agreement with Britain which fixed Liberia's boundary with Sierra Leone at the River Mano, to Liberia's disadvantage.

Similarly, the French annexed south-eastern Liberia between the Cavalla and San Pedro rivers in May 1891, taking advantage of its inhabitants' discontent with Liberia's trade policies and Liberia's lack of effective occupation of the district. Once again, the Liberians issued an emotional appeal to the 'civilized Christian nations of the world' to intercede on their behalf, but in vain.

To prevent further encroachments on Liberia, the Liberian government sent envoys to Washington and London in 1890 and 1892 respectively to obtain their commitment to the preservation of Liberia's territorial integrity; but neither would be committed. Liberia lost further territory to Britain and France between 1892 and 1914 as those powers advanced competitively to occupy Africa's heartland and subsequently demarcated their territories' boundaries with Liberia. In 1907, France, with the support of the United States, imposed a virtually unilateral treaty on Liberia which gave France a further slice of Liberian territory beyond the Makona river.

Apparently envious of the French gain of Liberian territory in 1907, Britain also insisted on acquiring the Kanre-Lahun district, which she had occupied by 1902. Between November 1909 and early 1910, the Liberian Government tried in vain to secure the Kanre-Lahun district from the British by persuasion. The matter was finally settled in January 1911 by an Anglo-Liberian treaty, by which Britain retained the Kanre-Lahun district but ceded to Liberia the much less desirable territory between the Morro and Mano rivers and £4000 'compensation' to the Liberian government with which to develop the territory ceded. (Liberia also won the right to free navigation on the Mano River.) The final delimitation of the new Liberian–Sierra Leone boundary occurred in 1915. Thus Liberia survived the British and French threats and aggression but not unscathed.

Ethiopia

European imperial designs against Ethiopia's territory and independence were no less dangerous than against Liberia (see 11.1). Their beginnings could be traced to 1869 when an Italian Lazarist missionary, Giuseppe Sapeto, purchased the Red Sea port of Assab from a local sultan for 6000 Maria Theresa dollars. The port became the property of a private Italian shipping company, the Societa Rubattino, and in 1882 was declared an Italian colony.

Emperor Yohannes, though a notable patriot, was less immediately concerned with the advent of Italy than with the departure of Egypt, which was then ruling much of the Red Sea and Gulf of Aden coasts of Africa, and their immediate hinterlands. He therefore readily concluded with Britain a treaty on 3 June 1884 in which, in return for the emperor's assistance, the British agreed to return the territories on the Sudanese frontier recently occupied by Egypt. The value of the agreement was, however, short-lived, for on 3 February 1885 the Italians seized Massawa and penetrated as far as the villages of Sahati and Wia. They did so with the consent of the British, who favoured Italian expansion in the hope of curbing that of France, their principal rival in the

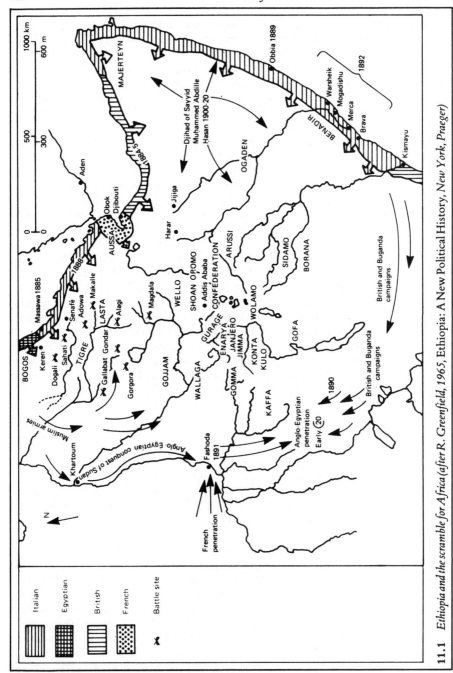

11.1 *Ethiopia and the scramble for Africa (after R. Greenfield, 1965, Ethiopia: A New Political History, New York, Praeger)*

Scramble for Africa. Ras Alula, the notable Ethiopian warrior, protested against this infiltration, but the Italians replied by fortifying the disputed areas and by sending more troops, which were intercepted by Ras Alula at Dogali in January 1887. The invaders thereupon evacuated Sahati and Wia, but, complaining of a 'massacre' at Dogali, blockaded all shipping bringing supplies to Ethiopia.

War between the Italians and Yohannes seemed imminent, but the former, anxious to avoid a difficult mountainous campaign, persuaded Britain to mediate. A British diplomat, Sir Gerald Portal, was dispatched to the emperor to ask him to agree to an Italian occupation of Sahati and Wia, and of the Senahit or Bogos area which the Egyptians had ceded in 1884. When those proposals were read out, Yohannes rejected them outright and angrily wrote to Queen Victoria, protesting that if she wished to make peace it should be when the the Italians were in their country and the Ethiopians in theirs.

Yohannes, faced with the growing threat from Italy, strengthened his defences by moving up a garrison stationed on the Sudan frontier. Finding the area unguarded, the Mahdists attacked there. The emperor hastened to Matamma to resist them, but, at the close of a victorious battle on 10 March 1889, was mortally wounded by a stray bullet. News of his death caused his army to flee. There was great confusion throughout northern Ethiopia, the more so as the country was suffering from a serious cattle plague and famine followed by epidemics of smallpox and cholera. During this period of difficulty the Italians advanced rapidly inland. By the end of 1889 they had occupied a stretch of the northern plateau, where they established their colony of Eritrea with its capital at Asmara.

During much of Emperor Yohannes's grim resistance against Egyptian and Italian aggression, Menelik, Shoa's ruler and nominally subordinated to the emperor, maintained cordial relations with Italy (see 11.2). Contact with Italy was valuable to Menelik since it enabled him to be supplied by the Italians with several physicians as well as numerous firearms. As a consequence of this friendship with Italy, Menelik was able as King of Shoa (1865–89) forcibly to acquire the rich regions of Arusi, Harar, Kulo and Konta to the south and south-east, and Gurage and Wallaga to the south-west. This friendship culminated on 2 May 1889 – less than two months after the death of Emperor Yohannes – in a Treaty of Peace and Amity signed between Menelik and Italy at the Ethiopian village of Wuchale.

The Wuchale (Italian: Uccialli) treaty, which was to constitute a turning-point in the relations between the two countries, contained articles of benefit to both. In it Menelik recognized Italian sovereignty over the greater part of the Eritrean plateau, including Asmara, while Italy recognized him as emperor – the first such recognition he had been accorded – and promised that he could import arms and ammunition through Italian territory. The most important section of the treaty, however, was Article XVII, which was soon to be the basis of disputes. The quarrel arose from the fact that the treaty had two texts, one in Amharic and the other in Italian, the sense of which differed materially in this article. The Amharic version stated that Menelik could avail himself of the services of the Italian authorities for all communications he might wish to have with other powers; the Italian text made this obligatory. On the basis of that clause, the Italians proclaimed Ethiopia a protectorate and this was duly recognized

11.2 *Menelik, King of Shoa, 1865–89; Emperor of Ethiopia, 1889–1913 (Harlingue-Viollet)*

by the European powers. In support of their claim the Italians occupied the town of Adowa in January 1890 and then informed Ras Mangasha, the son of Yohannes and the ruler of the Tigrai province, that they would not withdraw until Menelik accepted their interpretation of the Wuchale treaty.

Menelik refused to accept this interpretation and after several years' delay – which he turned to advantage by importing large quantities of firearms, especially from France and Russia, and conquering several provinces, including Kaffa, Wolamo, Sidamo, Bale, and eastern and western Boran Oromo ('Galla') – he finally denounced the Wuchale treaty on 12 February 1893. On 27 February he informed the European powers, and, referring to Italy's claims, alluded to the biblical phrase, declaring that 'Ethiopia has need of no one; she stretches out her hands unto God'. He spoke from a position of strength, for he was by then in possession of 82 000 rifles and twenty-eight cannon.

Fighting between the Italians and Ethiopians broke out in December 1894 when Batha Hagos, an Eritrean chief, rebelled against the rule of Italy. Early in January 1895 the Italians attacked Ras Mangasha in Tigrai and occupied much of that province. Menelik thereupon ordered the mobilization of his army on 17 September, and marched north with a large force which won significant victories at Amba Alagi on 7 December and Makalle at the end of the year. The Italians then fell back on Adowa, where, after a period of inaction, the final battle took place.

Menelik was in a relatively strong position. He had the support of the local population, whose patriotism had been intensified by the fact that the Italians had been expropriating Eritrean land for the settlement of their colonists. The inhabitants were therefore willing to show his troops good paths and report on enemy movements. The Italians, on the other hand, had to face the enmity of the local people, and had no accurate maps; they therefore moved in confusion in an almost unknown country. Menelik's army, moreover, was much larger. It was composed of over 100 000 men with modern rifles, besides others with antique firearms and spears, whereas the invaders had only about 17 000 men, of whom 10 596 were Italian and the rest Eritrean levies. The Italians had some superiority in cannon, but with fifty-six pieces as against Menelik's forty this was by no means decisive.

The outcome of the day's fighting at Adowa was a remarkable victory for Menelik, and a complete defeat for his enemies. During the battle, 261 Italian officers, 2918 Italian non-commissioned officers and men, and about 2000 *askaris*, or local troops, were killed. In addition, 954 Italian soldiers were permanently missing; and 470 Italians and 958 *askaris* were wounded. Total Italian casualties amounted to over 40% of the fighting force, which was almost completely routed and lost all its artillery, besides 11 000 rifles.

As a result of Menelik's victory, the Italians agreed, on 26 October, to the Peace Treaty of Addis Ababa, which annulled the Treaty of Wuchale and recognized the absolute independence of Ethiopia.

The Adowa campaign gave Menelik considerable international prestige. The French and British dispatched diplomatic missions to sign treaties with him, while other embassies arrived from the Sudanese Mahdists, the Sultan of the Ottoman empire and the Tsar of Russia.

The outcome of the battle was of major significance in the history of Europe's relations with Africa. The Ethiopians acquired prestige throughout the Red Sea area. Increasing interest in Ethiopia, the last indigenous independent state in black Africa, was also shown by black intellectuals in the New World. The Haitian, Benito Sylvain, one of the first apostles of pan-Africanism, travelled to Ethiopia four times between 1889 and 1906, carrying letters to and from President Alexis of Haiti, while William H. Ellis, a black American of Cuban descent, visited the country twice, in 1903 and 1904, with various plans for economic development and the settlement of black Americans. An Ethiopian impact was also felt in South Africa, where the biblical prophecy about Ethiopia stretching forth her hands unto God had aroused interest some years earlier. An Ethiopian Church had been established in South Africa by 1900. Increasing awareness of Ethiopia was later shown by the appearance in 1911 of the Gold Coast intellectual J. E. Casely Hayford's book, *Ethiopia Unbound*, which was dedicated 'to the sons of Ethiopia the World Wide Over'.

Economic and social developments and European intervention in Liberia's and Ethiopia's internal affairs, 1880–1914

Liberia

In addition to European threats and aggression, Liberia faced serious internal economic and social problems. The Scramble and partition forced the Liberian government to advance into the Liberian hinterland to subdue the indigenous ethnic groups and establish a colonial-type administration over them. Each administrative unit or district was governed 'indirectly' through its principal chiefs in collaboration with a government-appointed district commissioner. Up to 1914 most of the commissioners were Americo-Liberian or educated indigenous Liberian military officers. The administration was largely oppressive and corrupt. Most of the district commissioners, their aides and their troops, being poorly and irregularly paid and seldom supervised from Monrovia, lived off their districts by extorting food, labour for their private farms, and excessive fines and taxes.

Not surprisingly, the indigenous Africans resisted not only their military conquest by the Liberian government – just as Africans elsewhere resisted European conquest – but also the excesses of the Liberian administration. Until subjugated by the Liberian militia, the Liberian Frontier Force and American naval ships, the Kru resisted intermittently, and particularly in 1915–16; the Grebo in 1910; the Kisi in 1913; the Kpele and Bandi from 1911 to 1914; the Gio and Mano from 1913 to 1918; the Gbolobo Grebo from 1916 to 1918; the Gola and Bandi in 1918–19; the Joquelle Kpele from 1916 to 1920; and the Sikon in 1921. These protracted wars on different fronts and the cost and inefficiency of the 'native administration' encouraged foreign intervention and strained the government's human and material resources.

The government's revenues were never adequate. Foreign aid was meagre. Most Americo-Liberians preferred trade to agriculture and were seriously hurt by the worldwide depression of the late nineteenth century. By 1890 resident German, British and Dutch merchants dominated Liberia's external trade. Liberia's major export com-

modity from the 1860s was coffee. However, owing to the depression and adverse competition in the world market with better-prepared Brazilian coffee, the price of Liberian
coffee drastically fell from 1898 onwards. The consequent cuts in Liberian coffee output
and exports and the general contraction of the volume and value of Liberia's external
trade drastically reduced government revenues, which consisted mostly of customs dues
and other levies on trade and shipping. Besides, the government lacked the means to
collect effectively from reluctant Liberian and foreign merchants or to stop smuggling.

To avoid bankruptcy, the government borrowed frequently and heavily from
Liberian and resident foreign merchants 'to carry out its most ordinary operations':
$10 000 in November 1896 at 9% interest from the German trading firm, A.
Woermann and Company, 'to meet the current expenses of the Government'; $15 000
in February 1898 from the Dutch firm, Oost Afrikaansche Cie, to pay the expenses of
the Liberian legislature – to mention a few examples. Furthermore, the Liberian
government borrowed £100 000 in 1871, £100 000 in 1906 and $1 700 000 in 1912
from British and European financiers on harsh terms. For the repayment of these debts
the British took over the administration of the country's customs revenue as from 1896
and they were succeeded by an 'International Receivership' as from 1912.

The decline of Liberian trade and agriculture and of foreign aid as from the late
nineteenth century increased the Liberian government's exploitation of the indigenous
Liberians through the corvée, poll tax and other levies, as well as Liberians'
dependence on their government for jobs. Competition to control these jobs increased
between political parties and interest groups like the 'founding fathers' (or Americo-
Liberians who had settled in Liberia before Independence) and the 'sons of the soil' (or
Americo-Liberians born in Liberia).

Some social and economic developments did nevertheless occur. In 1900 the Liberian
government reopened the Liberia College (see. 11.3), which it had closed down in 1895
for lack of funds and progress. The following year, an Americo-Liberian engineer, T. J.
R. Faulkner, installed Liberia's first telephone linking Monrovia with several neighbouring Liberian towns. In 1900 a cable station in Monrovia, built by a German firm,
was opened and linked Liberia with the outside world. During 1906–7 a British firm,
the Liberia Development Company, built several motor roads from Monrovia inland,
using a part of the loan of 1906. Furthermore, several foreign firms obtained and
exploited rubber, mineral and other concessions in Liberia from the Liberian
government.

Ethiopia

Like Liberia, Ethiopia underwent significant economic changes from the last decades of
the nineteenth century on.

Menelik was desirous of modernizing his age-old country, and displayed keen
interest in innovations of all kinds. His reign therefore witnessed numerous innovations
without precedent in Ethiopia's history. The first, and one of the most important, was
the founding in the mid-1880s of the capital, Addis Ababa, literally 'New Flower',
which by 1910 had a population of some 100 000 inhabitants. The construction of the
first modern bridges was also effected at this time, and this improved the country's

11.3 *Teaching staff and students of Liberia College, 1900 (Sir H. Johnston, Liberia, 1906)*

difficult communications. In 1892 taxes were reorganized and a tithe instituted for the army, thereby ending the soldiers' traditional practice of looting from the peasants. In 1894 the first national currency was issued 'in order', a proclamation declared, 'that our country may increase in honour and our commerce prosper'. A postal system was also being brought into existence in the 1890s. Postage stamps, ordered like the coins from France, were put on sale in 1893, and a decree establishing post offices was issued in 1894. French advisers were used in developing the service, and Ethiopia entered the International Postal Union in 1908. A concession for a railway from Addis Ababa to the French Somaliland port of Djibuti was granted in 1894, but technical, financial and political difficulties were so great that its progress was very slow. Two telegraph lines had, meanwhile, been established at the turn of the century. Early in the twentieth century, the first modern roads were constructed between Addis Ababa and Addis Alem and between Harar and Dire Dawa, with the assistance of Italian and French engineers respectively.

The later years of the reign saw the establishment of various modern institutions. The Bank of Abyssinia was founded in 1905, as an affiliate of the British-owned National Bank of Egypt. The first modern hotel in Addis Ababa, the Etege, was established by Empress Taitu in 1907. The Menelik II School was set up with the help of Coptic teachers from Egypt in 1908. The Menelik II Hospital, founded to replace an earlier Russian Red Cross establishment set up during the Adowa war, was built in 1910, while a state printing press came into existence in 1911. Failing health, and the increasing complexity of government, had meanwhile caused Menelik in 1907 to establish the country's first Cabinet, which, according to his chronicler Gabre Sellassie, stemmed from a 'desire of implanting European customs'. Ethiopia by the end of Menelik's reign had thus been placed on the road of modernization.

The outcome of the Scramble and partition for Liberia and Ethiopia

The European Scramble for and partition of Africa did have some interesting but contrasting impacts on Liberia and Ethiopia. For one thing, they were the only two states in the whole of the continent that survived the imperialist onslaught and retained their sovereignty and independence. But, while, as indicated above, Ethiopia not merely survived but in fact expanded her southern and eastern frontiers during that period, Liberia lost a great deal of her territory to both Britain and France. The last question to be considered is why those countries survived while one lost and the other gained territory.

Both Liberia and Ethiopia survived for a number of reasons, and the first main one was the very strong belief of the peoples of both countries that they were destined by the Almighty God to survive, a belief which very much strengthened their determination to resist all European encroachments and aggression. Growing largely out of the experience of involuntary servitude in the New World, there was embedded within the Liberian consciousness a firm faith in a divine being as controller of the destiny of the nation. Several Liberian presidents were ministers of the gospel. Indeed, Liberians have always viewed each major event in their history as the result of divine intervention. It is this same belief that underlies the much-quoted expression of Emperor Menelik of

Ethiopia in 1893 that 'Ethiopia has need of no one; she stretches out her hands unto God'. There is no doubt that this firm belief on the part of the peoples of these countries filled them with a determination that should go some way to explaining their successful opposition to the European onslaughts.

The second main reason for the survival of Ethiopia and Liberia was diplomatic. On the one hand, both were able to play one European power against another and were able to resist by diplomacy the more indirect pressures of the colonial powers. Menelik certainly succeeded in playing Italy, France and Britain off against each other. Liberia also constantly played off France against Britain, and Britain against Germany, while she did not hesitate, whenever the going was tough, to bring in the United States to make the necessary threatening noises to ward off any of these powers.

On the other hand, there is no doubt that the determination of the imperial powers to prevent any one of them from gaining control of either of those states was a crucial factor in their survival. For mainly economic reasons, Germany, France and Britain were not prepared to see any one of them in sole control of Liberia while, for sentimental reasons, the United States was bent on ensuring its survival. Thus, there were times when the United States thwarted French and British ambitions to carve up Liberia (on the pretext that Liberia was unable to police her borders) by sending her gunboats to patrol Liberian waters. At other times, the United States employed diplomatic means to warn Britian and France of the moral judgement of history should either of them make any attempt to end the independence of Liberia. Thus, in 1879 and 1898, they warned France and Germany not to annex or establish a protectorate over Liberia. In the same way, for mainly strategic reasons, Britain, France and Italy were not prepared to see any one of them in sole control of Ethiopia.

However, in the case of Ethiopia, there is one unique and crucial factor that should be cited in explanation of her survival, and which also explains the fact that she was able to extend her territorial limits during the period under review, and that is her military strength. Had Menelik lost the battle of Adowa, Ethiopia would undoubtedly have become an Italian colony in 1896. But as shown above, thanks to her military strength, which was far superior to that of Italy in Africa, Ethiopia not only won that battle and thereby maintained her independence but was also able to extend her frontiers during the 1880s and 1890s.

But, if Liberia and Ethiopia did survive, the former did so mutilated and weakened, and this was the outcome of her military weakness and the hopeless internal conditions of the state. Liberia's navy in any year consisted of one or two gunboats. Her army was the Americo-Liberian militia up to 1908 when the Liberian Frontier Force (LFF) was organized to strengthen it. The militia numbered under 2000 men in any year up to 1914 and was mostly poorly trained, paid and equipped. It lacked the means of quick transportation to the scene of war. The LFF, no less inefficient than the militia, comprised in December 1913 three American and seven Liberian officers and little more than 600 enlisted men stationed in over a dozen detachments in the Liberian hinterland. Up to 1914, the officer commanding each detachment performed both military and administrative duties in his district. Consequently he received instructions from, and reported to, both the Department of War and the Department of Interior (neither of which co-ordinated with the other). Liberia's military weakness markedly contrasted with Ethiopia's military might and largely accounts for Liberia's inability to defend her territory from encroachment by Europeans during the Scramble. No less hopeless was the internal situation. As indicated above, and for reasons already given, the Liberian government was perennially near-bankrupt and owed huge debts to local and foreign creditors. By January 1908 Liberia's indebtedness to Britain comprised, according to the British consul-general at Monrovia, £60 000 a year 'for several years', while her indebtedness to German merchants in Liberia amounted to $120 000 by September 1905. This indebtedness enabled the imperial powers to constantly interfere in the internal affairs of Liberia during the period under review in a way that they never did in Ethiopia, where they were never provided with the cause or the excuse to do so. Throughout the last three decades of the nineteenth century, the imperial powers sent mission upon mission to Liberia to offer aid to pay her debts if she would come under their protection. France did this in 1879, Germany in 1887 and Spain in 1886, and each power offered to regulate Liberia's finances and organize her defence. At the same time, their resident ambassadors and representatives treated the Liberians with contempt and frequently imposed on her by denouncing her trade, customs and citizenship laws or bullying her to redress their nationals' grievances as Britain did in September 1869, August 1870, April 1871, February and June 1882, November 1886 and finally January 1909. Germany similarly brought in her gunboats to intimidate Liberia in February and October 1881, August 1897, January and September 1898 and December 1912.

Such European intervention in Liberia had far-reaching effects on Liberian politics and society. First, it divided the Liberians into pro-British and pro-American factions, who staged massive anti-Barclay and pro-Barclay demonstrations in Monrovia in January 1909. Moreover, the employment of Europeans at high salaries to implement the reforms demanded by the powers also greatly strained the Liberian government's already meagre revenues. But for the active intervention of the United States, thanks to the activities of the American Minister Resident in Monrovia, Ernest Lyon, an Afro-American thoroughly in sympathy with Liberia and her leaders' anxiety to obtain American support from 1909 onwards, there is no doubt that Liberia would have fallen victim to the other imperial powers.

Never at any time was Ethiopia subjected to such persistent intervention by the European imperial powers in her internal affairs. On the contrary, thanks to the Adowa victory, she was accorded every respect and accepted into the comity of nations more or less as an equal during the period that Liberia was virtually under the siege of the imperial powers. Granted the military weakness of Liberia, and, above all, her internal dislocation, due partly to her own economic weakness and the active interference of Europeans in her internal affairs, the surprising fact is not that Liberia survived anguished and emaciated, but that she survived at all.

12

The First World War and its consequences

It was during the last decade of the consolidation of colonialism in Africa that the First World War broke out. This war was essentially a quarrel between European powers but it involved Africa, both directly and indirectly, because at the outbreak of hostilities the greater part of it was ruled by the European belligerents. A great deal has been written about the European campaigns in Africa during the First World War, and the consequent distribution of German territory among the victorious Allied powers – the last chapter in the Scramble for Africa. Much less has been written about the impact of the war on Africans and on the administrative structures recently imposed on them by their European conquerors. It is with these themes that this chapter will be principally concerned. However, a brief account of the military campaigns is essential if we are fully to understand the implications of the war for Africa.

The war on African soil

The immediate consequence for Africa of the declaration of war in Europe was the invasion by the Allies of Germany's colonies.

The campaigns in Africa can be divided into two distinct phases. During the first, which lasted only a few weeks, the Allies were concerned to knock out Germany's offensive capability and ensure that her fleet could not use her African ports. Thus Lomé in Togo, Duala in Cameroon and Swakopmund and Lüderitz Bay in South West Africa were occupied soon after the outbreak of war. In German East Africa, British cruisers bombarded Dar es-Salaam and Tanga in August, and, although neither port was taken until later in the war, they could not be used by German warships. In Egypt, on the entry of Turkey into the war on Germany's side, the British defences of the Suez Canal were strengthened and a Turkish expedition repulsed in February 1915.

The campaigns of the first phase of the war in Africa were vital to Allied global strategy. The campaigns of the second phase were for the conquest of German colonies in Africa, both to prevent them from being used as bases for the subversion of the Allies' often tenuous authority in their own colonies, and to share them among themselves in the event of an overall Allied victory. German South West Africa was conquered within six months while the Cameroon campaign was rather protracted, lasting well over

132

fifteen months. The East African campaigns (see 12.1) lasted longer still. Von Lettow-Vorbeck, appreciating that he could not hope to win the battle against forces which outnumbered his own by more than ten to one, determined at least to tie them down as long as possible by resorting to guerrilla tactics. Right up to the end of hostilities he remained undefeated, leading his bedraggled column through Portuguese East Africa and then on its last march into Northern Rhodesia, where he learnt of the armistice in Europe.

The European exodus

The war saw a large-scale exodus of European administrative and commercial personnel from the Allied colonies in Africa, as they left for the Western Front or enlisted in locally based regiments for campaigns elsewhere in Africa. In some parts the European presence, already thinly spread, was diminished by more than half. Some divisions in Northern Nigeria, such as Borgu, were without any European administrator for much of the war. In Northern Rhodesia, as much as 40% of the adult European population was on active service. In French Black Africa there was general mobilization of Europeans of military age, while in British East Africa Europeans were registered for war work. In some parts, particularly the countryside, it was rumoured that the white man was leaving for ever.

The result of this exodus was a slow down, if not a complete stoppage, of many essential services manned by Europeans. In certain instances Africans were specially trained, as in Senegal, to fill the vacancies thus created. In British West Africa, some jobs hitherto reserved for whites were filled by educated Africans, which, as Richard Rathbone has pointed out, goes some way towards explaining the loyalty of the elites during the war. Only in Egypt was there a net increase in the European presence, since there was an enormous influx of British troops using Egypt as a base for the Allied offensive in the Middle East.

From the African point of view, perhaps even more remarkable than the apparent exodus of Europeans was the sight of white people fighting each other, a thing they had never done during the colonial occupation. What is more they encouraged their subjects in uniform to kill the 'enemy' white man, who hitherto had belonged to a clan who, by virtue of the colour of their skin, were held to be sacrosanct and desecration of whose person had hitherto been severely punished.

The African involvement in the war

Except in the German South West Africa campaign, African troops were a major factor in the Allied successes in their African campaigns. African troops were called on during the war not only to fight on African soil, but also to reinforce European armies on the Western and Middle Eastern fronts. Further, they were instrumental in putting down the various revolts against colonial authority, just as they had been instrumental in the European conquest of Africa.

Over a million troops were actually recruited during the war to supplement the generally small forces maintained by the colonial authorities. In addition to troops, carriers were recruited on a massive scale – some three carriers were necessary to keep

12.1   *German East African campaign: troops of the Nigerian Brigade disembarking at Lindi, December 1917 (Imperial War Museum)*

each fighting soldier in the field. Further, North Africans were recruited to work at factory benches vacated by Frenchmen conscripted into the army. The subsequent voluntary migration of Algerian labour to France has its origin in the First World War. All in all over 2.5 million Africans, or well over 1% of the population of the continent, were involved in war work of some kind.

Recruits for both fighting and carrier service were raised by three methods. The first was on a purely volunteer basis where Africans offered their services freely without any outside pressure. Thus, in the early stages of the war on the Palestine and Syrian fronts, large numbers of impoverished *fellāhin* (peasants) in Egypt offered their services in return for what were comparatively attractive wages.

The second method was recruitment, which was usually undertaken through chiefs, who were expected to deliver up the numbers required of them by the political officers. In some areas they had no difficulty in obtaining genuine volunteers; in others, men were impressed by the chiefs and presented to the political officers as volunteers.

The third and the most widespread method, however, was conscription. In French Black Africa, a Decree of 1912 aimed at creating a permanent black army made military service for four years compulsory for all African males between the ages of 20 and 28. After the outbreak of war, with 14 785 African troops in West Africa alone, it was decided to recruit 50 000 more during the 1915–16 recruitment campaign. Chiefs were given quotas of men to fill, and rounded up strangers and former slaves to avoid enlisting their immediate dependents or kinsmen. Desperate for more men and in the hope that an African of high standing might succeed where Frenchmen had not, the French government appointed Blaise Diagne in 1918 as High Commissioner for the Recruitment of Black Troops. Set the target of recruiting 40 000 men, his teams actually enlisted 63 378, few of whom, however, saw the front since the war ended in November 1918.

Compulsory recruitment was also used to raise troops and carriers in British East Africa, under the compulsory service order of 1915, which made all males aged between 18 and 45 liable for military service. This was extended to the Uganda Protectorate in April 1917. Forced recruitment of porters in all districts in Northern Rhodesia meant that for a large part of the war over a third of the adult males of the territory were involved in carrier service. In Algeria, Tunisia and even Morocco, which was still being conquered, colonial subjects were pressed into the war. Over 483 000 colonial soldiers from all over Africa are estimated to have served in the French army during the war, most of them compulsorily recruited. The Belgians in the Congo impressed up to 260 000 porters during the East African campaign.

While the war directly took an enormous toll in dead and wounded in Africa, it further accounted for innumerable indirect deaths in the Africa-wide influenza epidemic of 1918–19, whose spread was facilitated by the movement of troops and carriers returning home.

The African challenge to European authority

The war period saw widespread revolts and protest movements which challenged the authority of the colonial regimes in most parts of Africa – in French West Africa,

Libya, Portuguese and German East Africa and British West Africa. A number of themes run through the wartime risings: the desire to regain a lost independence; resentment against wartime measures, in particular compulsory recruitment and forced labour; religious, and in particular pan-Islamic, opposition to the war; reaction to economic hardships caused by the war; and discontent with particular aspects of the colonial system, whose full impact in many areas coincided with the wartime years. There is a final theme, particularly significant in South Africa, that of pro-German sentiment amongst the subjects of the Allied powers.

The desire to regain independence comes out clearly in the revolts of the Borgawa and Ohori-Ije in French Dahomey, of various Igbo groups in Owerri province of Nigeria, and of the majority of revolts against French authority in West Africa. In Egypt, the Wafd riots, which took place immediately after the war, were largely inspired by a desire to shake off the recently imposed British protectorate. In Madagascar 500 Malagasy, mainly intellectuals, were arrested at the end of 1915 and accused of 'forming a well-organised secret society with the aim of expelling the French and restoring a Malagasy government'.

Religious, and in particular pan-Islamic, considerations underlay some of the revolts. The activities of members of the Sanūsī brotherhood in Libya, where they were still resisting the Italian occupation of their country, and their invasion of western Egypt in November 1915 were partly in response to the Turkish call to *djihād*. Though driven back into Libya, members of the brotherhood as well as other Libyans inflicted a decisive defeat on the Italians at the battle of al-Karadābiyya, the worst defeat suffered by the Italians since Adowa in 1896. They then drove the Italians, who had to divert the bulk of their troops to the Austrian front, to the coast, so that by 1917 Italy was on the verge of losing Libya altogether. These victories led to the establishment of the Tripolitanian Republic (al-Djumhūriyya al-Ṭarābulusiyya) on 16 November 1918 in western Libya and the Emirate of Cyrenaica in eastern Libya. Italy recognized these states in 1919 and granted each one its own parliament. Further rights were granted by Italy under the Treaty of al-Radjma in 1920. In January 1922, these two states agreed to form a political union and elected Idris al-Sanūsi, the leader of the Sanūsiyya, as the head of the union and set up a central committee with its headquarters at Gharyān.

The Libyan risings directly influenced events in southern Tunisia, where 15 000 French troops were needed to suppress the revolt, and among the Tawārik and other Muslims in French Niger and Chad, where Islamic abhorrence of infidel rule, the drought of 1914 and intensive recruitment for the army had provoked considerable discontent. In December 1916 Sanūsī's forces invaded Niger, where they gained the support of Kaossen, leader of the Kel-Aïr Tawārik, Firhūn, chief of the Oullimiden Tawārik, and the Sultan of Agades. They took Agades and a combined French and British force was needed to defeat them.

Not only Islamic risings threatened the Allied powers in their colonies. John Chilembwe's rising in Nyasaland (now Malawi) of January 1915 had strong Christian undertones, whilst the Kitawala Watchtower movement in the Rhodesias preached the imminence of the end of the world and disobedience to constituted authority. The latter capitalized on the disruption caused in Northern Rhodesia by von Lettow-Vorbeck's invasion at the end of the war. Similarly apocalyptic was the widespread movement in the Niger delta area of Nigeria, led by Garrick Braide, otherwise known as Elijah II, who preached the imminent demise of the British administration. In Ivory Coast, the Prophet Harris was deported in December 1914 because 'the events in Europe demand more than ever the maintenance of tranquility among the people of the Colony'. In Nyanza in Kenya, the Mumbo cult, which grew rapidly during the war years, rejected the Christian religion and declared: 'All Europeans are your enemies, but the time is shortly coming when they will disappear from our country.'

Perhaps the most important cause of revolt was the forced recruitment of men for service as soldiers and carriers. Such was the hatred of forced recruitment that it was a major inspiration for nearly all the revolts that took place in French Black Africa, and evoked some resistance in the otherwise peaceful Gold Coast colony. John Chilembwe's rising was precipitated by the enlistment of Nyasas and their large death toll in the first weeks of the war in battle with the Germans.

Economic hardship caused by the war certainly underlay and even provoked resistance against the colonial authorities. The risings in the mid-west of Nigeria and the Niger delta during the early stages of the war cannot be understood except in the context of falling prices for palm products, and the drop in trade due to the exclusion of the producers' main customers, the Germans.

In South Africa the Afrikaner revolt of late 1914 against the government's decision to support the Allies was due both to pro-German sympathy and to hatred of Britain. In Uganda, shortly after the commencement of hostilities, Nyindo, Paramount Chief of Kigezi, was persuaded by his half-brother, the *Mwami* of Ruanda, to revolt against the British on behalf of the Germans.

In many cases, particularly Nigeria, wartime revolts were not directly attributable to specific wartime measures. Rather they were directed against obnoxious features of colonial rule such as taxation, which was introduced into Yorubaland for the first time in 1916 and, together with the increased powers given to traditional rulers under the policy of 'indirect rule', provoked the Iseyin riots. In French West Africa, the impositions of the *indigénat* (a discriminatory judicial code), the reorganization of administrative boundaries, and the suppression of chiefs or the exactions of chiefs without traditional authority were all major causes of the revolts that broke out in every colony of the federation.

These revolts were, whatever their cause, put down ruthlessly by the colonial authorities. 'Rebels' were impressed into the army, flogged or even hanged, chiefs exiled or imprisoned, and villages razed to the ground to serve as a warning. But not all protests were violent in character. Many people tried to avoid the source of their grievances by emigration or other forms of evasive action. Thus large numbers of French subjects in Senegal, Guinea, Haut-Sénégal-Niger and Côte d'Ivoire, estimated at about 62 000, undertook what A. I. Asiwaju has termed 'protest migrations' to the neighbouring British territories. To avoid recruitment teams, inhabitants of whole villages fled to the bush. Young men mutilated themselves rather than serve in the colonial army.

The economic consequences of the war

The declaration of war brought considerable economic disruption to Africa. Generally there followed a depression in the prices paid for Africa's primary products, while knowledge that henceforth imported goods would be in short supply led to a rise in their prices. In Uganda there was an overnight increase of 50% in the price of imports. The pattern of African trade with Europe was radically changed by the exclusion of the Germans from the Allied territories, where in certain cases, like Sierra Leone, they had accounted for 80% of the import–export trade. Germany, from being tropical Africa's major overseas trading partner, was now almost entirely excluded from trading activities in the continent, with the expulsion of her nationals and the seizure of their plantations, commercial houses and industries by the occupying powers.

The depression that followed the outbreak of war soon gave way to a boom in those products needed to boost the Allied war effort. Thus Egyptian cotton rose from £E3 a quintal in 1914 to £E8 in 1916–18. But increased demand was not always reflected by increased prices, for often the colonial governments controlled the prices paid to the producers. Certain countries, such as the Gold Coast, whose major export crop of cocoa was not so much in demand, suffered badly throughout the war. While prices of exports and wages by and large fell despite increased demand for raw materials and labour, the prices of imports, where they were obtainable, rose throughout the war. This affected the Africans in the wage-earning or export crop-producing sectors.

Furthermore, the war witnessed an increased level of state intervention in the economies of the African colonies, whether in the form of price control, requisition of food crops, compulsory cultivation of crops, recruitment of labour for essential projects or allocation of shipping space. Generally such intervention tended to favour the import–export houses of the colonial power controlling the colony concerned.

Demands for traditional subsistence crops, including yams, manioc and beans, for the feeding of the Allies in Europe and for the armies in Africa or the Middle Eastern front, added to the hardship of those outside the subsistence sector. And, where subsistence crops were requisitioned – as they widely were – or paid for at prices below the free-market price, the producers themselves suffered. Thus by the end of the war the Egyptian *fellāhīn* were hard put to keep body and soul together, what with inflation and the requisition of their cereals and animals.

Recruitment of troops and carriers resulted in shortages of labour in many parts of the continent during the war. The influenza epidemic at the end of the war in East and Central Africa particularly affected the returning carriers and created acute shortages of labour in Kenya and the Rhodesias. This shortage occurred among European as well as African personnel.

The shortage of imports may have led to a fall in production where agriculture, as in Egypt, was dependent on imports of fertilizers, farm implements and irrigation machinery, but it also encouraged the development of import substitution industries in some countries, particularly South Africa where the potentialities of overseas markets for local products came to be realized at this time. In the Belgian Congo, cut off from the occupied metropolis, the war was a great stimulus to increased self-sufficiency. The influx of British troops into Egypt and the injection of some £200 million into the economy during the war period was an important stimulus to industrial growth.

The war introduced the motor vehicle and, with it, motorable roads to many parts of Africa. In East Africa, the protracted campaign against the Germans and the problem of moving supplies led to the construction of a number of motorable roads. In those areas where there was sustained military activity, or where transit facilities were required, ports developed rapidly. Mombasa, Bizerta, Port Harcourt and Dakar are cases in point. In Nigeria, the Enugu coal mines were opened up during the war to provide the railways with a local source of fuel.

Generally government revenues diminished during the war, since they were largely dependent on duties on imported goods. Therefore, except where military needs made them necessary, public works came to a halt and development plans were shelved until after the war.

The socio-political consequences of the war

The social consequences of the war for Africa varied considerably from territory to territory and depended on the extent of their involvement, in particular the degree of recruitment or military activity in them. Compared with the research conducted on the political consequences of the war for Africa, comparatively little has been undertaken on its social consequences. Yet its impact on soldiers, carriers and labourers who were uprooted from the limited worlds of their villages and sent thousands of miles away and their impact on their societies on their return forms a major theme in colonial history.

There is no doubt that the war opened up new windows for many Africans, particularly the educated elite groups. In many parts of Africa the war gave a boost, if not always to nationalist activity, at least to the development of a more critical approach by the educated elites towards their colonial masters. In Guinea the return of the ex-servicemen heralded strikes, riots in the demobilization camps and attacks on the authority of chiefs.

If the war saw an end of attempts by Africans to regain the lost sovereignty of their pre-colonial polities, it also saw a rise in demands for participation in the process of government of the new politics imposed on them by the Europeans. These demands – inspired by United States President Woodrow Wilson's Fourteen Points which were made in reaction to the Soviet proposals put forward in October 1917 for the immediate conclusion of peace without annexation or indemnity – even extended to the right to self-determination. Sa'd Zaghlūl's Wafd Party in Egypt took its name from the delegation (*Wafd*) he tried to send to the Versailles Peace Conference to negotiate Egypt's return to independence. Similarly, in Tunisia, though the wartime Resident, Alapetite, had kept as firm a grip on the nationalists as the British had in Egypt, after the war their leaders sent a telegram to President Wilson to enlist his assistance in their demands for self-determination.

While Wilson's Fourteen Points did not inspire demands for immediate independence in Africa south of the Sahara, his liberal sentiments encouraged West African nationalists to hope that they could influence the Versailles Peace Conference and also encouraged them to demand a greater say in their own affairs. In the Sudan, Wilson's Fourteen Points, coupled with the inspiration of the Arab revolt of 1916, proved a turning-point in Sudanese nationalism, informing the attitudes of a new generation of politically conscious young men who had passed through government schools and had acquired some modern western skills.

In many territories where heavy contributions had been made in terms of men and material to the war effort, there was hope that these would be rewarded at least by social and political reform. Blaise Diagne was in fact promised a package of post-war reforms in French Black Africa if he could recruit the additional men France required for the European front. This he did, but the reforms were never put into effect. The Algerian contribution to the war effort was rewarded by economic and political improvements in the status of Algerians, which were, however, opposed by the settlers and perceived as too limited by the Emir Khālid, grandson of 'Abd al-Kādir, who strongly criticized the French administration and was deported in 1924. He has justly been described as the founder of the Algerian nationalist movement. In Tunisia a delegation of thirty men representative of the Arab community called on the Bey to initiate political reform, reminding him of the sacrifices Tunisia had made in the war. Certainly much of the impetus behind the foundation of the Destūr or Constitution Party in 1920 came from returned soldiers and labourers who were dissatisfied with their subordinate position in their own country. In British West Africa, the press, while generally extremely loyal to the British and critical of the Germans, believed that the reward for this loyalty would be a more significant role for the educated elite in the colonial decision-making process.

The war acted as a stimulus not only to African nationalism but also to white nationalism, particularly in South Africa. There, though the Afrikaner rebellion was speedily put down, the spirit which informed it was not. As W. H. Vatcher has put it:

> Thus, in a real sense, modern Afrikaner nationalism, conceived in the Boer War, was born in the 1914 rebellion. If the first world war had not taken place, the Boers might have been better able to adjust to the conciliatory policy of Botha and Smuts. The war forced on them the decision to organize, first [secretly] in the form of the Afrikaner Broederbond, then in the form of the 'purified' National Party.

In Kenya, the white settlers used the war to make major political advances *vis-à-vis* the colonial government. They secured the right of whites to elect representatives to the legislative council, where after 1918 they formed a majority. Other privileges won by them were the Crown Lands Ordinance, which made racial segregation in the White Highlands possible, and the Soldier Settlement Scheme, which allocated large portions of the Nandi reserve for settlement of white soldiers after the war.

A major stimulus to Kenyan nationalism was the reaction against such privileges gained by the white community, in particular with regard to land. Thus the Kikuyu Association, consisting mainly of chiefs, was founded in 1920 to defend Kikuyu land interests, while Harry Thuku's Young Kikuyu Association, founded a year later, aimed at defence of both land and labour.

In South Africa, the rise of Afrikaner nationalism and republican agitation during the war gave serious concern to African leaders in Swaziland and Basutoland (now Lesotho). They feared that their countries might be integrated into the Union, with its increasingly racist policies, exemplified by the provisions of the Native Land Act of 1913. Within the Union, the South African Native National Congress (later to become the African National Congress) presented a memorandum after the war to King George V of Britain, citing the African contribution to the war in both the South West African and the East African campaigns as well as in France, and recalling that the war had been fought to liberate oppressed peoples and to grant to every nation the right to determine its sovereign destiny. The Congress was informed by the British Colonial Office that Britain could not interfere in the internal affairs of South Africa and the Congress appeal was not presented to the Peace Conference.

Finally the war saw a major change in the climate of international opinion with regard to colonialism. Prior to the war, the European colonial powers had been accountable only to themselves. After the war, the idea of administering so-called backward peoples as a 'sacred trust', though evident in the 1890s in the prohibition, for example, of the sale of alcohol to Africans, was now enshrined in the mandates, where the victorious Allies took over the administration of Germany's colonies on behalf of the League of Nations, which was made 'responsible for the . . . promotion to the utmost of the material and moral well-being and the social progress of [their] inhabitants'. Theoretically this underlined the principle of international accountability. The right of self-determination, first enunciated at the Congress of the Socialist Second International held in London in 1896, had also been enunciated by the leader of a major world power, Woodrow Wilson, whilst the newly emerged Soviet Union was to attack all forms of colonialism in Africa.

Even if the lot of the subject peoples did not change much for the better in the years following the war, when even willing attempts at reform were aborted by the depression, searching questions about the morality of colonialism had begun to be asked. And it was in this climate that the seeds of the nationalist movement that was eventually to obtain independence for many African countries were sown.

Conclusion

The First World War, then, represented a turning-point in African history, not as dramatic as the Second World War, but nevertheless important in many areas. One of its most important legacies was the re-ordering of the map of Africa roughly as it is today. Germany was eliminated as a colonial power, and replaced by France and Britain in the Cameroon and Togo, by the Union of South Africa in South West Africa and by Britain and Belgium in German East Africa, the latter gaining the small but densely populated provinces of Ruanda and Urundi (now Rwanda and Burundi). The intricate negotiations that took place at Versailles over the re-allocation of these territories to the Allied victors belongs properly to the history of Europe, though the way in which Cameroon and Togo were divided, with little reference to historical and ethnic considerations, was to create considerable bitterness amongst certain sections of the population in these territories, in particular the Ewe of Togo.

The First World War thus marked both the end of the partition of Africa and of attempts by Africans to regain independence based on their pre-partition polities. Though it represented a period of immense social and economic change for many African countries, it ushered in a twenty-year period of tranquillity for the European administrations, except in places like French and Spanish Morocco, French Mauritania and Italian Libya.

However, ideas concerning the self-determination of peoples and the accountability of colonial powers had been sown during this war which, during the ensuing period of peace, were to influence profoundly the development of the incipient nationalist movements. But it was to take a second world war to provide the shock which translated the requests of the nationalists for greater participation in the process of government into demands for full control of it.

Methods and institutions of European domination

'Native policy'

Shortly after or during the military conquest and occupation of Africa by the imperial powers of Europe, various 'native policies' were adopted for the administration of the new colonies. Though these policies differed, there was general agreement both in theory and in practice that colonial rule could only be effectively secured through the use of indigenous personnel and institutions in some role. It was further agreed that the purpose of the European presence was to be defined in terms of a responsibility or trust or, according to Sir Frederick (later Lord) Lugard, a 'dual mandate'. This paternalistic attitude of a trust or responsibility which had thoroughly permeated European thought about colonial Africa was both internationalized and institutionalized with the mandates system that emerged from the First World War.

Behind such rhetoric, however, still stood an attitude of cultural and racial superiority, formed in the eighteenth and nineteenth centuries and regularly given expression in descriptions of the African as childlike or 'non-adult'. This latter attitude in turn gave birth to the widespread belief that European domination had to last for a very long time. As for those few areas already with large residential white minorities and receiving still more such immigrants at this time, European domination was to be permanent. Yet even in such territories – except South Africa where a policy of severely unequal segregation had already been imposed – notions of co-operative development were frequently expressed. Beyond such considerations, colonial policy was without clear and final objectives but vaguely included notions of self-government in its British form and of political integration in its French and Portuguese forms.

There were reasons for the general agreement on what might be called conjunctive administration or 'indirect rule' – that which used traditional African authorities in colonial administration but in an inferior role. First, the internal penetration of Africa during the late nineteenth century rapidly outpaced the numbers of European personnel available to administer the newly possessed lands. Secondly, since such penetration extended into many regions yet untouched by European cultural contact, direct rule of any kind would not have been possible. Thirdly, no metropolitan state was prepared to shoulder the high cost of administering colonies directly, while it was also generally believed that involving the traditional authorities in administration would cause very

143

little social dislocation and therefore ensure the co-operation of the people. The final reason was the failure of the assimilationist or direct administration policy which was the vogue in the nineteenth century. Whether in respect of the French in the Four Communes of Senegal or of the British with regard to the Crown colonies of Sierra Leone, Gold Coast and Lagos, assimilation had, by the end of the nineteenth century, been frustrated not only by the cultural resistance of the African peoples concerned but also by the growing conflict and friction between the European colonial elite and the locally produced western-educated Africans. It was, indeed, this loss of co-operation between the European colonialists and the educated Africans at the end of the century which created the artificial scarcity of administrative personnel, as the new regimes began to exercise restriction on the recruitment of highly skilled Africans into the administrations.

In the light of these considerations, no colonial power immediately sought to dispose completely of the socio-political structures already in existence. However, the basic demands of the colonial system everywhere had the effect of distorting the functions of and weakening basic African institutions. The very fact that most African states were acquired by conquest and the exile or deposition of some ruling chiefs in itself brought the whole institution of chieftaincy, for instance, into disrepute. The universal imposition of European-planned taxes was certainly another disruptive colonial measure, while even the modest efforts made in the direction of what is today called modernization also affected local institutions. For these reasons, indirect rule could not be fully practised and had to be modified in different ways by the different colonial powers.

Colonial rule and structure

From the palace of the Sultan of Morocco to the kraal of the East and Southern African chief, European colonial administrators sought and employed 'native authorities' as allies or agents through whom the demands of alien rule might effectively be made on the African populations at large. At the top of the administrative system stood the governor or resident-general, who, while ultimately responsible to his national government, frequently enjoyed the powers of a sovereign (see 13.1–13.4). He was usually assisted in the inter-war period by some form of consultative council or committee which included both 'official' or administrative and 'unofficial' or colonist or commercial interests. The centralized nature of colonial administration in the French, Portuguese and Belgian systems caused the retention of legislative authority in the metropolis. In the British African possessions, however, colonial councils did emerge as proto-parliamentary bodies with appointed or elected membership, or both, and with functions varying from the advisory to the legislative. However, their number and the means by which such representatives were appointed effectively guaranteed that European domination in the inter-war period would not be seriously disturbed or challenged.

The crucial institution of all colonial organization was the district or provincial unit, called a *cercle* in French West Africa. The continued use of this military term was a reminder of the nature of colonial acquisitions. Over the *cercle*, a European administrator exercised colonial authority and directed the activities of both his European subordinates

13.1 *Frederick, Lord Lugard (1858–1945). High Commissioner, then Governor, of Northern Nigeria 1900–07, 1912–14; Governor of Nigeria 1914–19 (Mary Evans Picture Library)*

13.2 *Louis-Gabriel Angoulvant, Lieutenant-Governor of Côte d'Ivoire, 1908–16 (Roger Viollet)*

13.3 *General Joseph Simon Gallieni (1849–1916), Commandant-Supérieur of French Sudan, 1886–8; Governor-General of Madagascar, 1896–1905 (BBC Hulton Picture Library)*

13.4 *Albert Heinrich Schnee (1871–1949), Governor of German East Africa, 1912–18 (BBC Hulton Picture Library)*

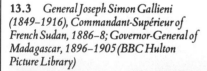

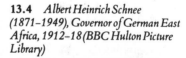

13.1–13.4 *Colonial governors and administrators*

and the African authorities enlisted in the colonial administration. The most important and most discussed African component was the local chief. Indeed, every colonial power in Black Africa depended on the chief, whether traditional or warrant in authority, as the basic element of the administrative structure. Although no observer or critic has doubted that chiefly activities were integral to the colonial system throughout the continent, there has been a considerable academic debate about the uses to which the European powers put these chiefs. The major question has centred on the difference between direct and indirect rule, between delegation of European authority to the African rulers and European control of traditional authority enjoyed by these rulers.

The most famous explanation of the importance of the 'native authority' to the colonial order was that of Lugard. For reasons already given, especially a shortage of men and funds and his belief that the use of existing indigenous institutions was the best method of colonial administration, Lugard ruled out direct in favour of indirect control or rule, which he now developed into a theory in his service as high commissioner for northern Nigeria between 1900 and 1907. The best résumé of his policy is found in a set of instructions he issued to his officers in 1906, in which he argues for 'a single Government in which the Native Chiefs have clearly defined duties and an acknowledged status, equally with the British officials'. The basis of what was to become the system of indirect rule was therefore one of co-operation, not subordination, with the British Resident acting primarily in an advisory, not an executive, capacity and with the African 'chief' – in this instance, the Fulbe emir – continuing in a traditional role which was now carefully guided, not rigidly fixed, by the imposed colonial administration.

If, then, the essential component of Lugard's rule was the use of existing authorities in existing capacities, something more was intended. Modifications along European lines were expected in matters such as justice and taxation. The task depended in large measure on the knowledge that European administrators had of local customs and institutions – and, of course, on the willingness of the native authorities to make such adjustments toward modernization within the context of their own institutions.

This broad sketch of indirect rule in northern Nigeria can be aligned with another which, like Lugard's, met with most success in regions overlaid with Muslim political institutions. Reaching beyond Africa in scope, this form of indirect administration was primarily given theoretical definition by the French. What they labelled a *politique d'association* (a policy of association) received considerable recognition at the turn of the century and was enthusiastically contrasted with the older ideal of the policy of assimilation. Originally suggested for Indochina and later extended as policy to Africa, 'association' was none the less geographically limited as a colonial practice. Only in Morocco did the French seriously consider it, and there primarily because of the attention given to indigenous affairs by the resident-general, Louis-Hubert Lyautey, who, in the initial years of the protectorate, ruled with few restrictions from the metropolitan government. Throughout Morocco, the forms of the Sherifian state were preserved, while at the local level administrative activities were strikingly similar to those proposed by Lugard. The French *contrôleur civil* was to perform in an advisory, not a supervisory, capacity with respect to the ḳāḍī, a Muslim official administering justice in accordance with the sharīʿa. A comparable arrangement existed in the

Spanish-dominated portion of Morocco where the *kādī* was guided in his role by the *Inventore*, the Spanish counterpart of the *contrôleur civil*. The *kādī* was also administratively retained as before in Italian Somaliland but there he was joined in the responsibilities of local government by assigned warrant chiefs.

In theory such indirect administration also applied to French colonial activities south of the Sahara, but in fact practice was quite different, for there the French used indigenous authorities not indirectly but directly and subordinately in their colonial administration. And in like manner so did the Portuguese.

Lugard's form of indirect rule was initially successful in northern Nigeria, although discredited by some critics as too conservative. It was then extended after the war throughout much of British Africa, including Buganda and the newly acquired German possessions of Tanganyika and the Cameroon. It was even adapted by the Belgians for their use in the Congo after 1920. Although conditions were nowhere else so ideal or the results so successful as in the Hausa–Fulbe region of Nigeria, the British tried to follow the contours of local custom so that even newly devised institutions, like local councils, were in tune with indigenous forms of organization. The notorious exception, however, was South Africa, where the concept of 'native authority' was the means by which the white minority assured local administration of Africans now displaced by the policy of segregation to territorial reserves.

Throughout sub-Saharan Africa during the inter-war period, the chief became an administrative agent and not a 'native authority' and his traditional roles and powers were greatly weakened or reduced. This shift in position, even in regions submitted to indirect rule, is easily explained. Most obviously, traditional functions were extended by new demands, such as the collection of taxes, the taking of censuses, or the recruitment of labour and military conscripts. Where there appeared to European eyes no satisfactory individuals in positions of traditional authority, other personnel, such as veterans, non-commissioned officers or clerks, were installed as chiefs. This was especially the case in French and Portuguese colonies, where the local rules for the recruitment of personnel for chieftaincy positions were more often than not violated. Then, chiefs were sometimes accorded a political importance which they had not enjoyed previously or on other occasions they were installed in societies that had no chiefs and where they therefore previously had no administrative purpose. Examples of these two developments are found among the Igbo of Nigeria, the Gikuyu of Kenya and the Teso of eastern Uganda.

With the establishment of European administration, chiefs were manipulated as if they were administrative personnel who might be reposted or removed to satisfy colonial needs. Chieftancies were abolished where considered superfluous and created where considered colonially useful. Perhaps the most striking example of this process occurred in the Belgian Congo (now Zaire) where, after 1918, the number of *chefferies* (kingdoms or states) was reduced from 6095 in 1917 to 1212 in 1938. Furthermore, an entirely new administrative unit, called *le secteur*, was introduced for purposes of consolidation. Along similar lines the French in West Africa also created a new unit, a grouping of villages into a *canton*, which, in the words of one governor, 'is placed under the authority of an *indigenous administrative agent* who assumes the name of canton chief'.

Operating as a disruptive agent in connection with these factors was the local administrator. Whatever his intentions, he invariably became a substitute or deputy chief. As Delavignette described the situation with satisfaction, the colonial administrator was not an administrator at all, but a commander and recognized as such by the African population under his control. His primary function, he asserted unequivocally, 'is to act as a chief'. The reserved and unobtrusive role which Lugard had hoped that the British resident would generally play in northern Nigeria was denied in their territories by the French and Portuguese administrators, both sets of whom were prominent in the exercise of local authority. While the administrators in Italian Somaliland came closest to the British in their relationship to the local chiefs, even among these two groups Lugard's dicta were necessarily modified by the needs of colonial rule and the personalities of the individuals exercising it.

Purposes and impositions of colonialism

Beyond the official rhetoric, practical purposes of colonization turned out to be quite limited. In their simplest form, they were the maintenance of order, the avoidance of heavy financial expenditure, and the establishment of a labour force, initially for porterage and later for the creation of roads and railways but also for commercial purposes. In general practice, these purposes were added to the functions of local rule and were fulfilled in three ways: redirection of systems of justice, use of forced labour, and the imposition of personal taxes.

The introduction of European judicial institutions was usually done with some attention to African customary law and to Muslim law where it also existed, as for instance, in Italian Somaliland; but it still had the effect of modifying local institutions. Frequently, there were colonial attempts at a dual judicial arrangement wherein civil litigation involving Africans was settled according to pre-colonial legal modes, while criminal law and litigation involving Europeans fell directly under colonial jurisdiction.

However, everywhere, with the noticeable exception of the Portuguese colonies, a court system was developed or reinforced according to African needs as perceived by the Europeans. In the first decade of the century, there were particular attempts by the Italians in Somaliland and the Germans in East Africa to extend the judicial function of African chiefs or magistrates. In the same period, the most elaborate and successful of such efforts was Lugard's implementation of 'native courts', which, in his mind, were an instrument by which to 'inculcate a sense of responsibility and evolve among a primitive community some sense of discipline and respect for authority'. Presided over by Africans, and directed primarily to domestic affairs, these courts were to stick as closely as possible to African customary law, modified only where basic customs were not in accordance with fundamental English practices. The Lugardian model was introduced into many British possessions and the mandated territories, and was also copied by the Belgians in the Congo.

In direct contrast to this method was the French, which tended to erode African authority, finally making the administrator the responsible judicial official. However, the most peculiar and inequitable element in the French system was the *indigénat*. First employed in Algeria in the 1870s, this device was imported into French West Africa in the 1880s and remained institutionally operative there as well as in Algeria until the end of the Second World War. Regularized by a decree of 1924, it allowed any French administrator to impose a punishment of up to fifteen days' gaol sentence and a fine for a series of offences ranging from failure to pay taxes on time to displaying discourtesy to French officials.

More pervasive in effect than the legal systems were the personal taxes which all African males eventually encountered. Primarily designed as one means by which to make the colonial effort pay for itself, they were also inspired by the notion that they would force the African into European economic enterprises and would extend the money economy. By the early twentieth century, these taxes were regularized as was no other colonial institution, having undergone what appears to be a clear cycle of development. The hut tax was an obvious form in the early years of domination and was also a source of considerable African contention and protest. It was generally replaced by about the second decade of the twentieth century with a poll or capitation tax, which remained the dominant form until the end of the colonial regime. Lastly, there was the income tax, introduced in the 1920s into several British territories and the Belgian Congo, but then primarily affecting non-Africans, who generally were the only ones with sufficient income to be required to pay it.

Within this general pattern, there were many regional distinctions, the most prominent being that connected with Lugard's idea of native authority. As he wrote in his *Dual Mandate*, the 'tax . . . is, in a sense, the basis of the whole system, since it supplies the means to pay the Emir and all his officials'. The institution through which the process worked was the 'native treasury', an idea originating with Sir Charles Temple, in service under Lugard in northern Nigeria. Each native authority was to be returned a percentage of the taxes collected in his district. This amount was to form part of a native treasury further enriched by various licensing fees and fines collected in the courts. From this sum, the emir or chief was to draw his own revenue and supply the salary of his subordinates. The remaining funds were to be used for public services and improvements. The arrangement, originally employed in the emirates, spread with indirect rule, not only to British possessions on both coasts but also to the Belgian Congo.

Of all the colonial devices, the tax system was the one which most obviously encouraged the bureaucratic development of colonial rule. It assigned a common function to the administrator and the African chief, who, in assessing and collecting the tax, often in conjunction with local councils of elders or notables, reminded everyone of the regulatory power of the new system. Furthermore, after tax collectors as such, there soon appeared administrative agents who became part of the new colonial elite. The most striking and controversial among them were no doubt the *akidas* used by the Germans in East Africa. Swahili-speaking officials who served on the coast before European domination, they were used in redefined positions both to collect taxes and to recruit labour for the German administration.

The introduction of money taxes was briefly accompanied by labour taxes, the most obvious expression of European attempts to exploit the human resources of their colonies. The *impôt de cueillette*, the tax by which wild rubber was harvested in the Congo Free State, was the most criticized of such taxes, though the French *prestation*, a labour tax required of all males in French West and Equatorial Africa unless remitted by cash payment, lasted till 1944. Conversely, the Germans in the Cameroon allowed the tax levied per head to be remitted by a labour 'payment'. And, in parts of Uganda, the British continued the *luwalo*, a pre-colonial public-work tax of one month's labour, until 1938, when it was replaced by a money tax. Yet such taxes were the exception to forced labour devices employed by all the colonial powers.

Consistently concerned with shortage of manpower for new projects and new employments which colonial rule supported, European administrators imposed their domination before the end of the century by a system of virtual impressment, or forced labour, frequently satisfying private as well as public purposes. It is true that such direct forced labour declined in the early twentieth century because of the decreasing need for portage as well as the increasing concern with international opinion. But its use, however modified, remained an integral part of colonial domination until the Second World War. At least this was the case with the French colonial governments, which, as in West Africa, still employed large numbers of Africans through *prestation*, particularly on railway building, until after the Second World War.

The most oppressive forms of labour regulations were those found in German South West Africa and in the Union of South Africa. Union policies were, of course, extended to South West Africa when it became a mandated territory after the war, but German policy before then was strikingly similar in nature and severity to that devised in the Union. Pass laws were imposed, as were identity cards, both regulating the movement of Africans; Africans without labour contracts were subject to vagrancy laws; and labour contracts were designed to give the German employer an enormous advantage. In the Union, there were also pass laws and Acts against vagrancy. The Native (Urban Areas) Act of 1923 and the Native Administration Act of 1927 reinforced previous pass laws, while other enactments, such as the Apprenticeship Act of 1922, effectively restricted the forms of employment an African might take.

Means of control and administration

As its most ardent advocates were willing to remark, colonial rule was won by the sword and so maintained. With this dictum in mind, all the European powers established armies or troops recruited from the indigenous population. Although organization and effectiveness varied according to both region and particular national purposes, such colonial troops primarily performed police functions in the inter-war era and were joined by newly created constabulary forces in this capacity. Yet, because they were frequently made to serve in geographical regions culturally and ethnically unfamiliar to them, African soldiers were thus alienated from their own society and were often received with hostility by the local populations they forcefully encountered. As a result of this condition and, furthermore, of the European denial of command positions to Africans, the army never came to play the political role in the independence movements that its counterparts in Asia and the Near East did.

However, even in the inter-war period, labelled by contemporaries as one of 'colonial peace', military activities still punctuated African affairs in a severe manner. The professed European desire to keep Africa as militarily neutralized as possible was in fact never realized. The French introduced a law of conscription in 1919 whereby an African contingent of 10 000 was to be annually obtained; the British developed a Sudan

Defence Force, uniquely staffed by Sudanese as well as by British officers, but primarily directed to imperial strategic needs in the Near East as well as in East Africa. The *Force Publique* of the Belgian Congo, exhibiting the qualities both of occupation army and police force, was frequently used during this era to quell resistance expressed in the form of syncretistic religious movements.

This account of military developments in Africa in the inter-war period does not seriously impair the assertion that divergent intentions of European colonial method and practice are those which, in retrospect, seem the most significant. There is little doubt that colonial bureaucratization did provide preparation for an unintended movement towards national independence. A new political elite, consisting of lower-echelon clerks and appointed chiefs in various colonial services, was slowly emerging, particularly in the British colonies. Training schools, such as the École William Ponty in Dakar, were undertaking the preparation of educators and administrators, upon whom the colonial administration, was more and more to depend. Principally in the urban regions, the 'wind of change' was slowly being generated.

Yet this was not what the European colonial administrators actually intended. Even when they emphasized 'native paramountcy', they did so with the thought that the welfare of the African populations could only be guaranteed and effectively structured socially and economically by them. Good government and independent government were, as Lord Cromer once remarked, opposing objectives in a colonial context. Thus the colonial system existed as an authoritarian one, and it was in no meaningful way calculated to confer political power upon the Africans it supposedly served. Its most common characteristic was paternalism, with shared responsibility at best only tolerated in areas of considerable white settlement.

Even where parliamentary institutions were introduced to provide a degree of responsible colonial government, this arrangement was effected so that white preponderance was guaranteed. In Algeria, for instance, a two-college electoral system, sanctioned by the Jonnart Law of 1919, provided proportionately lower Arab participation than European in the Délégations Financières, the incipient parliamentary body representing interest groups, not geographic areas. In South Africa, the African enjoyed no role whatsoever in the parliamentary procedures that were developed there. In these two major settler colonies, exactly as in all the other colonies in which residential Europeans were to be found, the demographic minority was in fact the political majority, the very opposite of democratic government on the European model.

Diversity of colonial method was not as important historically as the similarity in assessment of the colonial situation. Despite the pronouncements enshrined in the documents of the League of Nations, and in defiance of their weakened global positions as a result of the First World War, the European powers in Africa did not entertain thoughts of African political independence in the inter-war period. Egypt excepted, Africa was seen as the one continent in which colonialism would be of very long duration, and colonial methods were all designed to accommodate European interests and intentions. Therefore, the essential political activity was one of African adjustment to European objectives, regardless of whether the particular colonial practice followed was indirect or not.

Most important of all the historical developments of the inter-war period, the colonial system established the general administrative framework, in which national government would be housed in the first decade of independence. This incipient regularization of political activity within a European-arranged structure was the principal aspect of modernization that the Europeans introduced, but for their own purposes, to contemporary Africa at that time.

The colonial economy

Conquest and new production relations, 1880–c.1910

At the same time as the colonial powers were establishing various institutions and structures for the administration of their colonies, they were also establishing an economic system for the exploitation of the natural resources of those colonies. The colonial economic system cannot be said to have reached its prime until the coming of the Second World War.

Africans witnessed the first physical evidence of a new economy in the form of road, rail and telegraph construction. Transport and communication lines were a prelude to conquest and they were logistically necessary in occupied areas so that the latter could serve as the staging points for further aggression. However, few roads or railways were of purely military interest; and the same railways which facilitated conquest were used for the extraction of groundnuts, cotton and so on.

Coastal African economies were quickly made dependent upon the economies of the respective colonizing powers, while the interior peoples were usually the last to be brought into the network of produce collection, cash-crop cultivation and paid labour. Considerable expenditure was needed to provide certain African ports with deep berths and viable off-loading capacity; but this was less onerous than the capital which had to be invested in trunk roads or railways penetrating the hinterland. Therefore, distance from the coast was one of the determinants of how early the colonial economy could be set in motion.

The most decisive variable affecting the implanting of the colonial economy was the extent to which various parts of Africa had already been participating in the world economy. The slaving zones from Senegal to Sierra Leone, from the Gold Coast (now Ghana) to Nigeria and from the Congo river to Angola were the stretches of coastline first encroached upon by the European colonizers. In these localities, features of the colonial economy emerged before the formal advent of colonial rule, because of mutual African and European attempts to stimulate export commodities which served as 'legitimate' replacements for slaves. Rulers, professional traders and other sectors of the population in western Africa perceived advantages in maintaining the foreign trade nexus and access to imported goods.

On the eastern side of the continent, the Indian Ocean trade was not exclusively directed towards European countries, nor was the long-distance trade out of East Africa controlled by Europeans or Afro-Europeans. The colonizers had to supplant the Arab, Swahili and Indian merchants. Setting out from the Swahili coastal towns, European colonizers followed the Arab lead and sought the termini of the caravan routes in the Great Lakes region. By the mid-1880s, the Scramble was already taking place on Lake Victoria, on whose shores colonial enterprises were quickly grafted on to the already high level of African economic activity. When the British completed their railway from Mombasa to the Lake in 1902, it attracted freight which had been part of the caravan traffic which had previously existed further south at Tanga and Bagamoyo. As a result of British competition, the Germans too began a coast–hinterland railway in 1905, and this faithfully traversed the slave and ivory route to Lake Tanganyika. Deep within Central Africa, it was also the Arab trading network which provided the European colonizers with their first economic base.

North Africa combined some of the features of East and West Africa, and displayed these in a heightened form. The prelude to European colonization of Egypt goes back to the Napoleonic expedition of 1798. The European presence in the nineteenth century frustrated the economic innovations of Muhammad 'Alī. After contributing to the failure of Egyptian industrialization, Britain and France sought control of Egypt's trade and entered the internal market in land and mortgages. In Algeria, bitter resistance against the French was not yet over in the 1870s, but by then the country was already host to an entrenched settler agriculture, which was the principal feature of the Algerian colonial economy and which appeared in varying degrees in the rest of the Maghrib and in Libya. Tunisia entered the colonial epoch in 1881–2; while Morocco and Libya were partially annexed in 1912. Italian immigrants in Libya were fewer than their French counterparts in the Maghrib, and settler agriculture in Tripolitania had to await the complete defeat of the Libyan people by about 1931.

European powers reduced North African economies to colonial dependency mainly through the power of finance capital. North Africa entered the imperialist epoch when large amounts of capital were invested in the Suez Canal and when loans were thrust upon the ruling class from Egypt to Morocco. This process was at its height by 1880, leading to the increasing subservience of the local regimes and ultimately to the assumption of sovereignty by one or other of the interested European nations. Therefore, while the colonial economy had a long and early period of genesis in North Africa, it cannot be said to have been definitively established until the 1890s, when monopoly capital was to the fore in Europe. The same observations are applicable to Southern Africa.

By the time of imperialist partition, European settlement in South Africa involved tens of thousands of whites maintaining economic ties with Africans. African economic independence was undermined through the forcible alienation of land while African labour power was placed at the behest of the whites. During the nineteenth century, whites and blacks 'engaged in the formation of new economic and social bonds'. These new bonds were at first colonial ones only in the sense that they bound together an alien minority and an indigenous majority in a superior/inferior relationship, but they soon became the type of colonial relations determined by the intrusion of large-scale capital due to the discovery of diamonds and gold.

The mining of diamonds and gold in South Africa could not have been carried on without modern technology and relatively heavy concentrations of capital. Neither the British government nor the mining monopolies which emerged from the 1870s had any intention of leaving mineral resources under the control of the Boers or of allowing priority to settler agricultural concerns with arable land, water, pasture and cattle, when the subsoil and African labour promised huge surpluses exportable to the metropolises. After the Kimberley diamond finds (1870) and particularly after the Witwatersrand gold strike (1886), the bourgeoisie was determined to impose hegemony over all pre-capitalist social formations in South Africa, irrespective of race. The Anglo-Boer war (1899–1902) was also anti-imperialist resistance, albeit in a perverse sense, since at the same time it sought the further entrenchment of settler colonialism. The defeat of Boer attempts at settler autonomy and the crushing of the African peoples of the region, discussed in Chapter 9, marked the formation of a South African colonial economy which was unquestionably geared towards the transfer of raw materials, profits and other inputs to the capitalist metropolises.

Capital and coercion, c.1900–c.1920

African resistance helped substantially to dictate a slow pace of economic colonization for at least the three decades between 1880 and 1910. Besides, immediate interest on the part of European monopoly capital was low. Africa commanded high priority during the mercantilist era of accumulation, but the relative obscurity of the nineteenth century persisted into the early years of colonialism, in spite of the increase in politico-economic control which followed upon partition and conquest. Viewed in terms of the global investment drive of monopoly capitalism up to the First World War, figures concerning the growth of the African colonial economy are unimpressive. The most relevant of these figures concerned imports and exports, since the import/export sector was the central feature of the colonial economy. The volume of goods imported into Africa rose sluggishly and remained the same as that of the mid-nineteenth century, and that had not departed radically from the patterns of the slave trade era. Cotton piece-goods continued to dominate European exchanges with Africa throughout the period in question, although other items of domestic consumption, such as kitchen utensils, radios, bicycles and sewing machines, were later to gain in popularity.

Production of export commodities within Africa advanced slowly and not always steadily. The more usual performance graph of African staples in the colonial context comprised a first stage of insignificant quantities covering two decades of the present century, followed by a second stage of appreciable growth until 1930. Cotton, palm oil, coffee, groundnuts and cocoa illustrate such characteristics in the parts of the continent with which they are respectively associated.

Only small amounts of foreign capital were invested in African industry and agriculture during the early colonial period. South Africa was again the obvious exception, while to a lesser extent Algeria also attracted settler and mining capital. It was rather coercion, either bare-faced or clothed by the laws of the new colonial regimes, which was principally responsible for bringing labour and cash crops to the market-place. Undisguised forms of forced labour and barely disguised forms of slavery, such as the 'contract labour' practised by the Portuguese in São Tomé or King Leopold's

Congo, were prominent aspects of the entrenchment of the colonial economy in Africa. At the onset of colonial rule, private capital sometimes performed police functions and coerced people on its own behalf. This was the case with the chartered and concession companies which were active in Southern and Central Africa and in Nigeria and German East Africa. But chartered companies could not cope with coercive state functions. European states had to assume direct responsibility for their colonial territories – usually during the 1890s – and the locally established colonial state apparatus supervised the economy on behalf of private capitalists. The latter were usually compensated for surrendering their political privileges, making it clear whose class interests were being advanced by colonial regimes. Compensation was a means of financing these companies to place their enterprises on a more secure footing than had been the case when they were virtually in a state of war with the African people.

Metropolitan states and their colonial counterparts in Africa had to continue state coercion for economic exploitation, because the colonial economy had constantly to be established in the face of opposition from Africans. In many places, African land had first to be seized before the settler-type socio-economic formations could flourish. The necessary infrastructure of roads and railways could be laid down only by government assistance, one aspect of which was the compulsory recruitment of African labour. The use of taxation to build the money economy is a device which is too well known to be discussed at length here. Taxation undoubtedly provided the major factor driving Africans initially into wage labour or cash-crop production; and subsequent increases in taxation deepened African involvement.

Colonial states discriminated with regard to the type of force which they sanctioned in their colonies. Remnants of slavery were suppressed because they had become outmoded. Whipping and physical abuse of Africans by European employers was frowned upon and usually legislated against by the second decade of the twentieth century. Colonial states, like any others, tried to retain a monopoly over legal forms of violence. At the same time, they sought to reassure European investors or settlers that the power of the state was unquestionably at their disposal. Thus, whipping under the orders of employers was merely replaced by judicial floggings, which were resorted to in far greater measure than was the case with workers in Europe. African labour codes remained backward throughout the 1930s; breach of contract was treated not as a civil but as a criminal offence.

The combination of European capital with forced African labour registered a sizeable surplus in products destined for European consumption and export. Crops and minerals were exported and the profits expatriated because of the non-resident nature of the capital in the mining and plantation companies and the import/export houses. However, some of the amount accumulated was reinvested. This allowed Southern African capital to grow to massive proportions; and it speeded up monopolization among the West African commercial firms, enabling them to support and integrate with manufacturing and distributing enterprises in Europe. In Algeria and South Africa and to a lesser extent in Tunisia, Kenya, the Rhodesias (now Zambia and Zimbabwe) and Nyasaland (now Malawi), the first flow of profits from the colonial economy also permitted higher living standards as well as greater economic viability for the white settlers.

African participation in the colonial economy, 1920–30

Coercion in economic relations was decisive in the formative years of the colonial economies in Africa, but it grew less and less important, firstly in the British and German colonies, followed by the French and then the Belgian and Portuguese. Whenever it came, Africans contemplated the new colonial economy as a fact of life – a new order which they could not reverse and which in many instances they were prepared to welcome. A new phase, however, began in the 1920s when Africans began to influence the terms on which they were involved in this economy. During this period, they continued to play their role as wage-earners in the mines in South Africa and on the plantations in the Congos and East and Central Africa. These labourers were attracted from far afield. Tanganyika (Tanzania) had an influx from Nyasaland, Northern Rhodesia (Zambia), Mozambique and Ruanda-Urundi (now Rwanda and Burundi).

However, wage-earners of all categories remained a tiny minority of the adult African population. Undoubtedly, cash-crop farming embraced the largest proportion of Africans – providing the basis for what has been termed the *économie de traite*, an economic system in which imported manufactured goods were directly exchanged for cash crops which were unprocessed or minimally processed. Cash crops offered Africans slightly greater room for manouevre than wage labour. Occasionally, there was a choice between export crops. Food crops were grown for family consumption, sometimes for local cash sales and more rarely for export. African peasants used the limited flexibility in these circumstances to determine the nature and quantity of what they would plant or prepare for export. Prices were set by metropolitan agencies, but agricultural prices could be marginally affected where peasants switched from one crop to another or deployed stocks into a local market. In a few desperate instances, they turned to the technique of 'hold-up' of the sale of their produce, even though this meant serious loss to themselves.

While it was still being forced on some African communities, cash-crop farming was actively pursued by other Africans in the face of official indifference or hostility. They demanded the transport and marketing infrastructure, seizing the opportunity as soon as a railway line was completed. In many cases, they pioneered before the colonial governments had built bridges and feeder roads. Seed for new crops was taken from the colonial Africans who were already engaged in cultivation. Cocoa and coffee are the two best-known and most important of the cash crops whose extension relied mainly on African initiatives. Minor crops such as tea, tobacco and pyrethrum also bear out the same principle. Besides, Africans fought specifically for crops which were better money-earners than others. Thus, the latter part of the 1920s and the early 1930s saw a determined effort on the part of Africans in several highland areas of Tanganyika to cultivate *Arabica* coffee rather than hire their labour out or rather than growing the less profitable *Robusta* variety. The Africans won literally by planting coffee trees faster than the colonial administration could destroy them.

Where peasant cultivation established itself as an essential feature of the colonial economy, it functioned like mines and plantations in drawing labour resources from an area much wider than the actual zone of production. Senegambian groundnut farming attracted seasonal labour from the hinterland of the Senegal and Niger rivers; cocoa in the Gold Coast (now Ghana) and in the Ivory Coast drew upon Upper Volta; while Ugandan coffee-growers turned to Ruanda-Urundi and Tanganyika to expand output. Together, cash-crop farming and the wage labour of mines and agriculture accounted for the overwhelming majority of Africans who participated directly in the colonial economy. However, a host of other activities were generated or transformed by the new commodity relationships. An extractive timber industry arose early in Gabon and in varying degrees some such enterprise was pursued wherever forest reserves existed. The transportation network was a factor of more general significance. Thousands of Africans found wage employment at the ports and on the trains, especially when head porterage declined after the First World War.

As the colonial economy began to mature, hardly any sector of the African community could stand apart. In spite of their reputation for conservatism, all pastoral groups were drawn into the money economy by the 1920s, if not earlier. They sold meat for local consumption and occasionally for export along with hides. In the territories that were to become Somalia, this was the principal manifestation of the colonial economy. Africans naturally exerted themselves to earn in a manner which was remunerative and congenial. Colonial administrations, missionaries and private companies employed junior clerks, artisans and (in the case of the first two) schoolteachers. The drive to obtain education was related to these job opportunities, especially since they were closely connected with the growing popularity of urban living. The drop-outs from primary schools or those who for one reason or another could not arrive at more prestigious paid employment filled the interstices of the colonial economy as domestic servants or as members of the police or army or by reaching out for forms of urban 'hustling' such as prostitution.

Wages were kept abysmally low. Upward trends were resisted; purchasing power was eroded, partly because of the periodic inflations and partly because wages were depressed or allowed to lag behind commodity prices. Settlers and other residents and the managers of foreign enterprises combined to keep wages low and to keep labour semi-feudal through the issue of work-cards which severely limited the freedom to shift labour from one employer to another. Throughout the period in question, employers remained hostile to worker organizations which would have had an effect in raising the wage rate. The backward regime of task- or piece-work was widely pursued, and workers received no benefits for sickness, disability, unemployment and old age. Besides, the constant mobility of the largely migratory labour force, its low level of skill and the pervasiveness of racism all added to the disadvantages of the African worker in confronting the capitalists over wages and working conditions.

Dependence and depression, 1930–5

Colonial production relations were built within Africa over a span of years, during which the numerous self-sufficient African economies were either destroyed or transformed and brought under control. Their connections one with the other were broken, as in the case of the trans-Saharan trade and the commerce of the Great Lakes zone of East and Central Africa. Links previously existing between Africa and the rest of the world were also adversely affected, notably with regard to India and Arabia. A large number of discrete colonial economies came into being. Economic partition was not exactly the same as political partition, since stronger capitalist powers exploited the colonies of weaker nations. Even Britain had to accept the penetration of United States capital into South Africa after the formation of the Anglo American Corporation in 1917. Nevertheless, the arbitrary political boundaries were generally taken to be the limits of the economies, each of which was small-scale, artificial and separately oriented towards Europe. They lacked continental, regional or internal linkages.

Thus, by definition, the colonial economy was an extension of that of the colonizing power. African economies were integrated firstly into that of their respective colonizer and secondly into the economies of the leading nations of the capitalist world. Colonialism confined African colonies to the production of primary goods for export and in turn kept them dependent upon the developed capitalist countries for manufactured goods and technology.

This rigid international division of labour presented itself within the colonial economies as an ever-widening divergence between production and consumption. The bulk of the production within the growing money economy was never intended to meet local demand and consumption. Conversely, the variety of goods obtainable at the retail markets were increasingly of foreign origin. Local artisanship suffered heavily from European competition or manipulation, along lines already evident in the pre-colonial period. As the colonial economy became firmly rooted in the 1920s, Africans were producing that which they did not consume and consuming that which they did not produce. In effect, domestic demand did not stimulate the maximum use of domestic resources. Furthermore, the colonizers wasted some African resources and ignored others, because their yardstick was the usefulness of the given resources to Europe rather than Africa. From all this, it is clear that colonization did not produce economic development as used to be thought, but rather economic dependence, lopsidedness and underdevelopment.

The most significant event in the evolution of African economies in the inter-war period was the great depression of 1929–33. When this hit the interdependent capitalist economies, it necessarily struck at the dependent African colonial economies. Cyclical crises in the world economy since the nineteenth century had the effect of slowing down growth in Africa and imposing hardships on Africans already within the money economy. It was the severity of these tendencies which was new in 1930 when the repercussions were felt on the African continent. The depression entered via the most advanced sectors of capitalism in Africa – the mines, plantations and primary cash-crop areas. However, it spread through all the secondary and tertiary channels, causing hardships to Africans who sold food to workers or to other farmers, to pastoralists who found it uneconomical to part with their livestock at the prevailing prices and to those specializing in trade.

Each participant in the colonial economy took steps to counter the effects of the depression. The initiative lay with the capitalist firms. Banks and commercial houses cut back on their operations, so that in cash-crop areas they maintained a presence in key centres like Dakar, Lagos and Nairobi, while branches up-country and in lesser capitals were closed. Above all, the export houses achieved economy at the expense of the peasants by slashing producer prices when the 1930 crop came to market. As employers, they retrenched workers and cut wages drastically. Except in the gold industry, which was avidly pursued, retrenchment was the main response of all major employers in various spheres of production. Wage labour had increased considerably after the First World War, but sank by 50% or more between 1931 and 1934. Meanwhile, although many settlers and small businesses went bankrupt, the principal beneficiaries of the colonial system continued to make reduced but substantial profits.

Africans reacted to the crisis by struggling against attempted European solutions. To deal with lowered wages, workers resorted to the strike weapon with greater frequency and in larger numbers, in spite of the non-existence or lack of development of trade unions. Relatively little has been written on the spontaneous struggle of the African working class before the coming of trade unions, but business cycles and wars appear to have sharpened conflict, judging from unrest during the depression of 1920–1, during the major depression of 1929–33, and once more during the 1938 recession. Similarly, it could be no mere coincidence that farmers on the Gold Coast held up their cocoa and boycotted foreign stores in 1920–1 and again in 1930 and 1938.

Another line of defence on the part of Africans was withdrawal from the money economy. Areas which had been recently brought into the money economy or which were only lightly touched were the first to retreat. Many Tanganyikan peasants, who had a much lower level of involvement in money exchanges than their brothers on the Gold Coast, simply sought to abandon cash-crop farming in the years after 1930. In this they were not very successful, because the power of the colonial state was brought in to tilt the scales against what was considered to be a reversion to barbarism.

Most capital projects were suspended during the depression; and, where this was not so, the investment was associated with the expansion of cheap primary production and was undertaken with the use of forced labour, as with the French Office du Niger irrigation project. There was an overall revival of coercion in economic relations, indicating that the colonial economy had to be buttressed by non-economic means when in crisis. African labour and taxes kept the railways viable and maintained colonial revenues. Yet the African masses suffered most from the cutback on already skimpy social services. In the years of recovery after 1934, wages, prices and facilities for Africans remained retrenched in contrast to the return to high profit levels for private capital.

Colonial governments granted minimum relief to Africans suffering from the depression. They suspended tax collection, and they subsidized prices, as the French did for groundnuts. They also tried to check the crudest forms of middleman exploitation. These measures arose out of necessity, since no money was circulating and since lower prices in one country forced desperate peasants to march long distances and smuggle their produce out through an area where there was some marginal advantage. Africans emerged from the depression subject to more bureaucratic controls (designed to increase production) and still entirely vulnerable to manipulation by the import/export firms and their local compradors.

The dependence illustrated by the great depression indicates the degree of change in the lives of Africans some fifty years after the coming of colonialism. The impact in the early years was often slight, but a major transformation was caused by colonialism as it advanced. Consequent upon the growth of the money economy, African society became more differentiated and new classes were formed. The number of workers did not increase much, but the number of peasants did, and they even became divided into big and small peasants. All of the cash-crop areas witnessed during the 1920s the emergence of big peasants owning land privately, employing labour and occasionally capable of new techniques. A second well-known stratum comprised the privileged few who received education in the first years of colonialism, when certain skills were being introduced to make the colonial economy function. Finally, it is to be noted that the distribution networks were manned at the lowest levels by Africans, who achieved prominence in West and North Africa. Successful cash-crop farmers, African traders and the educated elite together created the embryonic petty bourgeoisie. They often had roots in the old possessor classes in quasi-feudal parts of Africa, and as such were often pampered by the Europeans. But the more portentous fact was that, irrespective of colonial policy, the operating of the economy favoured the advance of these classes, which were economically and culturally part of the dependent colonial order.

The colonial economy of the former French, Belgian and Portuguese zones, 1914–35

In the previous chapter, we discussed in general terms and from a continental perspective the main features of the colonial economies that were instituted by the various colonial powers in Africa during the inter-war period. In this and the subsequent two chapters, we shall discuss in some detail the colonial economies of the former French, Belgian and Portuguese zones, that of the British zones and finally that of North Africa.

Both in their general distribution and from the standpoint of colonial policy, the French, Belgian and Portuguese colonies, namely, French Equatorial Africa (AEF), French West Africa (AOF), Belgian Congo, Ruanda-Urundi, Mozambique and Angola share a number of similarities. They were colonies or federations of enormous geographical area, though in terms of population generally smaller than the average for British Africa (especially AEF and Angola) (see 15.1). In the economic field, the period was decisive; its beginning and end were marked by two profound crises, the First World War and the 1930 economic crisis. The former served to generate, despite the brief but acute crisis of 1921–2, an unprecedented colonial boom which in fact reflected the prosperity of the metropolitan countries during the 1920s. The depression ended this spectacular though short-lived expansion. All this led to great disruption in economic as well as in social and ideological terms. By the end of the period, the relations of French-speaking and Portuguese-speaking Africa with the outside world were transformed. The colonies, which on the whole had not been very dependent on the metropolitan countries, began from this time to be an integral part of the western capitalist system within the framework of a coherent economic system of colonial exploitation.

The financing of capital equipment

The main characteristic of the colonial economies of the period was the emphasis on the import of capital equipment, which was as profitable to the metropolitan states as it was sorely trying for the colonies. Not much capital had been risked there before the First World War; only £25 million in French Black Africa, £40 million in Belgian Africa and hardly any in Portuguese Africa. But the situation underwent a radical change after the war. In the Belgian Congo, the cumulative capital invested

162

15.1   *The resources of the French, Belgian and Portuguese colonies (after G. Grandidier, 1934, Atlas des colonies françaises, Paris: Societé d'Éditions Géographiques, Maritimes et Coloniales)*

rose sharply from B.frs 1215 million before the war to more than 3000 million gold francs in 1935. It increased rapidly between 1920 and 1924, more than doubled between 1924 and 1929 and dropped abruptly during the depression. Of these investments in 1932, 65% was in mines, transport and real estate or secondary agricultural or commercial undertakings related to the expansion of railways or mines. Capital invested in AOF and AEF, which was negligible by 1913, had grown to £30.4 million and £21.2 million respectively.

A great deal of this investment was acquired through borrowing since the colonies were too poor to take on the financing of expansion themselves. Starting in the Belgian Congo during the euphoria of the last years of the decade, the policy of borrowing reached a peak there between 1928 and 1932, when approximately B.frs 3500 million, or nearly 600 million Belgian gold francs, was borrowed. From 1931, AOF in turn began its serious effort at borrowing since the events of the 1930s convinced the government of the urgent need for a capital investment programme. However, despite the fact that it had a larger area and a larger population, AOF had to make do with a quarter of the Belgian amount, or only a third of the sum authorized by law. AEF, more poverty-striken and patterned more on the Belgian example, borrowed approximately 300 million gold francs between 1920 and 1936, which was spent almost entirely on the construction of the Congo–Océan railway.

The result was an increase in the external debt, which became all the more alarming for a balanced budget as the payments became heavier in the middle of the depression, precisely when export prices fell sharply. In 1933, the annual instalment of the Congolese debt (estimated at B.frs 298 million) represented nearly 88% of the budgetary receipts of the colony – almost half its expenditure or nearly half the value of its exports. Much less heavy, the amounts payable by AOF (F.frs 40 million in 1933) amounted to more than a third of its general budget during the worst years of the depression. Those of AEF then exceeded 80% (81% of the global budget in 1934). The Portuguese territories, on which there is little precise information, were also overwhelmed by debt. In 1936, Angola owed a total of almost 1 million contos, which is equal to £8.7 million or 220 million French gold francs. In general, the increase in the burden of instalments during the depression years was distinctly more rapid than in the most debt-ridden of the British territories.

A comparison between the Belgian Congo and AOF shows the differences in the modes of exploitation. The indebtedness of the former was infinitely heavier while the volume of her export trade was somewhat less despite the importance of the mining industries. Above all, her budgetary revenues were substantially more limited owing to lower customs duties and a lighter taxation of the Africans. The result was a more serious financial deficit at the time of the depression.

This apparent inconsistency is accounted for by the fact that the Congo was reaching the stage of exploitation by capital, whereas AOF was still more or less at the stage of the 'milking economy', that is, an economy based on the exploitation of the profit margins between imported goods sold at high prices to African producers and the purchase at low prices of crops left to the traditional sector, and also on heavy taxation without any subsidies from France. Despite the depression, which brought business to a standstill and at the same time wiped out African revenues, France refused any subsidy in aid to AOF. In the same way, the last subsidy paid out to the wretched AEF – which received in all, from 1910 to 1934, F.frs 375 million – occurred in 1928, the metropolitan state resigning itself only to assuming the servicing of loans at the height of the depression to the value of F.frs 80 million in 1935.

But the head tax continued to increase throughout the depression, or at least it scarcely receded; for AOF it was F.frs 156 million in 1929 and F.frs 181 million in 1931, its lowest point being F.frs 153 million in 1935. Though France finally agreed to make efforts to invest, this was strictly a temporary measure which took the form of state-guaranteed loans payable after fifty years at a rate of 4–5.5%. In other words, the French colonies were still essentially required to pay for their own capital equipment. Of course AEF was so poverty-striken that the metropolitan state finally took over its debt almost in its entirety. But in AOF the French share of expenses was reduced between 1931 and 1936 to only 16% of the total, allowing for servicing of the debt. In other words, it was indeed the labour of the inhabitants that was first used to develop the territory.

Since this archaic economy, that is, an economy that depended on taxation and plundering instead of production and investment, was fragile, the depression triggered off its bankruptcy. In 1934, the Economic Conference of Metropolitan and Overseas France was held to make the first attempt at setting up a programme of support. But this programme was in fact only carried out after the Second World War.

Although the depression was sudden and severe in the Belgian Congo, with the value of exports falling by almost two-thirds, from B.frs 1511 million to B.frs 658 million between 1930 and 1933, it was less pronounced in relative value and was more quickly overcome. This is evident from the fact that exports rose again to B.frs 1203 million in 1935. The fact that, following the depression, exports everywhere again took the lead over imports, proved that the capital equipment of the preceding phase had only helped develop to a further stage a policy still basically centred on exploitation from outside rather than on the development of the territories for their own benefit.

The workers' burden

This period – falling between two difficult phases marked by increasing exploitation of the workers, the First World War and the depression – was hard on the Africans. At that time of colonial 'development', Africans interested the colonizers only to the extent that they represented a commodity or an instrument of production. It was, moreover, to ensure their efficiency that the first measures for the protection of labour were taken. But the precarious living standard was sensitive to the slightest upset, and collapsed with the depression.

Labour

Although forced labour was officially repudiated everywhere, the shortage of labour encouraged coercion, whether direct or imposed through the expedient of taxes that had to be paid.

Compulsory service and provision of crops
Everywhere, the use of unpaid labour was common. The French federations, after the war, officially sanctioned unpaid labour for projects of local or colonial interest. Initially set at seven days per year, it soon rose to twelve days in AOF and fifteen in AEF.

The obligation, limited in itself, was the more unpopular because of the fact that the feeding of the workers, previously not even considered, remained the women's responsibility if the work was within a day's walking distance from the village. This labour obligation was in addition to forced (but paid) recruitment for railway work. From 1921 to 1932, 127 250 men, representing a total absence of 138 125 years, were recruited in AEF for building the Congo–Océan railway; probably some 20 000 lives were lost before 1928.

The period was also characterized by the institution of compulsory cultivation of crops. The principle, which originated as early as the end of the nineteenth century in the Belgian Congo, was revived during the First World War. In 1930, the 'state fields' covered more than a million hectares, producing 15 000 tonnes of rice and 30 000 tonnes of cotton. The innovation was particularly unpopular but was none the less adopted in the French federations in 1916 in connection with the 'war effort' and throughout the Portuguese colonies. In AOF and the Portuguese colonies this policy of compulsory cultivation of crops failed. In the former this was owing to the impossibility of solving the population problem and because of the low yields of an inferior cotton whose selling price fell from 1.25 francs in 1928 to 90 centimes in 1929, 70 centimes in 1931 and only 60 centimes from 1933 to 1936. In the Portuguese colonies, it was the failure of the administrative authorities to ensure the distribution of seed or provide technical instructions. It nevertheless prevailed in a particularly archaic form in the territory of the Mozambique Company, which was created in 1891 and enjoyed fifty-year sovereign rights over 160 000 sq km. It did succeed, however, in the Cameroon, Côte d'Ivoire and Ruanda-Urundi, where large-scale production of cocoa and, especially, coffee was launched at the turning-point of the depression.

The labour system and legislation
In French Africa, the administration controlled recruitment, which in theory, after 1921 in AEF, could not exceed 'one-third of the able-bodied male population having reached adult age'. In the Belgian Congo, recruiting was limited to 25% of the 'able-bodied adult males'. The limit was reduced to 10% in the middle of the decade because of the drying-up of the labour pool; but in general the official quota was very considerably exceeded. In the Portuguese colonies, a subtle distinction was established between 'penal labour', reserved for convicts and the labour – 'a moral and social obligation' – of men between 14 and 60 years of age for at least six months per year.

The wickedness of recruiters was particularly prevalent in the Congo, where the state delegated its powers of recruiting to companies such as the Bourse du Travail du Katanga (BTK), a private agency recruiting for the mines in the rural zones. In the Portuguese colonies, scandals broke out periodically, such as the scandal of forced and slave labour on the cocoa plantations of São Tomé and Principe at the turn of the twentieth century. They took between 2000 and 4000 'voluntary recruits' each year. In 1903, recruitment in Mozambique of miners for the Transvaal was entrusted to the

Witwatersrand Native Labour Association (WNLA). The average between 1913 and 1930 was 50 000 emigrants per year, or a total of 900 000 of whom 35 000 died and only 740 000 returned in satisfactory health. The hiring out of manpower thus constituted, with the transit of goods, the chief financial resource of the colony (two-thirds in 1928).

All the colonial powers felt, at approximately the same time, the need for labour regulations, which were introduced for the first time in the Belgian Congo in 1910, in AEF in 1902, in AOF in 1928 and in the Portuguese colonies in 1911. The regulations, which were similar everywhere, fixed the legal duration of the contract at three years maximum in the Congo and two years in the French and Portuguese colonies. These regulations were never fully observed.

The manpower crisis, particularly acute in the mines and on railway projects, led to the adoption of the famous policy of paternalism in the Belgian Congo after 1926, aimed at substituting permanent labour for one recruited under short-term contracts of six to nine months, as was the practice in South Africa. In line with this policy, the reorganization of the compounds was undertaken in 1926; within a year the cost of labour increased by 40% although wages no longer represented more than one-fifth of the budget. Leadership was provided in all sectors of life (leisure activities, religion, schooling, etc.). The result of these measures was that in 1930, for the first time, the birth rate exceeded the death rate in the Union Minière camps, which at the time offered the least unfavourable working conditions in Central Africa.

Taxation

Despite the progress achieved, the undeniable improvement in the economy had little effect on the living standards of Africans. To be sure, wage-earning became standard practice; the number of workers in the Congo increased tenfold within a decade, from less than 20% of the 'able-bodied adult males' in the Congo, of whom 2% in any case were Ruandese. Despite the rising curve of employment, wages failed to keep pace and tended to fall owing to the high inflation in the European countries (apart from Britain) in the 1920s, which was felt in Africa through the cost of imported goods. By 1926, the French franc had lost four-fifths of its pre-war value and the Belgian franc a little more, to say nothing of the galloping inflation of the Portuguese escudo.

The only effort that met with any success was the gradual substitution of payment in cash for payment in kind – imposed in the Belgian Congo from 1916 onwards and more slowly adopted in AEF. However, this led to cash payment of the tax, which was required of all able-bodied adults.

This problem of taxation weighed more and more heavily on the Africans, as it became the chief source of finance for expansion in the inter-war period and as the income of the peasants remained ridiculously low, especially among those planting compulsory crops; wages also fell. Between 1928 and 1932, in the Belgian Congo, 700 000 cotton-planters each earned an average of B.frs 165 a year; rice-growers did only a little better (B.frs 170). Results were even worse in AEF. The average monthly wage also fell in the Middle Congo from B.frs 25.45 in 1912 – admittedly a peak year (B.frs 19.30 in 1913) – to B.frs 19.35 in 1920.

In general, the burden of direct taxation on the African was far higher than his wages, and led him into debt and destitution – all the more so since taxes rose just at the moment when prices fell to their lowest level and dragged peasants' wages down with them. Despite the concurrent increase in speculative crops, all the evidence shows that poverty was acute.

Although comparisons between the territories with which we are concerned are difficult, certain similarities and certain differences in their evolution can be discerned. It was in the Portuguese colonies that the burden of the head tax remained consistently heaviest, since it corresponded officially to three months' labour, the tax being payable in labour. The corresponding daily wage was estimated as being 1 to 1.5% of its total. The head tax was also proportionately high in AOF. The average amount of the direct tax collected in 1915 per inhabitant was F.frs 2 in AOF, F.frs 1.55 in AEF and B.frs 1.35 in the Belgian Congo. The more the country was obliged to live off its own resources, the heavier was the tax.

As a general rule, the colonial budgets were all funded in the same way: 25% from customs revenues and 25% from the head tax. The tragedy was that, with the depression, the authorities tried to have the head tax make up the deficit in customs receipts, which everywhere had fallen to less than 20% in 1932.

The crises and their consequences

The crises discussed above had far-reaching effects on Africans. The first of these was the impoverishment of a majority of the masses. Burdened by taxes which they were no longer able to pay, Africans reacted to the fall in their incomes by stepping up production. As we have seen, it was at the height of the crisis that tropical plantation crops (coffee, cocoa, bananas, cotton) enjoyed a boom due solely to the production of small-scale indigenous planters. However, since the increase in the tax burden upon the producer occurred at the very moment when prices reached their lowest levels, the wages of rural workers declined correspondingly. Moreover, crop-farming helped to start off a process of social differentiation through the emergence of a class of indigenous 'new rich', small-scale landowners and commercial entrepreneurs who made their money by exploiting the destitution and indebtedness of the majority.

But for the mass of the poor small peasants, poverty appeared to be at its worst. The Africans dug into their meagre reserves, mortgaged their land and became share-croppers on the two-thirds and three-quarters system (the *abusa* of the Côte d'Ivoire cocoa plantation area). There was no longer even any need to constrain them by strict compulsory work legislation. From 1931 onwards the shortage of money (whose use could no longer be avoided) became acute; and it was less and less possible for them to fall back on the traditional life of subsistence food cropping, which no longer even ensured survival.

Food shortage, famine and epidemics

Another important impact of the colonial economy was the acute famine that it generated. The war economy of the years 1915–18 had some very serious implications. The most harmful step was the requisitioning of foodstuffs for the home country just when the troops (only 10 000 men in AEF, but a little over 160 000 in AOF) were draining the countryside. In Gabon, only a quarter of the compulsorily produced crops were left for local consumption. Even manioc (cassava) was exported from the Middle Congo and Oubangui–Chari. In AOF, as a consequence of the decision to export local staple crops, the authorities emptied the reserve granaries, which were already suffering from the succession of two years of semi-drought (1911–12) and one year of total aridity (1913). This drought had spread over the entire Sudan area, from Senegal to Wadai and Chad. From periodic shortages, the situation worsened to a devastating famine which claimed probably 250 000 to 300 000 victims.

In AEF, where forced sales continued into the following decade in order to provision the Congo–Océan railway projects, famine, which had began in 1918, spread to the northern half of the country (Woleu-Ntem) between 1922 and 1925; it probably reduced the Fang population by half, from 140 000 to 65 000 in 1933.

The weakened populations then fell prey to epidemics: renewed outbreaks of small-pox and especially the spread of Spanish influenza imported from Europe, from which perhaps one-tenth of the population of AEF perished.

Though not always accompanied by such disastrous results, the famine problem resulting from food shortages caused by the colonial system was a recurrent feature of the period. It recurred, for example, in 1928–9 in Ruanda, the 'granary' of the Belgian Congo, following another drought, and was indeed the sign of the fragility of countries exhausted by the *économie de traite* despite the rise in export figures.

Taken all round, however, the catastrophe was less spectacular. The famines were checked thanks to progress in transport facilities and the epidemics were halted by the first health campaign. But the fall in prices and loss of employment were everywhere cruelly felt.

It is revealing that, in Francophone Africa, large-scale urban immigration began precisely when the great crisis occurred. Notwithstanding the overall stagnation in population growth (in AOF 14.4 million inhabitants in 1931, as compared with 14.6 million in 1936), the towns and cities began to be swollen by the massive influx of destitute peasants. Between 1931 and 1936 the populations of Dakar and Abidjan increased by 71%, while that of Conakry doubled and that of Ouagadougou, an impoverished little town in the interior, increased by one-third over the same period. The overall stagnation in population growth during this period is particularly indicative of the prevailing state of poverty.

The economic balance sheet

Because they were held under strict control by the administrative authorities, and because of their very limited participation in social and economic changes, the populations, at the end of the period, were in a perilous situation, while the system itself was in the throes of change.

The private sector

The period was indeed marked by the rise of powerful firms which, at the turn of the century, had only just been founded. The Belgian Congo was at the forefront of this development. Just before the depression, there were 278 industrial and commercial concerns, and agencies for thirty-six foreign companies – not counting a scattering of privately owned local businesses. In all, the number of establishments had increased by more than a third in three years, rising from 4500 in 1926 to 6000 in 1929 and covering transport, banking, mining, agriculture, industry, commerce and forestry. From 1919 to 1930, the amount of capital invested had risen by 1000 million gold francs.

But, although the sectors covered were already diversified, the chief impetus was from mining and railway activities. Four principal companies (Société Générale, Empain, Cominière and Banque de Bruxelles), with more than 6000 million gold francs invested, accounted for nearly 75% of the capital. The leading company, the Société Générale, was itself responsible for half of this, controlling almost all the mining production (copper, diamonds, radium and a good share of the gold), the entire cement industry and the most important hydroelectric installations. It contrasted with the relative inactivity of the other concessionaire companies, most of which had not assembled sufficient capital to exploit their excessively vast areas. This was particularly true of AEF, paralysed since 1900 by an unfortunate thirty-year concessionary scheme that had sold off the territory to some forty enormous monopoly companies, most of which had already collapsed by the eve of the First World War.

On the eve of the depression, the combined capital of 107 firms totalled a nominal B.frs 309 million which – in gold francs – had scarcely doubled since 1913, when private shareholder capital reached B.frs 70 million. The dominant role in capital investment was still played by the state – the sign of a country considered to be poor, where the private sector had long abandoned to the public authorities the burden of the enormous expenditure for equipment.

AOF remained, in effect, the domain of commercial firms founded on agriculture for export. Even in this field, the lag was enormous compared with the Belgian Congo.

In 1938, the French federations numbered only some fifty commercial firms, whose registered capital barely exceeded F.frs 600 million. At the time, ten of them listed a capital of more than F.frs 20 million, among which only two accounted for a third of the whole: the Société Commerciale de l'Ouest-Africain (SCOA), founded in 1906 with a capital of F.frs 125 million, and the Compagnie Française de l'Afrique Occidentale (CFAO), founded in 1887, with F.frs 75 million.

The reason for this low investment was that trading – which consisted in collecting and routeing to the ports the products of the country to be exported unprocessed or in a semi-refined state, and in distributing in exchange imported manufactured commodities consisting chiefly of consumer goods – required little capital. Certainly the 1920s were the heyday of this form of trading, and inflation was a source of major profit: from 1913 to 1920, the foreign trade of AOF rose from F.frs 277 to F.frs 1143 million.

The depression was felt severely, for the basis of prosperity was largely speculative and ill-equipped to resist the collapse of commodity prices since the diversification of activities had scarcely begun, industrialization was as yet virtually non-existent, and the traditional trading economy still constituted the bulk of AOF activities.

As for the Portuguese colonies, they had as yet scarcely managed to choose between these various approaches. Mozambique, still largely under the concessionaire regime, was very seriously affected by the depression, as is evident from the fact that the value of exports fell by half between 1929 and 1933. In Angola, the first attempt at mining operations was that of the Diamang group with Belgian and British capital. Since 1920, it had figured as the chief financial support of the colony, despite its still relatively limited contribution of £600 000 sterling in 1929, or a quarter of the value of Angolan exports.

Equipment and production

With respect to capital equipment and production, the economic balance sheet still remained poor at the end of the period. The main achievement had been the railways; everywhere the state had replaced or largely financed the former private companies. The Belgian Congo network had expanded considerably. The investments in this field rose from 480 million gold francs in 1920 to 535 million in 1935 and the length of railway lines from 1940 km to 2410 km.

In AEF the grandiose railway projects launched in 1913, including the Gabonese railway and the Congo–Chad link-up, finally resulted in the laborious construction, at great cost in men and money, of the Congo–Océan line (less than 500 km, 1922–34). The latter opened up the territory previously dependent on the Belgian Congo. On the other hand, AOF, which suffered from the poverty of its mineral resources carried out only a few extension projects amounting to 550 km.

A more important innovation was the construction, in savanna country, of a road network which, by putting an end to the ravages of human porterage, transformed the conditions governing the collection and distribution of products. The beginning of the construction of the Oubangui network (AEF) dated from the war and, by 1926, 4200 km had been completed. However, only a few vehicles were seen using it and most of them were exclusively commercial. There were fewer than 1000 vehicles in 1930, 1500 in 1931 and only 2850 in 1945, 600 of which were for tourism.

AOF, especially, made up for its railway deficiencies with roads. By 1937, 27 000 km were open to 17 229 vehicles, including nearly 10 000 trucks and light trucks. Between 1926 and 1934 highway projects and port improvements absorbed almost as much capital as the railways, amounting to F.frs 475 million as against F.frs 520 million.

Nevertheless, the infrastructure provided hardly had time to affect the volume of exports before the onset of the depression. To be sure, a certain number of territories offered a wide range of products: cotton, coffee, sugar cane, sisal and maize in Angola; coconuts, groundnuts and rice in Mozambique; wood in Gabon and the Ivory Coast and bananas in Guinea. But exports continued to be based almost exclusively on minerals and oil-yielding plants. Few territories were as favourably situated as the Belgian Congo, whose improvement was based, at best, on two or three groups of products which, at least, were already partially processed. These were vegetable oil, whose production increased from 2500 tonnes in 1914 to 9000 in 1921 and 65 000 in 1930, and copper, which tripled between 1922 and 1931, from 43 000 to 120 000 tonnes.

Certainly, Angola seemed almost as well endowed potentially. However, Portuguese negligence left its haphazard agricultural production to the risks of the weather and of speculation, which led to its stagnation for ten years.

As for AEF, it was just emerging from the Gabonese forestry monopoly, which accounted for a little more than 400 000 tonnes of its exports in 1930. Although the tonnage exported from Cameroon had tripled since 1923 (from 48 000 to 124 000 tonnes), exploitation of the country was barely getting under way by 1934 with F.frs 73 million in exports, of which nearly 60% consisted of cocoa and oil palm products. Finally, AOF, despite the slow emergence of a few new products, still depended for more than half its exports on Senegalese groundnuts, almost all of them leaving the country unprocessed.

Conclusion

In short, the economic balance sheet at the end of the inter-war period was a negative one, both from the colonizers' standpoint – with production slumping and insufficiently diversified – and from the African angle – with the populations poverty-stricken and distraught. None the less, despite appearances, the available infrastructure and production facilities had profoundly altered the structure of the economy. In this respect, the crisis of 1930 drew attention to the need for a concerted policy directed by the state. It heralded the emergence of colonial planning, in which the international division of labour served to justify the organization of specialized intensified production zones.

A further feature of the period was the reversal of the population trend. In the case of the French-speaking territories at least, it would appear that the population decline was halted in the mid-1920s. Admittedly, by the end of the 1930s the population explosion had not yet begun. The resumption of population growth none the less helped to speed up the process of recovery. Certainly Portuguese colonies remained wretchedly poor. Belgian paternalism was always ready to invest, but accompanied this with a systematic rejection of internal advancement for the Africans. France, for its part, had finally awoken to the need to contribute on a massive scale to investment in production, even if such investment did not bring immediate returns. As early as 1936, it fell to the Popular Front government to put forward a coherent colonial programme that was both modernist and reformist. Even though lack of funds prevented it from going very far in this direction, it introduced into the French federations the very first reforms that were finally to permit the formation of African trade unions and political parties.

16

The colonial economy:
the former British zones

Not only did the nature and characteristics of the colonial economies established in the British zones differ in many significant respects from those established in the zones described in the previous chapter, but, even within those British zones, there were also some significant differences as well as similarities between those of East and Central Africa (Kenya, Uganda, Tanganyika, the Rhodesias and Nyasaland), and those of West Africa (Cameroon, Nigeria, Gold Coast, Sierra Leone and The Gambia).

The British, like other colonizers, did not develop a universal theory or practice of colonialism which could embrace all aspects of life in all colonies. Much was left to the administrators to deal with, depending on the local conditions. Even in the absence of a clear theory, however, there were some fundamental assumptions which seem to have acted as guidelines for both the framers and the practitioners of colonial economic policies. First, the colonies were expected to provide raw materials (agricultural products and minerals) to feed the machines of the industrial imperial power. Second, the colonies had to import manufactured goods from the imperial power. Third, the colonies had to be self-supporting. The colonized peoples had to raise revenue for the general administration and for whatever limited development projects that were undertaken. The fourth assumption, often confused by some colonial administrators and other apologists of colonialism, is the fact that the British, like other colonizers, went out to the colonies primarily, if not exclusively, to enrich themselves and promote their own interests, and those of their commercial firms, mining companies and banks. The development of the colonized was none of their business. Their main preoccupation was to create and maintain effective conditions for the 'orderly' running of economic activities in the colony. These included the maintenance of 'law and order' which facilitated effective exploitation of colonial resources, both human and material.

Ownership of the means of production

The basic and almost only means of production in the British dependencies in the period up to 1935 was land. British attitudes and policies towards land varied from region to region, and even, within each region, from colony to colony. It can be stated in general terms, however, that, whereas Africans remained in practice in control of their land in British West Africa, many of them were deprived of it in British East and Central

Africa. There were, however, some important variations from colony to colony in each region.

In Uganda and to a lesser extent Tanganyika, most of the fertile land was owned by the indigenous population, the Africans. Foreigners, mostly British, secured and held concessions on land with minerals and timber resources. With almost no exception, mineral wealth belonged to the British Crown or its agents and was disposed of in ways decided by the official agents of imperialism and the unofficial ones, such as mining companies and banks.

In Kenya and Central Africa, as was the case in Tanganyika under the Germans, Africans owned some land, but substantial portions of the most fertile arable lands were seized and sold to European settlers (see 16.1). In 1903 only about 2000 ha had been alienated to Europeans in Kenya. By 1914 the area alienated had risen to about 260 000 ha and to about 2 740 000 ha in 1930. This was a very substantial chunk of the arable land. The chief losers were the Gikuyu, but the Nandi, Maasai, Kipsigi and others also lost land.

The availability of land and the propaganda by the colonial authorities to popularize settler agriculture attracted many Europeans, both adventurers and genuine settlers. In 1903 there were only 596 Europeans in Kenya, two years later the number had reached 954, of whom 700 were South Africans; by the end of March 1914 the number had risen to 5438 and by the end of December 1929 to 16 663. Many of the early settlers, especially until 1910, acquired land at little or no cost. The land bought between 1902 and 1915 was held on ninety-nine-year leases. The Crown Lands Ordinance of 1915 extended the duration of the leases from 99 years to 999 years.

In Southern Rhodesia (now Zimbabwe) an even greater proportion of land was alienated to Europeans. Between 1890 and 1900 European entrepreneurs and adventurers poured into the country. Unlike the situation in Kenya, the European population increased very fast, rising from 11 000 in 1901 to 23 000 in 1911 and 35 000 by 1926. The increase in European population led to more alienation of land. By 1911 they had acquired about 7 700 000 ha, slightly less than the areas of the Native Reserves. In contrast, by 1925 Africans had purchased only some 18 000 ha of land outside the Native Reserves. This figure vividly illustrates their inability to compete with Europeans under the then prevailing circumstances.

In Northern Rhodesia (now Zambia) relatively less land was seized and sold to Europeans. During the mid-1930s land in Northern Rhodesia was divided roughly into three categories. Areas reserved especially for Africans totalled 28 740 000 ha. Land already allocated to Europeans was more than 3 430 000 ha. The remaining 60 700 000 ha comprised forest and game reserves.

In British West Africa, the British attempted even earlier than in East Africa to establish direct control over land, to create forest reserves and to offer land as concessions to European planters and concessionaires (see 16.2). As early as 1894, and again in 1897, the British introduced a Land Bill in the Gold Coast which was to establish direct British control over lands which were said to be vacant. The reaction of the people, as has been pointed out already in Chapter 6 was the formation of the Aborigines' Rights Protection Society in Cape Coast in 1897 by the educated elite and the traditional rulers, whose opposition to the Bill forced the Colonial Office to drop it. A move to introduce

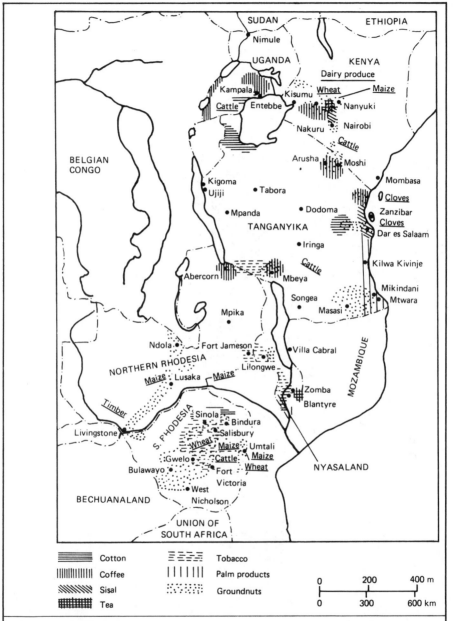

16.1 *East Africa: economic development in the former British zones; agricultural products (after R. Oliver and A. Atmore, 1972,* Africa since 1800, *Cambridge, Cambridge University Press, 2nd edn)*

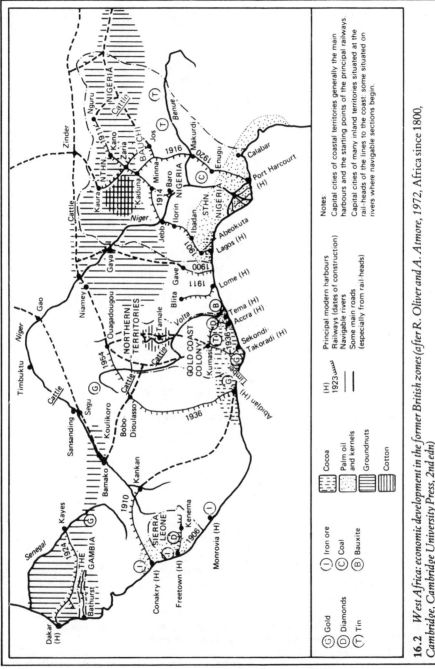

16.2 *West Africa: economic development in the former British zones (after R. Oliver and A. Atmore, 1972, Africa since 1800, Cambridge, Cambridge University Press, 2nd edn)*

a similar Bill in Lagos in Nigeria in the 1910s was also checkmated by the Anti-Slavery and Aborigines' Rights Protection Society founded by the elite led by Herbert Macaulay and the traditional rulers. As a result of these victories by the West Africans, the British abandoned the policy of direct control of land. Thus by 1930 only a relatively small proportion of land in British West Africa had been alienated for the use of the colonial rulers and other Europeans, and most of this was for mining purposes.

What prevented the wholesale alienation of land in British West Africa? The first answer was what A. G. Hopkins has termed 'a fortuitous geological fact' – that West Africa was found to be not profusely rich in mineral deposits. The second was the failure of the move to establish plantations in West Africa by individual Europeans, such as W. H. Lever, the Liverpool soap and margarine tycoon, and by societies, such as the British Cotton Growing Association, between 1906 and 1925. The third and most important factor was the success of the West Africans themselves in meeting the demand for export crops such as cocoa, groundnuts and oil palm, using their own simple methods on their small farms, which made the introduction of the plantation system in these areas totally unnecessary. Another factor was the opposition that any attempt to seize any large areas or introduce large-scale forced labour for plantations would have generated among West Africans. It was a combination of these factors that saved the people of British West Africa from the expropriation of their lands that was the fate of some of those in British East and Central Africa and in Portuguese and Belgian Africa.

Production

The colonial economies under discussion were characterized by two sectors – one producing mainly for the subsistence of the producers and for the home market, and the other producing essentially primary products for export. Production for subsistence had been well developed long before colonial rule. Plantains, yams, cassava, rice and maize were produced by West African peasants with the very simple technology which the British met at the end of the nineteenth century. Things were not different in the production of bananas, maize, cassava, millet and a variety of other crops in Eastern and Central Africa. This sector, however, was neglected by the colonial authorities because, unlike the export sector, it did not earn the badly needed foreign exchange with which to pay for imports, nor did it provide raw materials to feed the factories of the metropolis.

Cash crops

The export sector was basically concerned with the production of primary products – agricultural products and minerals. With the few exceptions of the areas where European settlers owned much land, the agricultural export sector in the former British dependencies of tropical Africa was almost wholly in the hands of millions of small-scale farmers. The main cash crops grown by such farmers comprised cocoa from the Gold Coast and western Nigeria, palm oil and palm kernels from Nigeria, Sierra Leone and, to a lesser extent, the Gold Coast; groundnuts from The Gambia and northern Nigeria; cotton from Uganda, Nigeria and Tanganyika; and coffee from Uganda and Tanganyika (see 16.1 and 16.2).

Contrary to what colonial historians would have us believe, the peasant export sector in the countries under consideration was established with little government initiative. Even the Gold Coast cocoa industry, of which the British were greatly proud, was essentially developed with local initiative. Starting from almost nothing in the early 1890s, by 1903 the farmers had put over 17 000 ha under cocoa. By 1928 there were 364 000 ha of cocoa, and in 1934 the Gold Coast produced 40% of world output. Yet until this time the industry had benefited little from scientific research carried out in the country.

In Kenya and the Rhodesias the production of cash crops increasingly passed into settler hands as the twentieth century advanced. During the first decade of the century African peasant producers in Kenya and Southern Rhodesia competed with white settlers quite effectively in producing most of the grain which fed the growing numbers of wage-earners. Indeed, until 1914, African farmers in Kenya contributed more to the cash and export sector than the settlers.

It was by using the colonial administration to push through certain measures that the role of African producers was systematically reduced to the minimum possible. These measures included seizure of more land from Africans, paying higher prices for commodities produced by the settlers, imposing taxes on the Africans which compelled them to go and work for the white man, forcing Africans to work for a certain number of days a year on public works and plantations and settler farms, and finally forbidding Africans to grow coffee, which was 'by far the most lucrative crop'. The main result of all these steps was to turn Africans from farmers or peasants into wage-earners (see 16.3). Thus, in Kenya, by 1927, between 83 700 and 117 000 Africans, or more than 50% of total wage labour, worked in commercial agriculture, producing mainly maize and coffee for European settlers, while in Southern Rhodesia they produced mainly maize and tobacco. By the early 1920s the settlers in Kenya had ousted African peasants from the production of and trade in the important crop of maize. A dominant feature of the economy in colonial Kenya was established.

Minerals

A number of the former British dependencies of tropical Africa were rich in a variety of mineral resources (see 16.2). Gold was mined in the Gold Coast, Southern Rhodesia, Tanganyika and Sierra Leone. Diamonds became an important industry in Sierra Leone and the Gold Coast. Copper mining was restricted to Northern Rhodesia, while iron-ore mining remained a speciality of Sierra Leone. Only Nigeria and Southern Rhodesia mined coal, an important source of power. Most territories had one or two minerals; only Southern Rhodesia and Sierra Leone had a variety.

With the exception of a few cases, mineral resources were exploited, as was the case in other zones, with foreign capital. Two main reasons accounted for this feature. First, there were cases where capital beyond the resources of Africans was required, for example in copper mining in Northern Rhodesia and iron-ore mining in Sierra Leone. Second, and this had a wider applicability, the colonial administrations deliberately and systematically excluded Africans from benefiting from the mineral resources of their country. Soon after mineral deposits were found a series of legislative measures were

16.3 *Tea pickers at work on a plantation in Nyasaland: the Lujenda estates, Cholo (BBC Hulton Picture Library)*

introduced to give monopolies to imperialist interests. Even where Africans had been working minerals for generations, as with gold and tin in the Gold Coast and Nigeria respectively, it became illegal for the African to be found in possession of minerals without a licence. No Africans were allowed to deal in diamond mining. The industry, both in Sierra Leone and the Gold Coast, was monopolized by the Consolidated African Selection Trust (CAST), a powerful multinational company engaged in mining a number of minerals.

Minerals have been regarded as 'the touchstone of economic development in most of Africa'. But clearly the contribution of minerals to colonial economies has been greatly exaggerated. It is true that minerals contributed substantially to the export sector of a few countries, especially the Rhodesias, the Gold Coast and Sierra Leone. However, minerals were not that important in the economies of Nigeria, Kenya and Tanganyika nor did they contribute that much to the general wealth. Moreover, as mining was established with foreign capital, the profits accruing from the industry were repatriated to swell the pockets of shareholders abroad, or to develop economies outside Africa. But, even where the colonial administrations nationalized minerals, as was the case in Sierra Leone, Kenya, Tanganyika and Uganda, little revenue (mainly from royalties and income tax) was realized. In Sierra Leone direct revenue from minerals in 1935 was £34 100, which was only 5% of total revenue.

Wages remained the only way by which the local population could have acquired a substantial portion of the proceeds from mining, but, as was the case in settler and plantation agriculture, they were kept so low that wage-earners had to be subsidized by the peasant sector.

The export sectors of the countries under discussion had two major characteristics. First, exports, both agricultural products and minerals, left the countries unprocessed, as was generally the case in the other zones. Thus, most exports were of relatively low value. Second, there was a tendency towards monoculture, or concentration on single cash crops. This made the economies of the countries which depended mostly on agricultural exports highly vulnerable. Only Nigeria, with three or so crops (including cocoa, oil palm and groundnuts), and Kenya developed somewhat diversified economies. The weakness of monoculture economics was vividly exposed during the great depression of 1929–34 by the panic and confusion displayed by colonial administrators.

Currency and banking

Like the other colonial powers, the British also introduced modern currencies into their colonies in place of the traditional system of barter, commodity currency and currencies such as gold dust and cowries. This was mainly to encourage production and export of cash crops and the importation of European manufactures. By 1910, European currencies were widespread in West Africa. These consisted of a wide variety of English coins. In 1912, the West African Currency Board was established to supply currencies to British West Africa. In 1913, the Board issued its first coins in denominations of 2s, 1s, 6d and 3d and three years later its first currency notes. In British East Africa, the British first introduced the currency system operating in British India. In 1920, however, one currency board was established to issue coins and notes for the three colonies. It should be noted that all these currencies were linked with the sterling in London.

One important consequence of the increasing use of currencies was the introduction of banking institutions in British Africa. In West Africa, the first bank to start operations was the Bank of British West Africa in 1894, followed in 1926 by Barclays Bank (Dominion, Colonial and Overseas). These two banks completely dominated banking activities in British West Africa throughout the colonial period. In British East and Central Africa, the National Bank and Grindlay's Bank also appeared and soon dominated the field. The operations of these banks impeded economic developments in the colonies in three main ways. First, the banks invested all their money in England, including the savings made by the Africans themselves. This meant that they promoted capital formation and therefore economic development of the rich metropolitan country at the expense of the poor colonies. Secondly, and this is more serious still, recent research has shown that, in their lending policies, all the banks discriminated against African entrepreneurs in favour of the British and Asian populations. Thirdly, since banking became the exclusive preserve of Europeans, Africans were denied the opportunity of acquiring training and experience in this vital field.

Marketing

Marketing was greatly neglected by the colonial administrators. The policy of *laissez-faire*, or free trade, was applied to varying degrees in all the countries under discussion. Being the champion of free trade till this period and concerned primarily with increasing revenue from customs duties through the expansion of the export trade, Britain tended to encourage whoever was likely to contribute to the revenue. Thus Indian traders were not only allowed but, to some extent, also encouraged to engage in trade in East Africa and, to a more limited degree, in Central Africa. The Levantine communities were allowed to operate in British West Africa. Britain did not even restrict the operations of non-British commercial firms and individuals in her dependencies. Before the emergence of the United Africa Company (UCA) in 1929, for instance, the two leading French firms – the Compagnie Française de l'Afrique Occidentale (CFAO) and the Société Commerciale de l'Ouest-Africain (SCOA) – competed quite effectively with British firms in the British dependencies of West Africa.

Yet there were no safeguards to protect the local population. First of all, general official policy, as would be expected in a colonial situation, was geared primarily towards the advancement of imperialist interests. Consequently, the local population was not protected from the devouring jaws of big firms. If anything, they were exposed for easy destruction. By the first decade of the twentieth century, following the construction of railways, European firms were squeezing African traders in two related ways, namely by underselling the Africans and by extending their business from wholesale to retail sale. Worse still, in most cases African businessmen could not secure bank loans because they had no collateral. In all these ways, the big indigenous West African merchants who emerged during the nineteenth century were pushed out of business. Nor did African peasant farmers fare any better since they were paid little for their produce and charged relatively high prices for imported goods.

Occasionally African producers defended their interests collectively through hold-ups (refusals to deliver produce to market) and boycotts of European goods. There were several such hold-ups in the Gold Coast, where cocoa farmers were substantially exposed to international market forces. The most serious cocoa hold-up occurred between October and December 1930, and there was another one during the 1937–8 cocoa season. The latter, which was staged against the most important cocoa exporting firms, which had formed an agreement to buy cocoa at a fixed maximum price, was extended to Western Nigeria. All the hold-ups, which threatened the very foundation of colonial economic relations, were forcibly suppressed by the British government.

Trade with Britain put African dependencies at a great disadvantage, as was the case during the great depression. In 1932 imperial preference was introduced in British dependencies. Imports from the British empire had customs duties fixed at between 10 and 50% lower than the general level. Since this did not keep out Japanese and other foreign manufactured goods, the tariff on these goods was raised to 100% in 1934, while a quota system was imposed on the importation of Japanese textiles. There were isolated protests against these measures but the colonized people had to pay high prices, thereby promoting imperialist interests at their own expense.

Infrastructure

One of the most important aspects of marketing is infrastructure. The construction of railways, roads, telegraph lines and harbours therefore received the attention of the colonial administrations quite early on. Though these facilities helped in the general administration, their main task was to move out exports. No wonder therefore that the location and general direction of railways and roads took little account of the general welfare of the dependencies. Most railways ran directly from the coast to interior sources of cash crops or mineral deposits. Only a few lateral and inter-colonial links were established.

Most of the railways were constructed, owned and operated by governments or official agencies. Construction of the first railway in British West Africa took place in Sierra Leone during the 1890s. The first train started operating in the colony in 1897, and by 1909 the main line, crossing the rich oil palm belt to Pendembu, in the east (365 km) had been completed. Soon after the work started in Sierra Leone, other dependencies followed her example with even better results. All major lines had been built by 1920.

Only in the Rhodesias and Sierra Leone did private capital contribute to railway construction. The main railway running northwards through the Rhodesias was a continuation of the South African system and was constructed by the British South Africa Company. Road construction was carried out by both the colonial administration and local authorities. African chiefs, where resources allowed, mobilized their people to integrate their economies with the wider world. But roads, as a rule, were meant to act as feeders, not as alternatives, to the railways, which were official undertakings. Thus the taxpayer had to maintain expensive and inefficient systems.

The most important contribution of modern transport was the dramatic reduction of freight rates, which had two related results. First, human porterage was replaced by machinery, thereby releasing scarce human resources for other productive activities. Secondly, the decreased cost of transport increased the profit margins of producers and encouraged the expansion of the cash sector. Only rarely, however, did African producers benefit from this development, the lion's share going to the commercial firms and others engaged in the export sector. In the settler regions, freight rates were manipulated in favour of Europeans, thereby forcing the African sector to subsidize settler agriculture.

Another part of the infrastructure, which was in existence in pre-colonial days but increased in efficiency and importance during the colonial period, was shipping. In British West Africa, this field was by 1900 dominated by one single British firm, the Elder Dempster Line and Co Ltd, which was an amalgamation in 1890 of all the British shipping companies operating on the west coast. In East and Southern Africa, shipping was dominated by the Union Castle Line.

South Africa, 1880–1935

Of the British African colonies and dependencies, so unique and so phenomenal and yet so notorious in their impact were the economic changes that occurred in South Africa during the period under review that they merit separate treatment here, however briefly.

By 1869, South Africa – consisting of the two British colonies of Cape Colony and Natal and the Boer or Afrikaner settler colonies of Transvaal and Orange Free State – was economically as poor as any of the other European colonies and settlements in Africa. The combined European population was only 260 000, about 20% of whom lived in the Cape Colony. The Cape had the only town with a population of over 10 000, namely Cape Town. There were only 3 km of railway by 1860 and no motorable roads. All transport was drawn by animals. Manufacturing was confined to the making of wagons, furniture and shoes and the tanning of leather. The exports of South Africa in 1860 consisted of primary products, with wool as the leading one, followed by iron, hides and skins, in total worth only £2.5 million a year.

Not only the economy but also the society of South Africa underwent a revolutionary change during the last three decades of the nineteenth century. This was primarily because of one single event, the discovery of minerals, first of diamonds in Griqualand in 1867 and Kimberley in 1870, and then of gold in Transvaal in 1886. Within five years of the discovery in Griqualand, more than £1.6 million-worth of diamonds was being annually exported. Even more rapid was the growth of the gold mining industry after its discovery in 1886. By 1890 £10 million-worth of gold was being exported, which made gold the leading South African export; this had risen to £25 million by 1905 and to between £45 and £50 million by 1910.

The effects of this mining boom in South Africa were truly phenomenal and all-embracing. Politically, the discovery of diamonds led first to the annexation of the Kimberley area and then of Transvaal itself in 1877 and finally to the conquest of Zululand in 1879 after the humiliating defeat of the British at Isandhlwana. Similarly, the discovery of gold led to the annexation of all the African states south of the Limpopo river, the Jameson Raid of 1896, and finally the Second Boer War of 1899, which ultimately resulted in the creation of the Union of South Africa in 1910.

Secondly, the discovery led to the pouring in of capital and technical personnel from Britian, Europe and the United States of America. Indeed, the bulk of the investments in colonial Africa between 1880 and 1939 went to Southern Africa alone. It was this investment that promoted not only the mining industry but also the infrastructure of South Africa, constituting the third effect of the discovery. The length of railway line rose from 110 km by 1869 to 1700 km by 1889, 3300 km by 1899 and 4190 km by 1905. Side by side with railways went the construction of roads. By the end of the First World War, 75 000 km of provincial roads and many more of farm roads had been constructed.

The fourth important impact was in the field of labour and land, and with it came the growth of urban centres. The demand for labour created by the diamond- and gold-mining activities was virtually inexhaustible. It was partly to ensure the supply of labour and partly to safeguard even more the positions of the whites that a whole series of Acts were passed, especially in the 1910s and 1920s, to compel the Africans to leave their farms and places of birth for the mining and other industrial centres. These Acts included the Natives Land Act of 1913, the Mines and Works Act of 1911 and its amendment in 1926, the Apprenticeship Act of 1922 and the Natives (Urban Areas) Act of 1923. The most notorious was the Natives Land Act, under which 88% of the land in South Africa was reserved for the exclusive use of whites, who constituted only 20% of its population. The remaining 12% was established as a series of 'native reserves' for the Africans. The Act caused the immediate displacement of thousands of independent African pastoral and agricultural farmers from their traditional homes and lands and from the white-owned farms.

The Mines and Works Act of 1911 and its amendment of 1926 and the Apprenticeship Act of 1922 also excluded Africans from many skilled occupations and laid down different scales of pay for skilled (largely white) labour and unskilled (largely African, Indian and Coloured) labour. In 1935, the white miner was receiving on the average eleven times what an African was receiving. The Natives (Urban Areas) Act of 1923, the Native Administration Act of 1927 and the Native Service Contract Act of 1932 all also jointly regulated the movement, residence and employment of Africans in the interest of white workers.

The total effect of all these measures was to drive Africans from their homes and farms into the new mining and industrial centres and to keep them on European farms as wage-earners. The number of labourers in the mines rose by leaps and bounds during the period under review. By 1906, the mines were employing 163 000 people – 18 000 whites, 94 000 Africans and 51 000 Chinese; by 1918 this number had risen to 291 000, of whom 32 000 were whites. It should be emphasized that, as a result of the various Acts, most of the Africans employed were not permanent but rather migrant or seasonal labourers. They were therefore compelled to spend their lives shifting back and forth between work on the white portions and the 'native reserves'.

Another important impact of the mining boom was on urbanization. Since the workers migrated into the new mining and industrial areas, completely new towns came into existence while some existing ones saw very rapid growth. Thus, Kimberley, which was not in existence in 1866, had become a town with a population of 18 000 by 1877, while Johannesburg had grown from a small village into a large town with a population of 166 000 by 1900. The percentage of whites living in towns rose from

35.8% in 1890–1 to 65.2% in 1936 and that of Africans from 13% in 1904 to only 17.3% in 1936.

Two other sectors of the South African economy also saw some tremendous development, partly as a result of the mining boom. These were the agricultural and manufacturing sectors. The great increase in the population of South Africa and the new urban populations created new markets for both agricultural products and manufactured goods, while the new infrastructure of roads and railways facilitated the transportation of these products. Between 1927 and 1937, the government also introduced a number of measures, such as protective tariffs and the establishment of various marketing boards and extension of banking facilities, to assist the white farmers at the expense of black farmers. The result was that not only were white farmers producing enough for home consumption but they also began to export maize from 1907, meat and eggs after the First World War and sugar and dairy products from the late 1920s onwards. But by now Africans had been virtually eliminated from commercialized farming and had become mere wage-earners on these farms. To worsen their plight, their wages either remained static or were increased only very slowly.

Even more revolutionary were the changes that occurred in the manufacturing sector and this is all the more interesting since this did not occur, as we have seen already, in most other parts of colonial Africa. Taking advantage of the facilities referred to above, the whites began to promote economic development, and by 1912 a number of industries had been established. These included fruit-preserving, jam-making, brewing, soap-making, candle-making, small-scale engineering industries making windmills, pumps, water-boring drills, gates and fences, and boots, shoes and clothing. The growth of this sector was particularly encouraged during the First World War with a view to diversifying the economy of the country, minimizing its dependence on the mining industry and providing employment for the 'poor whites'. The manufacturing sector saw even more rapid growth after the depression of the 1920s and early 1930s and by 1939 it had become the second leading contributor to national income, with mining in the lead.

It should be obvious from the above that, unlike that of most colonies, the economy of South Africa definitely experienced a revolutionary development during the period between 1880 and 1935. By 1932, the gross national product was as high as £217 million and this rose to £320 million in 1937. It also became highly diversified, unlike the economies of most other African countries, depending, as it did, on mining, manufacturing and agriculture. And all this was due primarily to the discovery of gold and diamonds.

However, all this phenomenal development was achieved at the expense of the non-white peoples of Africa, especially the Africans and the Coloureds. In the reserved areas overpopulation and poverty were widespread; this had caused mass migrations into the towns and mining centres, where the Africans were packed into slums and ghettos. What was even worse, they were not allowed to settle permanently in these places with their families so that most of them became temporary migrants moving between town and country. Displaced, landless, underpaid and discriminated against, the Africans of South Africa suffered economically and socially far more than Africans in any other part of Africa during the period under review.

The colonial economy: North Africa

The colonial economies of the countries of North Africa were not very different from those of the countries of the zones already discussed for the simple reason that the whole region was colonized by the same imperial powers. Tunisia, Algeria and Morocco were colonized by the French, Libya by Italy, and Egypt and Sudan by the British. (See 17.1). However, it would appear that, on the whole, apart from industrialization, they had more in common with the colonial economies of the Portuguese, French and Belgian zones than with those of the British.

The economy of Tunisia, Algeria and Morocco

By the end of the First World War, the French had established political, administrative, economic and financial institutions in Tunisia, Algeria and Morocco and had set in motion the process of dispossessing the *fellāhīn* and draining wealth away for the benefit of the metropolitan country. These processes were slowed down by the war but they were resumed at high speed once hostilities ended, first in the field of agriculture, then in mining and infrastructure and finally in finance (see 17.1).

Agriculture

In the field of agriculture, in Algeria the process of 'official colonization', in which land was taken from the indigenous people, made up into lots by the authorities and allocated to European settlers, was started again, even faster than before, and by 1930 there were 25 795 settler estates with a total area of 2 334 000 ha.

In Tunisia the process of dispossessing the *fellāhīn* had started as soon as the protectorate was established in 1881. 'Colonization by capital' (1881–2), which had allowed big capitalist firms (Compagnie des Batignolles, Société Marseillaise de Crédit, Société Foncière de Tunisie, etc.) to gain control of nearly 430 000 ha, had been followed by 'official colonization', whose main aim was to increase systematically the French population in Tunisia and promote 'colonization by Frenchmen'. Considerable sums of money were allocated to it. In addition to legislation tending to transfer Tunisian-occupied land into French hands, the protectorate authorities gave settlers major financial help. In 1931 settler estates in Tunisia amounted to some 700 000 ha, mainly in the best-watered and most fertile parts of the country.

In Morocco the protectorate administration, which wanted to bring about heavy

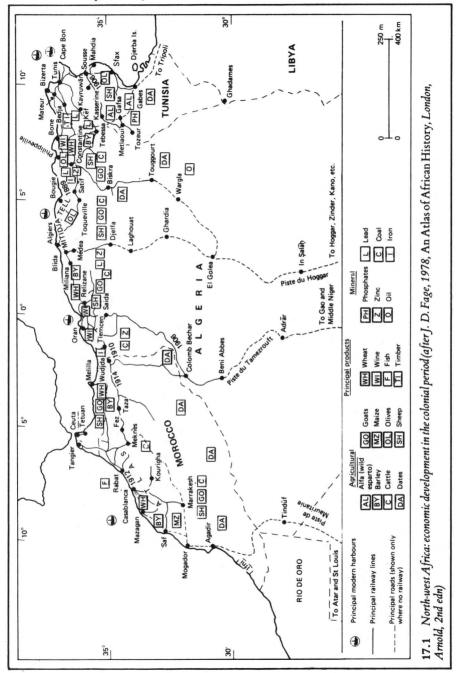

17.1 *North-west Africa: economic development in the colonial period (after J. D. Fage, 1978, An Atlas of African History, London, Arnold, 2nd edn)*

European settlement throughout the Sherifian empire, likewise methodically organized official colonization. It made available to the settlers – 60% of whom came from Algeria – state land transferred in the form of settler estates of varying sizes, and communal land. This land was not granted free as in Algeria but sold at low prices, as in Tunisia, and several facilities were provided, such as subsidies for land-clearing, exemption from customs duties on imports of agricultural equipment, and so on. During the same period (1922–32), private colonization managed to take over more than 350 000 ha.

The features of agricultural colonization
Despite considerable efforts by the authorities to increase the French rural population, official colonization did not manage to establish many French settlers in the countryside of North Africa. Apart from smallholders in vineyards and orchards (Italians in Tunisia, Spaniards in Morocco), European settlers did not constitute a real peasantry such as existed in France at that time. They were mainly large farmers owning enormous estates, a wide range of agricultural equipment and often impressive farm buildings.

The agriculture they practised was essentially speculative and aimed at exporting their produce rather than selling it on the home market. Most settlers specialized in a single crop, such as vines in the Oran area in Algeria and cereals or olives in Tunisia.

This agriculture, in which tractors, tractor-drawn equipment and later combine harvesters and highly mechanized methods were used, often reached a high level of productivity. Yields in all sectors increased continuously between 1919 and 1929; wine production in Tunisia made a great leap, rising from 498 148 hl to 918 583 hl between 1920 and 1925; and in Algeria average annual wine production, 6 853 000 hl in the years 1916–20, rose to 18 371 000 hl in the years 1931–5. The Moroccan *fellāhīn* obtained only 1 316 000 quintals of grain from a larger area (222 815 ha). Local markets could not absorb the increasing quantities of agricultural produce.

What about the indigenous people? On the eve of the First World War, the majority (more than 80%) of the population of North Africa lived off the land in rural areas. The system of land tenure broadly comprised *melk* land (private property), '*arsh* or communal land and, in Tunisia and Morocco, *habous* (land property in mortmain). In areas of *melk* land there was a whole hierarchy of landowners, the top consisting of a minority of large landowners who concentrated in their hands a major part of the arable and pasture land. These large landowners were particularly common in Morocco. In Algeria too, despite the great growth of settler land, large Muslim holdings on the morrow of the First World War covered a sizeable area. In Tunisia also there was a landed aristocracy, living in Tunis. Their land was mostly in the cereal-growing Tell (areas of Bēdja, Mateur and the Kēf). This land was farmed by fifth sharecropping, the *khammāsāt* practised throughout North Africa, which did not allow much development of techniques or methods of cultivation.

Smallholdings were legion around the towns, in the fertile grain-growing plains such as those of the Sa'is in Morocco and the middle Medjerda in Tunisia, in the mountains where there were settled farmers (Kabylia, Rīf and the western High Atlas) and in the oases.

Agricultural production and herd populations were liable to wide fluctuations because of the irregular rainfall; famines, though on the decrease, were still frequent. In addition, usury still caused havoc in the countryside, and only large farmers had access to the credit institutions set up by Europeans. But early on in Tunisia (1907) and later in Morocco (1922) *sociétés indigènes de prévoyance* (indigenous provident societies) were set up, mainly to make seed loans to small *fellāḥīn*. The colonial authorities' financial help for settlers was incomparably bigger.

Mining

European settlement in the three countries of North Africa meant not only the seizure by settlers of much of the best land, but also the working of underground resources, mainly for the benefit of foreign companies. These resources were prospected very early and exploited quickly. In Algeria the first mines were opened in 1845; in Tunisia the phosphate deposits at Ḳafṣa were already discovered by 1885–6 (only four years after the establishment of the protectorate) and exploited from 1889 on. In Morocco, serious mining did not begin until after 1928, when prospectors and applicants for mining concessions fell on the country like a swarm of locusts. By 1930, Morocco was seemingly one of the North African countries richest in mineral resources, producing iron ore, manganese, cobalt, lead and tin, with phosphates as the leading mineral whose export rose from 8232 tonnes in 1921 to 1 179 000 tonnes in 1930.

In Algeria and Tunisia deposits of phosphates (Kuwayf and Ḳafṣa), iron ore (Beni Sāf, Wenza and Djarisā), lead, zinc, etc., had already been brought into production before the First World War, and nearly the whole output was exported to France and other West European countries. This mineral wealth was exploited entirely by foreign companies, particularly French, which provided the capital, the technicians, the managers and so on.

Communications and ports

To link the various mineral deposits to the export ports, railways were built very early in Algeria (from 1844) and in the early years of the protectorate in Tunisia and Morocco. By 1919 the main lines of the Algerian and Tunisian railways were already set up: they linked the large towns (mostly near the coast) with each other and the mines with the main export ports (Oran, Algiers, Annāba, Tunis, Safāḳus and Sousse). In Morocco railway development, undertaken entirely by foreign companies and designed entirely to serve the mines and the large towns, was slower and it was not until April 1923 that the first line, Casablanca–Rabat, was inaugurated. The road network was also planned to serve the big towns, where most of the European population lived, and those parts of the countryside where settler estates had been established. The same was true of the port infrastructure, which was planned and developed essentially in order to open up the countries of North Africa to French and foreign manufactured goods and to export minerals and agricultural produce.

The customs and fiscal system

The customs system

Algeria being a colony, Algerian and French merchandise was reciprocally admitted duty-free into the other country. Foreign goods imported into either France or Algeria were likewise liable to the same tariffs; and under the flag monopoly French shipping had the exclusive right to sail between Algeria and French ports. Thus there was a true customs union between France and Algeria. But this union condemned Algeria to remain an exporter of raw materials and agricultural produce and an importer of manufactured goods.

The customs system in Tunisia on the morrow of the First World War was governed by the Acts of 19 July 1890 and 2 May 1898. The latter gave a preferential position to French manufactured products, especially metal goods, machinery, textiles, etc. Similar foreign goods, however, were not liable to duty under the French tariff, so that the Tunisian market was flooded with manufactured products from France and foreign countries. A partial customs union was introduced in 1928: Tunisian agricultural produce admitted free of duty was no longer subject to quotas, but French goods were given either complete exemption from duty or protection against similar foreign goods.

Commercial and customs relations between Morocco and foreign countries were even more iniquitous and unequal. The Act of Algeciras (1906) laid down the principle of strict economic equality between signatory countries on the Moroccan market. Wherever they came from and whatever ships they were carried in, goods entering Morocco were liable to a flat 10% *ad valorem* duty plus an additional 2.5% duty for the Caisse Spéciale des Travaux Publics (Special Fund for Public Works). This 'open door' system allowed the big exporting countries to flood Morocco with their manufactured goods and agricultural produce. To protect her infant industries, Morocco resorted to indirect protectionism, restricting access for certain foreign foodstuffs such as wheat, barley and flour.

The nature of North Africa's exports clearly demonstrated the nature of the North African economy and its customs system. The imbalance in the type of goods bought and sold by North Africa was responsible for the almost continual deficit in its balance of trade, imports by value being far higher than exports for all three countries. Finally, the customs system was largely responsible for the ruin of the rural and urban craft industries.

The fiscal system

One of the first things the French authorities did when they took over North Africa was to reorganize the financial and fiscal system. They set up a Financial Administration whose first task was to draw up a budget and check expenditure. Budgetary strictness and discipline enabled them to balance receipts and expenditure, and this balance was frequently achieved between 1919 and 1930.

Revenue came mainly from customs duties and from taxes on land, agricultural produce (*tartib* in Morocco) and consumption goods (indirect taxes). All this fell mainly on the indigenous population, whose burden often became very heavy.

In addition, in order to purchase equipment, the three North African countries had to borrow at frequent intervals. In 1930 Algeria owed France 2000 million francs, while in 1932 Morocco owed a total of 1691 million francs. The equipment acquired by dint of these loans benefited first and foremost the modern sectors of the economy, which was dominated by European concerns; yet the bulk of these loans was redeemed out of Muslim money. In 1931 the servicing of Morocco's public debt absorbed more than a third of the country's budget.

The crisis and the major sectors of the economy

The great economic crisis of 1930–5 hit North Africa a little late. Its full effects were felt from 1932 onwards; but it came on earlier in Morocco than in Tunisia or Algeria, the former being then right in the development phase of its economic potential.

One of the first sectors of the economy affected by the crisis was settler agriculture, which was highly dependent on credit and foreign markets. Once prices collapsed and foreign outlets were shut off or became scarce, the mechanized but debt-ridden farmers could no longer honour their commitments to the various credit bodies to which they were indebted. It was the same situation in mining, which was totally dependent on foreign markets because mineral raw materials were hardly processed or used at all in the producer countries.

The domestic economy was also hit by the crisis, its contribution to the export of agricultural produce being affected by the slump and the fall in prices. So were the craft industries, which played an important role in the economy of the big towns in Morocco (Fez, Meknès and Marrakesh) and in Tunisia (Tunis, Kayrawān and Safākus), and whose foreign outlets were practically cut off.

The first European agricultural sector affected by the crisis was the one most dependent on foreign markets, especially the French market, namely the wine industry. The average selling price of a hectolitre of wine, which in 1927 reached 168 francs, fell to 108 francs in 1931 and 54 francs in 1934. The crisis also affected the olive oil industry, especially the Tunisian one. The quantity of oil exported from Tunisia fell from 409 800 quintals in 1930 to under 200 000 in 1936. The third agricultural venture, essential both to *fellahin* and settlers, which was affected was cereal-growing. Here a drop in prices went hand in hand with a fall in exports; the value of European exports of Tunisian wheat, 291 408 000 francs in 1931, fell to 60 845 000 francs in 1934.

The mining industry also suffered. Shipments of Moroccan phosphate fell from 1 779 000 tonnes in 1930 to 900 731 tonnes in 1931; and Tunisian shipments from 3 600 000 tonnes to 1 623 000 tonnes in 1932. The crisis led to the closure of a great many mines, especially those that were marginal or split up.

Effects of the crisis

It is not surprising, in these circumstances, that in the three North African countries the overall value of external trade fell steadily between 1931 and 1936. The value of Tunisian external trade fell in 1936 by nearly 40% compared with 1927–8. In Morocco the total value of external trade fell from 3 780 606 francs in 1929 to 1 750 518 francs in 1935, and that of Algeria from 9 983 000 francs in 1930 to 6 702 000 francs in 1936.

This crisis had extremely serious social effects. The debt-ridden settlers and North African farmers who could not honour their commitments were faced with bankruptcy. A great many of those who were not yet in debt had to take out loans and mortgage their possessions. The small and middling farmers, who did not have access to the banks or agricultural credit institutions, had to turn to moneylenders in the countryside or the towns in order to pay off their debts.

The crisis considerably sharpened social divisions by enabling financiers (often also moneylenders), big businessmen and rich owners of blocks of plots in the town and the country greatly to increase their wealth. Property and farming became increasingly concentrated in the hands of a minority of big property owners from the country (and often too from the towns). With the farming crisis and natural calamities, drought and famine became commonplace in several parts of North Africa, particularly in the steppe areas.

Other consequences were the intensification of the flight from the countryside of a considerable number of *fellāhīn*, ruined, starving or pursued by tax collectors, to the towns, and the establishment or growth of shanty-towns on the outskirts of these towns. Finally, the economic depression led to the stoppage of building work and the closure of mines and workshops, and so brought about massive unemployment among townspeople, craftsmen and workers in all occupations.

A crisis of such proportions could not leave the authorities unconcerned. The main measures taken by the colonial authorities and the government in France had to do with the agricultural sector. The steps taken to help the wine industry included increasing the quotas of wine admitted duty-free into the metropolitan country and the banning of extension of new vineyards throughout North Africa. To assist cereal-growing, stocks of hard wheat and soft wheat were built up and a minimum price for them was fixed, the scale of stockpiled cereals was staggered and loans were granted.

The distress in the rural communities, and the resultant nationalist unrest, led the French authorities to investigate the lot of the North African *fellāhīn*. From 1933 to 1935 a peasant policy was introduced in the three countries of North Africa. In Algeria an Act of 9 July 1933 established a Fonds Commun des Sociétés Indigènes de Prévoyance (Pool of Native Provident Societies), which enabled the administration to give loans and grants to Muslims alone through the Sociétés Indigènes de Prévoyance. The Pool also helped to get the *fellāhīn* out of debt by giving them consolidation loans. A 'social economy' department in the Directorate of Native Affairs instituted certain measures to modernize the *fellāhīn*'s production techniques; it gave long-term loans for tree-planting, and made advances for the purchase of fertilizers, ploughs, etc. But all these measures, useful though they were, were far from adequate.

In Tunisia and Morocco the state also set out to inject credit into the countryside, settle land-tenure problems and diversify the *fellāhīn*'s agricultural production systems.

Finally, to end the predominant system of monoculture (especially among European farmers), whose dangers were clearly shown by the crisis, the government promoted crop diversification by encouraging the extension of orchard farming and market gardening and developing irrigation through the building of dams.

Enormous orchards of orange, clementine and lemon trees were planted in the

Mitidja in Algeria, on Cape Bon in Tunisia and in the Casablanca, Khenifra, Meknès, Wudja, etc. areas in Morocco. Semi-governmental bodies such as the Office Tunisien de Standardisation were set up to organize the packing, sale and export of the fruit.

Nevertheless the economy of North Africa remained essentially agricultural. There were only a few processing industries using as raw material local agricultural produce, such as flour-mills, oil mills and distilleries. Firms, mostly small, were almost entirely in the hands of Europeans, and the number of workers in industry was not large: 40 000 for the whole of Algeria in 1938. Despite the highly under-industrialized state of the country, the towns of North Africa were growing very rapidly because they drew the poor countryfolk into them. Casablanca, which had only 20 000 inhabitants in 1900, had 257 400 in 1936.

On the eve of the Second World War the economy of North Africa was thus a typical colonial economy. The sectors of the economy in which North Africans predominated suffered from arrested development because of lack of finance, the survival of archaic practices, small land holdings and the fact that they had been driven back to the marginal land. North Africans were in fact excluded from the modern sectors of the economy (banking, mining, processing industries and development project planning). But these sectors themselves, dominated as they were by foreign capital, were closely dependent on outside decision-making centres and markets, over which the North Africans had no control.

Libya, Egypt and the Sudan (see 17.2)

Libya

During the colonial period, the economy of Libya evolved around two main activities, namely agriculture (including animal husbandry) and trade. Agriculture was carried out in the rural areas while trade was conducted in the cities. These two activities were the main occupation and source of income for most of the population. No attempt was made by the Turkish rulers to change this situation. The Italians, however, tried to introduce some drastic changes in the economy. The first part of this section deals with the late years of the Ottoman rule, while the second part describes the economy under the Italian occupation.

The economy was stagnant during the period of the Ottoman administration (1880–1911) and economic activities were confined to agriculture, trade and small handicrafts. Agriculture remained traditional during the Ottoman rule. Animal-drawn wooden ploughs were used to till the soil. The main crops were wheat and barley. Other crops were dates, olive oil, citrus fruit and livestock. Agricultural production depended to a large extent on rainfall, which varied from season to season. Huge numbers of livestock were raised in the plains of Cyrenaica and Tripoli.

In the field of trade, due to the lack of paved roads and the absence of modern means of transportation, caravans were used not only to carry merchandise between local cities, but also between the main cities in Tripoli and other neighbouring countries as well as to Borno and Hausaland.

The caravan trade carried glassware, dresses, silk, spices and paper to Borno and

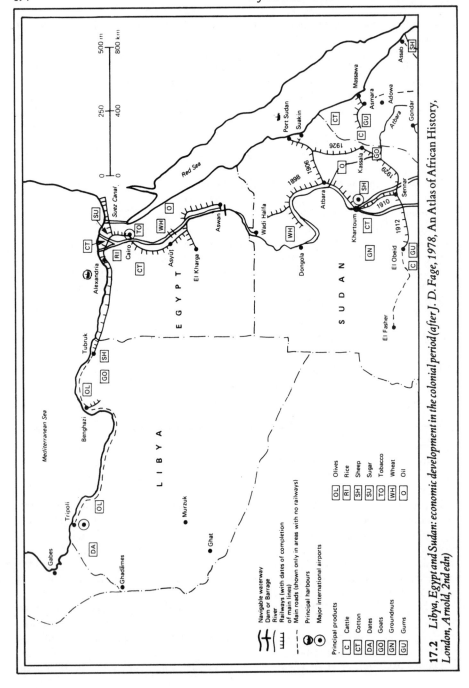

17.2 Libya, Egypt and Sudan: economic development in the colonial period (after J. D. Fage, 1978, An Atlas of African History, London, Arnold, 2nd edn)

Wadai and brought back other commodities such as leather, ivory and ostrich feathers. But, from the end of the nineteenth century, the caravan trade started to decline. The colonization of other African countries brought about new and cheaper routes. Modern and more efficient methods of transportation replaced the old ones. Consequently, the importance of the caravan trade slowly diminished. On the other hand, Tripoli and Benghazi, the main ports, did a brisk business with Europe and other neighbouring countries. The exports to these countries included cattle, sheep, wool, camel hair, dates, barley, wheat and esparto grass. Imports included cotton and silk textiles, glass, firearms, rice, sugar, tea and coffee.

Industry was carried out on a small scale and was confined to a few handicrafts. These small industries included textiles, mat-making, tanning, soap and some gold and silver works.

Although the second Ottoman reign in Tripoli lasted for more than seventy years, little effort was made to develop the Libyan economy. There was no conscious policy to improve the economic infrastructure such as roads, ports and the education system. Few technical schools were operating in the country at the time.

All that the Turkish administration seemed to care about was to collect taxes. The tax system which was implemented in Tripoli during the Ottoman rule included a head tax on male adults, a tithe on agricultural products and an income tax. Other taxes were real-estate tax, inheritance tax, a tax for exemption from military services which was levied on non-Muslim male adults, a tax on stamping gold and silver, and customs duties which were imposed on exported and imported goods. Furthermore, the government gained sizeable revenues from monopolizing salt and tobacco. These taxes added to the burden of the economy and contributed to its sluggish growth. They also precipitated several revolts, which caused political instability and weakened Turkish control of the country.

Economic policy during the period of Italian occupation
When Italy invaded Libya in 1911, she had a dream of making her new colony a source of raw materials for Italian industry, a market for Italian products and a means of solving Italy's population problem. The Italian intention was to make Libya an integral part of Italy and every effort was geared towards accomplishing this aim. The Italians invested heavily in agriculture, industry and infrastructure.

Agricultural settlements and industry
The Italian agricultural programme in Libya passed through two distinct stages, namely private settlement and colonial settlement. To encourage colonial settlement of Libya in the early stages of the Italian occupation, the Italian government granted large estates to wealthy Italians in order to develop them for agricultural purposes. These were either government lands or lands which were seized from their original owners. By 1929, about 58 087 ha of land had been acquired. The estates were leased to Italian farmers for ninety years and they were expected to settle more Italian farmers on their estates with the assistance of government subsidies and loans. However, only about 2031 families were settled according to this plan, which was far below the Italian expectations.

Shortly after the suppression of the national resistance, which was not accomplished until 1932 (for details see Chapter 5 above), the Italian government set out to implement an ambitious development scheme with the goal of resettling about 300 000 Italians in a period of twenty-five years. The scheme, which was entrusted to private and semi-public institutions, included clearing land, providing a water supply, erecting farm buildings and related facilities and providing stock and equipment for the settlers. Up to 1936 the settlement project had cost about £800 million and only 85 000 Italians had been resettled.

The Italians did not establish major industries in Libya. However, they developed some of the small industries which already existed before the Italian invasion. A small tuna-processing plant was established in Tripoli, and the capacity of the olive oil-processing plant was increased to 2200 tonnes annually. During the period under study, there were about 789 factories, producing salt, shoes, tobacco, building materials, asphalt, gunpowder, fats and soap, etc., most of them in Tripoli. The local handicrafts industry continued to exist during the Italian occupation because of its character and the smallness of the market.

Developing the infrastructure
Prior to the Italian occupation the infrastructure of Libya was grossly underdeveloped and the Italian government therefore had to invest massively in it. It built roads, railways, ports, a modern communication system, irrigation works and public buildings. The investment expenditure in these areas amounted to 870 million lire for the period between 1913 and 1936. The purpose of such massive investment in the infrastructure was to develop the economy for the benefit of Italy.

This huge investment, however, was not without its cost to the Libyans. The Libyan population had been reduced by the war. Many people died fighting the Italian occupation. Others perished in concentration camps. Moreover, large groups migrated to neighbouring countries. Those who survived the concentration camps were herded, in semi-slave conditions, to build the coastal road and the new agricultural development projects. The Italian aim was to drive out the local population to the marginal land in the interior and to resettle the surplus Italian population in the most fertile lands of Libya.

The Italians also reduced the number of livestock in Libya. For years the Libyan population in the interior had been dependent on sheep and camels for food, as a source of raw materials and as a means of transportation. Huge numbers of livestock were either killed or confiscated by the Italians. What remained of these animals was further reduced by starvation when they were moved from the pastoral land to inhospitable areas near the concentration camps. Thus the number of sheep fell from 810 000 in 1926 to 98 000 in 1933, that of goats from 70 000 to 25 000, and that of camels from 75 000 to 2000. Though the Italians tried to encourage animal husbandry after 1932, it took years before the animal wealth could be restored to its original level.

Finally, to make things worse, the Italians did not train the Libyans in administration nor did they provide them with adequate education. As K. Folayan has pointed out, 'while the Italians (about 10% of the total population) had in 1939–40 eighty-one elementary schools for their children, the Libyans, who constituted more than 85% of that population were given only ninety-seven schools'. There were also seven secondary schools for the Italians and only three for the Libyans. Even in the police and military services, no Libyan national could be promoted beyond the rank of sergeant. The lack of trained personnel impeded economic development in Libya for many years to come.

Egypt

During the period under consideration, the economy of Egypt was characterized by two main trends. The first was towards concentration on agriculture, especially cotton, for export. The second was towards industrialization. Several structural changes were made in the light of these trends.

The period witnessed an impressive infrastructural development of the country. This was, however, concentrated on activities related to cotton and its export. Major irrigation projects were undertaken. The Aswān dam, the largest in the world at that time, was completed in 1902 and made higher in 1907–10. Thus the cultivated area rose from 4.76 million *feddāns* in 1881 to 5.66 million in 1911. The bulk of the increase was used up by cotton, not only because it was more profitable than other crops but also because of British encouragement since cotton was both a cash crop which enabled Egypt to pay her debts and a much-needed raw material for Lancashire.

The need to move the cotton crop required an expansion of the transportation and the communication network, on which most effort was consequently concentrated (see 17.2). Railways connecting all major cities of the Delta and from Cairo to Upper Egypt were completed. The first railway was opened in 1853 and by 1877 there were 1519 km of standard-gauge railways. These railways were more than doubled during the British occupation, reaching 3200 km in 1909. In addition there were 1600 km of light railways. Harbour facilities at Alexandria were modernized and repeatedly enlarged, and new ports at Suez and Port Said were built on the Suez Canal, which was opened for navigation in 1869. Such developments greatly facilitated the transformation of the agricultural sector from subsistence farming to the cultivation of cash crops on a large scale for export to international markets.

The import-substitution phase
There is no doubt that the British administration carried out many reforms that benefited the Egyptian economy. The major achievements were in the financial field, irrigation works, and in efficient administration. However, it is equally true that the British administration did not promote industrialization until the late 1920s, when several important changes were introduced marking the beginning of a new era when attention was directed towards industry.

After the country had achieved fiscal autonomy with the expiry of the Anglo-Turkish Treaty of 1838 in February 1930, the government imposed tariffs of 15 to 20% on a wide range of consumer goods likely to compete with domestic products. The following decades saw tariff protection extended to all competing foreign goods. Several indices showed the growth of industry. The first was the rise in industrial employment. In 1937, about 155 000 persons worked in manufacturing establishments employing ten persons or more as compared with 30 000 in 1916. Another index was the increase in industrial output. For example, sugar production increased from 79 000 tonnes in 1917 to 159 000 tonnes in 1939; cement output rose from 24 000 tonnes to 353 000 tonnes over the same period; and the production of mechanically woven cotton cloth increased from 7.2 million sq m in 1917 to 132.6 million sq m in 1939.

Another important development was the emergence of national enterprises during the 1920s. The first purely Egyptian-owned and-managed bank, Bank Misr, was founded in 1920. It pioneered the development of large-scale manufacturing firms. The bank managed to attract private capital away from the traditional investment channels; by 1940 the Misr group included twenty-one affiliated companies. It was estimated that the share of Bank Misr industrial companies amounted to 45% of the increase in the total paid-up capital of all joint-stock industrial companies during the 1922–38 period. Thus, Bank Misr gave a big push to the industrial development of Egypt during the inter-war period. Investment during the period showed increasing participation of local capital.

In conclusion, the period under consideration witnessed several attempts at achieving economic development. After the failure of Muhammad 'Alī's plan to carry on a forced programme of industrialization without having adequate infrastructure, the economy was led to specialization in one crop for export. This trend was reinforced under the British occupation, which encouraged the expansion of cultivable land and cotton exports. The result was an export-oriented economy. On the other hand, the first three decades on the twentieth century were characterized by a greater emphasis on industrialization.

The Sudan

During the period under review, the Sudan witnessed two administrations, the Mahdist government from 1881 to 1898 and the Anglo-Egyptian administration from 1898, and each of these administrations pursued its own economic policies.

The Mahdist state set up its own type of administration as well as a judicial system. One of the outstanding achievements of the Mahdist administration was the establishment of a simple and practical tax system which was based on Islamic teachings. *Zakāt* comprised the bulk of the revenue. It was levied at the rate of 2.5% on money and at the rate of 10% on livestock and grain. Owing to the simplicity of this tax system and its adaptibility to social conditions, it continued even after the fall of the Mahdist regime. The Mahdist administration encouraged both agriculture and trade because these activities were geared to support the army and equip it with arms and ammunition.

The main contribution of the British administration in the Sudan during the colonial period was the development of the infrastructure and the introduction of a modern agricultural system. Railways, ports and dams were built (see 17.2). The first railway was constructed during the period from 1896 to 1898 to be used for the military campaign. It was later extended to Atbara and was used for transportation between the northern part of the Sudan and the Mediterranean via Egypt. When Port Sudan was built in 1906, a new railway was constructed to connect it with Atbara. Then in 1910 the main line was extended to Sennār. Another line was laid in 1924 between the Djazīra and the Red Sea. Steamboat services were also used to link the south with the north of the country. These modern and efficient means of transportation helped to convey agricultural products and considerably reduced transportation costs. Furthermore, measures were taken to improve the utilization of soil and water resources. A few pumping stations were built and several canals were dug for irrigation purposes.

From the beginning, the British realized the great agricultural potential of the Sudan. They started the experimental cultivation of cotton so that they could supplement the Egyptian production of this crop. When the first experiment in Zaydab in 1905 showed promising results, it was extended to the Djazira plain between the Blue Nile and the White Nile, which contained the most fertile soil in the Sudan. An ambitious plan was drawn up for the Djazira plain which envisaged the irrigation of about 200 000 ha on which cotton, millet and fodder were to be cultivated. This was not successfully implemented, however until the 1920s. The success of the Djazira scheme stimulated the development of other related activities such as transportation, irrigation and ginning factories for cotton.

To finance these schemes, the existing tax system was supplemented by an agreement between Britain and Egypt by which the latter would provide the Sudan with financial aid and loans for development projects and budget purposes. The Egyptian contribution to the Sudanese budget amounted to £E 2.8 million for the period from 1899 to 1916, while the Egyptian loans to the Sudan totalled about £E 5.4 million for the period from 1900 to 1910.

To stimulate land use, a quarter of the cultivable land was taxed after two years. Then, the whole land would be taxed after eight to ten years. Other taxes included a herd tax which was levied on an ethnic group as a whole. A poll tax of between 25 piastres and 80 piastres per head was collected. In 1912 property tax was introduced.

The impact of British colonial economic activities on the Sudan
Compared with those of the French and the Italians in the Maghrib and Tripoli respectively, British colonial economic activities in the Sudan were laudable to some extent. Land was not appropriated by foreigners nor was it concentrated in the hands of a few people as was the case in the other colonies. The Djazira scheme also proved quite beneficial both to the British and to those people of the Sudan who were directly involved in it. The development of a modern transport system together with the construction of ports and irrigation facilities also helped the growth of a modern agricultural system in the Sudan. However, there is a negative side to this story. First, the infrastructure that was provided was totally inadequate and was clearly meant to promote the interests of Britain more than those of the Sudanese. It is most significant that not one single mile of motor road was constructed in the whole of the Sudan in the period under review while the railway was built initially to facilitate British military campaigns and later to promote their cotton and gum projects in Djazira and the western areas respectively. As in most of the colonies, industrialization was completely neglected. However, the greatest indictment against British colonialism in the Sudan is its total neglect of Southern Sudan economically and socially. This neglect is undoubtedly one of the most important contributory factors to the creation of the southern problem in the Sudan, a problem which has still not been solved.

18

The social repercussions of colonial rule: demographic aspects

The imposition of colonialism on Africa not only affected the political structures and economy of the continent but also had far-reaching social repercussions, which form the subject of this and the next three chapters. In this chapter, we intend to look at one of the themes often neglected by historians of colonialism in Africa, namely, its demographic impact or its impact on the population of Africa. From the available evidence, it seems clear that two main changes occurred in the demographic situation in Africa. These were the rate of population growth and its spatial distribution.

Population growth

From the point of view of population growth, it seems clear that while the period from 1880 to about the end of the First World War witnessed a drastic reduction of the rate of growth and therefore a decline in population in many parts of Africa, the period after that saw an increase in population. It is true that, from recent calculations, there was an overall increase in population from 120 million in 1880 to 129 million in 1900 and 142 million by 1920. However, apart from some parts of North and Southern Africa and possibly the Gold Coast, which witnessed an increase in the growth rate, most other parts of Africa, and especially the whole of Middle Africa, witnessed a sharp decline in growth rate. Indeed, in spite of the increase in numbers between 1880 and 1920, the rate of population growth declined to as low as about 0.25% by about 1900 and rose to an average of only 0.5% by 1920.

The reasons for this reduction of the rate of growth between 1880 and 1900 and its very sluggish rise between 1900 and 1920 are not difficult to come by. The first of these was the heavy loss of life arising not from the original extension of colonial administration, as some authorities think, but rather from the suppression of subsequent revolts and of the ensuing punitive expeditions, which apparently often inflicted most damage because of the starvation resulting from the upsetting of the subsistence farming cycle. Examples include the thousands killed in Senegal in 1886 when opposing the building of the railway and in the Ndebele War in Southern Rhodesia in 1893, the long-drawn-out suppression of the Batetela Rebellion in the Congo Free State from 1895 to 1907, and a series of episodes in German South West Africa (now Namibia) between 1901 and 1906. Greater disasters racked Tanganyika, (now Tanzania), where the Germans adopted a 'scorched earth' policy in the 1905–6 Maji Maji rebellion, resulting perhaps in hundreds of thousands of deaths, largely from starvation, and where fighting between British and German forces throughout the First World War undoubtedly raised mortality levels again.

The second crucial reason centres on the so-called 'labour question' and on the concessionaire schemes of Middle Africa. In the late nineteenth century it was the central belief of colonizers that colonies should be profitable. Whether this could be achieved or not depended entirely on African labour. Profits depended on moving goods and this meant human porterage in most of tropical Africa, for the tsetse fly often prevented the use of draught animals and the lack of roads or railways prevented powered and wheeled vehicles from being used. In Middle Africa the most profitable produce was at first ivory, which entailed huge quantities of labour for carrying tusks. With the development of the pneumatic bicycle tyre in the late 1880s and the pneumatic car tyre in the 1890s a huge demand for rubber was created, which could not be met for a generation by plantation rubber (the first Malayan plantation came into production in 1910). In the mean time, tropical Africa and South America met the demand from wild rubber, and this needed great quantities of labour for its collection and initial processing.

The difficulty was that subsistence farmers had few needs and often felt that regular employment savoured of slavery and that these tasks were women's work. Europeans, frustrated by seeing large profits slipping away from them, resorted to primitive and often brutal solutions. For government purposes forced labour was used, with the chiefs designating those who were to work. Individual and hut taxes were imposed, with, in some areas and more frequently in the earlier years of the system, the possibility of commuting payment to labour. In addition Africans were recruited and conscripted into armies and police forces. Everywhere there was movement of labour, mainly to concentrate it in places where it was needed.

Much of this labour movement in the third of a century after 1880 was accompanied by appallingly high mortality. The labourers were often shifted to areas which exposed them to diseases new to them as well as those recently introduced into Africa, such as typhoid fever. In addition, Africans apparently immune to malaria in their home areas developed not only virulent malaria in distant areas but even blackwater fever. Certainly the conditions of the work camps encouraged the spread of venereal disease and diarrhoea. The workers, carrying within themselves the great load of worms and agents of diseases commonly found in tropical Africa, worked more strenuously at times than they had learnt was possible for them, and came down with sickness. Many of the labourers were weakened by hunger, partly because they were offered diets astonishingly different from their usual ones, but partly because porters and others were underfed, apparently because Europeans either did not care or, in some unanalysed way, believed Africans lived off the land.

Little is known of the nineteenth-century death rates, but in 1915 the British Consul on São Tomé and Principe claimed a death rate of 100 per thousand among the indentured labourers there, while a similar rate has been calculated for forced labour on the railway from Brazzaville to the sea in 1922. The latter rate was exceeded by that of 150 per thousand for the pre-First World War Cameroon railway. The Mosi made a proverb out of the situation, saying 'White Man's work eats people'.

Death rates were still enormous in the mines of Southern Africa in the early years of the present century; a 1907 commission reporting on the situation in Transvaal drew attention to death rates in the mines at the time of 71 per thousand for tropical Africans compared with 28 for Africans from the temperate south and 19 for whites, the rates having declined from 130, 35 and 20 respectively two years earlier. Similarly bad conditions prevailed on plantations, as is evidenced by the loss in 1902 of one-fifth of the work force a year in Cameroon. The worst situation developed in Middle Africa, in the Congo Free State (later Belgian Congo and then Zaire), French Congo (later French Equatorial Africa) and German Cameroon, in almost exactly the area of the low fertility belt.

Undoubtedly disease and famine followed the break-up of the village organization of labour and the flight of whole villages. No one kept adequate population records but enormous declines in population were widely agreed upon. Probably the evidence for such declines was based upon exaggerated estimates of pre-partition populations, and from the evidence of vanished populations along the tracks and riverbanks from which the people had fled. But it is difficult to avoid the conclusion that population probably did decline in the Middle Africa region between 1890 and 1910 or even later.

After the First World War, however, the colonial demographic impact was the very reverse of what it was before, as it led to a great increase in population. From recent calculations the overall population rose from 142 million in 1920 to 165 million in 1935. This great increase was partly due to the establishment of an economic base, which is evidenced by many developments discussed in several of the chapters above. Some of the more spectacular of them were the development of palm-oil exports from the Niger delta, the discovery of diamonds and then gold in Southern Africa in the years from 1870 to 1900, the development of an indigenous cocoa-growing industry in the Gold Coast in the 1890s and the discovery of huge deposits of copper between the Congo and Northern Rhodesia (now Zambia) in the early years of the century.

However, a development which probably contributed more to the increase in population was the spread of roads and railways. By the end of the 1920s most of the railway system had been built and roads were improving; by the late 1930s lorries in limited numbers were reaching almost every part of the continent. This system made it possible for food to be sent by governments or traders to famine areas. The very existence of a transport network together with a currency acceptable over great distances encouraged the production of a surplus of food for the market. From about 1920 famine deaths, relative to the size of the rainfall deficit, fell consistently, and the great mortality peaks, which kept up the average level of mortality, began to be under major attack. Until that time, even countries like Uganda could experience over a hundred thousand famine deaths in a single year, as it apparently did in 1918–19.

Missionaries probably had a small but real impact on mortality, quite apart from the setting up of hospitals. One authority argues that 'their pupils imbibed . . . at least some sense of mastery over the new conditions of life created by the colonial system'.

Finally, what effect did western medicine have on Africa? Africans were subject to many diseases. These included malaria, syphilis, yaws, leprosy, spirillum fever, dysentery and worms, to which must be added such epidemic diseases as yellow fever, small pox and sleeping sickness and the new imports of tuberculosis and cholera. But Europe was not medically well equipped for its African ventures. At the beginning of the nineteenth century Britain's expectation of life at birth was less than 40 years; while, by the end, those of Britain, France and Germany had reached about 47 years with death rates close to 20 per thousand and infant mortality rates near to 200. Furthermore, the medical revolution was late in turning its attention to tropical disease. Although smallpox vaccination had been known since the eighteenth century (largely because the disease was not a specifically tropical one), even the methods of transmission of elephantiasis, malaria and yellow fever were established only in 1877, 1897 and 1900 respectively. Apart from quinine, and a limited use of arsenical compounds against syphilis and yaws, the development of drugs and vaccines to combat tropical diseases really dates only from the 1920s. Nevertheless, schools of tropical medicine were established in Europe as early as 1897 in Liverpool and London, 1900 in Hamburg, 1901 in Brussels, followed later by Paris, Bordeaux and Marseilles, and in Africa by 1912 in Cape Town and 1918 in Dakar.

In tropical Africa governmental medicine was long a military concern although small civilian hospitals began to appear in the 1890s. From 1840, when the first mission doctor arrived in Sierra Leone, there were across West Africa a scattering of medical missionaries including some Africans (mostly Sierra Leoneans). These services were concentrated very largely on saving the soldiers, administrators and missionaries, although some care was also extended to African troops, government workers and mission personnel. Real success was achieved only at the beginning of the present century, as is shown by the crude death rates for European officials in the Gold Coast which fell from a level of 76 per thousand in the last two decades of the nineteenth century to 31, 22 and 13 respectively in 1902, 1903 and 1904. Even taking age composition into account, this compared favourably with levels in Britain from about 1912. The explanation was held to be sanitary measures against malaria and yellow fever, improved methods of treating tropical diseases, and segregated living quarters. The sanitary measures must have had some impact on the relatively small number of Africans living in the chief administrative centres, especially in Lagos after the measures taken in the first years of the present century by Governor William McGregor and Dr Ronald Ross (who had identified the mechanism of malaria spread).

The use of European methods to improve African health was relatively insignificant, partly because Europe offered more temptations after the First World War and partly because colonial powers cut back on health expenditures with the onset of the depression of the 1930s. In 1924 Nigeria had a theoretical medical establishment of one doctor for every 200 000 persons, but in fact only a quarter of these posts were filled. Indeed, by 1939 there was a lower ratio of doctors to population in the country than there had been in 1914. Even these figures exaggerate the chance of an African receiving health care, for in the 1930s twelve hospitals met the needs of 4000 Europeans, while fifty-two hospitals catered for 40 million Africans.

In the absence of many doctors, extensive treatment services really depended on whether rural clinics could be established providing adequate care with the services of medical auxiliaries and whether local self-help projects could be organized. In Nigeria, a dispensary was opened in Ibadan in 1904 and others followed in Yoruba towns in succeeding years. By 1910 the Sierra Leonean government was awarding prizes to the chiefs of the two villages in each district which had shown the greatest improvement in sanitation. By 1934 Uganda had hospitals in all major centres and eighty-eight sub-dispensaries in rural areas which recorded 1 378 545 attendances during the year. One should not exaggerate the significance of these changes: in many dispensaries drugs were few and attendants uncertain about what to do, as has remained the position in much of rural Africa until the time of writing. André Gide, visiting health facilities at Bétou on the Oubangui river in the late 1920s, commented scathingly that the only supplies received to combat the diseases of Middle Africa were iodine, boracic acid and Glauber's salts.

The major reduction in African mortality (certainly in the period covered by this chapter) was probably achieved by attacking the periodic peaks in mortality caused by famine and epidemic disease. With gathering momentum from the early years of the century, the campaigns against epidemic disease apparently gained some success. The British attacked sleeping sickness by keeping the tsetse fly away from people, preventing game from using waterholes in inhabited areas, clearing bush, and, more spectacularly, moving populations, as they did from the foreshores of Lake Victoria. The French treated huge numbers of individual cases, especially noteworthy being the work of Dr E. Jamot using the arsenical compound, atoxyl. One area of 124 000 people in the Cameroon which was treated in this way was recorded in 1924 as having a crude death rate of 81 per thousand of which 36 points could be attributed to sleeping sickness; by 1930 the epidemic there was being beaten. In Uganda, where sleeping sickness was first identified in 1901, it was held to have caused over 200 000 deaths by 1906 when the large population transfers began; but by 1918 there was sufficient confidence that the disease was being contained to allow some people to move back to their old areas.

Outbreaks of bubonic plague were far from rare in the first third of the present century: in the first decade Egypt reported 6000 cases of whom half died; almost 60 000 deaths had been recorded in Uganda up to 1932; and there were outbreaks in Accra in 1908, Lagos in 1924 and more generally in Yoruba areas of Nigeria in 1925. Control measures in British West Africa indicated that the disease could be contained; during the Accra outbreak the town had been sealed off and 35 000 doses of Haffkine's vaccine were administered.

Yellow fever epidemics have occurred from Senegal to Sudan at unpredictable intervals. By 1927 a vaccine had been developed in the Rockefeller laboratories in Yaba on the outskirts of Lagos, but, as it was not used on a large scale until the Second World War, any success against the disease up until 1935 was due to the suppression of mosquitoes in urban areas and the use of mosquito netting. It is doubtful whether leprosy declined in this period; alepol oil was used in Nigeria from the early 1920s but by 1938 it was estimated that 1% of the population still had the disease. Smallpox vaccination was on such a small scale that by the late 1930s a significant reduction of the disease had probably taken place only in the Gold Coast and southern Nigeria. In most of the continent little progress had been made against the greatest scourge of all, malaria, which weakened when it did not kill and explained many deaths attributed to other causes.

Demographic movements up to 1935

However, there was not only an overall increase in African population between 1880 and 1935 but also population redistribution and urbanization. These fifty-five years witnessed a flow of population that was to do much to determine the nature of the new Africa. An addition of 45 million meant that everyone could not be fitted into exactly the same space as was occupied by their ancestors and the movement of people to unoccupied land speeded up. More significantly, from the 1890s in West Africa – earlier in South Africa and somewhat later in East Africa – labour migrants began to move great distances looking for paid employment. At first they were impelled by the need to pay taxes, but later the desire to purchase goods and to go to distant places became stronger; at first they were nearly all seasonal migrants but longer-term migration steadily assumed significance. By the late 1920s, almost 200 000 migrants a year were pouring from the savanna into the Gold Coast and Nigeria. Governments put few restrictions on who moved, except in South Africa and Southern and Northern Rhodesia where the movement was restricted to temporary, adult males because of fears of settlement and pressures from white trade unions.

Ultimately, a larger proportion of these migration streams flowed not to the plantations and mines but into the towns, thus eventually ensuring centres in most regions large enough to support national administrations and secondary industries. Africa had, of course, ancient cities in the lower Nile valley, and more recent ones in the Maghrib savannah, West Africa, Nigeria's Yorubaland and the central Gold Coast. Nevertheless, by 1880 only about one person in three hundred lived in centres with populations of over 100 000, compared with perhaps one in fifty in Asia and one in fifteen in Europe.

The real change occurred in our period, especially in sub-Saharan Africa. In tropical Africa, if we exclude Nigeria, and list sixteen towns which were to be of major significance in the twentieth century, we can estimate a combined population in 1880 of about 80 000; by 1930 this had multiplied five-fold to over half a million (thus establishing a base for a multiplication of over ten times in the next forty years). By 1931 Dakar had grown to 54 000, Freetown had reached 44 000 (but this was only a doubling of the population of half a century before), Accra 60 000, Addis Ababa 65 000, Nairobi 48 000, and Dar es-Salaam 25 000. In Nigeria the scale was different: Ibadan had a population of 400 000 but probably had 150 000 inhabitants at the beginning of the period; Lagos had perhaps doubled to 126 000.

In the Sahel, the population of the historic cities was undoubtedly declining, partly because they had not become the main French administrative centres; by 1931, Timbuktu, Gao and Mopti had a combined population of only about 15 000. In North Africa, many of the historic towns had retained their importance; in our period Cairo, Alexandria and Algiers had all trebled their populations to over a million, about 600 000 and a quarter of a million respectively; by 1931 fourteen other old towns of the Maghrib had attained a total approaching one and a half million, which represented at least a doubling in half a century, and in Sudan, Khartoum–Omdurman had 159 000 people.

By 1931 the fourteen largest towns of Southern Africa (South Africa, Southern and Northern Rhodesia, Angola and Mozambique) had a total population of well over a million, perhaps a tenfold increase in the previous half century, and Johannesburg was approaching 400 000. In sub-Saharan Africa, people were pouring into the new ports, mining towns and administrative cities, which were doubling in size about every twenty years.

A basis for the future

By 1935, Africa had successfully withstood the demographic shock of European colonization. Its births now far exceeded its deaths, and in many parts of the continent, especially in the growing towns, life was no longer very precarious. Admittedly its death rates were still very high – in the continent as a whole the death rate was probably still well over 30 per thousand and the expectation of life at birth barely more than 30 years – but it was the diseases of tropical Africa, more than any other factor, which had held the invader largely at bay and prevented Africa from becoming another Latin America. Even as it was, the white population of the continent had increased thirty times from 25 000 in 1800, found mostly in the Cape, to three-quarters of a million in 1880, of whom five-sixths were in South Africa, Algeria and Egypt. By 1935 it had multiplied again to 3.75 million, of whom half were in South Africa, a quarter in Algeria and a further fifth in the rest of North Africa. During the same period, Asians (almost entirely Indians except for a few small Chinese communities, of which the largest was on the Rand) increased from about 50 000 to over a third of a million of whom over two-thirds were in South Africa.

In 1935 Africa stood on the brink of a rapid population growth which would take its numbers – which had already grown according to our estimates from 120 million in 1880 to 165 million – to 200 million by the late 1940s, 300 million by the mid-1960s and inevitably to 400 million in the mid-1970s. Of the latter number, 50 million would be in cities with more than 100 000 inhabitants, a far cry from the Africa of the partition of the 1880s with its debate about creating a labour force.

Finally, it is pertinent to ask whether these massive changes were largely or even entirely the result of the colonial penetration. Without doubt the upsetting of stable populations, leading in the Congo Free State and elsewhere in Middle Africa to an upsurge in the death rate, the slow reduction in mortality in other parts of the continent during the nineteenth century and generally in this century, and the accelerating concentration of population in towns and on mining fields owed nearly everything to the industrial revolution and to increasing contact with people from industrial societies. Much of this process would have occurred even without colonial rule: the traders would have provoked trading centres into growth; European medical schools would have become interested in the problem of protecting the traders and others from tropical disease; missionaries would have laid the foundations of a hospital system.

Nevertheless, direct colonial rule certainly speeded up all these processes. Eventually, and certainly towards the end of our period, it helped to reduce the great peaks of mortality by increasingly and effectively importing and utilizing epidemic control technology and creating a modern transport system which could distribute food in areas of famine. The need for administrative centres provided a nucleus for new towns, and colonial administrations' guarantees of personal safety and investment security to the nationals of their metropolitan countries hastened the growth of commercial settlements, mining camps and plantations. Without colonial administrations European entrepreneurs might have been even more rapacious and murderous than they were. Europeans usually justified the colonial penetration by pointing to these achievements. Yet the history of Latin America and China shows that in time most of these gains would have been achieved in any case; the growth of industrialization was irreversible and a *modus vivendi* with Africa and other developing areas, from which needed raw materials were secured, was essential.

The social repercussions of colonial rule: the new social structures

In the previous chapter, it was seen that, mainly as a result of the colonial impact, the population of Africa not only increased numerically but also became redistributed, giving rise to the rapid development of existing urban centres and the rise of completely new ones. At the same time, African societies underwent other social changes.

The new social structures

The first of these social changes that occurred, and one that was a direct result of the establishment of colonialism, was the superimposition on the pre-existing class structure of the continent of at least an extra layer of alien leaders and pacesetters. On top of the old political and religious elite was now placed a new class of European bureaucrats and businessmen. In East Africa, where it encouraged Asian immigration, colonialism in fact superimposed two classes. In each colony Europeans had the monopoly of political, economic and educational power, except in East Africa where a fraction of the economic power fell into the hands of Asians. In this situation the Africans became the underprivileged and looked up to the Europeans, and at times to the Asians, for leadership and example.

This structure of social relationship was backed by a bogus racial theory which sought to arrange the different branches of the human family in a hierarchical order of civilization with the Africans (the Negroes) occupying the bottom of the ladder while the Europeans (whites) occupied the top. In Southern Africa, in particular, where white settlers found themselves locked in conflict with numerically superior Bantu peoples, the racial theory was especially stringent.

In practical life the ascendancy of this racist theory led to a policy of denying Africans, no matter how well educated, equal rights and opportunities with the whites in the colonial service. In West Africa this meant a retreat from the liberal policies of the middle years of the nineteenth century which had made it possible for Africans to hold the same posts as the Europeans. The theory also led to a policy of segregating Africans from the Europeans in the urban areas. Not only were there European housing reserves, but there were also European hospitals, European clubs and so on, distinct from those established specifically for the use of Africans. One effect of all this was to induce in the African a feeling of inferiority, a tendency to lose confidence in himself and his future – in short a state of mind which at times encouraged an uncritical imitation of European powers. Luckily, however, some African path-finders were motivated by it all into questioning the whole social and ideological façade of colonialism using facts from history and Christianity. By so doing they helped to prepare the way for post-Second World War radical nationalist thinking.

Besides introducing a new class of leaders, colonialism also altered the existing class structure in Africa, leading to the emergence of a new urban proletariat and a new elite. Though pre-colonial Africa provided many avenues for people of ability to rise in social status through personal achievement, its class structure tended to give undue weight to birth. This was so to the extent that not only political offices but also certain honoured professions like priesthood and smithing ran in families. Foreign rule brought about far-reaching changes in African social structure by simply laying emphasis on individual talent and achievement rather than birth, and by providing many openings for advancement which lay beyond the control of the traditional manipulators of African social structure and institutions. Furthermore, its desecration of many African institutions and systems tended to undermine the authority and respect of the old nobility and to erode the awe in which they were held. Colonial legal and moral codes, by abolishing slavery and proclaiming the equality of all before secular and divine law, offered even the most underprivileged in traditional society the opportunity to rise in status, each person according to his ability and destiny.

The new and growing urban centres reinforced the effects of the legal and moral revolution by providing for ex-slaves and their like an arena of action where they could operate unencumbered by history. Similarly, the urban centres, for reasons advanced in the previous chapter, irresistibly attracted other classes of people in the rural areas. Those immigrants who were well educated or highly skilled rose fast to become members of the new elite, or to hover on the fringe of that class as sub-elites. The less fortunate immigrants who had little or no education and who in addition were barely skilled or unskilled, sank to the bottom of the urban society to become the urban mass, also called the urban proletariat by some scholars. Many of these found themselves at the mercy of the employers of labour, while others learned some trade and established independent businesses of varying viability.

Both the new elite and the urban proletariat were important as agents making for change in rural colonial society, but the former were indisputably the more important in the political, economic and social history of colonial Africa. Their greatest advantage over the traditional elite and the urban and rural masses lay in their literacy (see 19.1). The fact was that for the non-Muslim areas of Africa probably the most important single innovation of foreign rule was literacy. To know the amount of power, authority and influence which the first generation of African clerks, interpreters and teachers exercised is to have some idea of the spell which literacy cast over many African peoples. Literacy gave the elite access to the scientific and social thought of the western world, equipped them to enter into dialogue with the colonial powers over the destiny of Africa, and familiarized them with the social fashions of Europe which made their life style an example to be imitated by their less fortunate countrymen (see 19.2).

But not all those classified as belonging to the new elite in colonial Africa owed their membership of that class to education, nor did all those who owed it to education attain

19.2 *Colonial cricket: producing the new elite (Royal Commonwealth Society)*

a uniform standard. As Professor Lucy Mair and a number of other scholars have shown, some gained entry into that class because they had made money from either large-scale farming or business and could help to finance the political agitation of their better educated but poorer brethren. Some cotton and coffee farmers of Uganda, cocoa farmers of western Nigeria and the Gold Coast, coffee farmers of the Côte d'Ivoire and groundnut farmers of Senegal and The Gambia were able to gain membership of the new elite class on grounds of their success in that profession. Similarly, in West Africa especially, where many indifferently educated Africans were able to interpose themselves as middlemen between the primary producers and the big European commercial companies, commercial success also provided a ready passport to the new elite status. On the contrary, in East and Central Africa relatively few Africans gained admission into the elite group as a result of the deliberate policies pursued by the colonial rulers and the activities of the Indians and Portuguese and Greek petty traders.

During the early part of this century, except in Liberia and Sierra Leone where for much of the period the new elites were made up of people who were not indigenous to these territories, the new and old elites built up a tradition of co-operation – the new elite being regarded as those who mediated between their indigenous societies and western culture. In the Gold Coast and in Egbaland (Nigeria) they had worked closely with the traditional elite in an effort to build a new society and ward off European rule. But these efforts had failed.

However, as colonial rule took deeper root, strains and stresses appeared in the relationship of the two groups. The new elites had wrongly hoped that Europe was out to modernize Africa and would use members of their group as the instruments for achieving that goal. But under colonial rule it was European bureaucrats who assumed the role which the new elites had cut out for themselves. And, instead of taking the new elites into partnership, the administration tended to prefer the traditional rulers, whom they relegated to the area of local government. This was particularly so in British-ruled Africa, where a determined effort was made to preserve the old ruling families, and to some extent in Belgian-ruled Africa after 1906. Even in the French territories, where most of the great paramountcies were destroyed, the old ruling families at times survived in attenuated forms to be used at the village and district levels.

Because of their exclusion, the new elites went into open opposition against the colonial powers. In this open opposition the traditional rulers could not join them. Their continued survival depended on the colonial power and this tied their hands. Also for the most part the traditional rulers were not sufficiently educated to participate meaningfully in the ongoing debates. In any case if they accepted the arguments of the new elites, they would be consigning themselves to second or even third place. Because they did not side with the new elites, the latter regarded them as the lackeys of imperialism. They in turn regarded the new elites as revolutionaries who wanted to destroy immemorial custom and turn the world upside down.

To make matters worse the two were driven by imperialist propaganda into engaging in a struggle over who spoke for the people. The new elites said they did. This the traditional rulers denied, claiming the honour for themselves. The colonial administration agreed with them. The kind of bitterness which this disagreement at times generated could be seen in the dispute between the king of Akyem-Abuakwa in the Gold Coast, Nana Sir Ofori Atta, and the leaders of the National Congress of British West Africa in the 1920s. It could also be seen in the quarrel between Harry Thuku's Young Kikuyu Association on the one hand, and the Kikuyu Association dominated by the traditional rulers on the other, and in the struggle between Blaise Diagne and the traditional Muslim leaders in Senegal.

Yet one cannot conclude from the foregoing that in the period 1880 to 1935 the normal relationship between the new elites and the traditional rulers was invariably one of conflict. The nature of the relationship varied both in place and time. In the French territories neither the new elites nor the traditional rulers flourished under alien rule. And, when after the Second World War the stranglehold of colonial autocracy came to be progressively relaxed, those who emerged as the leaders of French African nationalism included traditional rulers and their descendants.

In the Gold Coast the leading political party until the ascendancy of Dr Kwame Nkrumah – the United Gold Coast Convention – represented some kind of *rapprochement* between the new and traditional elites. In places like Ethiopia, Egypt and Buganda, where the traditional rulers had responded positively to western influences, no logical conflict developed between them and the new elites. It was the same in societies like that of the Igbo where the traditional elites did not have the kind of stature that survived far into the colonial period. In any case the new elites were not all the 'uprooted natives' of imperialist imaginings, nor were all the traditional rulers the obscurantist opponents of change of latter-day nationalist agitation. Both groups had more in common than was often admitted in the heat of occasional debate.

The rise of new organizations

Apart from giving rise to the new structures discussed above, colonial rule introduced other changes into the structure of African society. Here we have in mind the rise of new organizations which assisted the adjustment of many individuals and their rural homes to the new demands and norms of colonial society. Africanists are agreed on the social conditions which brought these organizations into being. It has been found that they generally originated in the urban centres, although some of them, like the ethnic-based ones, in time established home branches. The fact was that, as Professor Wallerstein has aptly put it, migration from 'the traditional rural to the modern urban area' led to 'dislocation and disorientation for the individual'. Since neither the traditional society nor the colonial administration had the means to step in and meet the new needs of such migrants, they had to evolve their own institutions, systems and norms for achieving meaningful existence in the strange and difficult social world of the town.

The studies of Godfrey Wilson in East Africa have shown that there was a clear link between the pressure of colonial society and the formation of these organizations. Thus Kenyan Africans, whose traditional culture came under unusually severe pressure from colonial rule and settler aggressiveness, had stronger and many more ethnic associations than Africans in neighbouring territories like Tanganyika and Uganda. There was thus an element of individual self-protection and self-stabilization in the formation of the associations. Furthermore, urban conditions of existence created opportunities that made it relatively easy to form such organizations since, as Thomas Hodgkin has put it, it provided 'physical centres . . . where men and women, with particular interests in common, can collide with one another'.

Three main kinds of associations emerged during the period under review. In the first group are those organizations which could be described as purely 'social', that is, devoted to promoting entertainment and relaxation. These were made necessary by the absence in the towns of traditional forms of amusement, relaxation and citizenship training – such as masquerades, age-grade associations and traditional festivities. There was also the attraction of forms of modern European social life as advertised in the life of the European community in each colony. In this category were the football clubs, Scout and Girl Guide movements, debating societies and old boys' associations.

In the second group are the ethnic unions. These were an extension of rural ethnicity to the urban areas. They existed in a hierarchy of village, clan and ethnic unions. These had two main functions. One was to help the individual who had migrated newly to the town to adjust as smoothly as possible to the conditions of urban life. Through such associations new arrivals obtained accommodation and jobs while members got help when in difficulty. They could get loans to continue their business if they sustained crippling losses. Funeral, marriage and other expenses approved by the association could also be met with loans or donations from the group, as the case might be.

The other function of the ethnic unions was to provide a channel for progressive public opinion at home, by maintaining an organized link between the sons at home and the sons abroad. At first this won the associations the opposition and obstruction of suspicious colonial officials. In south-eastern Nigeria, for instance, their activities became, on occasion, the object of secret intelligence inquiries.

In the third group were the trade unions, which came into being largely for economic bargaining. For the most part, modern urban centres grew up at vital commercial, mining and communication points which had openings for the employment of skilled and unskilled workers. In these towns, therefore, there soon came to be concentrations of people who earned their living mainly by means of salaried or wage employment. There were also the self-employed artisans who supplied certain needs of the urban population.

The life of these urban dwellers was tied to the vagaries of the world economy and market, whose structure and behaviour they did not understand. To protect themselves in this unfamiliar economic world, those in waged or salaried employment formed trade unions for the purpose of effective negotiation with their employers for higher pay and better conditions of work. The self-employed craftsmen also formed craft guilds which helped to fix prices, standards, conditions of apprenticeship and so on. The trade unions and craft guilds also functioned at times as friendly societies, helping members in difficulty with money and advice, and providing fitting funerals, educational facilities, scholarships and occasional feasts.

The years 1880–1935 saw something of the beginnings of these new organizations. Professor Kilson has, in a recent summing up, shown that by 1937 there were all kinds of tradesmen's and workers' organizations in Nigeria, Sierra Leone, Kenya and elsewhere. But his study and others clearly show that the golden age of these organizations did not arrive until after the Second World War.

The reasons for this were many. These associations depended to some extent on the spread of education, and the impact of this, as of urbanism, took time to appear. Outside the coastal areas of West Africa, the Maghrib, Egypt and Kenya, this generally took more than three decades. In South Africa, however, although the conditions should have been ideal owing to an early industrial and communications revolution, the growing harshness of Boer nationalism and the opposition of other whites stifled African initiatives. The rise of these associations also depended to some extent on the development of a capitalist economy, but colonial Africa is said to have had only 'a rudimentary capitalist economy', which depended substantially on migrant workers – a species of labour which is said to be very resistant to trade union organization. And, even after the Second World War, there were very few wage-earners in colonial Africa. In the 1950s their number was estimated at between 4 and 5 million. And finally the autocratic and exploitative colonial regimes either prohibited these unions or refused to give them legal recognition until the late 1930s or early 1940s.

The social effects of foreign rule were far from uniform throughout the continent. With respect to the spread of education, the triumph of the new economic forces, the expansion of urbanization and therefore the rise of the new elites, West Africa would appear to have witnessed the greatest advances, followed by Egypt and the Maghrib, South Africa, East Africa and Central Africa. In terms of colonial blocs rather than geographical regions, greater changes took place in the British territories, followed by those of the Belgians and the French with the Portuguese limping far behind. And, even among the British territories, there was also a differential impact. The British colonies where substantial changes were registered included Egypt, the Gold Coast, Nigeria, Uganda and Sierra Leone, followed by Kenya and the Rhodesias (now Zambia and Zimbabwe). And if we take individual colonies we discover that more changes took place in the southern than in the northern parts of the Gold Coast and Nigeria. In Francophone Africa, on the other hand, the West African colonies would come first, followed by the North African colonies and then French Equatorial Africa. Within French West Africa, Senegal and Dahomey (now Benin) led the way with the other colonies lagging rather far behind.

The reasons for this differential impact of the forces of change on the different regions and countries of Africa are not hard to come by. The first was the question of the length and extent of contact which the particular territory or geographic region had enjoyed with Europe by the time colonial rule was imposed. West and Southern Africa had maintained fairly regular contact with Europe from the sixteenth century. By the beginning of the nineteenth century, therefore, quasi-urban conditions of life had come into existence at several points along the coast – at Saint-Louis, Banjul, Accra, Lagos, the Oil River's ports, Luanda, and the Cape. These provided good stepping-stones for the forces of western education, western Christianity and western commerce to penetrate the interior. The east coast of the continent, on the other hand, came under sustained European contact only from about the 1870s.

The second reason was the illiberal racial policies pursued by the colonial rulers, which placed all kinds of obstacles in the way of free African participation in education and commerce. The extent of the change therefore came to be determined by the kind of educational and economic opportunities made available to the Africans. This surely explains why more changes took place in the colonies of the British, the least illiberal of the colonial powers.

The third factor was the presence of white settlers. There were very few European settlers in West Africa and this to some extent explains the relatively rapid progress of the West Africans in educational and economic matters. But settlers were present in force in Algeria, Kenya, the Rhodesias, South Africa and the Portuguese territories. The interests of these settlers clashed with those of the Africans and they used their influence with the colonial administration to obstruct or stultify African development.

Finally, there was the question of differing African responses to foreign influences. In Nigeria, the Igbo embraced westernism much more enthusiastically than the Fulbe did. In Kenya, the Gikuyu saw the advantages of western education long before their neighbours. Islamic cultural conservatism and resistance, especially in the Western Sudan, tended to hinder the spread of western influence, especially western education. In North Africa and Egypt, on the other hand, sections of the ruling elite sought to ensure the survival of Islamic culture through the introduction of western science and commerce. Their stand led to a fruitful marriage between Islamic culture and western scientific thought. Because the Western Sudanese Muslims failed to show comparable initiative in this matter, they found themselves unprepared to meet the challenges posed by colonial rule. As a result it was possible for the British and the French to determine what types of western influences to admit into the region and in what doses.

By 1935, then, mainly as a result of the colonial impact, Africa had not only witnessed population growth but also some social changes. New social structures, new classes and new organizations had emerged and these provided the foundation for the even more radical and fundamental changes that were to take place in the following three decades.

20

Religion in Africa during the colonial era

Another aspect of social life that was affected by the imposition of colonialism was that of religion. On the eve of the imposition of colonial rule on Africa three religions had become established. These were traditional religion and the two guest religions of Islam and Christianity. It is generally agreed that, while the overwhelming majority of Africans were adherents of the first religion, thanks to the Islamic revolutions and the Christian and Muslim activities of the nineteenth century which have been dealt with in the earlier volumes, both religions had gained considerable followings. Islam was by then predominant in the Sudan belt and North Africa while Christianity was still confined mainly to the coastal peripheries in the regions south of the Sahara, with the exception of South Africa and a few areas of West Africa where it had penetrated some miles inland.

African traditional religion and colonial rule

Of the three religions, there is no doubt that traditional religion came under the heaviest attack and lost far more ground than the other two. The entire European intervention during the colonial period was based on the assumption that, to bring about development, African culture had to be modified if not destroyed altogether. Since African culture was so intricately intertwined with religion, it is easy to see how a European colonial policy could clash violently with some of the tenets and practices in African traditional religion which underpinned African society. These included belief in spirits, supernatural forces, gods and cults, witchcraft, sorcery, sacrifices, rituals, taboos, veneration of ancestors, and ceremonies of rites of passage such as naming ceremonies, initiation rights and customs associated with deaths and burials. It is these same tenets and practices which the Christian missionaries preached against and attacked so vehemently. Thus they weakened the influence of African traditional and spiritual leaders such as priests, priestesses, magicians, rain-makers and divine monarchs.

The colonial administrators thus adopted a hostile attitude towards certain traditional religious practices, abolished some and tried to suppress certain cults and deities. In the Gold Coast (now Ghana), the British colonial administration prohibited the cult of Katawere, the tutelary deity of Akim Kotoku, in 1907. Prior to this the German government had destroyed the shrines of the cult of Denteh of Kete-Krachi in the 1880s and the priest of Denteh was imprisoned and executed by the government. The Krobo people were forced to abandon their settlements on the Krobo mountain by the British colonial administration, which destroyed their settlements and suppressed the cult of their tutelary shrines of Kotoklo and Nadu.

New cults arose to protect people from witchcraft in West Africa, for example the *Aberewa* (Old Woman) cult in the Gold Coast, which was suppressed by the administration in 1908. The most widespread of the witchcraft eradication movements was the Bamucapi cult of south-eastern and Central Africa, which spread widely over Mozambique, Nyasaland (now Malawi), the Rhodesias (now Zimbabwe and Zambia), southern Tanganyika (now Tanzania), and the Belgian Congo (now Zaire).

The colonial administration used other methods to eradicate witchcraft. In Uganda, for example, a Witchcraft Ordinance was passed in 1912; this was revised in 1921 to make the punishment severer by increasing terms of imprisonment from one to five years and also making the possession of witchcraft articles, in which the power of witchcraft is believed to reside, a punishable offence.

Another attack on African traditional religion, especially in East Africa, took the form of measures against initiation rites into adulthood which involved circumcision for both boys and girls.

Africans responded to these attacks in many ways. In the first place, many Africans simply ignored or rejected these attacks and steadfastly clung to their traditional beliefs and practised the essential rites either openly or secretly. Others, on the other hand, responded by using their gods, ancestors and cults to resist both the Christian missionaries and the colonial administrations. In the first two decades of this century, the Igbo warriors of south-eastern Nigeria resorted to such means to defend themselves from alien invaders. The Esza people of Abakaliki, the Uzuakoli and the Aro may be cited as examples. Some cults were clearly a focus for resistance to colonial rule, such as the Mwari in Southern Rhodesia, (now Zimbabwe), or secret associations like the Poro in Sierra Leone and other parts of West Africa. War-charm movements also occurred in Madagascar and the Congo basin. In East Africa, especially Kenya, African prophets arose to provide spiritual support and inspiration to resist colonialism, such as occurred in the Machakos district among the people of Kilungu in the early months of 1922 (see Chapter 22 below). One of the best-known movements which used both religion and magic to resist colonial rule and oppression was, as we have seen already, the Maji Maji movement in German East Africa during the first decade of the twentieth century.

Another cult similar to the Maji Maji was the Nyabingi cult, which also covered a wide area, including Ruanda (now Rwanda), north-western Tanganyika (now Tanzania) and Uganda. It began during the late nineteenth century and gathered momentum until it finally broke out in 1928 in revolt against European occupation in the Kigezi region of Uganda. The Germans, and the Belgians who took over Ruanda from them after the First World War, failed to suppress it, and, even after the suppression of the 1928 uprising, the cult lingered on until it was finally wiped out in 1934.

Others chose the method of direct confrontation, and this was particularly true in East Africa over the issue of circumcision. In the diocese of Masasi in southern

Tanganyika and in the Central Province of Kenya, we find examples of the most serious confrontation between Christian missions and African peoples on the matter of circumcision. In the former, a policy of adaptation was pursued, and it resulted in attempts to modify the *jando* (male circumcision) and the *malango* (female circumcision) by performing them under Christian auspices and eliminating whatever elements were thought or judged to be 'un-Christian'. This policy avoided a head-on collision between traditional initiation and Christian missions and practice.

But in Central Kenya no such compromise could be reached and a head-on collision therefore ensued in the early 1920s and 1930s. For example, independent schools were established among the Gikuyu whose aim was to restore the practice and to provide education for those children who could not get admission into mission schools on account of the female circumcision issue. In 1929, a dance song, called *muthirigu*, which ridiculed missions and Christians who were opposed to female initiation, spread quickly among the Gikuyu but was banned by the British colonial administration the following year. Furthermore, African opposition expressed itself in the secession of many members from the Protestant and Anglican Churches among the Gikuyu, Embu and Meru peoples. An independent church, the African Orthodox Church, arose in 1928, while in 1930 a prophetic movement sprang up among the Gikuyu, preaching God's impending judgement upon Europeans and missions, but was quickly banned by the colonial administration.

African protest continued to express itself in many forms, including disturbances, attacks on mission schools, attempts to prevent preachers from conducting services, and even the murder of a missionary at Kijabe. Combined with the African protest against the missionary attitude to female circumcision was also a growing nationalism which eventually resulted in political resistance against foreign rule.

Partly as a result of the attacks upon it described above and partly because of the inroads made by Islam and Christianity as discussed below, African traditional religion lost ground numerically. However, because of the African reactions to these attacks, the religion was on the whole greatly reinvigorated by the 1930s.

Islam and colonial rule

It would appear that Islam fared far better than traditional religion during the period of colonial rule. In the areas where Muslim rule was established before the arrival of the colonial power, Islamic law had provided territorial rather than ethnic uniformity and it commanded obedience to authority. This was good for efficient administration and commerce and Muslims were also able to proselytize and make more converts. The development of communications made it possible for Muslim agents to penetrate into areas which had not been open to them before, and, with the trading routes being redirected from the desert to the coast in West Africa, the number of Muslims, which had been scanty along the coast in the early days of colonial rule, now began to increase. In Sierra Leone, for instance, the percentage of the population that was Muslim rose from 10% in 1891 to 14% in 1911 and 26.12% in 1931.

The Muslim presence along the West African coast was also further increased by the Ahmadiyya Muslims, who came as missionaries using the coastal sea routes. Although considered heretical by some, they were important in fostering an interest in western education among Muslims.

The attitude of colonial administrations towards Islam was mixed. Some felt that Islam was a more enlightened form of religion than traditional African religion, or regarded Muslim institutions as socially advanced and able to be used in the interest of the colonial administrations. Islamic law courts were therefore allowed to be set up, Muslim rulers were given greater authority in some areas, and Muslims were employed by the colonial administrators in subordinate positions as guides, agents and clerks, and thereby given further opportunities to spread their religion.

Not all colonial administrations looked favourably upon Islam. The administration in the Belgian Congo was especially hostile to Islam and saw in it a threat to its 'Christianizing' and 'civilizing' mission. Only a few mosques were allowed to be built and there was a total ban on Muslim schools in the colony.

Other Europeans, especially the French, attempted to impose European culture on their subjects, Muslim and non-Muslim alike, believing that they had an obligation to raise the standard of their colonial subjects by imparting to them the 'benefits' of French culture. Unlike the British, whose policy towards the Muslim states was based on the belief that they could secure the co-operation of Muslim rulers, the French thought otherwise. They initially tried to limit the areas under Muslim control in their bid to conquer the bulk of the Western Sudan. To oppose effectively the spread of Islam and Islamic jurisprudence, they also tried to build up traditional religion and codify African customary law as a counterforce.

The colonial powers, however, later came to encourage Islam and not merely to tolerate it as before. This was because they came to prefer to deal with Islamized Africans rather than with their Christianized counterparts. The modernizing influence of Islam was also appreciated by the colonial powers, who were said to have regarded it as a 'bridge between the narrow particularism of traditional society and the wider impulses and requirements of modern life and economic interests'. Submissive Muslim leaders were therefore greatly encouraged and frequently received official favours such as national honours and awards. Mosques and Ku'ranic schools were built for them, and they were also helped to go on pilgrimages and study tours. But at the same time those Muslims who did not toe the colonial line and showed defiance were disciplined and often harassed.

But Muslims opposed colonial rule on both religious and political grounds, and, although colonial administrations, such as the French, succeeded in gaining a measure of Muslim support in their West African territories, there were large numbers of Muslims who were bent on preserving the purity of Islam and who could therefore not tolerate submission to a Christian infidel administration, and they sought to rid their countries of French colonialism. Such a desire led to the reappearance of Mahdism in many parts of the Sudanic zone of West Africa as an expression of anti-French sentiment, namely in Upper Guinea, Mauritania and Senegal, especially from 1906 to the First World War.

Other Islamic movements which expressed an anti-French or anti-colonial posture were the Hamalliyya movement, founded by S̲h̲ayk̲h̲ Hamallah, which was active in Senegal, French Sudan, Mauritania and Niger, and the Sanūsiyya brotherhood, founded by Muḥammad b. 'Alī al-Sanūsī in Libya, which became the force which led the

Libyans against Italian colonialism from 1911 to 1932. Between 1860 and 1901 the Sanūsiyya spread to Tunisia, Egypt, Central Sahara, central Sudan and Senegal.

Some of the most vigorous opponents of the French invasion of Upper Volta in the late nineteenth century were Muslims, most of whom were reported to have told local Mosi people that the whites would leave their country as soon as the blacks became Muslims. Furthermore, the conquests of Samori in West Africa and Rabah in the Chad area in the last quarter of the nineteenth century brought them into conflict with Europeans and helped to identify Islam with opposition to colonial rule.

But Islam prospered under colonial rule as a result of the many advantages it had over the Christianity imposed by the missionaries, as well as the disruption of traditional life which colonialism gave rise to. Islam was seen by many as an indigenous religion, spread by Africans, whose adherents did not separate themselves from the community but instead mixed with them. This was unlike the Christians, who tended to create their own separate communities and followed an essentially European way of life. It is thus no mere accident that the Temne (Sierra Leone) word for both Christian and European is 'poto'. Besides, unlike mission-imposed Christianity, Islam was able to accommodate more African traditional social and religious institutions, such as magic, divination, polygamy and communalism. Becoming Muslim did not therefore require the radical break with tradition which Christian missionaries insisted upon.

Christianity in the colonial era

The imposition of colonial rule also considerably aided the work of the Christian missionaries. In the first place, both colonial administrators and missionaries shared the same world view and sprang from the same culture. Secondly, the colonial administration was favourably disposed to the work of the missionaries and often subsidized mission schools. Thirdly, the imposition of colonial control over each territory ensured peace and order within which the missionaries had the protection of colonial administrators. Fourthly, the introduction of efficient means of communication and the establishment of the money economy gave impetus to trade and commerce and helped to usher in a new way of life which was to prevail all over Africa and which was characterized by a breakdown of communalism in favour of individualism.

There is no doubt, however, that it was the introduction of education and literacy by the Christian missionaries that made the greatest contribution to the rapid spread of Christianity. It was through the innumerable schools established by the missionaries that many Africans came into contact with Christianity, and in fact the school was the church in many parts of Africa. Moreover, the writing down of many African languages, as well as the teaching of European languages in schools, introduced literacy into many parts of Africa. As a result, written literature in many African languages came into being, and all this helped the spread of Christianity. Thanks to these factors and using the spoken word, or direct evangelization, schools and medical work, missionaries made many converts, and the late nineteenth century was marked by a phenomenal success for Christian missions. As a result of this, many Christian communities sprang up where before there were none.

It should be emphasized that the spread of Christianity during the colonial period was not due exclusively to European missionary initiative. African converts, catechists and ministers played an active role. Among the most famous were Canon Apolo Kivebulaya, who worked in the Belgian Congo, Samuel Ajayi Crowther in Nigeria and Prophet William Wade Harris in the Côte d'Ivoire and the Gold Coast.

The missionaries also played quite an important role in the introduction of a money economy in Africa. Mission stations developed plantations in many parts of Africa and, in addition to growing local foodstuffs and introducing new crops, they helped in the diffusion of commercial crops like cocoa, coffee, tobacco, cotton and sugar cane.

Above all, Christianity infused many ideas. Some of these were not entirely new, and there were points of convergence between what the missionaries preached and what the Africans believed, such as the belief in God and obedience to His will as the final Judge and Creator of men.

The missionaries, however, had a negative attitude towards African religion and culture and were determined right from the start to stamp them out. As pointed out already, the missionaries preached against and condemned all kinds of traditional belief and practices and also denied the existence of gods and witches and other supernatural powers which Africans believed in. On the whole, becoming a Christian meant, to a large extent, ceasing to be an African and using European culture as a point of reference. Thus Christianity had a disintegrating effect on African culture.

The African response to the missionary endeavour expressed itself in three distinct ways: acceptance, rejection and adaptation. There is no doubt that many Africans readily accepted the new faith and that Christianity gained far more ground in Africa during the period under review than it had done in the previous two or three centuries. The first group of Africans to embrace Christianity would appear to be those who were regarded by the Africans as social outcasts and the downtrodden, such as lepers and others who suffered various forms of social disabilities in traditional African societies.

There were also those Africans already dealt with above who rejected the message of Christianity altogether and stuck to the religious and cultural traditions of their forefathers, seeing in them more meaning and significance than what the missionaries preached. Some of these participated in the persecution and isolation of those who became Christians but others also carried on the sacrifices and observances that were intended to keep human beings in harmony with the spiritual forces. Out of their ranks came the religious and cultural leaders as well as herbalists and it is they who have been largely responsible for upholding African values and for providing knowledge about traditional African cultures.

Separatist churches

Finally, there were those whose chose to adapt the new religion by founding what have come to be known as separatist or independent churches, and this development represents the fourth stage in the history of Christianity in Africa. These churches were of two main types, namely, those which broke away from already existing independent churches and those which sprang up independently of any existing religious groups. In most instances, these churches sought to incorporate a larger measure of African beliefs and practices into Christian life than was permitted in churches under missionary control. They were an expression of the desire of Africans to find 'a place to feel at home', and include African ideas of worship in their Christian liturgies.

The breakaway churches, in part, represented the African reaction or adaptation to colonialism and were emancipatory in character. Especially in areas of European settlement where political repression was intense, such churches multiplied and attracted African nationalists. The Ethiopian churches in South Africa, which emphasize African self-improvement and political rights, are a case in point. Nehemiah Tile broke away from the Methodist Mission Church in 1882 and two years later founded the Tembu Church, one of the first independent churches ever to be formed in Africa. The second, which was the first to be called 'Ethiopian', was founded by Wesleyan minister, Mangena M. Mokone, in 1892, again in South Africa. The 'Ethiopian' movement spread to other parts of Southern and East Africa.

In other areas of colonial Africa, breakaway churches often expressed open hostility to the colonial administration. John Chilembwe (see 20.1) founded his Province Industrial Mission in Nyasaland (now Malawi), vehemently attacked the British colonial practices of taxation and military recruitment and eventually led an abortive armed resistance to the British colonial administration in 1915, in which he was captured and executed. Around this time, the Watchtower Movement began to grow and spread from Nyasaland to Southern Rhodesia among the Shona, becoming a religious movement with strong political overtones. It traced its origins to the separatist church movement in the area founded by Elliot Kamwana in northern Nyasaland in 1908. It became known as the Kitawala (Kingdom) or the Church of the Watch Tower, and in Northern Rhodesia its millennial preachers predicted the total collapse of colonialism and the end of the world.

Similar developments took place in other parts of Africa, especially in the early years of the First World War. Simon Kimbangu founded his Église de Jésus-Christ sur la Terre par le Prophète Simon Kimbangu (EJCSK) in 1921 in the Belgian Congo. His followers refused to pay taxes to the Belgian colonial administration and declared their intention to withhold their labour in the face of the forced labour which the administration had introduced. He was therefore arrested and kept in prison until his death in 1951. But Kimbanguism continued to spread from its original base in the Lower Congo River. The neo-Kimbanguist Mission des Noirs, founded by Simon-Pierre Mpadi, which became known as the 'Khakista', spread from the Lower Congo to the French Congo and Oubangui-Chari (now Central African Republic).

Similar in orientation to the movements founded by Kimbangu and Mpadi were those founded in Uganda by an ex-serviceman in the King's African Rifles, Ruben Spartas Mukasa, who dedicated his life to work for the redemption of all Africa at whatever personal cost. His African Progressive Association and the Christian Army for the Salvation of Africa, as well as a branch of the African Orthodox Church which he started, expressed the political and social purpose of all these movements. In Nyasaland, Jordan Nguma's Last Church of God and His Christ was of the same stamp as Mukasa's in Uganda.

Other churches, in the spirit of the Reformation, emphasized certain aspects of Christian theology which the mission-founded churches had neglected. The Zionist churches of South Africa emphasized possession by the Holy Spirit, healing and

20.1   *The Reverend John Chilembwe (1860s/1870s-1915), churchman and leader of the 1915 rising in Nyasaland, pictured with his family (Edinburgh University Press)*

prophecy and spread widely in Southern and East Africa. The Dini ya Roho (Holy Ghost Church), which grew up among the Abaluyia of Kenya and was founded by Jakobo Buluku and Daniel Sande in 1927, regarded baptism by the Holy Spirit, speaking in tongues, and the free confession of sins as a necessary prerequisite for full membership of the church. This same emphasis on the Holy Spirit also led Alfayo Odongo to found his Joroho (Holy Ghost) Church among the Luo of Kenya in 1932. Various African and Aladura churches in West Africa also emphasized possession by the Holy Spirit.

Other churches were set up specifically to accommodate those who had not been able to comply with the missionary churches' insistence on monogamy and had been expelled, as well as those who could not join the Church because they were already polygamous. An example of such a church was the African National Church, which thrived in the Rungwe district of Tanganyika in the 1930s.

Indigenous Christianity

Besides these churches, another set arose which were not the product of anxiety alleviation or stress in society but rather derived their inspiration from a more positive ideology. From the earliest days of the process of presenting Christianity to Africans, some converts had accepted the new faith lock, stock and barrel. Others, on the other hand, accepted it but adapted it in the light of the basic underlying concepts of African traditional religion. In other words, some African Christians used certain aspects of Christianity to strengthen aspects of traditional beliefs that needed strengthening, and at the same time used traditional beliefs to strengthen aspects of Christianity where they were found wanting. Thus they came out with what they sincerely believed to be a meaningful religion, and their Christianity can be seen as an expression of the African way of being religious. This is why we had termed it indigenous Christianity, and believe that it is an expression of religious creativity and cultural integrity, and not a mere reaction, response or adaptation to outside stimuli, as some scholars are wont to assert.

In these churches forms of worship are provided to satisfy the spiritual and emotional needs of members, thereby enabling Christianity, like traditional religion, to cover every area of human life and fulfil all human needs. Included in these is the concern for healing, whose centrality in both traditional religion and indigenous Christianity cannot be over-emphasized. In addition to healing, the religious needs of divining, prophesying and visioning are also fulfilled, for there is the firm belief that God reveals the future and the causes of misfortune through visions. While mission-founded churches deny the existence of evil forces such as witchcraft and sorcery, the indigenous churches recognize their existence and provide a Christian source of protection against these evil powers, firmly believing that Jesus Christ can effectively protect and heal.

The emergence of these churches has provided the opportunity for the exercise of African leadership and ability in Christianity, and in these churches a truly African Christianity has been expressed. And with this development has come the beginning of an African Christian theology.

Examples of indigenous Christian churches that emerged in the colonial period and are still very much alive are the Apostolowa Fe Dedefia Habobo (Apostolic Revelation Society) in the Gold Coast (Ghana); Dini ya Nsambwa (The Church of the Ancestors) in Kenya; Calici ca Makolo (Church of the Ancestors) in Nyasaland (Malawi); the original Church of the White Bird among the Zazuru of Southern Rhodesia (Zimbabwe); Church of Christ for the Union of the Bantu and Protection of Bantu Customs in South Africa; eglise des Noirs in the Congo; and the Herero Church of South West Africa (now Namibia).

The example of the Musama Disco Christo Church

A typical example of these indigenous Christian churches which we wish to examine briefly here is the Musama Disco Christo (Army of the Cross of Christ) Church of the Gold Coast (now Ghana). The founder of the church, Prophet Jemisimiham Jehu-Appiah, successfully adapted Christianity by reorganizing it on the Akan pattern and portrayed Christianity in terms which are comprehensible in the Akan view of things. The church began as a prayer group, the Faith Society, within the Methodist Church at Gomoa Oguan, in the Central Region of the Gold Coast in 1919. But, when its leader, Catechist William Egyanka Appiah, and his followers were expelled from the Church, it was established as a full-blown Church in 1922.

The founder not only founded a Church and became its General Spiritual Head, but also organized it on the traditional Akan state (*Oman*) structure based on a military formation with its wings. At the head of the *Oman* is *Nana Akaboha*, who combines both spiritual and temporal power and whose family constitutes the royal dynasty (though succession follows the patrilineal rather than the matrilineal rules so typical of the Akan). The wife of the founder, the Prophetess Natholomoa Jehu-Appiah, became the *Akatitibi* (Queen-mother) of the Church; and the King and Queen therefore became the supreme authorities in the Musama Disco Christo Church.

The headquarters of the Church, Mozano, functions as an *ahenkro*, capital town of an Akan traditional state. Here the *Akaboha* (King) resides and all major decisions affecting the Church emanate, and it is here that the annual festival, *Asomdwee Afe* (Peace Festival) is held (see 20.2). At the *ahenkro*, there are shrines and holy places where the faithful pray and receive healing. The Church has its own language, '*osor kasa*' (heavenly language), which is used in salutations and greetings and upon entry into houses; and the names used in the Church are also from this language.

The Church draws heavily on Akan religion and culture in its search for satisfactory answers to the problems of contemporary life and combines elements of Methodism with a strong African polity. It represents a further extension of Christianity in Africa, based as it is on the conviction that a Christian society can be built on the foundations of African culture.

Conclusion

The period of colonial rule in Africa from 1880 to 1935 saw not the destruction but rather the confirmation of religious pluralism in Africa. Orthodox Christianity and Islam gained much ground at the expense of traditional religion during the period

20.2   *Prophet M. Jehu-Appiah, Akaboha III, grandson and successor of the founder of the Musama Disco Christo Church (Gold Coast/Ghana) riding in a palanquin during the Church's annual Peace Festival (K. Asare Opoku)*

thanks to some of the activities of the colonial administrators. However, traditional religion, as the host religion, formed the foundation upon which many of the new sects that emerged from the new religions were based. The fact of religious pluralism created rivalries, competition and even conflict in many parts of Africa, but at the same time the opportunity for inter-religious dialogue was created.

The arts in Africa during the period of colonial rule

From the point of view of the arts within the context of social change, the period under review saw the survival, even renewal, of cultural values in the face of external domination and exploitation in Africa. Punitive raids by colonial forces, missionary intolerance and lack of understanding – all these had thoroughly disrupted the accustomed cultural directions of the continent. The Muslim dimension was unique in its own right and left strong cultural impressions on the landscape. Yet the reality that we extract from that period is the survival and even increased vitality of the forms and values of the true cultures of the peoples of Africa.

African art

It is difficult to assess the qualitative impact of imperial commerce on artistic productivity. Certain media remained obviously unaffected – for instance, the 'bead-paint' technique of the Cameroon artists or the art of religious sculpture among the Yoruba (see 21.1) the Baule, the Bakota, etc. Yet subtle changes had begun to take place in other art media, both in form and content. While retaining much of its colour, the Mbari mural art of the Igbo (Nigeria) had begun to undergo 'pop' crudities at the hands of urban returnees, the result of sudden access to paints in all tints and textures. Formerly such mural art was controlled by the very nature and sparse range of the dyes of local manufacture.

Local genius was hardly a match for the factory, whose products began to flood African markets even at the early stages of the colonial venture. The loss of the integrative role of art in normal community development may be seen in a decline in the art of the *forowa* and the *kuduo* (finely worked containers for snuff, unguents, etc.) of the Asante, whose decorative motifs were, as is much the case in Africa, symbols for traditional lessons, proverbs, moral counsels and episodes of history. The production of *forawa* was now largely taken over by factories in Britain, which additionally could experiment with a variety of metals.

African architecture

A more than cursory look at the layout, exterior and interior of some of the truly harmonious traditional living-spaces would reveal the existence of an effective,

21.1 *Wooden figures from a Yoruba shrine to the god Shango (Werner Forman Archives)*

sophisticated expression of the architectural genius of the people of Africa, one which contrasted vividly with the regimenting 'grid'-planned housing into which Africans were being forced at this time, by Belgian and (especially) French forms of plantation slavery. Urban architecture of the time did not borrow from the structural lessons of traditional architecture but was developed in rigid 'grid' forms. Nevertheless, it must be conceded that pockets of traditional housing were successfully inserted in the heart of the alien structures which rose all over the landscape. Tucked neatly away in the 'high-rising' centres of even the capital cities of the Belgian Congo (now Zaire), Senegal, the Gold Coast (now Ghana), Nigeria, Angola, etc, are traditional compounds, overshadowed by the concrete edifices, which date back to the nineteenth century. They are usually centred on a communal well. The contribution of the Brazilian returnees to the continent was, in this respect, quite immense. Even in the minor cities of the African hinterland, isolated instances of an arrested development of traditional architecture from this period continue to create a sense of aesthetic loss. The modern urban city in Africa constantly reminds one that the environment was never transformed on its own terms, but in the image of the colonizers.

African music

The real music of the people of Africa continues to remind us that it remained undisplaced despite all the assaults on it. This is not surprising for, to Africans, music has a social function, for it is through music, more than any form of art, that the *lived* cultural reality of the peoples is most readily grasped. When the Kuyu, for example, perform their dusk-to-dawn sequence of song, dance and symbolic mime in the funeral ceremonies for a famed woman farmer, who was regarded as being exceptionally proficient in the cultivation of manioc (cassava), we are made aware of the continuity of life, and it is even a practical demonstration of economic survival for the living.

But music did not minister only to the mysterious and the profound. Oratory, her twin-sister, has always, in any community, constituted a favourite medium of formal social exchanges including political arrangements and the administration of justice. Its role in warfare hardly requires emphasis. The combination of music and oratory in formal judicial structures may, however, be regarded as being yet another property of cultures in which music is not simply an isolated activity of society, but an integral one. The Idoma of north-eastern Nigeria and the Watutsi of Central Africa had a tradition of judicial processes which utilized a semi-choric pattern within a predominantly theatrical setting.

The large claims on behalf of music in the lives of the African peoples cannot be denied. According to a contemporary Shona musician:

> Much of African history has been handed down . . . in song. [As you play *mbira* and sing] you can see the panoramic scenes of those bygone days and the vague dreamy figures of the past come into . . . focus in the modern time . . . You can almost see your ancestors limping towards the living world again.

What has been written about the griot in Malian, Senegalese, Gambian and Guinean societies, not merely as the leaven of social occasions, but as recorder, historian, cultural formalist of society, is more than applicable also to the Shona musician, whose instrument, the *mbira* (a plucked board set in its classic form within a gourd), inspired the comments quoted above. To move from the griot's home in the Western Sudan southwards to Central and Southern Africa is to come across his counterpart and the epic of his survival in a phase of even greater violence and instability. Even for Southern Africa, with its history of epic empire-building and its attendant warfare and violent subjugations, the five decades across the turn of the century were singularly insecure for the inhabitants and recorded numerous violent dispersals.

The *mbira* survived this culture-fragmenting process; indeed it succeeded in creating an identity of culture among its practitioners, with all its social structures of the religious and the secular. *Mbira* music was considered by the Shona a gift of their great common ancestral spirit Chaminuka, who appears to have been a living person, a king in the early part of the nineteenth century. The music entered wholly into social life, penetrating it so thoroughly that it became indispensable to the various activities of healing, weddings, funerals, field labour, births, initiations and a host of other social undertakings.

Unlike a number of other forms of African social music, *mbira* was no court art but a true music of the people, of the entire scattered communities. That its practitioners were so highly respected within the community and their work so valued is explained by the fact that they were regarded as the people's artistic medium with the other world. Moreover, they were accessible and professional and became a symbol of ethnic cohesion during a period of violent upheavals. And such was the mastery of the artists over their forms that, in spite of the predictable early hostility, even the missions were eventually won over. In the 1920s *mbira* instruments had begun to trickle into church orchestration in Southern Rhodesia. Experimental compositions, based on *mbira* melodies, had crept into the missions' seasonal festivals, and schoolchildren no longer faced certain expulsion for plucking the 'devil's instrument' at playtime.

In or out of the mission compound, however, the socially integrating role of music remained the strongest feature of cultural life on the continent. As spiritual medium or as social entertainer, as historian or even as court retainer ministering to a privileged class, the musician was a vital feature of the cultural devices.

The theatrical arts

The theatrical arts were, in most instances, an extension or elaboration of the musical, and indeed it is quite difficult to demonstrate the dividing line between the two. However, as the theatrical arts on the West African coast evolved in the nineteenth century through contact with outside influences, they do offer, more specifically than in music, evidence of change under the double assault of Islamic structures and Christian evangelizing. The latter was in turn supported by the influence of returnee slaves in Sierra Leone and Liberia, who brought with them the entertainment forms of their countries of exile, their manners, values, costumes and idioms.

Throughout the nineteenth century, there were full-time professional theatrical groups in the Oyo empire which enjoyed the protection of the kings. The disintegration of the empire under the attacks of the Fulbe from the north, and the ravages of the ensuing civil war led simultaneously to the spread of the professional troupes to the south and across the border to Dahomey, and to their disappearance in its place of origin. The victorious Muslims banned most forms of theatrical performance, and most definitely those festivals of the ancestors whose representation of human figures was anathema to the Muslim religion.

The missionaries who had begun to push inland from the coast completed the task which Islam had begun by not only forbidding their adherents membership of any cult but also by banning the instruments which were associated with such theatre arts. A vacuum was thus created into which the returnee slaves' culture neatly stepped. As the century entered its last three decades, the west coast came under the creative influence of these returnee Christians, confident in the superiority of their acquired arts, eager to prove to the white colonials who now controlled their existence that the black man was capable not only of receiving, but of practising the refined arts of the European.

The new (Euro-American) forms of theatrical activity initiated largely by expatriate life in Liberia, Senegal and Sierra Leone spread eastwards, receiving ever-increasing blood transfusions along the line. The bastardized vaudeville or music-hall variety entertainment of the 'Nova Scotians', as some of the returnees of Sierra Leone called themselves, did enjoy a long run along the coast. However, its arrival in the more easterly countries of the Gold Coast, Dahomey and Nigeria brought about its transformation in both form and content. It is not an exaggeration to claim that, by the first decade of the twentieth century, a completely new form of theatre had achieved distinct form in West Africa: the 'concert party'.

'Academies' were formed for the performance of concerts which were modelled on the Victorian music hall or the American vaudeville. The Christian churches organized their own concerts, schools were drawn into the concert rage – prize-giving days, visit of the district officer, Queen Victoria's birthday, etc. The black missionaries refused to be outdone – the Reverend Samuel Ajayi Crowther was a famous example, a black prelate prominent in the patronage and encouragement of this form of the arts, while the Reverend James Johnson turned the famous Breadfruit Church in Lagos into a springboard for theatrical performances. The Brazilian returnees added an exotic yet familiar flavour, their music finding a ready echo in the traditional melodies of the west coast and the Congo. Christmas and New Year at the turn of the century and in the first decades of the twentieth witnessed the streets of the capital cities of Freetown and Lagos transformed by mini-pageants reminiscent of Latin fiestas, of which the *caretta*, a kind of satyr masquerade, appears to have been the most durable.

Cultural nationalism was, however, constantly at work against a total take-over by imported forms. On the one hand, traditional theatre withstood the attack, not only preserving its forms but turning itself consciously into a base of resistance against Christian culture. Indeed, it even influenced the new forms of theatre that evolved. On the other hand, unable to accept the excesses of the Christian cultural imperialism, such as the embargo on African instruments and tunes in a 'universal' Church, the breakaway movements began. From 1882 to the early 1930s as has been pointed out in the earlier chapters, many secessionist movements took place, mostly inspired by a need to worship God in the cultural mode of their forefathers. And now commenced also a unique 'operatic' tradition in West Africa, especially in Lagos, beginning with church cantatas and moving to the dramatization of biblical stories, until it asserted its independence in secular stories and the development of professional touring troupes.

The new 'vaudeville' troupes prospered. Names of groups such as we encounter in 'Two Bobs and their Carolina Girl' of the Gold Coast tell us something of the inspiration of much of these. Master Yalley, a schoolteacher, is credited with having begun the tradition of the vaudeville variety act in the Gold Coast. His pupil Bob Johnson and his 'Axim Trio' soon surpassed the master and became a familiar figure on the Gold Coast cultural landscape. By the mid-1930s, Bob Johnson had become sufficiently established to take his brand of vaudeville to other West African cities. West Africa in this decade could boast of a repertoire of shows displaying the most bizarre products of eclectic art in the history of theatre. Even cinema, an infant art, had by then left its mark on West African theatre – some of Bob Johnson's acts were adaptations of Charlie Chaplin's escapades, not omitting his costume and celebrated shuffle.

Again, another irony of colonial intentions. While Bob Johnson was preparing his first West African tour, a European educationist, Charles Beart, in Senegal was beginning to reverse the policy of European acculturation in a leading secondary school in Senegal, the École William Ponty. A famous teachers' college, it served Francophone Africa in the same way as did Achimota College in Anglophone West Africa and Makerere College in East Africa. They were all designed to provide a basic European education for would-be teachers and low-echelon civil servants. Such cultural education as came into the curriculum of the École William Ponty was of necessity French – French plays, poetry, music, art, history, sociology. Beart, however, during his principalship embarked on a new orientation of the students by encouraging them to return to their own societies for cultural directions. Assignments were given which resulted in the students' exploration of both the form and the substance of indigenous art. Groups from every colonial territory represented at William Ponty were then expected to return from vacation, armed with a theatrical presentation based on their researches, the entire direction being left in the hands of the students themselves.

Though the influence of this new theatre spread widely through different social strata of French-speaking Africa and though the experiment was not without its instructive value, it was really not an authentic development of the culture from which it derived. The 'community' represented by William Ponty was an artificial one. It was distanced from the society whose cultural properties it rifled, both in qualitative thought and in cultural ends. The situation was of course not peculiar to William Ponty but was common to the other schools and institutions set up by the colonizer for the fulfilment of his own mission in Africa. Thus the theatre of William Ponty served the needs of exotic satisfaction for the community of French colonials, but remained a curiosity that left the social life and authentic cultural awareness of the people untouched.

The literary renaissance in Egypt

In the sphere of literary culture, Egypt and the Western Sudan provide instances in the first case of literary renaissance and in the second of both direct and indirect mutual assistance in the cultural penetration of Africa during the colonial period by basically contending interests.

Bonaparte's occupation of Egypt, Muḥammad 'Alī's reforms in the military, social and economic fields, his sending of educational missions to Europe, especially France, and the establishment of a printing press in Bulaq in 1822 paved the way for the beginning of a new relationship between two worlds – the West and the Islamic East – and ushered in a new age in Egypt. This preparatory stage in Egypt's literary renaissance was accelerated during the reign of Khedive Ismā'īl Pasha (1863–79) and reached the high road of decisive development from the latter half of the nineteenth century onwards.

The creation of a necessary environment for the flowering of a modern Arabic culture was brought about by several factors. The first was the migration into Egypt from the 1870s onwards of largely Christian Libano-Syrian intellectuals, such as Farah Antun (1874–1922), Yagub Sarruf (1852–1927) and Jurji Zaidan, who were escaping the autocratic rule of the Ottomans and were imbued with ideas adopted from the West on politics, science and literature. The second was the emergence amongst the Muslims within Egypt itself of a new elite group filled with the Islamic modernist views of al-Afghāni and 'Abdūh. The third was the return home of Egyptian scholars from Europe, where they had been exposed to a programme of studies with a humanistic bias, providing several crops of writers with varied viewpoints and interests. The fourth was the economic development and transformation of the country as well as the establishment and founding of academies, learned societies, a national library (in 1870) and secular universities, the reforming of existing religious universities (e.g. al-Azhar) and the creation of a modern system of education. All this gave birth first to a public endowed with the leisure, education and interest to form an audience and then to a truly literary and intellectual renaissance. However, local literary output was still heavily reliant on the translation of European works, undertaken before the establishment of the British protectorate over Egypt and continuing to flourish under it. In time, this gave way to adaptations and imitations and finally creative works of originality.

This cultural awakening and the changing political climate of Egypt towards the end of the nineteenth century were reflected in the very extensive development of the press. By 1898, there were already 169 papers and journals in existence, with their numbers increasing to 282 in 1913. Under the influence of the eminent Muslim reformer al-Afghāni, the periodical press was widely acclaimed as an educating or politicizing instrument. It became increasingly the preferred medium of expression for a whole generation of literary personalities as well as intellectual leaders after the First World War. Thus, newspapers equally became vehicles for experimentation with new literary forms such as the short story, the drama, etc. The need to express and interpret the newly acquired foreign ideas led to the evolution of a 'neo-classical Arabic'.

This transformation of culture in Egypt under foreign rule during this period led to a greater political awareness that later found expression in the nascent nationalist movement.

Literary culture in the Western Sudan

It would appear that basically contending interests penetrated the Western Sudan during the colonial period, the colonial or European and the Muslim represented by the

Joola. The latter's penetration into the countries of the Western Sudan had commerce for its basic end; their immigration into towns such as Bobo-Dioulasso, Kong, Bonduku, and so on, followed the trade patterns from gold sources in the Gold Coast (Ghana), Upper Volta (now Burkina Faso) and other mines in the tropical belt, ending along the caravan trails of the Sahara. The Joola (a name which itself described their main occupation, trade) were, however, equally concerned with the preservation and promotion of their Islamic culture and served as the link for further Moorish and Arabic penetration into the rain-belts of the west coast.

And, while admittedly the literary culture of Islam which penetrated areas of West Africa was largely conservative, rhetorical and stereotyped, its methodology consisting of learning by rote rather than by recognition, its content restricted essentially to Islamic exegesis and the Law (*hadīth* and *fiḳh*), the continuing movement of scholars between the west coast and North Africa and the Middle East right into the twentieth century and the valuable trade in manuscripts which flourished side by side with the more mundane material of Joola commerce testify to the more enquiring nature of Arabic scholarship among its African adherents. Historical writings owe as much to the Arabic scholars as to their counterparts of the Europeanized coastal towns or émigré products of western literacy. For instance, a survey of the libraries of *mallams* of the west coast, largely around the Côte d'Ivoire in 1920, revealed manuscripts which covered history, language (Arabic grammar), poetry, mathematics, logic, jurisprudence, etc.

We have already commented on some devices employed by the 'autochthones' against the mechanisms employed by European colonialism to condemn African culture; the Islamic culture, in the proselytizing polity of the Joola, was to encounter the same resistance. In some cases, the Joola community became thoroughly assimilated into the local community. Such instances of total assimilation were rare, but I. Wilks, in his informative study, points to one example – the Tagara of Jirapa in north-western Ghana. In other cases, where the Africans retained the custodianship of their land both physically and ritualistically, the Joola became displaced.

Not all the West African westernized authors at the time were prepared to see the Muslim cultural challenge as necessarily opposed to the true genius of the African or indeed as incompatible with the Christian values then feverishly expanding through missionary stations set up by black converts along the Niger, the Volta and the Senegal. For sociologists and educationists like the Abbé Boillat (or his gallant compatriot, the scholar-soldier Paul Holle), Arabic language and (Islamic) culture deserved study, preferably in higher institutions in France where they would leave no contaminating influence on impressionable Africans. Bishop Samuel Ajayi Crowther of Nigeria went further and was prepared to have them studied and taught. It might even lead, through the translation of the Bible and catechism into Arabic, to an amelioration of the 'grosser aspects' of Islamic beliefs and society.

The St Thomas-born West Indian, Edward Wilmot Blyden, who migrated and settled in Liberia, was, however, of the firm conviction that Islamic culture was, of all the major civilizations of the world, best suited to the temperament and cultural realities of the African. Islam was for him only a component – although a major one – in the reformulation of an African culture for the African, with its own guaranteeing structures and institutions. This forerunner of *négritude* believed in nothing less than a complete reorientation of African education from its Eurocentric bias to a more African-attuned direction. Muslim-Arabic civilization, which had impressed him with its 'literary cultivation and intellectual activity', was to play a major role in this.

But it was not merely history in antiquity which formed the main material of Blyden's fight for the African's cultural reorientation. Recent events in the history of the African, the extension of his culture and genius even into a disadvantaged environment in the 'New World', prompted Blyden to examine the history books and declare that the history of European figures such as Admiral Nelson must be discarded for the history of black heroes such as Toussaint L'Ouverture and to propose the founding of a university in West Africa in which the Arabic language and culture were to be given special attention. Not surprisingly, such a university never became a reality in his lifetime, but the evidence we have today is that this West African 'returnee', versed thoroughly as he was in western traditions, precipitated the breakup of the Christian missionary monopoly on the West African coast. For, on 2 January 1891, he gave a speech to a crowded audience in the assembly hall of the Breadfruit Church in Lagos, stressing the incompatibility of European ecclesiasticism with the society and traditions of the African. A few months later, in Lagos, the first schism occurred in the 'orthodox' Breadfruit Church, giving birth to the United Native African Church, with consequences – as already described – for the cultural life of the African as the movement spread westwards and northwards of West Africa.

Literature in European languages

Literary culture in European languages in West and Central Africa may be said to have constituted the highest force of colonial confrontation. Oral literature retained its place as a satirical outlet, and mime, dance and innovations in masquerade forms took note of and made commentaries on the colonial phenomenon. But it was the colonial-language literatures in journalistic form and in poetry, drama and the novel, which mobilized the literary imagination in the service of anti-colonialism. The West African coast, from Liberia to Lagos, nourished the pamphlet industry on a scale that is comparable to eighteenth-century England. So did Kenya although, in the East African case, this appears to have been largely in the hands of the Asian community, as were most of the journals. The brief tract, cheaply printed and easily disseminated, vehemently attacked foreign domination and exploitation, acts of deceit by the colonial administration and the ever-increasing encroachments on the life-style and social dignity of the peoples. Portuguese Luanda for its part obtained its first printing press in 1841 and with it the commencement of active journalism in the championing of the Africans' cause. It was a period remarkable for its stylistic consciousness – no matter in which colonial language. Accusations against French colonialism of racism from Ahmadou Dugay Cledor of Senegal reveal meticulous prose in flights of indignation. Petitions to the British Colonial Office became an art, a study in diplomatic prose.

J. E. Casely Hayford published, in 1911, his *Ethiopia Unbound*, one of Africa's earliest novels, an attempt in a mixture of styles, ranging from caustic sarcasm to passionate indictment of the greed and racial arrogance that went into the partitioning and colonization of Africa. Casely Hayford's writings throughout his life kept permanent vigil on the fate of the black continent, a refusal to the last to accept the act of colonization or accord it authority in his own thinking. *Ethiopia Unbound* curiously did not give birth to known imitators during this period and remained in an exclusive class of its own. By contrast, however, Africa did produce scholars and literate public figures of a differing school of thought, such as Bishop Samuel Ajayi Crowther of Nigeria and Bakary Dialo of Senegal. Like the Abbé Boillat, they defended European colonialism as a positive and laudable experience for Africa. For Crowther, a Protestant theologian weighed down by the horrors of his 'pagan' origin and society, Christianity represented, in the most primitive sense, a divine instrument for the salvation of a heathen continent. Bakary Dialo was, for his part, simply overwhelmed by the virtue of French culture.

Even for the most radical anti-colonials, a manifest fascination with and preference for European culture as experienced in their society, and as encountered in the expanded intellectual horizons of the individual, was often discernible in their writings. The tragedy of the gifted poet from Madagascar, Jean-Joseph Rabéarivelo (??–1937), who committed suicide, it was believed, through his failure to resolve this internal conflict in his colonial personality, was a dramatic example. This gave a discernibly ambiguous quality to the writings of many articulate Africans in the early period of the colonial order. It facilitated the policy of cultural assimilation, especially in the French, Portuguese and Spanish territories, resulting in the deliberate withdrawal from, even denial of, the authentic sources of African creative genius by the new elite.

Exceptions, especially notable in the settler situation, who turned the policy of *assimilado* into political art were poets like Silverio Ferriera, Antonio José de Nascimento and Francisco Castelbranco, whose poetry from the turn of the century denounced the racial bigotry of the settlers. But, simultaneously, in Angola and other Portuguese territories (as indeed in *all* colonial territories), an escapist form of response to the daily reality of humiliation evolved. An example is found in the poetry of Caetano da Costa Alegre (São Tomé), whose sentimental love lyrics, glorifying the beauty of the black woman, were published after his death. His poetry may be regarded as forerunner to the literary school of black self-reclamation that became celebrated in the movement called *négritude*.

The principal midwives of *négritude* were Aimé Césairé (Martinique), Léopold Senghor (Senegal) and Leon Damas (French Guyana); the cradle was France. *Négritude* produced a flowering of poetry, not all of it 'propaganda' poetry in the manner of da Costa Alegre, but one which nevertheless owed its existence to the renewed consciousness of an African reality. It was a revolt, to summarize it quite simply, a revolt against the successful assimilative strategy of French and Portuguese colonialism, products of which the initiators of the movement realized they were. But the genesis of the movement can be attributed with justification to the 'manifesto' in one issue of the journal *Légitime Défense*, published by three students from Martinique. In this manifesto, they rejected the 'bourgeois' conventions' of European culture, rejected a number of European literary models and the false personality which they imposed on the black man.

Négritude, which rounds off the period under study, held undisputed sway for the next two decades, and not merely among the Francophone colonial writers and intellectuals but the Lusophone, and even Anglophone. Among the most uncompromising opponents of *négritude* today – convinced Marxists who hold a view of history irreconcilable with the tenets of *négritude* – are some African leaders who gave *négritude* a new lease of life in their own struggle against Portugal's *assimilado* policies in the early 1950s. Thus, it is accurate to say that *négritude* was a historical phenomenon which was called into being by a particular set of circumstances and has since lost its affective hold as those circumstances disappeared, and as society became subjected to more comprehensive forms of analysis and radical prescriptions.

22

African politics and nationalism, 1919-35

If the period between 1880 and 1919 was the period of African resistance to the imposition of colonial rule, the period from 1919 to 1935 was that of African nationalism. A preliminary point to make is the distinction between the nature of nationalism in Europe from the nineteenth century and that in colonized Africa in the period between the two world wars. Nationalism in Europe has been the expression of the desire of communities which were culturally identical and shared a common historical past for an independent, sovereign existence in political organizations (states) of their own. The struggle was to ensure that the cultural nation and the state became the same. As the Greek, Italian and German examples illustrate, what emerged from the nationalist movements were, by and large, nation-states.

In Africa, however, most of the colonies that had been created were made up of several culturally and historically diverse nationality groups without a common historical past and for whom, for the most part, the fact of subjection to a common alien ruler was the main base for unity. The expression of nationalism in Africa then was a desire of these different communities or cultural nations to forge new identities that would serve them well in their struggles against the atrocities and shortcomings of the new colonial administrations. They also began to see the units of the colonial administrations as proto-states around which they sought to develop a sense of common belonging.

Another interesting difference was that the attitudes of African leadership elites were shaped partly by the form of colonial administration. Where, as in the French colonial federations, the administrations were regional in structure and/or policy, the African leaders tended to adopt a regional outlook. Hence, champions of African nationalism in the inter-war period have been referred to as being primarily pan-Africanists rather than nationalists in the European sense. In other words nationalism was taking a reverse course to the expression of that phenomenon in Europe. Contrary to what happened in Europe, the state was created before the cultural nations that would make it a meaningful political community were welded together.

That Africans living in these colonies with the artificial boundaries imposed by colonialism should develop this sense of identity and common belonging should not surprise us since it was more or less a direct product of the colonial situation itself. In the first place, colonialism imposed an alien system of values, norms and definitions of political and social developments, embodying inequality based on racial discrimination and resting upon some kind of racialism and above all upon a negation of the culture of the colonized. It was therefore bound to arouse discontent and protest. It is not surprising that racial consciousness became basic to the growth of African nationalism and that one of the primary concerns of African nationalism and politics in the inter-war period was cultural revivalism.

Secondly, colonialism in general requires a social base for its survival. This is usually provided by raising a new group of elites among the colonized society through a diffusion of the culture of the colonizer through education. However, this diffusion almost invariably involves not only harmonious culture contacts but also culture conflicts, which could find expression in violent reactions from the subject people. Apart from this, there is always the problem of conflict of interests as between the colonizer and the colonized, the former working to perpetuate control, the latter struggling for self-fulfilment either through accommodation within the colonial system or through the recovery of independence and sovereignty.

As M. Crowder has shown above (Chapter 12), the First World War raised the hopes of the emergent educated elites all over Africa that they would be given greater opportunities and be absorbed and accepted as colleagues by the colonial rulers. These hopes, however, were steadily frustrated after the war. Even where educated Africans were given employment, not only did they find themselves assigned to inferior positions *vis-à-vis* the European personnel of comparable training and experience with whom they served in the same colonial administrations, but they were also kept in the background socially. All this became a source of resentment, bitterness and agitation against the colonial regimes.

Moreover, for reasons of economy and effectiveness, the colonial administrations made varied use, as R. F. Betts has shown above (Chapter 13), of traditional institutions and leadership elites to facilitate their control of the subject peoples. Indeed, in the search for such personnel, the colonial officials often created new ones which they could understand and use. Such were the 'warrant chiefs' of south-eastern Nigeria, the native authorities among the Maasai in Tanganyika (now Tanzania) and in parts of Uganda outside Buganda, and most of the so-called chiefs (*chefs de paille*) under the French, Belgians and Portuguese. But, even then, the elites so recruited to sustain colonial rule were hardly any better treated than the Africans who were raised through education in the colonial system. Like the new educated elites, the 'traditional' rulers fell between two stools. Having lost their traditional positions and roles in the eyes of their people, they were treated in most cases like mere instruments of control by the colonial masters and not as real partners. The loss of real power and social status and prestige was a source of discontent for many of them. Moreover, as will be seen later, these colonial administrators generally tried to play the traditional elite against the educated elite, and often acted as the protector of the 'traditional' leadership and system of government. In this situation, neither set of elites was satisfied with the colonial regimes.

But colonialism did not affect only the educated elite and the traditional rulers. To see African nationalism in the inter-war period only as an elitist and urban phenomenon, as has hitherto been done, is wrong. Recent research is showing more and more that a great deal of discontent and anti-colonial feelings were aroused among the masses of the people and in the rural areas mainly as a result of the new economic and financial measures, the new system of administering justice and, above all, the economic depression of the 1930s. All these factors have been discussed already and there is no doubt that they caused the feelings of oppression in not only the urban but also the rural areas that fuelled the nationalist movements.

Another factor which caused a great deal of anger and sense of frustration was the neglect of education. As European powers concentrated on making colonies pay for their administration and services, relatively little was done to spread western education. In several areas of colonized Africa between the two world wars, primary schools were still few and far between and secondary education was a rarity. In British Central Africa, French Equatorial Africa, and Portuguese Angola, Mozambique and Guinea, there was practically no access to secondary education before the Second World War. This general attempt to limit the quality and scope of education was based on the fear that European education and political and social ideas were destructive of colonialism as a system of relations. It was this fear that explains the general denunciation of education in the humanities at all levels, and the preference for rural schools, vocational schools, and technically-orientated post-secondary institutions which were concerned with intermediate manpower, but not universities. The idea was to avoid the example of India where the spread of liberal education had been a major lever for the expansion of anti-colonial and nationalistic politics. This is the explanation for the orientation and scope of colleges such as École William Ponty in French West Africa, and the Yaba Higher College (Nigeria), Achimota College (Gold Coast), Gordon's College (Sudan) and the Makerere College in British East Africa. But the attempt to regulate the measure and type of social change that could take place in the colonies was itself another source of anti-colonial grievances that generated the nationalist movements.

The final internal cause for the rise and intensification of African nationalism, especially in the middle thirties, was the Italo-Ethiopian War which began in 1935, and the eventual Italian occupation of Ethiopia. These major events furthered the feeling of alienation on the part of the colonized, especially the educated, against the colonial regimes. The tone of the Italian invasion, and of fascism and Nazism in general, emphasized the racialist nature of European colonialism in Africa. Those who had nursed hope in the League of Nations were sadly disappointed. The desire to protect the wounded pride of the African partly explains the resurgence of pan-African ideas and ideologies like *négritude* at this time. It also contributed to the setting up of international organizations in defence of the independence of Ethiopia, a country which symbolized the hope of the educated African for eventual independence.

African nationalism did not owe its rise and development to the internal colonial situation alone. In the pursuit of their aspirations, African nationalists were aided by developments on the international scene. Such were, for example, the impact of the First World War already referred to and discussed in Chapter 12 above, and the League of Nations' expression of the desirability of regarding the development of the colonized as a major objective of colonialism, and as a yardstick against which the performance of imperial masters, especially in the mandated territories, would be judged. The introduction of the idea of accountability to the international community in respect of the mandated territories served as a source of encouragement to some of the nationalists.

On the political plane, international ideological movements like the Leninist anti-imperialist Communist International (Comintern) and other socialist movements, as well as the march towards independence in other continents of the world, were also an incentive to African nationalists. So also was anti-imperialist pan-Africanism inspired by Sylvester Williams, Marcus Garvey, William Du Bois and other black American and Caribbean influences, which will be discussed later.

An international congress which was convened under the auspices of the Comintern at Brussels in February 1927 resulted in the formation of the League against Imperialism and for National Independence (known simply as the League Against Imperialism). The Congress was attended by about 180 delegates from Western Europe, North, Central and South America, the Caribbean, Asia and Africa. The Congress brought together Communists, left-wing socialist groups like the Independent Labour Party, represented by its general secretary, Fenner Brockway (later Lord Brockway), radical socialist intellectuals and representatives of national movements in colonial territories. Participants from Africa included Messali Hadj and Hadjali 'Abd al-Kādir (Maghrib); Muḥammad Hafiz Bey Ramadan and Ibrāhīm Yūsuf (Egypt); Lamine Senghor (French West Africa); Jomo Kenyatta (Kenya); and J. T. Gumede and I. A. La Guma (South Africa). Also represented were members of the Inter-Colonial Union, including Max Bloncoux, while Carlos Deambrosis Martins came from Haiti.

There were also movements concerned with protecting the rights of man and citizenship and anti-slavery bodies which operated both in Europe and in several colonies in Africa. Movements which originated from America, like Marcus Garvey's Universal Negro Improvement Association, first launched in 1917, exerted influence in several colonies in Africa.

The expression of African nationalism and politics

Although the colonial and the general international environment were broadly the same, the actual expression of African nationalism and politics, phenomena neatly summed up by the Swahili word *siasa*, varied from place to place, even in territories under the same imperial master. Factors which conditioned the form and intensity of action by nationalists (*wanasiasa*) in the colonies included the type of leadership, the variations in the spread and intensity of European influences in the form of ideas and institutions; the number and significance of the settler (white) population; and, lastly, the colonial ideologies and practices.

In nearly all cases, the nationalist movements and the attendant colonial politics were led and dominated by the new western-educated elites, who were the best equipped to understand the European political culture and therefore to challenge the colonial regimes effectively on the terms enunciated by the latter. Sometimes they co-operated actively with members of the 'traditional' leadership elites, even if there were tensions in their relations. Such co-operation featured in territories like the Gold Coast (Ghana) with the Aborigines' Rights Protection Society, Southern Nigeria, Morocco, and among the Gikuyu of Kenya. In some cases, leadership remained within the ranks of the 'traditional' elites as in Libya and Morocco. In most cases, however, since those who represented or were recruited to represent traditional leadership elites were preferred by colonial regimes as instruments of control, the tendency was for the expression of nationalism to involve treating the traditional elites as accomplices and for them to be attacked as such.

Intensity of variations in European influences in the form of ideas and institutions also influenced African reactions. The Africans in the areas which had been the most exposed to European education were well equipped and willing to adopt the European model of political and social development. They tended, therefore, to be constitutional in their agitations for desired change. The existence of a forum for doing this in the colonial legislatures was an incentive.

In places like Egypt and the Anglo-Egyptian Sudan, Algeria (especially the three departments of Algiers, Constantine and Oran), the French protectorates of Morocco and Tunisia, and the coastal areas of British and French West Africa, African activities were characterized by constitutionalism, and the employment of techniques of exerting political pressures that were appropriate to Western European political processes. One reason for this was that the African nationalists were addressing themselves both to the immediate colonial authorities and to liberal political groups and opinions in the imperial metropolis.

The constitutional approach found an ever-widening social base as the groups of educated Africans expanded and as new economic and social groups emerged as part of the dynamics of the colonial economy and following upon measures, especially educational institutions, which were adopted to ensure African manpower for economic and social activities.

The role of the different official ideologies enunciated by the colonial powers was another determinant. The differences in the orientation and style of African nationalists derived in part from the fact that the various groups had different ideologies to guide their expectations and by which to assess their achievements. Hence, among African nationalists under French control in Algeria and Senegal, where the possibility of ending colonialism through the policy of 'assimilation'—by the attainment of French citizenship for individuals with full rights and responsibilities—had been demonstrated, the tendency was to continue to press for the extension, both in scope and territorially, of the implementation of the policy. On the other hand, nationalists in British territories, with the hope of eventual independence as separate sovereign countries, though as members of the British Commonwealth, were understandably more explicitly concerned during the period under consideration with reforms and participation which would prepare them ultimately for independence. The difference was not as to the objective of freedom, which they all wanted, but rather as to method.

Related to ideology as a factor is the settler factor. The settler factor showed in the relative intensity of colonization as a process, the frustration of the expectations of the colonized or the lack of responsiveness to African claims. This factor explains the differences in tone and intensity in the expression of African nationalism as between settler-ridden Algeria on the one hand, and, on the other, French territories which did not have Algeria's settler problem. The same happened as between settler-dominated Kenya, Rhodesia and South Africa, on the one hand, and other British colonies. The different experiences of these territories resulted from the settlers' firm determination to perpetuate the subjugation of the indigenous population by practising what has been described as 'ultra-colonialism'.

Serving as channels for the expression of the aspirations and claims of African nationalism, and of specific grievances, were political parties and youth organizations. Political parties were meaningful in the few places where there were colonial legislatures. In Egypt, the granting of a parliament by the British, who had unilaterally declared a sham independence in 1922, provided a purpose for the organization and operation of political parties. The constitutional situation made it possible for Sa'd Zaghlūl's Wafd Party and the Nationalist Party to play a very important role in the struggle for the restoration of full independence and sovereignty to Egypt. The introduction of constitutional changes, though of less importance, in Nigeria and the Gold Coast (Ghana) in British West Africa paved the way for the appearance and meaningful operation of political parties like the National Democratic Party of Nigeria. So also did political parties play important roles in Senegal, where the General Council, which, after 1920, became the Colonial Council, provided the forum.

Youth organizations, ethnic associations, old boys' associations and other movements dedicated to the achievement of civil liberties and the rights of man fulfilled an invaluable role in all the colonies, irrespective of their constitutional situations. They were an unavoidable political and social force, especially in areas where open political activities were made impossible by the repressive nature of colonial rule. Youth organizations which acted as catalysts in nationalist, anti-colonial politics, and whose activities will be discussed in the next chapters, included the Gold Coast Youth Conference, which was founded in 1929, the Lagos (later Nigeria) Youth Movement, Young Egypt, Harry Thuku's Young Kikuyu Association, founded in Kenya in 1921, the Sudan Graduates' Congress, the Young Gabonese (Jeune Gabonais) and the Young Tunisians. Some of the movements were inter-regional while others were trans-territorial. The former included the North African Star under the leadership of Messali Hadj, the National Congress of British West Africa, the South Africa Congress and the West African Students' Union, led by the Nigerian Ladipo Solanke, which drew its membership from all of British West Africa.

Social organizations which contributed to the expression of African nationalism, and anti-colonial politics included the several branches in Africa of Marcus Garvey's Universal Negro Improvement Association, which had been founded in America in 1917. Such was the Nigerian Improvement Association (1920). We also have bodies like the League for the Rights of Man and Citizenship in Gabon (Ligue des Droits de l'Homme et du Citoyen); the Liga Africana at Luanda and Lorenço Marques in Portuguese Angola and Mozambique; André Matswa's Société Amicale des Originaires de l'Afrique Equatoriale Française with membership from Libreville, Bangui and Brazzaville; and La Ligue Universelle pour la Défense de la Race Nègre (1925), led by Tovalou Quenum (Dahomey, now Benin), Le Comité, and La Ligue de Défense de la Race Nègre, led by Kouyaté Garang (French Soudan, now Mali) and Lamine Senghor (Senegal). There was also, at the international level, the Comité Mondial Contre la Guerre et le Fascisme and various pan-Africanist congresses organized by Sylvester Williams and William Du Bois. Trade unions and other working-class movements also became important agents in the fight against the colonial system, though they became even more important after the Second World War.

Multifarious were the weapons that were fashioned during the inter-war period for the attack on the colonial system. Revolts and rebellions, which were so common in the previous period, were reduced to a minimum. Instead, newspapers, books, pamphlets, petitions, protest migrations, strikes, boycotts, the ballot box, the pulpit and the mosques became the stock-in-trade of the nationalists. The newspapers became a particularly vital organ for the dissemination of the views for these political and social organizations. The appearance of these papers varied from daily to weekly, fortnightly or monthly. Others were published only when it was possible. A number of the newspapers and periodicals had been in existence before the First World War. Such were *al-Liwa*, an Arabic newspaper founded in 1900 to popularize Egyptian nationalist ideas, *La Démocratie du Sénégal*, and *The Lagos Weekly Record*, founded in 1891. The majority, however, were founded in the inter-war period. Such were the *Times of Nigeria* (1921–30) and *Lagos Daily News* (1925–38), *Le Périscope Africain* and *Le Courrier de l'Ouest-Africain* (Dakar), the *African Morning Post* and *The Gold Coast Times* (Accra), *L'Action Tunisienne* (1932), and *La Presse Porto-Novienne*, with subtitles and a section in Yoruba. Newspapers in African languages other than the Egyptian *al-Liwa* included the Yoruba language paper, *Akede Eko* (Lagos, 1932 onwards), and *La Voix de Dahomey*. From outside Africa came communist-inspired and pan-African periodicals like the *Race Nègre*, *Negro World* and the *African Times and Orient Review*. Besides newspapers, plays, pamphlets, tracts and many books were written by some of the nationalist leaders, in which the colonial system was sharply criticized and ridiculed.

The newspapers and periodicals, both local and foreign, naturally served as vehicles for the transmission of anti-colonial and anti-European nationalism. It was to checkmate this development that various repressive administrative and legislative measures were taken against the mass media, including the slowly-expanding radio services. Efforts were made to prevent or limit the circulation of books, newspapers and periodicals, and of radio sets, even when these emanated from the home countries of the colonial administrators. The local press was in nearly all cases rigidly controlled through censorship and sedition laws. All these were to facilitate the operations of the colonial administrations, which became characterized by greater intolerance of nationalist aspirations and by deprivation of civil and personal liberties and rights.

Other instruments used by African nationalists during our period were traditionalist or 'nativistic' socio-religious movements. Of particular relevance, as we have seen already in some of the earlier chapters, were the messianic movements which expressed indigenous ideologies as well as those which reflected Islamic and Christian ones. They were movements which were emancipatory in character, expressing what is essentially a universal phenomenon in situations in which communities had to express their dissatisfaction with their living conditions and desire for regeneration.

Prominent examples of such movements in our period, some of whose activities have been discussed in Chapter 20 above, were Ethiopianism in South and East Africa, and the movement spearheaded by millenarian preachers in Southern and Central Africa, notably the Kitawala (African Watch Tower) with its large following in Northern and Southern Rhodesia and spreading to the Congo and Nyasaland; the Kimbanguist movement with its following in Belgian and French Congo and the neo-Kimbanguist Mission des Noirs, founded in the Lower Congo by Simon-Pierre Mpadi. Otherwise known as the Khakists, the movement had influence among the population of French

Congo and Oubangui-Chari (now Central African Republic). Others were Ruben Spartas Mukasa's African Progressive Association and the Christian Army for the Salvation of Africa in Uganda and Jordan Msuma's Last Church of God and His Christ in Nyasaland. Some of these movements were inspired by their acceptance of Christianity but disenchantment with the expression of the religion in the organized Church of the colonial societies. Like the reformation movements in Europe and elsewhere, the churches and movements founded by African nationalists aimed at applying Christian ideologies, like the ideas of the brotherhood of man and the essential oneness of believers, without distinction as to race or colour and at ending discrimination and oppression.

Islam also represented a counterpoise to colonial ideology as well as a forum for the expression of messianism. The Mahdī is for the Muslim what the Messiah is for the Christian. Mahdism haunted colonial authorities in North and West Africa, the Sudan and Somaliland. The Sanūsiyya in Italian-dominated Libya, as we have seen already, presented perhaps the clearest example of the expression of African nationalism and anti-colonialism through Islam. Pan-Islamism, the religious side of the culture-bound pan-Arabism, and the idea of *Salafiya* also played a prominent role in the nationalist and anti-colonial politics in Egypt, the Maghrib and northern Anglo-Egyptian Sudan. The Sanūsiyya influence as an anti-colonial force spread to parts of West Africa. The colonial authorities found Islamic movements like the Hamalliyya, the Tijaniyya and the Mouridiyya a constant threat to the security of the colonial system.

These Islamic movements provided a strong link among adherents who found themselves under different colonial regimes. From the First World War, as Crowder has shown in Chapter 12 above, pan-Islamic ideology being disseminated from Turkey was a worrying issue to colonial authorities in many parts of Africa. It was a problem colonial rulers sought to tackle through the exchange of information and inter-colonial co-operation.

Regardless of the degree of exposure to western influences experienced by the colonized African, a common base for the expression of African nationalism was the cultural movements of different forms. The point has been made about the resilience and continuing relevance of African cultures and institutions throughout Africa for the colonized. Even the most westernized of African educated elites were faced with the reality that they were essentially Africans whatever their degree of acculturation. Most of the youth movements already referred to, and as will be seen later, showed an awareness of the crucial importance of their culture to the preservation of their self-identity in spite of the inroads of Europe by way of the school system. The various Gikuyu associations were a good example. So also were the pan-African movements and the rather fluid concept of *négritude* which, as has been shown in Chapter 21 above, found expression from the early 1930s, as well as the so-called 'nativistic' and 'religious' movements already referred to.

In the inter-war period, colonialism and African nationalism were in a state of conflict. African nationalism and anti-colonial activities did not achieve much success in the inter-war period but they did cause some concern among the colonial officials. All the repressive anti-colonial measures taken during the period reflect this concern. Their responses to the challenges posed by African nationalism amounted to wanting to screen off Africa from general currents of development in the world. Not only was this unrealistic and self-contradictory, but the attempt also acted as a catalyst that hastened the growth of African nationalism and anti-colonialism, which, with the impact of the Second World War, soon led to the movement for the overthrow of the colonial system.

23

Politics and nationalism in North-East Africa, 1919–35

Introduction

Two forms of nationalism competed for supremacy in North-East Africa in the inter-war years – secular nationalism on the one side and religiously inspired patriotism on the other. The continuing legacy of the Mahdī in the Sudan and of Sayyid Muhammad in Somalia managed to fuse religion and patriotic sentiment the most directly. On the other hand, Egyptian nationalism in the inter-war years was getting more secular. Basically secular also were the protests in southern Sudan. It was in northern Sudan and Somalia during those inter-war years that the religious factor was the more difficult to disentangle from the political.

In addition to the dialectic between religion and secularism in politics during these years, there was the dialectic between nationalism and economic problems. This period included some of the worst years of economic depression in the history of the modern world. By the end of the 1920s the imperial powers themselves were experiencing the pressures of a deepening recession, culminating in the great depression. The colonies of North-East Africa had been feeling the economic squeeze a decade or two before the great depression hit the industrialized world.

For North-East Africa yet another characteristic of the inter-war years was that they witnessed both a further expansion of imperialism, on one side, and a new militancy against imperialism on the other. The years between the two world wars were the years of imperialism's last territorial push in Africa as new territory was annexed and colonial rule was consolidated. But the same years also witnessed the rise of anti-colonial militancy among the colonized peoples and the beginnings of effective political organization in pursuit of freedom and equality, especially in Egypt. However, it would appear that during these years Egyptian nationalism was still tainted by a form of expansionism of its own. The leaders of the new nationalist movement in Egypt still regarded the Sudan as an Egyptian dependency and sought to recover effective Egyptian sovereignty over it.

These, then, are the basic contradictions of the inter-war years in North-East Africa – the dialectic between economic and political forces, between religion and nationalism, between the last frontier of imperialism and the new frontier of anti-colonialism, and between local patriotism and local expansionism, especially, in Egypto-Sudanese relations.

Let us now look at these developments in greater detail, country by country.

Egypt

The 1919 revolution

One of the significant consequences of Britain's declaration of a protectorate over Egypt in 1914 and the ending of the First World War and the ensuing negotiations was the formation in November 1918 of al-Wafd al-Misri, or the Egyptian Delegation, by Sa'ad Zaghlul (see 23.1), the distinguished Egyptian leader, and two of his colleagues. Its ultimate objectives were openly to win complete independence for Egypt and secretly to ensure Egyptian sovereignty over the Sudan and abolish the Capitulations which granted special privileges to foreigners resident in Egypt.

Zaghlul and his colleagues represented not only the new Egyptian elite of modern administrators, lawyers and other secular professionals, but also a new group of landowners from the provinces bent on wresting leadership from the hands of the older alien Turco-Egyptian and Albanian aristocracy.

The Wafd reverted to militant tactics to strengthen its leadership and mobilize countrywide support for its position. It distributed leaflets, organized public meetings, and collected signed statements from all representative organizations in the country to the effect that the Wafd was the official representative of the Egyptian nation, solely authorized to negotiate its future. It described the unilateral British declaration of a protectorate over Egypt in December 1914 as humiliating and illegal and advocated its immediate abolition in fulfilment of President Woodrow Wilson's doctrines and the Allies' promises of freedom for small nations.

The many social and economic problems that beset the Egyptian society during the First World War created a widely felt sense of deprivation among the masses which helped the nationalist cause. Peasants were forcefully recruited in large numbers to serve in the Allied labour and camel corps. Their grain and animals were seized without adequate compensation. The sharp rise in the cost of living was particularly harmful to government employees and unskilled labourers. Landowners were unable to profit substantially from the rise in the price of cotton because Britain limited its acreage of cultivation, fixed its prices, and restricted its export. The Wafd repeatedly blamed Britain for this injustice and persuaded the Egyptians to rally behind it in order to redress it. This energetic campaign led to the gradual alienation of all classes from Britain. By 1919 an inflammable state of discontent prevailed throughout the country. The British government's insistence on maintaining the status of the protectorate and its subsequent stubborn refusal to allow Husayn Rushdi, the wartime prime minister, and Zaghlul to present Egypt's case in the Paris Peace Conference worsened an already explosive situation. But what touched off the 1919 revolution was the arrest on 8 March 1919 of Zaghlul and two of his colleagues and their deportation to Malta.

A series of violent demonstrations and massive strikes by transport workers, judges and lawyers broke out. Students from al-Azhar university and secondary and professional schools actively participated in the nationalist struggle. Soon the provinces joined in the general protest, and attempted more daring attacks upon railway and telephone

23.1 *Nationalism in Egypt: Zaghlul Pasha (c. 1857–1927) speaks at a demonstration demanding the withdrawal of British troops, c. 1920 (Harlingue-Viollet)*

communications. Frequent attacks were also made on British military personnel, culminating in the murder of eight British officers and men on a train from Aswān to Cairo at Deyrūt on 18 March. In short, the country was brought to a standstill and Britain's position in Egypt was seriously threatened. The Wafd now emerged as the sole representative of the nation and Zaghlūl dominated the national political scene until his death in 1927.

The 1919 revolution is indeed a significant event in the history of modern Egypt. For it mobilized, for the first time, all Egyptian classes (peasants, workers, students, landowners and intellectuals) and religious groups (Copts and Muslims) against British colonialism. It also clearly demonstrates the new secular nature of Egyptian nationalism.

The Declaration of Independence of 28 February 1922 was the most significant result of the 1919 revolution. Under the pressure of the nationalists, Britain unilaterally abolished the protectorate and recognized Egypt's independence on condition that the status quo would be maintained in the following matters (usually called the Reserved Points) until the conclusion of an agreement with Egypt: the security of imperial communications, the defence of Egypt, the protection of minorities and foreign interests, and the Sudan. Egypt's independence was formally declared on 15 March 1922, and Sultan Fu'ād assumed the title of Fu'ād I, King of Egypt. But was this a genuine case of decolonization? It was not, for the independence granted by the Declaration was diluted by the Reserved Points, particularly by the reservation which provided for the continued British military occupation of Egypt. Secondly, foreigners continued to enjoy their extra-territorial privileges. Thirdly, the 1923 Constitution did not establish constitutional rule and parliamentary democracy in Egypt since it gave extensive powers to the monarchy, such as the right to select and appoint the prime minister, dismiss the cabinet and dissolve parliament.

This inability to achieve all the nation's aspirations was, in the main, the outcome of the progressive breakup of the national unity achieved in 1919. This was caused by a serious split in 1920 between the moderates led by 'Adlī Yakan and the militants led by Zaghlūl. The former advocated compromise with Britain while the latter insisted on the continuation of the struggle until Britain yielded to all the nation's demands. Britain's colonial diplomacy of 'divide and rule' made extensive use of this split in the Wafd's ranks. While suppressing the militants, Allenby accommodated the moderates and negotiated the Declaration of Independence with them.

The era of negotiations 1924–35

In the post-Declaration period, the nationalist struggle was predominantly focused on liberation from the crippling Reserved Points through a negotiated settlement with Britain. Four negotiations took place between 1924 and 1935 – in 1924, 1927, 1929 and 1930. But they all failed because Britain refused to make any concessions that might relax its occupation of Egypt or change the status quo in the Sudan.

Britain remained so intransigent mainly because of its relations with the Palace, which became a strong anti-Wafdist centre of power. After supporting the Wafd-led independence movement in 1919, King Fu'ād soon came to suspect that Zaghlūl was planning to overthrow the monarchy and declare Egypt a republic, and so mounted an attack on the Wafd. To prevent the Wafd's accession to power, Fu'ād suspended the 1923 Constitution three times in less than seven years – in 1924, 1928 and 1930 – and in each case appointed his own prime minister. The various Palace governments that ruled Egypt before 1935, particularly that of Şidķī (1930–5), took repressive measures against the Wafd. Its leaders were imprisoned, newspapers were banned and supporters were dismissed from their posts in the government and civil service. Besides endorsing these extreme measures, the colonial administrators occasionally took direct measures to humiliate the Wafd. For instance, Zaghlūl was not allowed in 1924 and 1926 to be prime minister though his party had a majority in parliament.

This Palace–Residency suppressive campaign led to a gradual decline in the Wafd's popularity and erosion of its unity. Dissatisfied with what they called the 'uninspired leadership' of Nahhās, Zaghlūl's successor, a group of Wafd leaders deserted the party in 1932. Being less able and willing to confront colonialism, the majority of the Wafd leaders therefore decided in the mid-1930s to strengthen themselves against the Palace by a deal with Britain. This decision led to the conclusion of the 1936 treaty that legalized British occupation of Egypt and maintained the British-dominated administration in the Sudan.

The Sudan

Sudanese resistance to British colonial rule expressed itself in the aftermath of the First World War in various activities and sentiments. The educated elite and the Mahdists, the religious nationalists, organized this opposition in the northern Sudan while the protest movements in the southern Sudan were predominantly local in nature.

Young protest movements

The recently emergent educated elite, composed mainly of students and 'graduates' of Gordon Memorial College and Khartoum Military College, played a distinctive role in the development of Sudanese politics during the period 1919–25. They formed their own associations, the earliest being the Graduates' Club of Omdurman in 1918 and the next two, which were clandestine, being the League of Sudanese Union (LSU) in 1919 and, more importantly, the White Flag League (WFL) in May 1924.

The Sudanese nationalist movement of the early 1920s has been dismissed by many British writers as unrepresentative and its proponents as mere agents and pawns of Egypt. But recent studies by Sudanese scholars have demonstrated that, though tactically, culturally and ideologically closely connected with Egypt, this movement was indigenous and mainly concerned with the overthrow of British colonial rule. The call for unity with Egypt by the nationalists was apparently more of a political slogan than a tenet of nationalist faith and was largely calculated to gain the sympathy and support of Egypt, which was undergoing a national struggle herself.

Inspired by the example of the Wafd, Sudanese nationalists developed local grievances into an ideology of opposition to alien rule. They did not, however, formulate their opposition in religious terms, but dwelt upon the economic and political grievances, always emphasizing the greed and foreignness of the colonizer.

The main technique used by the nationalists for the dissemination of their ideas and propaganda on a mass level was at first hand-outs. Leaflets were mailed to different addresses in the country and sometimes posted in public places and scattered on the streets. Moreover, the nationalists occasionally smuggled some material for publication in the sympathetic Egyptian press.

By 1923, however, the nationalists had abandoned these ineffective clandestine methods of propaganda for more revolutionary tactics aimed at broadening the nationalist base and mobilizing popular support for its ideals. In 1924 they organized violent political agitation in Khartoum and some provincial capitals and towns. The WFL organized a series of demonstrations and riots in Atbara, Port Sudan, al-'Obeyd and Shendī, particularly after the arrest of its founder and president, 'Abd al-Laṭīf, and two of his colleagues in July. The secular side of Sudanese nationalism was more pronounced in these riots.

The Sudanese military were particularly susceptible to the ideas and propaganda of the WFL. The cadets were incited to demonstrate in some northern and southern towns. The Sudanese officers, many of whom were, incidentally, of Dinka origin, planned and executed the important military revolt of November 1924 in Khartoum. The main political motive of this revolt was to show sympathy and solidarity with the Egyptian troops, whose withdrawal from the Sudan had been ordered by Britain. Sudanese troops marched from their barracks to join the Egyptian units in Khartoum North. But the British troops fired on them *en route*. The result was a fierce battle that continued throughout the evening and night of 27–28 November, and claimed the lives of more than a dozen Sudanese troops. The total collapse of this revolt, coupled with the hostility of the colonial regime and its determination to suppress open political action, forced the educated class to abandon militant action during the following decade and to fall back on literary, religious and social activities. They formed small study groups in various towns and pioneered several short-lived but lively newspapers and magazines.

The first nationalist movement of the early 1920s was thus not successful and the main reason for its failure was that since it neither sought nor wished to ally itself with local and religious forces, the two reservoirs of mass following in the country, it lacked popular support. Nevertheless, it is significant first because it emerged earlier than nationalist movements in other tropical African dependencies, and secondly because its most important political slogan—the Unity of the Nile Valley—was picked up by the Unionist political parties in the 1940s.

Mahdist resistance to colonial rule

Mahdism was one of the early weapons that the Sudanese used in their struggle against colonialism outside the metropolitan province around Khartoum. Hardly a year passed during the first generation of Condominium rule (1899–1955) without a Mahdist rising against colonialism. Though this type of opposition subsequently gradually died down in the sedentary parts of the Sudan, the Mahdists remained active in Dārfūr. Many assumed for themselves messianic prophecy and declared a *djihād* against the 'infidel' British rule. The most important of them was *faḳī* 'Abdullāh al-Sihaynī, the leader of the Nyala revolt of 1921.

Like its predecessors, the Nyala revolt aimed at the overthrow of the 'infidel' colonial rule and the restoration of the 'glorious' Mahdiyya in the Sudan. Beside this fundamental religious drive, the imposition of a centralized colonial administration and increase in the herd tax were other factors that provoked the people in Dārfūr to join the revolt.

Led by al-Sihaynī, a force of about 5000 warriors attacked Nyala fort and the market on 26 September 1921. They seized the fort and set fire to a nearby building. Al-Sihaynī launched a second attack that could have driven the enemy into confusion had he not been seriously wounded. Though al-Sihaynī was publicly hanged on 4 October, his adherents continued the struggle. Faced with this challenge, colonial officials sent a strong punitive force that arrested many people, burned their houses, seized their cattle and confiscated their property. By May 1922, this revolt had been suppressed.

The Nyala revolt was certainly the most important revolt against colonialism in the Sudan before 1924. Though the rising failed to destroy colonial rule, its limited success was taken as a warning by the British.

Neo-Mahdism

After the failure of the militant religious form of opposition in the 1920s, some of the nationalists, such as Sayyid 'Abd al-Rahmān, the posthumous son of the Mahdī, resorted to neo-Mahdism. Since 1914, al-Sayyid had felt that armed rising could only lead to total destruction and that the interests of both the Sudanese nation and the Mahdist sect would best be served by co-operating with the British on the motto of the Sudan for the Sudanese. Al-Sayyid was also shrewd enough to realize that political and religious agitation required financial backing. Consequently, he enlarged his agricultural and commercial enterprises until, by 1935, he had become a large landowner and a wealthy capitalist, and he used this wealth to strengthen the Ansār organization. Seeing that political nationalism was beginning to supersede religion as the principal motive power in the east, al-Sayyid made special efforts in the 1930s to gain the support of the educated class.

By 1935 neo-Mahdism had thus become an important anti-colonial political force. The potential unity that it achieved between a sizeable section of the intelligentsia and the traditional and religious elements became the nucleus for the Independence Front, which played an important and unique role in achieving the independence of the nation in 1956.

Local protest movements in the southern Sudan

The African peoples of the southern Sudan continued their risings with a view to ending British colonial rule in that region. Of this major wave of resistance, two risings deserve particular attention: the Aliab Dinka uprising (1919–20) and the Nuer revolt (1927–8). African traditional religion affected the nature of these revolts.

The immediate cause of the Aliab Dinka uprising was the malpractices of the Aliab's immediate colonial administrator, the *ma'mūr*, particularly his extortion of cattle and women. It began on 30 October 1919, when a force of some 3000 warriors attacked the police station at Minkamman, south of the Sobat river. The station itself was overwhelmed by the Aliab, though the *ma'mūr* managed to escape. On 2 November the

Aliab struck again, attacking a rest-house and killing two policemen. Although this Dinka assault was eventually repelled, the campaign proved very costly for the colonial rulers.

The Nuer peoples offered another formidable challenge to colonialism in the southern region. In spite of the successive punitive patrols of the British forces, they did not accept defeat, and their resistance reached its climax in their revolt of 1927–8. Led by the powerful and influential Prophet Garluark, the western Nuer refused to obey the orders of the administration. In December 1927, a crowd of several thousand Nuer warriors attacked and killed the district commissioner of the area, who was on an inspection tour, together with eighteen of his people.

Simultaneously, the Nuer people in Lou country south of the Sobat river rose against colonialism. Their influential leader, Prophet Gwek Ngundeng, refused to see colonial officials, including the Governor-General himself. Knowing that Ngundeng could strike at any time, colonial officials took strong measures to suppress his movement.

The extreme and indiscriminate violence used against these risings led to widespread death and destruction. Nevertheless, the gallant resistance of the Dinka and the Nuer impressed the British colonialists that violence alone would not work. It forced them to launch in the early 1930s a new conciliatory and 'caring' policy towards the peoples of the southern Sudan.

Somaliland

The Somali people had for long had a deep-rooted common sentiment of Somali-ness, accompanied by a virtually uniform national culture, and reinforced by a strong adherence to Islam. Like both their predecessors and successors, the inter-war Somali nationalists appealed to this national identity in their struggle against Italian, British and French imperialism in Somaliland.

Besides this underlying factor, other forces at work related to changes that colonialism introduced into the Somali social fabric. Colonial forces had, in fact, destroyed the traditional social and political institutions by introducing in all parts of Somalia a centralized system of administration that vested all effective power in the hands of colonial administrators and appointed chiefs. The latter, known as *akils* in the British protectorate and *capos* in Italian-ruled Somalia, operated in an advisory capacity only and as vehicles for colonial directives to the people. With their fierce sense of independence and traditional hatred for all foreign elements, especially white Christians, the Somali people were bound to resist this radical change.

Furthermore, before the colonial era, the Somali were not subject to government taxes other than *kādi* fees and import and export duties. But the colonial powers instituted direct taxes for the first time and forcefully recruited labour for their enterprises. The French recruited 2000 Somali to work for them as manual labourers during the First World War while the Italians sent frequent gangs to seize the required labour for their plantations in Somalia. All this hardship and exploitation produced a widely felt sense of resentment to colonialism.

Somali resistance to colonial rule during the period 1919–35 was thus a direct response to these social changes. It expressed itself in two types of protest movements: local and elitist.

Local protest movements

By and large, Somali resistance in the inter-war period was local in nature and took the form of a series of local risings which are too many and too diverse to be enumerated here. But what they stood for may be seen from studying some of them.

The directive of the colonial administrators to all Somali chiefs and elders to surrender firearms and ammunition was rejected outright by Hādj dji Hasan of the Galjal Haya. Though Hādj dji Hasan was captured, the spirit of resistance could not be killed, for the Bantu Eile people waged another rising near Bur Acuba.

The resistance to the Italian attempt to incorporate in their colony the two northern provinces, Obbia and Midjurteyn, was another example of the determination of the Somali people to maintain the traditional and free social fabric of their society.

Though Obbia was annexed in 1925 and the Italians pensioned Yūsuf off to Mogadishu, a daring rising occurred at al-Būr. It was led by 'Umar Samatar, a Midjurteyn clansman appointed by the Italians as chief of the local population. Samatar seized al-Būr's fort and entrenched his forces in its central building. The Italian forces that besieged him were in turn besieged by the surrounding population, led by Herzi Gushan, Sultan 'Alī Yūsuf's district military commander. On 15 November the colonial forces retreated to Bud Bud, leaving behind thirty-eight dead, among whom was the Italian Resident himself. On 30 November the Italians suffered another defeat in an ambush at Bot.

The Italians faced an even more serious resistance in the Midjurteyn Sultanate. Its reputable Sultan, 'Uthmān Mahmūd, refused the inferior status assigned by the colonialists to himself and his people. In spite of colonial repression, his movement continued to thrive, and he held out against the invaders for almost two years. He was, however, arrested towards the end of 1927, to be treated in the same manner as his kinsman Yūsuf. But the struggle continued under the leadership of his son and heir apparent, Herzi Bogor, until he left for Ethiopia.

Meanwhile the ever-present memory of Sayyid Muhammad's revolt entrenched the spirit of resistance in the hearts of many Somalis in the Protectorate, and some of Sayyid Muhammad's supporters, like Farah 'Umar and Hādj dj Bashīr Yūsuf, continued the struggle, particularly in the west and along the eastern borders. The introduction of western education in the Protectorate in 1920 and 1935 was interpreted by religious leaders as an instrument for Christian missionary activities and consequently a threat to Islam. It therefore aroused fierce resentment that culminated in two riots: at Burao in 1922 and Baro in 1936.

Equally significant were the local risings of the Somali people against French colonialism. Both the Afar, and the Isa Somalis, the two main ethnic groups in French Somaliland, displayed a hostile attitude towards colonial administration. The Afar Sultanates of Tadjura and Gobaad were particularly active in this respect. The French had in fact summarily deported the Sultan of Gobaad to Madagascar in 1931. The Sultan Yayu of Awsa, who had for long opposed French penetration in the area, also continued his resistance during this period. He ambushed and arrested Lippmann, the newly appointed governor at Dikhil. His successor, Albert Bernard, and sixteen of his Somali troops were murdered at Morheito in 1935. The activism of the Sultan of Awṣa further increased after the Italian conquest of Ethiopia in 1935.

These local risings against colonial rule in Somaliland failed for two main reasons. The first was that the Somali did not constitute a single autonomous political unit but were rather divided into a number of often hostile clans, which were further split into numerous kinship groups, each usually composed of a few thousand men only. They therefore failed to present a united front against colonial rule. The second was the tough policy that the colonial powers adopted against them. Nevertheless, these risings provided an element of continuity with the former era and laid the foundation of further popular resistance to colonialism in Somaliland.

Elitist protest movements

While these uprisings were going on in the rural areas, the Somali educated elite in the towns were also attacking the colonial system through the 'young' associations that they organized.

The first of them was the Somali Islamic Association, founded in Aden by Ḥādj dji Farah 'Umar, a former colonial official and a pioneer modern politician. He had been exiled to Aden by the British for protesting in the 1920s against the excesses of colonial administration, and campaigning for the improvement of economic facilities and expansion of education. Though not a political organization as such, this association promoted Somali interests. Ḥādj dji Farah brought the Somali national aspirations to the notice of the British public through articles in Aden newspapers and petitions and letters addressed to the British government, press and members of parliament.

Political clubs were also established by merchants and junior colonial officials in the main towns of the Protectorate in the mid-1930s, which played a role in expressing people's grievances and promoting political consciousness in towns and urban centres. In French Somaliland, too, the Seamen's Union, established in Djibuti in 1931, did not confine itself to sailor's affairs but campaigned for Somali representation in government and their share in the territory's economy.

From these tentative beginnings the Somali National League (SNL), the most important 'young' association in the inter-war years, emerged in 1935. From its inception the SNL saw itself as a pan-Somali organization striving to break down all traditional resistance to a national patriotism. The SNL continued to exist under various titles, and in 1951 it emerged as a full-fledged political party in the British Protectorate.

Like the rural nationalists, these elitist associations did not achieve much for two main reasons. First, the educated elite that formed these movements was too small in number to be effective since western education during the inter-war period was virtually ignored in all parts of Somaliland. Secondly, the colonial authorities took prompt steps to neutralize the few activists among the educated elite by, for example, dismissing them from government service or posting them to remote areas. Nevertheless, the limited awareness founded by these associations developed into a stronger political consciousness in the years after the Second World War.

In this connection one has to mention the invention in about 1920 of an indigenous alphabet for the Somali language, the 'Osmania Alphabet', so named after its inventor 'Uthmān Yūsuf Kenadid. Both the conservative religious leaders, who favoured Arabic as a medium for writing Somali, and the Italian colonialists opposed its usage. Nevertheless, it gained restricted usage and was later heralded by the nationalists 'as a symbol of Somali achievement'.

Conclusion

From the above, it is evident that the inter-war years witnessed intensive nationalist activities in North-East Africa, inspired not only by the changes introduced by colonialism but also by religious considerations. It is equally evident that unlike most other parts of Africa, the nationalist leaders did not fight for accommodation within or reform of colonialism but rather for its overthrow. Though it was only in Egypt that these nationalist activities bore substantial fruits, there is no doubt that the seeds of liberation were indeed sown in the Nile Valley and the Horn of Africa in these inter-war years.

Politics and nationalism in the Maghrib and the Sahara, 1919–35

In the rest of North Africa, that is, in Libya and the Maghrib, the inter-war period witnessed three main political activities. The first was the continuation of the resistance or opposition to imperialism's last territorial push in Africa by some North Africans with the principal objectives of maintaining their sovereign and independent existence. This was particularly true of the political activities in Libya and in the High and Middle Atlas of Morocco. The second was a genuine anti-colonial or nationalist activity, aimed at either the overthrow of the colonial system or its reform, which took a particularly militant form immediately after the war. This phase ended in 1923 in Algeria and Tunisia, with the simultaneous departure of al-Thaʿālibi and Khālid, though not in Morocco, especially the Rīf area. It would appear, however, that nationalism in these areas was more religious and cultural, like that in the Sudan and Somaliland, rather than predominantly secular, as was the case in Egypt and southern Sudan. In the 1930s, however, as a result of the impact of the world depression, which was particularly felt in the Maghrib from 1932 onwards, anti-colonial and nationalist activities were resumed, though different tactics and methods were resorted to. These three features or phases of politics and nationalism in Libya and Maghrib form the themes of this chapter.

Open war and passive resistance

More than the peoples of the other states of Northern Africa, the people of Libya were virtually throughout the period under review still preoccupied with the problem of maintaining their sovereignty and independence in the face of the aggressive imperialism of Italy. This struggle, which continued well into the 1930s, has been treated in Chapter 5. Libya is therefore not dealt with in this chapter.

The 'dissidence' or *sība* of the Berbers, then practically general in Morocco, was also clearly a continuation of a pre-colonial phenomenon. The penetration of the French into the Middle Atlas region during the period in question encountered more difficulties than that of the sultans, despite the fact that it was still effected in the name of the 'legal government' or *Makhzen*. The defence of the nation took the form of xenophobia and holy war, and resistance spread over all the High and Middle Atlas. In the Algero-Moroccan marches, the area to the north of present-day Mauritania and the western part of the Sahara, known as the Rio de Oro, there were communal raids or *rezzous*, while at the same time attempts at organization were made by the successors of the great religious reformer, Mā-'al-'Aynayn. North of the Tāza corridor, the greater part of the coastal region ceded to Spain remained unsubdued. Far to the east, on the other side of the Algerian Sahara, independent organizations functioned in Tripolitania, and the Sanūsī were able to consolidate their position in the oases. To consider such a widespread phenomenon as mere unruly conservatism is certainly to underrate it. The main impetus behind it was a tradition of communal liberty.

Anti-colonial resistance and nationalist activities in the 1910s and 1920s

While this opposition to the establishment of colonialism was going on in the aforementioned areas, genuine anti-colonial and nationalist activities were raging in those areas where the colonial system had already entrenched itself. These activities took different forms in Algeria, Tunisia and Morocco and were in evidence both in the urban and rural areas, among the intelligentsia as well as the workers and the peasants.

In Algeria, resistance to the colonial system took a militant turn during the brief electoral career of the Emir Khālid. A former captain in the French army, grandson of the great 'Abd al-Kādir, Khālid enjoyed a short period of popularity. In the name of his 'Muslim personality' he extolled the honour of Algeria and emphasized her claims to France's gratitude for all the soldiers she had supplied. Khālid's party, which defeated the moderates in the Algiers town council election, seemed to the authorities so dangerous that they annulled the election. The Emir then won a second and a third election, but was finally obliged to leave Algeria for France in 1923. His departure certainly slowed down the pace of the nationalist movement in Algeria.

The energetic Berber resistance in the towns helped to turn public opinion in rural Algeria into quite a strong social force, and it was to contain this force that the law of 4 February 1919, known as the Jonnart Law, and of the two decrees putting it into effect were passed. It gave Algerians who possessed certain qualifications (such as having served in the army, being able to read and write French, etc.) the right to take part in electing the communal assembly, or *duwār-commune*, and town councils, including the mayor. Nearly half a million Muslims made up this primary electorate; this included about a hundred thousand with the right to vote for departmental and central assemblies too. But this did not end inequality, and the measures fell far below what had been asked for.

In the 1920s, the principal demands of the Algerians were for assimilation, that is, to become part of the French commonwealth, and for some of the Algerians to be given the right to elect deputies to the French Parliament, without losing their other voting rights, based on their 'personal status'. This demand for assimilation, which should probably be interpreted as a desire for emancipation, is evident from the series of articles published by Ferhāt 'Abbās between 1922 and 1927, which he brought out in 1931 under the title *Le Jeune Algérien* (The Young Algerian). In these articles, he denounced colonization as 'power without thought, brain without soul'. The campaign was led by the 'Ulamās Association founded in 1931. One of its leaders, Shaykh 'Abd al-Hamīd ben Bādis, prepared a programme which, while not defying French sovereignty, insisted on an intellectual and moral reform, and in so doing raised the question of identity, touched on the impulses of the majority, and echoed similar movements in the Middle East. He thus appealed to a model which compared well with that of western democracy. Above all, he addressed himself to clearly existing signs of social dispersion and moral deterioration.

Another, less well-known aspect is the geographical one. As the *nasabs* (lines of descent) show, the leadership of the movement included several provincial names: not only those of the Constantine aristocracy, like Ben Bādīs, but also Tébessa, Mīla and Sīdī 'Ukba. Not content with having established the 'Circle of Progress' over the central plateau, especially Algiers and other urban areas, the movement also aimed at covering 'the unknown country'. Shaykh Bashīr al-Ibrāhīmī stirred Tlemcen to its depths, and attempts of this kind grew more and more numerous, in the form of sermons, friendly societies and mutual benefit associations.

The resulting spread of the movement is often attributed only to theological controversies which are almost incomprehensible to outsiders. But all these stirrings represented, for communities which up till then had been quite cut off, the first contact with a worldwide problem. Shaykh Ben Bādīs and his friends set an example by giving North African Islam a doctrinal shake-up which had not been attempted for centuries. The period was a turning-point in the social history of Algeria.

Strange as it may seem today, the celebration of the centenary of the French landing in Algeria did not provoke the hostile reactions that we in this age of decolonization tend to attribute restrospectively to the colonized. To the many Algerians who were then concerned with the claim for justice and equality, the festivities brought first a renewal of hope, though this was swiftly followed by disillusion. The Muslim dignitaries of the regime – elected members, *caïds* and *bachagas* – vied shamelessly with one another in flattering the French, thereby discrediting what remained of the authority of the traditional aristocracy and those who benefited from the policy of compromise. The extravagant expression of praise that arose to the glory of the settlers unfortunately convinced the French of the soundness of their policies in Algeria, a conviction that they held for a very long time.

It was in Tunisia that nationalist activities closely paralled those in Egypt. During the period under review, Ottoman nostalgia was replaced for the enlightened bourgeoisie by hope in the Wilson principles, and nationalism, as in the case of the Egyptian Wafd, changed its tune. Shaykh 'Abd al-'Azīz al-Thaʿālibī (Taalbi) and his friends decided to plead their cause before public opinion in metropolitan France, especially the socialist sector. Their pamphlet, *La Tunisie martyre* (The Martyrdom of Tunisia) (1920), presented a vigorous analysis of colonial deterioration. By founding the 'constitutionalist' or Destūrian party in February 1920, they intended to restore Tunisia to her independent existence. However, going back on its initial radical proposals, the Destūr published a reformist manifesto which 'played into the Protectorate's hands'. Bey Nāsir's quasi-ultimatum of 3 April, 1922 was countered by intimidation. But, in the following year, various beylical decrees and Resident-General's orders set up *caïd*-al, regional and central representation by election at various levels. A Ministry of Justice, entrusted to the son of the reformer Khayruddīn, had already been created. These were scanty results for a campaign which had managed to win over both local sovereigns and the French Chamber. Shaykh al-Thaʿālibī served several months in prison but his release did not contribute to the unity of his party; it broke up into two groups, not equally active. In the colonial context, as Maître Guellati's experience showed, moderation is always suspect.

But anti-colonial activities in Tunisia were not confined to the intellectuals only during our period. They involved the masses though the leadership was concentrated in the hands of a small group educated in the ways of European trade unionism. Two of such leaders were Muhammad 'Alī and Tahār al-Haddād. The adventurous life of the former had brought him into contact with German socialism and made him a friend of Enver Pasha, probably the man with the clearest sense, then, of the ways in which the leading ideas of the West might combine with the nationalist upsurge of the Islamic peoples. Haddād supplemented the foreign experience of Muhammad 'Alī with an examination of the domestic problem. He discussed both the subject of the workers and that of women, showing a clear grasp of the nature of each question. The dockers, first of Tunis and then of Bizerta, the cement-workers of Hammām Lif and others gave a practical response to Haddād's dual drive.

At Bizerta on 12 October 1924, nine regional unions became affiliated: they had the support of the French Communist Party (PCF), but were strongly criticized by the French section of the Workers' International (the SFIO), which was worried by the new group's nationalist affinities. The Destūr dissociated itself from what it considered to be a compromising collusion. But it joined, on a reformist basis, a coalition which in February 1925 brought together the Destūr, the traditional section of the Grand Conseil (Great Council), the socialist party and the French General Confederation of Labour (CGT). The complexity of these alliances and controversies, with their quarrels and reconciliations and changes of position, tends to obscure the spontaneous character of such movements. However, these movements in Tunisia were repressed with the arrest of the organizers of the workers and the banishment of their leader Muhammad 'Alī. It was not until September 1932 that Tunisian trade unionism was legalized and not until 1937 that it resumed independent activity in the context of the events of the Popular Front.

Even more determined and for a time very successful was the resistance against Spanish and French colonialism organized by the Rīf leader Muhammad ben 'Abd al-Khattābī ('Abd al-Karīm) (see 24.1 and 24.2). To describe this as a 'revolt' and treat it as a mere episode is to underrate the significance of facts which we now recognize as the forerunners of much later developments.

The Rīf had never given up the struggle. 'Abd al-Karīm's military talent had inflicted on Spain (at Anwāl, July 1921) one of the most famous disasters of the colonial wars. The Spaniards suffered an equally heavy defeat in November 1924, when they had to evacuate Shafshāwīn in order to straighten their front.

'Abd al-Karīm, the son of a *kādī* (judge) of the Spanish protectorate, and thus born and brought up in a situation of compromise, had studied for a time at the religious university of Karāwiyyīn at Fez, where he probably first came into contact with Islamic modernism. It was no less as a Muslim reformer than as a political leader that he made a position for himself among his contemporaries. As well as military skill, he possessed an open-mindedness and political dexterity which enabled him to play a more influential part internationally than the Libyans who may to a certain extent be regarded as his

24.1 *'Abd al-Karīm (1882–1963), kāḍī of Melilla, leader of Moroccan resistance to Spanish imperialism during the Rīf war, 1921–6 (Harlingue-Viollet)*

24.2 *The Rīf war: Spanish troops display heads of 'Abd al-Karīm's soldiers (Longman)*

counterparts – Sulaymān al-Barunī, Ramdān S̲h̲atiwī, and especially 'Umar al-Mukhtār. The change he brought about in his own clan, the Benī Warig̲h̲īl, and the neighbouring communities was a lasting one. He led these groups, ridden by clan vendettas, back to Islamic law, banning collective oaths and membership of brotherhoods, and forbidding married women to dance. Even before the victory at Anwāl, a meeting at al-Ḳāma between Benī Warig̲h̲īl, Temsamān, Benī Tuzīn and Rukkūya produced a 'crystallization of the Rīfian state structure'. The 'Rīfian Republican Nation', proclaimed according to some on 18 January 1923, was thus an attempt to reform the traditional state without destroying its positive aspects, such as certain practices facilitating group consultation and co-operation.

'Abd al-Karīm had established relations with the PCF, which actually called a strike in his support. During this strike, which occurred on 12 October 1925, many French workers demonstrated against the colonial war in Morocco. There was also a strong campaign of the masses at the national level against the war, organized by the PCF, the Young Communists, the CGTU (the CGT Unifié), ARAC (Association Républicaine des Anciens Combattants), etc. From the spring of 1926 onwards, the Third Republic resorted to exaggerated force to bring 'Abd al-Karīm to heel, and this was accomplished in May 1926. But the rest of Morocco did not react. Nevertheless, the military solution, which enabled Spain to establish itself in the Spanish zone, did not wipe out the significance of the 'Abd al-Karīm experiment.

In Morocco itself, the Berber *zahir* (royal proclamation) of 16 May 1930, which incorporated Berber customary law into the French colonial judicial system, provided middle-class youth with an opportunity to appraise the position and with a first springboard for mass action. It was regarded as an attack on Islam and an attempt to divide the country, carried out in contempt of the undertakings of 1912. Though intended as a local and localizing measure, it had repercussions throughout the Muslim world, while on the spot it brought out into the open an opposition hitherto limited to small clandestine groups in two or three large towns.

In the three months from 20 June to 30 September, 1930, there were more than 120 incidents. Most of them occurred in mosques, the dogmatic setting for the *laṭif*, the Muslim prayer in distress. These activities were considered such a threat to public order that the authorities met them with summonses, imprisonment and beatings. A delegation from the town of Fez went to the capital, and on 31 August three of its members were imprisoned, among them 'Allāl al-Fāsī, 'a young scholar from Karāwiyyīn', and Ben Ḥasan al-Wazzānī, 'graduate of the School of Social and Political Sciences in Paris'. The pair represented an almost symbolic combination of the two driving forces of resistance – orthodox tradition and modernity – and, appropriately enough, repression played the role of catalyst. The number of arrests rose to 150. Many shops closed, as before, in protest. Despite the official ban, the *laṭif* rang out again from the mosques. There were clashes in the streets. The spell of the protectorate was well and truly broken.

Nationalist activities and politics in the 1930s

Out of the twenty years between the two world wars, half thus went by without any significant progress in the relations between France and the Maghrib. Of course, the economic situation was scarcely favourable. Hardly was the immediate post-war depression over than the world slump began. It reached the Maghrib in 1932, accentuating the depressive tendency that had reappeared in 1825 and was to last for a whole decade. This embittered relations between capital and labour, that is, between the French settlers and the Algerians. Progress in mechanization, planning, co-operatives, and even the unionization of public servants enabled the French element to strengthen its stranglehold on the colony. The regime showed itself incapable of moderating the damaging effect of this stranglehold upon those it ruled. The connection between economic deterioration, which aggravated inequality, and political demands is plain, but needs working out in more detail. It seems that social change and the desire for a restored collective identity were even stronger factors than inequality in the awakening of North Africa. At all events, various motives combined to produce an aspiration which largely overrode party groupings. The Waṭaniyyīn, or Moroccan 'Patriots', were then for the most part members of the bourgeois intelligentsia. The Etoile nord-Africaine (North-African Star), founded in Paris in 1924 among the *émigrés* from the Maghrib, had scarcely established itself in Algeria. The Destūr was still imprisoned in unreality. The PCF did not back up its radical theories with enough support on the spot. Most drives for action remained implicit. Political expression was to be found in clubs, committees and groups without a name, or even just in the spreading of attitudes, rather than in political parties as such.

The administration, though unable to understand these nuances of expression, was very good at exploiting personal interests and rivalries. But it played down political protest. It had superiority of means on its side, as well as continuity, and even an apparent consensus. But it was oblivious of the forces which were gathering beneath the seemingly normal surface. If there happened to be an outburst, the government blamed 'trouble-makers', local or abroad, or the 'Reds', an attitude which excused both ultra-conservatism and repression.

New tactics and obstructions to action

It was not all or nothing – far from it – but a deliberately temporal or even secular foothold on the political scene that Bourguiba and his friends Baḥrī Kīka Tahār Safār and Dr Matari, among others, aimed at. They defended the conformist president of the Tunisian Co-operative, because by so doing they were able to rally public opinion. As regards the Great Mosque and the Tunis bourgeoisie, which provided many recruits for the Destūr, they did not conceal their criticism or their sarcasm. It was already apparent that the whole movement would be coloured by the fact that the men of the Sāhel had become militant, and politicizing the country districts was to be one of the aims of the Neo-Destūr. It was not by chance that the split which brought it into being took place at a vividly rural congress held at Kaṣr Hilāl (12 and 13 May 1933). Meanwhile clashes with the Residency became more and more violent, for example at Monastir and Moknīn. Obnoxious decrees were introduced to legalize repression, and Bourguiba, who applied that adjective to them, was imprisoned with his friends in the south (3 September 1934). But even though he was 'down' he still went on pleading the cause.

In Algeria the administration tried to limit the spreading influence of the *'Ulamā'*, mustering against them both the religious brotherhoods and the official clergy, the latter of extremely low standard. The authorities, seeing the people flock to hear the new preachers, whom they instinctively recognized as presenting a necessary updating of Islam, decided to forbid them to preach in the mosques. On 16 February 1933 the 'Michel Circular' – named after the official who drew it up – and three supporting decrees set up an official monopoly to this effect. Not only believers but also trade unionists and militants of the extreme Left took part in the demonstration that followed – a coalition which might have proved effective. Admittedly there occurred at that point a kind of 'divorce' between the Communist and nationalist trends, which was far from healed by the reunification of the CGT and the CGTU in 1935. After several years of clandestine activity, the Étoile nord-Africaine resumed open activity in Algeria itself in June 1933. Mesali Ḥādj, its president, had been using the word independence since 1927. And now, amidst the growing uneasiness, there was an anti-Jewish riot at Constantine in August 1934. Whether this was a plot, a mere explosion, a diversion, or the result of provocation was not clear. But, whatever it was, it was a street outbreak which frightened all the politicians by its violence. Yet at the next elections, in January 1935, the opposition list of Dr Bendjellūl carried the day in Constantine: this showed in which direction the sympathies of the majority were tending. Although the victor was a convinced assimilationist, he aroused the prevailing powers to a fury of preventive measures. Clearly, what mattered in this vague radicalization of public life in Algeria was not the theory expressed but what it suggested or actually provoked.

In Morocco, the settlers, embittered by the slump and irritated by such few limits as the administration imposed upon them, issued an ultimatum. This development, full of symbolic significance, occurred on the same day as the disorders in Paris on 6 February 1934. The same period saw in Morocco the rise of a nationalist press. The Moroccan Action Committee, in which 'Allāl al-Fāsī was beginning to stand out as a leading figure, put forward a 'Reform Plan' on 1 December 1934, which if adopted would have developed its real significance and object in the course of the protectorate. In the Spanish zone, opposition was already being expressed more openly through Torrès and Nāsiri; it established contacts up-country, and almost compromised the future Mohammed V in a demonstration in Fez on 10 May 1934.

The introduction of the Plan coincided with the wiping out of the last centre of dissidence in the south. Henceforth, history was to take quite a different course from the archaic, almost legendary one that had been prolonged beyond its natural span by Lyauteyism and the Ministry for Native Affairs. The coincidence had a bearing outside Morocco itself. The ending of the resistance was also potentially the end of the 'Arab bureaux'. In Algeria and Tunisia too, social change, which weakened old solidarities, also created new ones. The streets of the large towns and even village market-places became the scene of mass action which class and party ideology were able to organize across traditional groupings. In all three countries of French North Africa, and especially in Algeria, where Régnier, the Minister, carried out a showy inquiry, the government's only answer to these material and intellectual developments was to manipulate elections and bring its repressive arsenal up to date.

This refusal of the administration to act cannot be explained entirely by the mounting dangers beyond the Rhine and the arguments this lent to the conservatives in France. The attitudes which the three parties concerned – metropolitan France, the colonialists and the nationalist movement – had taken up enjoined the first two to defend a status quo which the third was not yet in a position to challenge seriously. In return for the slavish allegiance which forbade Europeans in North Africa any originality, metropolitan France gave them her unconditional support. Those in Algeria, for example, who called themselves 'Algerians', carried particularism far enough to get super-profits out of it, but not far enough to risk finding themselves alone, face to face, as a 'dominion' or under some other arrangement, with the Muslim majority. Algeria was France, as they said, but France without democracy. The situation was to all intents and purposes the same in Tunisia and Morocco.

Provisional conclusions

Not everything has emerged into the daylight about the period we have just been examining. But we hope to have suggested that the situation in the Maghrib at this period is, more than many others, to be interpreted in terms of a kind of underground movement, where what was implicit was more important than what was explicit. An approach to bourgeois democracy, international socialism, the reaffirmation of a separate identity – we know now that of these three alternatives it was the third which prevailed. Yet at the time it was not unequivocal, but left the alternative open between two rival camps – Islamic and secular, westernizing and pan-Arab, moderate and revolutionary. In 1935 no one could have said which of the two tendencies would prevail, or even if either would prevail over the colonial set-up. What we may conclude is that history probably left in suspense other possibilities which might have come – perhaps may still come – to govern in other forms other phases of the future.

Politics and nationalism in West Africa, 1919-35

25

In contrast to nationalism and political activities in North Africa, those in West Africa in the inter-war period were primarily secular. Secondly, the objectives of these activities were not .the overthrow of colonialism, as was the case in many of the countries of North Africa, but rather its reform. However, it would appear that, as in North Africa, these activities were far more in evidence in the urban centres and involved the intelligentsia and the bourgeoisie far more than the masses and the rural people, though, as will be seen below, the latter were neither entirely unaware of nor totally unresponsive to the colonial situation. Finally, as in North Africa, nationalism in West Africa was also basically a product of the colonial situation, an awareness or consciousness arising out of the iniquities, oppressiveness and racialist nature of the colonial system.

African nationalism and political activities in western Africa during the period under review were shaped by a number of factors which clearly bring out their secular nature. The first was the impact of the First World War on Africa. This has already been discussed in detail in Chapter 12 above. Suffice it to state here that the compulsory recruitment of many Africans as soldiers aroused a great deal of anger, especially in the former French African areas. Secondly, the war proved to the African that the white man was after all not a superman and could therefore be resisted. Thirdly, after the war, 'loyalist' West Africans were expecting rewards for their loyalty in the form of more concessions and more participation in the running of their own affairs. All these considerations undoubtedly made a good number of West Africans more ready than before to participate in the anti-colonial and resistance movements.

The second factor was the colonial system itself. This became consolidated during the period and its authoritarian and racialist nature became even more evident. It was during this period that various ordinances were introduced which greatly increased the powers of the traditional rulers and virtually eliminated the new educated elite and professional groups from participation in the administration of their own countries. What made this situation all the more explosive was the fact that the period saw a substantial increase in the size of this educated elite and professional group, following the spread of western education locally and the education of more and more people overseas.

But even more important as a factor were the economic conditions of the inter-war period. The economic crisis and changes in the colonial economy, which again have been discussed already, drastically affected the colonial elite of lawyers and merchants, the sub-elite of teachers and civil servants, and the workers, and made them even more conscious than before of the oppressive nature of the colonial system. In Sierra Leone, the frustration of the educated classes, the African traders and the unemployed in the big towns was given open expression in the rice and anti-Syrian riots of 1919 and in the workers' strike the same year. In The Gambia, too, rising prices had their social and political effects, leading to sporadic outbursts of looting and petty theft, as well as a seamen's strike for better wages, and to the formation of unions, notably the Gambia Native Defensive Union. The 1921 slump also led to more agitation from West African merchants a few of whom were financially ruined. All these economic hardships led the West African press to advocate the formation of a common front to press for a reform of the colonial system.

The final background factor was the launching of the pan-Africanist movement and, in particular, the activities of Dr W. E. B. Du Bois and Marcus Garvey, especially in the 1920s. These themes are discussed in great detail in Chapter 29. But let it be mentioned here that the various pan-African congresses organized by Du Bois, and attended by participants from West Africa – in Paris in 1919, in London, Brussels and Paris in 1921, in London and Lisbon in 1922 and in New York in 1927 – first and foremost internationalized nationalist activities and the struggle against colonialism in Africa in general and in West Africa in particular. Secondly, they very much strengthened the consciousness of blacks throughout the world of their common plight as a downtrodden and oppressed race and won more converts to the nationalist cause in West Africa.

Against this background, let us examine the organizations and movements that were formed during the inter-war period for the articulation of nationalist grievances and demands, first in British West Africa and then in Francophone West Africa.

Politics and nationalism in British West Africa

Youth leagues and movements

The most common of these organizations were ethnic unions and youth movements or associations. The inter-war period certainly saw the formation of an increasing number of ethnic, welfare, literary, old boys', voluntary and youth associations, clubs, societies and movements in many countries in West Africa. Numerous Igbo unions were formed in the cities of Nigeria such as Ibadan, Abeokuta and Lagos. In the Colony and Asante regions of the Gold Coast (Ghana) alone, there were as many as fifty of such clubs and associations by 1930, most of them formed between 1925 and 1930. It was some of these clubs and associations that J. B. Danquah organized into the Youth Conference Movement, which held its first meeting in Accra in 1929. In the Gold Coast and Sierra Leone, I. T. A. Wallace Johnson founded his Youth League and the West African Youth League, while the Nigerian Youth Movement was formed in 1934.

All these clubs and associations were led either by the missionary-educated elite or by young lawyers, doctors and businessmen. Though the aim of these leaders was to wrest political leadership from the old conservative nationalist leaders, none of them – with the sole exception of the West African Youth League – made any radical demands in spite of the deteriorating economic conditions of the 1920s and 1930s. Their demands were confined to better and more educational facilities, university education, higher wages and salaries, equitable representation on the legislative and executive councils, abolition of racial discrimination, admission into the higher grades of the civil service, provision of economic opportunities for Africans and better relations between the colonial administration and the Africans. Such certainly were the demands made by the Gold Coast Youth Conference at its first meeting in Accra in 1929, and similar demands were made by the Nigerian Youth Movement (NYM).

The only radical youth movement was that led by Wallace Johnson, a Sierra Leonean trade unionist who had studied in Moscow in 1931–2. He returned to West Africa with the aim of creating a new political force, based on wage labourers and the unemployed in the urban areas, for the overthrow of the colonial system. He founded the Youth League in the Gold Coast by organizing the workers and arousing them against the colonial system by his near-seditious and violent articles and by his skilful manipulation of local grievances, especially the unemployment situation, rising food prices and the frustration caused by the reduced value of cocoa exports since 1929. Because of his activities, he was deported to Sierra Leone, where he established branches of the Youth League in Freetown and Bo, and started a newspaper, *The Sentinel*, which agitated against labour conditions and the Education Ordinance.

Apart from newspaper campaigns and petitions, these youth movements took part in local elections and also resorted to strike action. Thus, they were involved in the demonstrations, riots and strikes in Freetown in Sierra Leone (1926–31), and in Bathurst (now Banjul) in The Gambia (1929). In Accra, the Youth Movement led by Kojo Thompson, an Accra barrister, and Nnamdi Azikiwe participated in the Accra municipal elections under the umbrella of the Mambii Party against the older and more conservative nationalists like Dr F. V. Nanka-Bruce, while the Youth League took part in the Cape Coast local elections. The Nigerian Youth Movement, backed by Azikiwe's *West African Pilot*, also took part in the elections in Lagos in the 1930s.

However, the youth movements did not achieve much. Their electoral successes of the 1930s failed to dislodge the conservative leadership. Nevertheless, the political style of the post-1945 nationalist movement in British West Africa owed much to the experience some of the leaders gained in the youth movements.

Political parties

In addition to these youth movements, a number of political parties were formed to agitate for reforms. The best known of these was the Nigerian National Democratic Party formed in Nigeria by Herbert Macaulay in 1923. Among the points of its programme were the election of the Lagos members of the Legislative Council, the development of higher education and the introduction of compulsory education throughout Nigeria, Africanization of the civil service, free and fair trade in Nigeria and equal treatment for traders and producers of Nigeria. The party employed the usual methods to achieve its aims – participating in elections in Lagos, which it won in 1923,

1928 and 1933, holding mass meetings and sending deputations to the governor, as it did in 1930. This party dominated the politics of Lagos until its defeat by the Nigerian Youth Movement in the Lagos elections of 1938.

Trade unions

Another vehicle for the articulation of anti-colonial sentiments and nationalist grievances was the trade union movement. Even though trade union activities were not allowed or encouraged officially during this period, a number of them did emerge, mainly as a result of the high cost of living. They included the Railway Workers Union of Sierra Leone, the Nigerian Mechanics Union, formed in 1919, and the Gambia Native Defence Union. The typical weapons of these unions were strikes, boycotts and hold-ups. The first series of strikes occurred among the railway and mine workers. Thus a railway strike occurred in Sierra Leone in 1919 and again in 1926. The workers of the Ashanti goldfields went on strike at Obuasi in the Gold Coast in 1924 while the Enugu coal-mine strike occurred in 1925. All these strikes were for higher wages and better conditions of service.

Inter-territorial movements and international movements: the National Congress of British West Africa

In addition to these associations, parties and movements that were local or territorial in organization and outlook, an inter-territorial movement in British West Africa and international movements in the metropolitican capitals of the colonial rulers were formed. The former was the National Congress of British West Africa (NCBWA) in West Africa and among the latter was the West African Students Union (WASU), formed in London.

Undoubtedly, the NCBWA was the most interesting of the nationalist movements that emerged in West Africa in the inter-war period. It was founded through the efforts of J. B. Casely Hayford, a Gold Coast lawyer and intellectual, and Dr Akiwande Savage of Nigeria, and, throughout, its leadership was dominated not by the traditional rulers but by professional men such as lawyers, doctors and businessmen.

The objectives of the NCBWA are obvious from the resolutions passed at the first conference, held in Accra from 11 to 29 March 1929 and attended by delegates from Nigeria, the Gold Coast, Sierra Leone and The Gambia. In these resolutions, the delegates demanded not the destruction but the modification of the existing structures of colonial administration. Constitutional changes advocated included the reconstitution of the West African legislative councils so that half of the members be nominated by the Crown, and the other half elected by the people. They condemned the restriction of senior official posts to Europeans. They asked for municipal institutions, and for the establishment of a West African university. They complained of the post-war financial and economic controls and the growing power of extra-territorial firms. Legal reforms were also proposed, especially the establishment of a West African Court of Appeal. They also resolved to set up a West African Press Union in recognition of 'the important part the Press plays in National Development'.

Sanitary and medical reforms, residential segregation of races and the position of African doctors in government service were also thoroughly dealt with. The important land question was also discussed, with the conference declaring that 'the average British West African is quite capable of controlling and looking after his own interests in the land'. Finally, they denounced the partitioning of Togoland between the English and the French governments and the handing over of the Cameroon to the French government without consulting or paying any regard to the wishes of the peoples in the matter. All these resolutions show the moderate if not conservative nature of the NCBWA.

A delegation, in which The Gambia, Sierra Leone, the Gold Coast and Nigeria were represented, went to London in 1920 to petition His Majesty's Government to grant elective representation to the four colonies (see 25.1). Casely Hayford of the Gold Coast led the delegation. However, mainly because of the opposition of Sir Hugh Clifford, Governor-General of Nigeria, and Gordon Guggisberg, Governor of the Gold Coast, as well as the opposition of some of the Gold Coast chiefs led by Nana Sir Ofori Atta, the NCBWA petition was rejected.

The Congress met again in Freetown (January–February 1923), Bathurst (December 1925–January 1926) and Lagos (1930), though most of the agitational politics of the movement was conducted by the individual territorial committees set up in The Gambia, Sierra Leone, the Gold Coast and Nigeria. The Freetown session, fully supported by the Freetown social elite, ratified the constitution of the movement, dealt with inter-West African economic co-operation, and laid down the functions of the president, general secretary, executive council, financial secretary and central executive committee.

The Bathurst session resolved that the time had arrived for the elective system of representation to be fully applied to the colony of The Gambia, and that the various sections of the Congress should seriously consider the question of a British West African Federation with a Governor-General. Also advocated were the establishment of national schools, compulsory education in all urban areas, industrial and agricultural education for the rural areas, and the establishment of agricultural banks and co-operatives, and the 'commercial and economic independence' of West Africa was called for, as well as the creation of a West African Appellate Court and the appointment of Africans to higher posts in the judiciary.

What did the NCBWA achieve? Although it continued its activities throughout the 1920s, its main achievement was the introduction of new constitutions in Nigeria in 1923, Sierra Leone in 1924 and the Gold Coast in 1925 in which the principle of elective representation was conceded. The NCBWA also succeeded in developing a feeling of unity and common political destiny among the British West African political leadership. It did not succeed, however, in achieving economic independence, the unification of the four British colonies or any other amelioration or weakening of the colonial system. On the contrary, by the middle 1930s, colonialism was even more firmly entrenched than it was in the 1920s.

Rural politics and rural mass nationalism in the inter-war period

It would appear from recent research that African nationalist activities were not confined to the urban centres but were also evident in the rural areas, and here the

25.1 *The deputation of the National Congress of British West Africa that visited London in 1920: left to right, seated: Dr H. C. Bankole-Bright (Sierra Leone), T. Hutton Mills (Gold Coast), Chief Oluwa (Nigeria), J. E. Casely Hayford (Gold Coast), H. Van Hein (Gold Coast); standing: J. Egerton Shyngle (Nigeria), H. M. Jones (The Gambia), Herbert Macaulay (Nigeria), T. M. Oluwa (Nigeria), F. W. Dove (Sierra Leone), E. F. Small (The Gambia) (Clarendon Press, Oxford)*

principal actors were the commoners and farmers, both literate and illiterate, on the one hand, and the traditional rulers on the other. The latter were seen at times acting in co-operation with their subjects against the colonial system and at times being attacked by their subjects as agents of the same system.

The main objectives of the rural people were to acquire representation on the newly created state councils and, above all, to curb the increasing powers of their traditional rulers and the district commissioners and the abolition or reduction of some of the fines and taxes being imposed by them.

As recent research in Ghana has shown, two main instruments were fashioned in these areas for the attainment of these ends, namely, the traditional instrument of the *asafo* companies, that is, permanent organizations of commoners for military and social purposes outside the control of the traditional rulers or political elite, and new associations such as the Cocoa Farmers' Association and the Gold Coast Federation of Cocoa Farmers, formed in 1910 and 1928 respectively. The methods that these bodies employed were petitions, cocoa hold-ups and the destoolment (deposing) of chiefs. Between 1910 and 1944, there were at least thirty-three destoolments of divisional chiefs in the state of Akyem Abuakwa alone. The charges were usually abuse of power, improper sale of land, the imposition of extortionate fines or enforcement of levies, or compulsory labour, imposed by the colonial administration. As for the method of cocoa hold-ups, in 1921–2, 1930–1 and 1937–8, the cocoa farmers, led by John Kwame Ayew and Winifried Tete-Ansa, refused to sell their cocoa until better prices were paid.

It seems evident from the Gold Coast case, then, that politics and nationalist activities in the inter-war period were not confined to the urban areas alone but were in evidence in the rural areas and involved the commoners and farmers.

The outcome of nationalist activities in British West Africa

The question, then, is why did the nationalist movement in British West Africa achieve so little during the period under review? The first and most important answer is that neither the NCBWA nor the youth movements ever commanded mass followings, nor did any linkage occur between urban and rural politics. The leaders could therefore be written off as being unrepresentative of the people, which, in fact, both Sir Hugh Clifford and the Colonial Office did. Secondly, in spite of all the rhetoric, neither the leaders of the NCBWA nor those of the youth movements were prepared to use any radical methods to achieve their objectives. Thirdly, there was a great deal of conflict among the leaders of the movements, which greatly impeded their activities. In all the colonies, conflicts occurred between the conservatives and the moderates, and between both of them and the old traditional elite of kings. Such, indeed, was the conflict between the leaders of the NCBWA and those of the Aborigines' Rights Protection Society, and between the leaders of both, on the one hand, and the traditional rulers, led by Nana Sir Ofori Atta, the Paramount Chief of Akyem Abuakwa in the Gold Coast, on the other. These conflicts greatly weakened the nationalist movement in that country. Similarly there were internal dissensions and personality conflicts in the Lagos branch of the NCBWA. Fourthly, it would appear that the limited elective representation granted between 1923 and 1925 had the effect of politically dividing and thereby weakening the national movements. The final blow was the death of Casely Hayford, the main spirit behind the NCBWA, in 1930. For all these reasons, then, by the end of the period under review, politics and nationalism in British West Africa were at their lowest ebb.

Political activities in Francophone West Africa, 1919–35

From the rather limited evidence available now, it would appear that there was a relative lack of political activity in the French West African colonies during the inter-war period. This was due partly to France's more hostile attitude towards African political activities and organizations, and partly to the absence of a vigorous African press in French West Africa comparable to the African newspapers in Sierra Leone, the Gold Coast and Nigeria. However, like the activities in British West Africa, those in French West Africa had their local as well as their international aspects. Indeed, a good deal of Francophone African political activity took place in Paris between 1924 and 1936. However, as most of these political groups were radical and aligned to radical French political parties and trade unions, the impact of their anti-colonial agitation on the French authorities was limited. Among these groups was the Ligue Universelle pour la Défense de la Race Noire, founded in Paris by a Dahomean lawyer and nationalist, Prince Kojo Tovalou Houéou, in 1924. Another was the Comité de la Défense de la Race Nègre, under the leadership of another Francophone West African Marxist, Tiémoho Garan-Kouyaté of Sudan. Interesting as these movements were, however, they did not operate in West Africa.

Politics and nationalism in Senegal

The two French West African colonies where there was some African political activity in the inter-war period were Senegal and Dahomey. In Senegal, this centred around Blaise Diagne, who founded the Republican Socialist Party in 1914 to unite the various ethnic groups in Dakar and Saint-Louis and to contest the elections to the French Chamber of Deputies in 1914. He was able to gain the support of the *grands marabouts* (leaders of Islamic orders) in the urban areas and of ethnic groups other than his own in Dakar and Saint Louis as well as the political sponsorship of the Jeunes Sénégalais (Young Senegalese) and some liberal-minded Frenchmen. Throughout the campaign, Diagne emphasized the importance of maintaining the right of citizenship and the right to vote of the Africans in the four *communes*, while his European and *métis* opponents (who had dominated the politics of the *communes* since 1900 and had come to regard the electoral seats as their personal or family fiefs) largely ignored these issues and dismissed Diagne as a candidate of no consequence.

Diagne, however, not only campaigned for the electoral rights of the Africans, but also advocated official recognition of Ku'ranic law and custom. He also called for more commercial concessions to the Africans, the creation of a Colonial Council to manage the finances of the French colonies, the establishment of a medical school in Dakar and the right to organize trade unions. Largely through his energetic campaign, the secret ballot and the political support of the Muslim groups in the rural areas, Diagne emerged victorious in the 1914 elections, and became the first African deputy to the French Chamber of Deputies in July 1914. His electoral victory was in itself a revolution in the participation and organization of the Africans in Senegalese politics. The African voters had become a significant political factor and not just mere pawns in the hands of the *colons* and *métis*.

Politics and nationalism in Dahomey

In Dahomey, apart from the usual African protest through the local branch of the Ligue des Droits de l'Homme, which was perhaps the only permissible forum of 'political' activity, 'politics' was largely a question of conflicts within the religious groups and the interaction of these conflicts with chieftaincy and succession disputes. The most significant Dahomean political activist during this period, who combined participation in chieftaincy politics (he supported the Sognigbe faction of the Porto Novo Muslim community against the Jose Paraiso group of Yoruba Muslims) with anti-colonial agitation, was Louis Hunkanrin. Hunkanrin was educated in Senegal, worked for some time in Dahomey and returned to Senegal in 1913. He wrote critical articles against colonial maladministration in Dahomey in French and Senegalese newspapers, and assisted Blaise Diagne during the latter's election campaign in 1914. Through Blaise Diagne, Hunkanrin was given a job in Paris, but got involved with radical political groups there and was sent back to Dahomey in 1921.

On his return home, he revived the local branch of the Ligue des Droits de l'Homme as well as a branch of the Comité Franco-Musulman. Through colleagues in these local branches, radical and communist newspapers from France and the United States of America reached Dahomean intellectuals, and petitions expressing grievances against the local administration were sent to Paris.

In February–March 1923, partly because of increased taxes and the lower price for palm kernel following the depression of 1919 and 1920–1, and the subsequent price inflation and shortage of metal coins, workers in private firms went on strike and public meetings were organized by Hunkanrin's friends in the Comité Franco-Musulman and in the Ligue. The army had to be called out to break up meetings, and the Africans reacted by mounting a passive resistance movement which lasted from 13 February to early March. There were also strikes in Whydah. Some of the chiefs even requested fellow chiefs to resist the new taxes. The colonial administration countered by arresting the leaders of the resistance, calling for more troops from Togo and Côte d'Ivoire, and declaring a state of emergency which lasted until June 1923. With the arrest and exile of nearly all the leaders of the protest movement, including Hunkanrin, nationalist agitation in Dahomey came to an end, and a period of political calm, as in the other French West African territories, followed.

Apart from the demonstrations and riots in Porto Novo in 1923, nationalist movements organized along the lines of the NCBWA or Herbert Macaulay's Nigerian National Democratic Party scarcely figured in French West Africa during this period.

26 Politics and nationalism in East Africa, 1919–35

Unlike the situation in West Africa, politics and nationalism, terms neatly summed up by the Swahili word *siasa*, involved in the inter-war period not only the intelligentsia or educated elite but also the masses. The political activities there were mass activities. Secondly, unlike those of West Africa but like those of North Africa, nationalism and political activities were both secular and religious. However, as in both West and North Africa, nationalism in East Africa arose out of a consciousness of colonial wrongs while there was the same interaction between politics and economic conditions. Moreover, the objectives of nationalist activities as well as the weapons fashioned for their implementation were virtually the same as those of West Africa. In East Africa, as in West Africa, these objectives were not the overthrow of the colonial system but rather the improvement of and accommodation within the system. And among the weapons used were religion, youth movements and elitist associations.

Religious protest movements

One of the weapons that East Africans used even more actively than West Africans from early on in their struggle against colonialism was religion. Resistance called for mobilization, and in many regions, as has already been seen, religious leadership arose to fulfil this role. These traditional religious resistance movements continued during the first decade after the First World War and this provided an element of continuity with the former era. But as colonial forces dug in and restructured or destroyed the existing social and political institutions during the second decade, the need for a stronger spiritual means of standing up against colonialism was felt by the colonized Africans. The spiritual need was filled in two ways: first by the emergence of a new generation of African prophets, and secondly by the founding of African independent churches alongside the European Christian churches.

Examples of these new religious protest movements, which started from the second decade and continued throughout the 1920s and 1930s, and were joined by many more after the Second World War, can be seen among the Kamba and the Abagusii of Kenya. During the first two decades of this century, the colonial situation produced a widely felt sense of deprivation and frustration among the Kamba masses as the colonial authorities campaigned to appropriate Kamba resources in the form of taxes, land and

279

labour, using their newly-appointed chiefs, who had very little regard for traditional authority. The compulsory recruitment into the Carrier Corps in the First World War years and the failure of the colonial authorities to deal with the many social and economic problems that beset the Kamba masses after the war worsened their plight, while the impact of the world-wide economic crisis of 1920–1 and the increasing burden of taxation after 1920 served to increase the numbers of those who were ready to answer a call for a spiritual solution to the tensions in society.

Such a call came with the emergence of Ndonye wa Kauti, who began to preach a prophetic message to the people of Kilungu in Machakos district in the early months of 1922. He claimed to be a prophet, asserting his ability to foretell the coming of rain, and invited women to perform a religious dance (*kilumi*) at his home. He also stated that God, *Ngai*, had selected him to lead the people in a New Age about to come on this earth. At the onset of this new era, Europeans would be driven out, following which the earth would be as good as it was before colonialism, with plentiful water, and no taxes. Ndonye's movement grew as the economic conditions continued to deteriorate. As one would expect, such a leader would not be tolerated in a colonial situation; and indeed the district commissioner arrested him and deported him to Siyu along the Kenya coast. Ndonye was never to return again, for, like many activists before and after him, he died in exile.

Not so easy to suppress was the Mumbo cult, a movement contemporaneous with Ndonye wa Kauti's prophetism. This movement was rooted in the resentment of colonial authority which the Luo and the Abagusii shared. This resentment dated back to the wars of occupation the British had fought against the Abagusii in 1904 and 1908, and against the Luo of Alego in 1908–10. But it was further deepened by the introduction of compulsory labour for road construction and for the settler farms and the hated hut tax. The paternalist attitude of the missionaries further fuelled this mood of resentment. As in Ukambani, the Abagusii began to look for a better world view and they found this in the Luo Mumbo cult, a traditional lake spirit cult which was at the height of its influence in the nineteenth century, and in its mouthpiece, one Onyango Dunde of the Seje clan in Alego. Through him, the Mumbo spirit told the people: 'The Christian religion is rotten . . . All Europeans are your enemies but the time is shortly coming when they will disappear from our country.' Because its message was simple and correctly reflected the political situation, the movement spread very quickly from Alego in Siaya District to South Nyanza, appearing in Gusii in 1914 through the agency of another Luo prophet, Mosi wuod Auma, who was predicting 'the early departure from Kisii of all white men after which the natives would possess their land in peace'.

The message about the imminent departure of the white men appeared to be coming true when in 1914 the Germans attacked the British stockade at Kisii township, and so the Africans rose up and plundered colonial and missionary centres in the district. The British suppressed the revolt with brutality, killing about 150 Abagusii. But this did not deter the adherents, who continued with their activities in the inter-war years, in spite of frequent arrests and deportations of the leaders. In Gusiiland the Mumbo cult got mixed up with the more indigenous cult of Sakawa. Repressed by the colonial administration, these movements continued to thrive in Gusiiland throughout our period. Persecuted, deported, forbidden in the district, the Mumboites continued to preach while the spirit of resistance could not be killed but simply went underground, surfacing later in the 1950s to gall the British administration in Gusii yet again.

Equally significant, and the second strand of religious resistance, was the emergence of Christian independent churches. As we have seen in Chapters 12 and 20, many such churches emerged in East Africa in earlier decades but even more and a greater variety did so during the period under review. Some were 'Ethiopian' churches in that they emphasized, as K. Asare Opoku has pointed out already, African self-improvement and political rights, while others belonged to the 'Zionist' school, with their emphasis upon possession by the Holy Spirit and upon healing and prophecy.

The earliest independent African Church in this region, the Nomiya Luo Church, founded in 1910 by Johana Owalo, has already been dealt with in Chapter 7 of this volume. The second example, the Watchtower Church, which had begun in Central Africa and southern Tanganyika during the First World War, was a religion of the masses and was an attempt to solve the problems of colonized rural peoples. By rejecting the authority of the chiefs, the missionaries and British officials, and setting up new villages for the believers, the adherents sought to create new societies where they could feel at home. By 1919 the movement had entered Tanganyika, and had caught on substantially in the Kasanga, Mambwe, Ufipa and Mbozi areas. Matters came to a head in 1923 when the British accused the Church's leaders of vilifying the missionary churches; seventeen men were arrested and gaoled. This did not deter the followers and the religion continued to spread throughout the colonial period.

But some of the churches were started with a narrower scope than the Watchtower Church, being concerned with single issues. For example, the African National Church, which thrived in the Rungwe district of Tanganyika from the 1930s onward, was set up specially as a Christian Church for those who had been expelled from or would not be admitted into the missionary churches for being polygamous. Likewise, the Dini ya Roho (Holy Ghost Church) was founded among the Abaluyia of Kenya in 1927 as a breakaway from the Friends African Mission. The followers of Dini ya Roho insisted that in order to count oneself fully a Christian one had to accept 'baptism by the Holy Spirit', speaking in tongues, and the free confession of sins. This emphasis on 'baptism by the Holy Spirit' also led Alfayo Odongo Mango to found his Joroho (Holy Ghost) Church among the Luo in 1932.

Although regarded by many colonial authorities merely as 'impulsive negative retorts', these religious protest movements clearly demonstrate the strength and vitality of the African spirit and were, so to speak, the 'illegitimate uncles' of African nationalism. And the basis of their support was the people, the rural masses.

The 'young' associations

Much prominence has been given in the recent historiography to the educated elites, the *asomi* or *josomo*, in the development of African politics during these years. This newly emergent group consisted of those few men (and handful of women) who had attended the missionary schools of, for example Maseno, Budo, Thogoto and Zanzibar, and subsequently became teachers, catechists, clerks and artisans. Working in opposition to the colonial-appointed chiefs and to the local administration, these people organized

'Young' Associations as protest movements through which to conduct their political campaigns. These associations therefore had a mass following. Typical examples were the Young Baganda Association, the Young Kavirondo Association and the Kikuyu Central Association.

The young Baganda Association emerged as a result of the basic tensions in Ganda society, caused mainly by the Buganda Agreement of 1900 and the behaviour of the newly created chiefs. Under that Agreement, the colonial-appointed chiefs were awarded substantial personal and official estates and therefore became the enemies of the traditional clan-heads (the *bataka*), the peasants (*bakopi*), and the 'young' men, both Catholic and Muslim, who were left dissatisfied. As the Kabaka of Buganda was the biggest individual beneficiary of the Agreement, the questioning eyes, tongues and pens of the 'young' men did not spare him. The behaviour of the new chiefs left a lot to be desired. Being colonial bureaucrats and not traditional leaders, they too willingly flouted the patron–client relationships that had obtained in Buganda in favour of their new masters. Moreover, as agents of colonialism, they were meant to enforce regulations such as those dealing with health and sanitation, which were unpopular with the peasants. Those members of the western-educated elite who were not co-opted by the hierarchy exploited these grievances to the full.

Leading in this revolt were the young men, the most pre-eminent of whom was Z. K. Sentongo, an articulate pamphleteer who founded the Young Baganda Association in 1919. The aims of the Association were to improve Uganda in every way, to assist every Muganda in distress and to promote education. In their many testimonies and writings, these leaders also complained about the chiefs in Buganda, accusing them of imprisoning the people without trial by jury. Their other grievance was economic: they wanted the many restrictions which had been imposed on the cotton trade by the Uganda protectorate government to be removed. From this modest beginning, the Young Buganda Association became more intransigent in the following three years. By 1921 it had become racialist and anti-Asian. Writing in the *Uganda Herald* in that year, Sentongo accused the Asians of being the immediate exploiters of the Africans. By 1922 the Young Buganda Association had become anti-monarchical as well, attacking the chiefs and the Kabaka, and suggesting that Uganda should be a republic. In that year Yowasi Paito, Joswa Naluma and Yusufu Mukasa, three medical assistants at Namirembe Hospital and all of them old boys of Budo High School, wrote a letter attacking the Kabaka Daudi Chwa for his personal immorality, for his failure to run the *lubiri* (palace) properly, and for supporting the chiefs. Obviously neither the chiefs nor the Kabaka would let them get away with all this. Under a law passed by the Lukiko, making it illegal to abuse the Kabaka, the three letter-writers were imprisoned in July 1922. Partly because of this and partly because some of its supporters were bought off with minor chiefly positions, the Association steadily fizzled out.

The Young Kavirondo Association was founded in the latter half of 1921 by the alumni of Maseno School in Nyanza. Its formation was precipitated by the conversion in 1920 of the British East Africa Protectorate into a Crown Colony – the Kenya Colony and Protectorate – a move which the Association's future leaders interpreted to mean an ominous attempt by the British to change the status of Africans and possibly to expose the lands of western Kenya to European settlement. It was at the public meeting to discuss these grievances, held on 23 December 1921 that the Association (YKA) was set up with Jonathan Okwiri, a teacher, as chairman, Benjamin Owuor Gumba as secretary and Simeon Nyende, another teacher, as treasurer. Resolutions were passed calling for, among other things, the abolition of the infamous *kipande* (identity card), the reduction of hut tax and poll tax with a view to excluding women from taxation, an increase in wages, the reversion to protectorate status, the granting of individual title-deeds to land, the abolition of forced labour and the building of a government school in central Nyanza. Following this, a delegation went to see first the provincial commissioner and then the governor with these resolutions. None of the requests were immediately granted. However, alarmed by this impressive demonstration of mass mobilization by this nascent elite, the colonial administration decided to contain them by the weapon of colonial patronage, through an agreeable missionary, Archdeacon Owen. In 1923 the leaders of Young Kavirondo Association felt that he would be a good go-between for them and therefore handed the presidency of their movement to him. Owen proceeded immediately to make the organization respectable by subverting it. He thus shifted the basis of its support from the masses to the elites and its emphasis away from agitation towards new demands for better houses, better food, better clothing, better education and better hygiene. In other words, Owen removed the mass political sting from the Association, which from then on took on the impotent title of Kavirondo Taxpayers' Welfare Association (KTWA) and resorted to writing memoranda as the main method of expressing political grievance. The Association was rendered even more ineffective by its split into Luo and Abaluyia factions in 1931 with the Luo wing limping on under Owen's leadership until 1944.

More intractable was the Kikuyu Central Association (KCA), movement that gave vent to Gikuyu rural grievances, beginning from 1924. Its headquarters was at Kahuhia in Muranga, where it was launched under the leadership of Joseph Kang'ethe and James Beauttah. Its principal objectives were, first and foremost, 'to get back the land Europeans had taken from us', to protest against the excesses of the colonial situation and in particular against the racial indignities which the Gikuyu suffered, against the Crown Lands Ordinance of 1915 which had made all Africans tenants at will of the Crown and against the banning of the growing of cotton and coffee by Africans.

The fortunes of the KCA improved when Jomo Kenyatta became its general secretary in 1928. Kenyatta's efforts as party secretary led to a cultural revival. In his efforts to build up grassroots support for the Association, Kenyatta appealed to the Gikuyu through *Mwigwithania*, a Gikuyu-language newspaper he founded, to be proud of their cultural heritage. The pages of the monthly *Mwigwithania* were full of riddles, proverbs and stories which encouraged the leaders to think of themselves as Gikuyu.

From 1928, the Gikuyu placed their land grievances at the centre of their problems. In that year the KCA sent a delegation including Jomo Kenyatta to London to present a petition to and give evidence before the Hilton Young Commission. The gist of their grievance was captured in this statement of evidence: 'We have tried for many years to make the government give us title deeds for our land but we have not got them and we cannot know whether it is our land or whether it is Crown Land.' This concern with security of tenure in the African 'reserves' was reiterated by Kenyatta when in 1929 the KCA sent him to London to articulate their demands. The KCA also helped the Gikuyu lineages to prepare the evidence which they submitted to the Kenya Land Commission in 1931. When the report of that commission came out, the KCA marshalled all the Gikuyu political groups to draft a unanimous memorandum of rejection and protest. It was because these protests went unheeded that the question of land assumed the central place in Gikuyu politics that it did, leading to the Mau Mau war two decades later.

These 'young' associations did not succeed, and yet it would be unfair to write them off as total failures. Although they were not effective because they were regularly undermined by the co-option of some of their leaders and the detention of others, their lasting legacy is that they expressed the grievances of the Africans against the colonial system.

Segmentary associations

Besides these associations, whose activities and demands were wide in scope, there emerged during the period numerous small associations formed to deal with specific issues and whose scale of operation was therefore local. Most of these issues centred on the new provincial and district boundaries created by the colonial rulers for internal administrative purposes, which cut across many ethnic groups, clans and lineages. These segmentary associations were formed, therefore, either to regain lost lands, or to be allowed to rejoin clansmen in a different sub-location, or to be given distinct administrative boundaries.

The Ugenya Kager Luo Clan (South Bank of River Nzoia) Association, which was set up by the Luo-speaking Kager clansmen in 1932 with a view to recovering 'lost territory' from their Wanga neighbours, was a typical example of this type of association. Another was the more famous Mubende Banyoro Committee, which persistently sought the return of the 'lost countries' of Huyaga, Bugangaizi, Buwekula, Buruli and Rugonjo to the kingdom of Bunyoro in Uganda. By and large, the colonizers refused to satisfy the demands emanating from these segmentary associations.

Of minor political significance during this period were the many commercial associations formed by African farmers and businessmen. Quite often they set out with specific aims but they very soon found themselves acting as vehicles of protest against all that was wrong with the colonial system within their areas. A case in point was the Kilimanjaro Native Planters (Coffee) Association (KNPA), which was founded in 1925 'to protect and promote the interests of the Native Coffee Growers on the mountain', but found itself pushed by the activities of the European settlers and various British administrative officials to take up other matters, such as land registration, land alienation and use, political rights and representation in the Central Legislative Council and the Moshi District Water Board, and to oppose chiefly authority. Another was the Bukoba Bahaya Union, formed in 1924 by government clerks and local traders in Bukoba, such as Clemens Kiiza, Suedi Kangasheki, Ludovic Kaitaba and Herbert Rugizibwa, 'for the development of our country and for the seeking of a system for the simple way to civilization to our mutual advantage.' The two avenues open for the attainment of this 'civilization' were literacy education and the planting of coffee. Throughout the 1920s and 1930s this organization championed these causes, and in the process regularly clashed with both the colonial and the chiefly authorities, which they considered to be standing in the way of progress.

In East African historiography these organizations have been described as 'improvement' associations led by 'modern' men. Their emergence was an indication that a new generation of elites had developed outside the chiefly elite that had been set up by the colonial authorities fifteen or twenty years earlier and which was demanding that the former should hand over to them. The contribution of these modernizers to the political awareness of the African is being debated by East African historians. Some scholars emphasize their vision for the African people while others regard them as primarily self-seekers and would deny them any legitimate role in African political radicalism. On the whole, since the improvers set off primarily to defend their own and their class interests, it is difficult to accord them a leadership role in the politics of mass activism. Championing popular causes was to be the task of these elites only in the post-Second World War years.

What of direct trade union organization? In East Africa as in West Africa, trade unions as such were not allowed by the colonial administration. What were allowed were staff associations, provided they took on a welfare mantle rather than direct union activities. It was for this reason that a number of such associations were formed. However, once they emerged, they did make political demands. Among those that were formed were the Tanganyika Territory African Civil Service Association in 1922 and the Kenya African Civil Service Association sometime before 1933. The former was founded by Martin Kayamba 'to promote social and educational development among its members' and 'to foster the welfare of its members in the various Government Departments'. It was partly a trade union and partly a social club whose activities included sports and evening classes. This organization was largely concerned with elitist privileges. Although Kayamba had hoped to build a countrywide organization, his Association seems to have faded out in the late 1920s as its supporters were absorbed into the colonial administration. Its achievements, therefore, were limited even while it lasted.

The exact origins of the Kenya African Civil Service Association are obscure, but it submitted an important memorandum to the Commission of Inquiry into the Administration of Justice in Kenya, Uganda and Tanganyika Territory in Criminal Matters, which was set up in 1933. It requested that all the laws of the country should be translated into Kiswahili, asked for an assessor jury in all criminal trials, and demanded the repeal of the *kipande* system. The memorandum also criticized the provisions of the Vagrancy and the Collective Punishment Ordinances, and urged the abolition of payment of tax by widows, the unemployed and those over fifty years of age. Apart from this memorandum not much is known about what else the Association did. Equally little is know about the Kenya African Teachers Union, which was formed in 1934 under the leadership of Eliud Mathu and James Gichuru.

But generally it can be stated that the activities of the elite were ineffective in comparison with those of the workers, which were characterized throughout our period by the recurrent resort to strikes in the factories, ports and workshops and also in the settler farms. Unfortunately, very little is known as yet about these individual strikes but it cannot be overemphasized that the feeling of deprivation was recurrent amongst African labour.

26.1 *Harry Thuku (1895–1970), a founder and leader of the East African Association, the pioneer nationalist organization in Kenya (East African Publishing House, Nairobi)*

Efforts at territorial politics

This narrative has so far been concerned with the politics of local concern articulated at various levels. When it comes to the question of attempts at territorial politics, the experience is one of failure. Indeed, only two serious efforts were made, that of the East African Association (EAA) and the Tanganyika Africa Association (TAA). The EAA was founded in 1921 in Nairobi by Harry Thuku, (see 26.1), Jesse Kariuki, Job Muchuchu and 'Abdullāh Tarrara. Africans from other territories were also prominent, including the indomitable Z. K. Sentongo of the Young Baganda Association and an unnamed Nyasa man from Nyasaland (now Malawi). It was certainly trans-ethnic, and its name reflects its Kenya-wide concern. But its membership was predominantly Gikuyu. It was led and inspired by Harry Thuku, a clerk working in the Treasury.

Thuku was one of a number of young Gikuyu then living in Nairobi who felt the need to organize themselves into a body that would rival the chief-dominated Kikuyu Association. More important, Thuku and the young men in Nairobi felt that there was a need for a Kenya-wide African organization. As he wrote to the *East African Standard* in 1921, it was felt 'that unless the young people of this country form an Association the Native in Kenya will always remain voiceless'. This quest for a united front is what led Thuku to fraternize with the Kamba, Luo and Ganda young men then living in Nairobi. Thus, on 1 July 1921, they formally launched the East African Association.

The organization passed resolutions on the subject of *kipande*, forced labour, excessive taxation, and education. Thuku cabled these resolutions directly to the Colonial Office in London.

Of especial importance for this analysis were the efforts by Thuku to involve non-Gikuyu in his Association at this time. He succeeded in winning over the Kamba living in Nairobi but not those in the rural areas. In Nyanza, Thuku's Association found a corresponding body in the Young Kavirondo Association. By December 1921 the leaders of the latter group were in touch with Thuku and had assured him that they were 'struggling' with him for the country, and had contributed to his funds. Thuku also won support among the western-educated and urban Maasai elites, all of whom had been educated at Thogoto or at the African Inland Mission schools in Kijabe and Siyiapei, and who had been enraged by the seizure of their land by the British.

Thuku also had support from the Kampala-based Young Baganda Association, whose secretary, Joseph Kamulegeya, corresponded with Thuku on a number of issues. Kamulegeya introduced Thuku to the Black American world, and Thuku wrote to Dr W. E. B. Du Bois, Marcus Garvey and the Tuskegee Institute for Black American Aid Missions to East Africa. No lasting associations were created, however, although Garvey's paper, the *Negro World*, was sent to Thuku.

As one would expect, the colonial administration was upset by Thuku's activities and therefore arrested him on 14 March 1922. This arrest touched off a massive demonstration in Nairobi two days later, which the police fired upon, killing twenty-one Africans.

Following this incident, Thuku was deported to Kismayu and his Association collapsed. Politics in the Gikuyu countryside from this time on took on a more ethnic dimension. The new organization that emerged was the Kikuyu Central Association. British gunpowder put an end to any pretensions that the Nairobi Africans had entertained on multi-ethnic political organization in the inter-war years.

Prospects in Tanganyika were not much better than in the other territories, as the example of the Tanganyika African Association (TAA) reveals. The TAA was founded in Dar es-Salaam in 1929. Under the leadership of Cecil Matola, Kleise Sykes, Mzee Bin Sudi and Ramadan 'Ali, the Association stated its aims as being 'to safeguard the interests of Africans, not only in this territory but in the whole of Africa'. In practice, however, the parameters of the TAA did not extend beyond Dar es-Salaam in the subsequent six years unless some member was transferred to work up-country, as happened in 1933 when Mack Makeja was posted to Dodoma and founded a branch there. Moreover, even within Dar es-Salaam, its achievements were limited to building a club house. It also unsuccessfully petitioned the government for the appointment of an African town magistrate. Internal conflicts reduced its membership in the years of 1931 and 1932 and it was not until 1934 that the Zanzibar branch took the initiative in reviving the Association.

That attempts at political organization at territorial level failed should not surprise us. Quite apart from the fact of colonial repression, political consciousness had not developed to embrace the boundaries of the colonial state. Apart from a few exceptions such as Jomo Kenyatta, Akiiki Nyanbogo and Mbiyu Koimange, who after travelling and studying abroad in Europe and America saw the colonial situation in an imperial perspective, most others saw it in local or regional terms. There were politically no Kenyans or Ugandans or Tanganyikans in the inter-war period.

Conclusion

This chapter has attempted to narrate the extent, nature and limitations of African politics and nationalism in East Africa in the period between 1919 and 1935 through examining the various forms of activism. The main actors were the masses, while the main organizers of politics (*siasa*) during these years were the 'young' men, people who had benefited from the introduction of missionary education in the first two decades of the century, and were competent to articulate African grievances before the colonial authorities. They largely concerned themselves with local grievances, agitating against those ills that colonialism had brought in its train. Their attempts at political organization were often thwarted by the colonial power, and none of the associations succeeded in all their aims. But, while they lasted, these organizations were a reminder to the colonial authorities that 'the African voice' could be heard through channels other than the structure of the colonial administration.

27

Politics and nationalism
in Central and Southern Africa,
1919–35

As has been seen in the earlier chapters of this volume, European capitalist colonialism was more oppressive and became more firmly entrenched in Southern and Central Africa than in other parts of Africa during the period under review. The whole situation was worsened by the settler problem with its mass appropriation of land and racial discrimination in Southern Africa, and the exploitative plantation system and its attendant forced labour in Central Africa. These features of the colonial system in the regions under review affected the African societies there much more directly and much more deeply than in the other regions of Africa. As one would expect, therefore, African politics and anti-colonial activities were far more widespread and far more militant and had far stronger international ties than those in other parts of Africa. Particularly unique were the use of religion as an instrument of protest and the roles that the working class or proletariat, which became far more developed in Southern Africa than in most other parts of Africa, and the peasants played, especially in South Africa and Mozambique. This chapter examines the changing nature of popular protest in Southern and Central Africa with particular attention being given to South Africa, the Belgian Congo and the former Portuguese colonies.

Popular protest, nationalism and politics in South Africa
and the surrounding territories

Opposition to colonial rule and capitalist exploitation in South Africa took four principal forms: peasant protest, independent churches, elitist organizations and, finally, working-class movements.

In response to the increased impoverishment and economic uncertainty which accompanied the transformation of much of the rural South African area from a peasant economy to a labour reserve, peasants engaged in a number of actions designed to protect their land and livestock and to protest against increased taxation and labour demands. Often these were individual and sporadic acts such as flight, tax evasion, violation of registration laws and attacks on loyalist chiefs and police. In other cases, they represented more coherent and organized forms of opposition. Such was the widespread campaign throughout the Transkei, Pondoland and Fingoland, which lasted from 1913 to 1917, in which the peasants refused to pay the dipping tax, organized boycotts and dynamited and destroyed dipping tanks. In 1917, rural women in the Transkei organized a series of boycotts against European merchants to protest against price fixing and refused to supply basic commodities on credit. Ultimately state intervention and threats from loyalist chiefs undercut the boycott.

Peasant uprisings surfaced periodically in South West Africa, where the South African government only began to consolidate effectively its power after the First World War. Thereafter the government of Jan Smuts cruelly put down the Bondelswart people, one of the Nama cattle-raising peoples living in the south, who had risen to protest against a rise in taxes. In May 1922, a punitive military operation was launched against them involving 400 troops armed with machine guns and aircraft. About 100 Africans were killed and over 150 gaoled.

Three years later, an equally cruel treatment was meted out to the 'Coloured' community on the Rehoboth river in the central part of the country. The village was surrounded by troops, as aircraft appeared in the sky. The villagers offered to 'surrender' and about 640 of them were taken prisoner. Though the question of the Bondelswarts and Rehobothers was discussed at the League of Nations because South West Africa was a trusteeship territory, no measures were taken to prevent similar brutalities in the future.

Much broader-based and better organized were those protest movements organized by independent churches, of both the Zionist and the Ethiopian varieties, which were particularly widespread in South Africa. Their number increased rapidly rising from 76 in 1918 to 320 by 1932 and more than 800 by 1942. The peasants provided the social base for these movements, although city-dwellers often took an active part in them.

Despite close state surveillance, independent churches periodically engaged in explicit insurgent activities. As early as 1884 Nehemiah Tile, a Methodist preacher, urged his adherents in Tembuland to disregard state officials. In 1921 an Ethiopian sect known as the Israelites, under the leadership of Enoch Mgijima, forcibly resisted removal from a squatter settlement in Queenstown. They were, however, attacked by soldiers, armed with machine guns, who killed 163 of them and wounded 129.

Other militant independent churches combined a prophetic vision with an abridged form of Garveyism. The most important was the Wellington movement, named after its founder, Wellington Butelezi, which flourished from the early 1920s until the mid-1930s. Butelezi assured his followers in the Transkei that American blacks in airplanes would come to their aid and help to liberate them. Though he and several of his lieutenants were arrested and deported by state officials, his influence persisted and a whole series of separatist schools and churches were organized to spread his word.

By the latter half of the 1930s, Afro-Christian movements had ceased to be effective vehicles of anti-colonial struggle. In the southern as well as in other parts of the continent that role was passing to new and more developed forms of political organization which emerged during the period under review. These were the elitist and the working-class organizations, which were not based on ethnic community. The first, and by far the most important, of the new elitist organizations was the African National Congress (ANC), founded in 1912. It was originally set up as an African organization for all the countries of Southern Africa which were part of the British empire. Its constitutional congress was attended by representatives from the Rhodesias,

Basutoland, Bechuanaland and Swaziland. Later, national organizations sprang up in each of these countries which, as a rule, were under heavy ANC influence. Many national organizations in Southern, Central and even East Africa borrowed not only the name of the ANC but, to varying degrees and at different stages, also its structure, programme, rules and methods.

By the beginning of the inter-war period, the ANC had behind it seven years of stormy activity. However, its formative period did not end until 1925, when, at its annual conference, it adopted the name of African National Congress. (Previously, it was called the South African Native National Congress.) In the same year, the anthem and flag of the Congress were adopted. The anthem was called *Nkosi Sikelel' i'Afrika* ('Lord, Bless Africa') and the tricolour flag – black, green and gold – symbolized the people (black), the green fields and veld (green) and the country's main wealth (gold). Between 1919 and 1935, the ANC experienced various degrees of successful political organizing. In 1926 it initiated a mass campaign against a new series of racist Bills, which the government of the then South African prime minister, J. Hertzog, tried to put through. In February 1926 the ANC called a national convention in Bloemfontein which sharply condemned all racial segregation, demanded constitutionally guaranteed equality of all citizens irrespective of skin colour and decided to boycott puppet 'native conferences' being called by the government.

At the end of the same year, the ANC, together with a number of other African organizations, as well as with the African Political Organization (APO), which was the major political organization of the 'Coloured' people, and the South African Indian Congress, which had been set up shortly after the First World War, called the First Non-European Convention in Kimberley. This convention condemned the racist practices in the country, sharply opposed the new Hertzog legislation and called for 'closer co-operation among the non-European sections of South Africa'. That marked a breakthrough, an early step towards creating a united anti-racist front in Southern Africa.

The ANC was also active outside the country. It contributed to the long-standing participation of South Africans in the pan-African movement. Sol T. Plaatje, one of the ANC founding fathers and leaders, attended the Pan-African Congress of 1919 and in February 1927 ANC President J. J. Gumede visited the Soviet Union.

However, the late 1920s and early 1930s saw a decline of the activities of the ANC, mainly because its leadership fell into the hands of moderates who feared communist influence.

In neighbouring Southern African countries, the emergence of African political organizations proceeded in much the same direction, although it did not go as far as in South Africa. As a rule, there were initially 'native associations', 'native conventions' and 'welfare societies', which dealt with local matters at first but gradually expanded the range of their activities.

In Nyasaland, the first 'native association' sprang up on the eve of the First World War, and from the late 1920s such associations mushroomed throughout the country. In 1933 alone, fifteen were formed in the major cities, such as Zomba, Blantyre and Limo. In Northern Rhodesia, the first 'welfare association' was set up in 1923 and was directly modelled on similar organizations in Nyasaland. Among its founders was David Kaunda, the father of Kenneth Kaunda. From 1930 onwards, similar associations were formed in Livingstone, the protectorate's administrative centre, and in many other places, particularly in the Copper Belt towns and along the railway track.

In Southern Rhodesia, too, political organizations of a new character came to be formed in the early post-war years. Set up in January 1923, the Rhodesian Bantu Voters' Association sought greater voting rights for Africans and the return of seized lands. Its activity was confined to the Bulawayo area and several districts in Matabeleland. There was a welfare society in Gwelo and a Rhodesian native organization in Mashonaland.

In the British protectorates of Basutoland, Bechuanaland and Swaziland, which were closely linked with the Union of South Africa, anti-colonial forces had close ANC associations. The most active organization in Basutoland was Lekhotla la Bafo ('League of the Poor'), which played an important role there throughout the inter-war period. The social base of Lekhotla la Bafo was provided by peasants many of whom were seasonal miners in Transvaal. Partly because of its very radical stand and partly because from 1928 it began to draw closer to the Communist Party of South Africa, it scared the ANC leaders. The British authorities ordered the chiefs to ban the League meetings. But in August 1928 Lekhotla la Bafo staged a protest demonstration in Maseru against the ban. That was the first mass demonstration in Basutoland history and it was attended by several thousand people.

The social base of all these early political organizations in Southern Africa was not broad. Often it consisted of members of the educated elite who had become professionals. Nor did they often have a clear action programme. Yet they paved the way for other organizations, more numerous, durable and effective.

Working-class movements in the industrial areas provided another new form of anti-colonial struggle. The first mass movement in the Union of South Africa occurred in the Transvaal mines in early 1918 with the boycott of the company shops through which the mine owners sold food and manufactured goods to workers.

The next was a strike which took place in Johannesburg and involved sewage and garbage collectors. The strikers were fewer in number but better organized. The strike was quelled and its participants were put on trial, at which 152 of them were sentenced to two months of forced labour. On 1 July 1918, 15 000 Africans working in three mines downed tools. Police forced them into the mines after a fierce clash in which workers used axes, picks and lengths of metal pipe as their weapons. In February 1920, a new strike swept twenty-two mines in Transvaal in which 71 000 African workers, coming from different ethnic groups, took part. Troops and police were used to put down the strike. It was the largest in African history until 1946, when an even larger strike took place, also in the Transvaal.

In the Rhodesias, the first organized mass working-class action was recorded on 22 May 1935 at the Muflira mine in Northern Rhodesia; it spread to the Nkana mine on 26 May and to the Luansha mine on 28 May. Miners demanded higher wages and a cut in taxes and protested against poor working conditions and various forms of racial discrimination. Twenty-eight strikers were killed or wounded in clashes with the troops and arrests were made among the workers.

On the crest of the wave of industrial action which swept Southern Africa in the early post-war years, the largest African proletarian organization, the Industrial and Commercial Workers' Union of Africa (ICU) was formed in January 1919 in Cape Town by Clements Kadalie, a schoolteacher and a seasonal worker from Nyasaland, during a strike of African and Coloured dock workers. Its membership rose from less than thirty at its launching to 30 000 five years later and to 100 000 by 1927, with affiliates far beyond the Union of South Africa. The ICU, which was strongly influenced by socialist ideas, as the preamble to its constitution clearly indicates, promised its members to seek higher wages, better working conditions, pensions, sick and unemployment allowances and protection of the workers' rights. It proclaimed the whole of the African continent to be its field of activity. It reached the peak of its influence in the mid-1920s, but suffered a sharp decline in the late 1920s and early 1930s because it found itself split into three factions.

Socialist influence was also felt in an earlier African proletarian organization, the Industrial Workers of Africa. The International Socialist League had played no small role in its formation and activities. The League, set up by South African white socialists and working-class activists, was gradually coming to realize the need for proletarian solidarity, irrespective of the colour of the skin. That became particularly evident in its appeals in a number of leaflets issued to black and white workers.

The International Socialist League and several other South African socialist organizations merged at a congress in Cape Town in 1921 to form the Communist Party of South Africa, the first Communist Party on the African continent. Initially, its membership consisted only of whites, but, by the early 1930s, Africans formed the majority of the Party's membership and its general secretary was a Zulu, Albert Nzula (1905–34). National liberation became the focus of the Party's effort.

The Belgian Congo

Increased state control, an elaborate patronage policy and a wave of epidemics reduced the effectiveness of social protest in the Belgian Congo. Nevertheless, popular opposition continued, although on a smaller scale.

Peasant opposition in the Congo, often sporadic and barely visible, took a variety of forms all of which were designed to avoid or minimize the disruptive impact of the colonial capitalist system on their way of life. Tax evasion continued with great frequency in the years immediately following the First World War. Thousands of Congolese peasants fled across the open borders to the adjacent regions of Angola and the French Congo, while others disappeared into the bush just prior to the arrival of state tax officials. Many members of the rural population used a similar strategy to avoid working on state projects, in mines and on European plantations. Still other peasants refused to cultivate the obligatory cotton or rice or planted less than the required amounts.

As the colonial system was extended into the more remote areas and a network of loyalist chiefs was created, direct confrontations, which had frequently occurred in the period preceding the First World War, almost disappeared. Occasionally, alienated peasants attacked the symbols of oppression – loyalist chiefs, African police and tax collectors. Far more hazardous were the peasant revolts which were reported in the Bas-Congo in the period between 1920 and 1922, and a major uprising by the Pende peasants and workers in Kwilu, which occurred in 1931. The latter was precipitated by a sharp increase in taxes, a 50% reduction in the price peasants received for their commodities and the decision of Unilever to lower wages on its plantations. This uprising was immediately suppressed, and more than 400 Pende and one European lost their lives in the process.

As in South and East Africa, numerous religious–political movements emerged in the Congo to protest against the political system. These included Muvungu, Lukusu, Mpewe and the 'Talking Serpent' sects and the 'Black Mission' Tunzi and the 'Leopard' people movements. These movements attracted even larger peasant followings, which may be partly due to the fact that the colonial authorities had imposed a strict ban on political organizations. Their appeal also reflected the growing sense of anxiety and frustration brought on by the economic uncertainties of the 1921 recession and the depression a decade later.

The largest of these movements was Kimbanguism, named after Simon Kimbangu, a Bakongo peasant. A catechist, he proclaimed that he had been touched by God, which gave him the power to cure the sick, combat witchcraft and resurrect the dead. Kimbangu also proclaimed in a general but vague way that he was to deliver Africans from the yoke of colonial oppression. His anti-colonial speeches, his growing popularity and the militancy of some of his followers led to his arrest by the Belgian administration and his subsequent deportation to Katanga on 14 September 1921, where he died a martyr thirty years later.

Although Kimbangu himself was not revolutionary, his followers made his movement strongly anti-European rather than simply religious after his deportation. The Kimbanguists exhorted the people not to work for the Europeans, not to grow the export crops imposed by the colonial administration, not to pay taxes and levies, not to send their children to missionary schools, and generally to disobey the Belgians. In both towns and villages, his adherents actively participated in the struggle against colonialism, and their propaganda efforts even affected the strikes of railway, white-collar and oil-mill workers in the lower Zaire from 1921 to 1925. Although cruelly repressed, the Kimbanguists were undaunted. Various offshoots of Kimbanguism sprang up throughout the Congo, where Kimbanguists established links with Afro-Christian churches of Nigeria and Uganda and with the opponents of French colonialism in the French Congo.

Another major independent church movement – the African Watchtower, known more commonly in the Congo as Kitawala – appeared at about the same time that Kimbangu began his activities. Its initial bases of support seem to have been in Northern Rhodesia, Nyasaland and Tanganyika, from where it spread into Katanga province, where it had become firmly entrenched by 1926. Under the forceful leadership of Tomo Nyirenda, the Kitawala movement became explicitly anti-colonial. Along with militant slogans such as 'Africa for the Africans' and 'Equality of the Races', Nyirenda and his principal lieutenants urged their followers to assassinate Europeans and their African allies, especially loyalist chiefs. Pursued by the Belgians, who were alarmed by his increasing influence, Nyirenda fled to Northern Rhodesia in 1926, where the British authorities detained and ultimately executed him. As in the case of Kimbanguism, the execution of the prophet actually increased popular support for Kitawala and it continued to spread into the rural areas, where its priests organized protests against taxation and fanned hostility to appointed chiefs.

Working-class protests against colonialism were also in evidence in the Congo, though these developed much more slowly here than in South Africa. It was the discovery of copper, tin and uranium in Katanga, of diamonds in Kasai and of gold in Kilo Moto that precipitated the growth of an industrial working class. By the 1920s over 60 000 labourers were involved in mineral extraction.

As in other parts of the continent, the initial response of Africans to the low wages and harsh working conditions of the mines was desertion. Large numbers of peasants fled from Katanga and Kasai provinces to avoid the recruiting agents. Others resorted to strike action and boycotts. In 1921, a large number of miners at Luishi, for example, walked off the job and proceeded to Elizabethville to complain to government officials of ill-treatment and poor rations. Two years later, a similar work stoppage occurred at the Kakontwe mines. Ever during the depression, work stoppages and labour 'riots' erupted at the Union Minière mines of Kipushi, Ruashi and Mswenu Ditu in 1931, temporarily paralysing operations. In the same year, workers organized a boycott in Elizabethville to protest against the high prices charged for basic commodities by the Union Minière company stores and independent European merchants. The growing militancy continued throughout the 1930s culminating in the great strike of 1941, in which several thousand African workers walked off their jobs at tin and copper mines throughout Katanga province.

As in the case of a working-class movement, political associations and nationalist parties developed much more slowly in the Belgian Congo than in South Africa. Indeed, explicit nationalist organizations, such as the Association de Bakongo (ABAKO), did not emerge until the late 1950s. During this period, however, many closed associations, known as Mbeni, emerged. These were brought back to the Belgian colony by African servicemen who had been stationed in German East Africa during the First World War. The Mbeni were essentially dance societies which also provided a self-help network for members. Although not primarily anti-colonial, their songs and dances often ridiculed European officials and expressed deep-seated popular resentment against colonial rule. However, government harrassment, gang warfare, rivalries among and within Mbeni societies, and the urban dislocation created by the depression combined to reduce the influence and significance of these societies by the mid-1930s.

Popular opposition to colonial rule in Angola

Regarded as nonentities by the Europeans and subject to corporal punishment and sometimes arbitrary treatment at the hands of the colonial authorities, to the demands of labour-recruiters and to collusion between government officials and the resident Portuguese, the Africans of Angola became outcasts in their own country. They did, however, develop several means of escaping the pressures that were brought to bear on them.

The first form of resistance consisted of taking up arms, but this was steadily abandoned from the end of the First World War since it was ultimately doomed to failure. The second alternative was going into hiding in areas furthest from the reach of the colonial authorities. The third solution was even more radical, namely, massive clandestine emigration into the Belgian Congo, Northern Rhodesia and even South West Africa. Often members of the rural population travelled great distances through harsh terrain with young children on their backs to free themselves from the tyranny of Portuguese colonial rule.

The fourth type of resistance to colonial rule was the religious or messianic cults founded by Africans in reaction to the colonial religion. Unlike the situation in the Belgian Congo, the independent churches, mostly introduced from outside, had a relatively small following and short life. The revolt of the Mafulu in 1918 is sometimes cited as the first Angolan messianic protest to have led to armed revolt. Followers of Simon Kimbangu gained a number of adherents among the Bakongo living inside the Angolan border. Despite the serious efforts of the colonial administration to suppress Kimbanguism in 1921 and 1922, an underground network continued to operate.

Other more obscure sects surfaced, such as Maiaigni, which was detected in the Cabinda enclave in 1930 and the short-lived Cassongola movement among the Mbundu between 1924 and 1930. Kitawala also spread from the Belgian Congo and Northern Rhodesia into eastern Angola around 1932. Although the data are extremely fragmentary, these religious expressions of protest seem to have had a minimal impact. Only in the 1950s with the advent of Tokoism did an independent Church attract a large permanent following.

While most of these protests were rurally based, assimilated intellectuals and journalists in Luanda and Lisbon spoke out against the abuses of colonialism and reaffirmed their identity. The best known of these proto-nationalists were canon Antonio José de Nascimento (1838–1902), the lawyer and journalist José de Fontes Pereira (1838–91), the writer Joaquim Dias Cordeiro da Matta (1857–94) and possibly the members of an association formed in connection with a virulently anti-colonial work entitled *Voz d'Angola clamando no deserto*, published in Lisbon in 1901. In Angola itself, Liga Angolana, a small association of Angolan civil servants, gained formal recognition from Governor-General Norton de Matos in 1913. Almost immediately a split in this association led to the emergence of Gremio Africano. These organizations, however, lacked a substantial following and had extremely limited influence.

Of far greater potential importance than the formation of any of these associations was the Cuanza Norte 'conspiracy' of 1916–17, which momentarily linked a number of alienated intellectuals with Mbundu peasants living in the Luanda hinterland. It was led by António de Assis Júnior (1887–1960), a lawyer, novelist and journalist. He vigorously condemned colonial oppression and the preferential treatment given to the settler community. Fearing a growing alliance between *assimilados* and peasants and concerned about the spate of uprisings, the colonial state acted swiftly. António de Assis Júnior was arrested and narrowly escaped being deported.

In Lisbon, the Junta de Defensa dos Direitos de Africa, formed in 1913 by Africans living there, had very little power. A dissident offshoot of the Junta founded the Liga Africana in 1919, to which the Liga Angolana de Luanda was affiliated. The Junta de Defensa was reorganized as the Partido Nacional Africano in 1921, to avoid being taken over by left-wing elements.

A year after his return in 1921, the High Commissioner Norton de Matos, an unyielding opponent of the Liga Angolana and the Gremio Africano formally clamped down on the two associations. He ordered that António de Assis Júnior be arrested, that several influential members of the Liga Angolana be deported, and finally that the Liga Angolana be formally dissolved. He also banned 'nativist' newspapers and curtailed promotion opportunities for *assimilado* civil servants. After this blow, organized nationalism in Angola went underground.

Conditions became so difficult in Angola, especially after the establishment of the military dictatorship by the Salazar regime in 1926, that African associations adopted a policy of co-operation with the government. 'Purged' of its hard-line elements, the Liga Angolana was allowed to reappear in 1929–30 under the name of the Liga Nacional Africana. The Gremio Africano, which had collapsed because of the numerous restrictions in the 1920s, also re-emerged as the Associação dos Naturais de Angola (ANANGOLA). Sapped of their vital force and rendered politically impotent, the two organizations were induced to pursue purely social aims. Thus, the new forms of political protest centring around elitist organizations and working-class movements so active in South Africa failed to take root in Angola.

Popular opposition to colonial rule in Mozambique

The mode of popular protest in Mozambique was similar to that in Angola though it varied somewhat in scale and intensity. There were fewer armed insurrections and the literary tradition and connections with the pan-Africanist movement were less well developed. The number of documented examples of peasant and worker opposition, on the other hand, is appreciably greater in Mozambique than in Angola and independent churches were far more numerous and politically significant.

Peasant opposition posed a recurring challenge to the colonial capitalist system. For peasants the central arena of struggle was against the appropriation of their labour and its products. As in the early years of the colonial period, tax evasion recurred with great regularity throughout all of rural Mozambique. Peasants developed a variety of different strategies to reduce or avoid the annual payments. They commonly falsified their age or marital status, thereby reducing their financial burdens. Thousands of rural Mozambicans, compelled to grow cotton or to work on settler farms, plantations and state public work projects, withheld their labour entirely by fleeing to neighbouring colonies. By 1919, it was estimated that more than 100 000 northern Mozambicans had resettled in Nyasaland alone.

Other deserters, reluctant to break all links with their families and traditional homelands, fled to sparsely populated backwater areas. In some instances, they created permanent refugee communities, several of which were able to maintain their independence for a number of years, surviving both the harsh environmental conditions and armed colonial intervention. The most common form of protest by cotton-producing peasants and rural workers, however, was the withdrawal of their labour.

Given the factors which tended to divide both the peasantry and migrant workers and frustrate any sense of class solidarity, it is hardly surprising that rural resistance rarely took a collective form. Occasionally, however, rural dissatisfaction was expressed in a more radical form. From 1917 to 1921 peasants throughout the Zambezi valley, angered by forced labour, increased taxation, mandatory cotton production, sexual abuses and military conscription, joined in a rebellion, directed by descendants of the Barue royal family and Shona spirit mediums, with the aim of liberating their home-lands and dismantling the oppressive colonial system. During the next two decades, there were also a series of localized peasant uprisings in Erati, Moguincal and Angoch in northern Mozambique, precipitated by taxation and forced labour.

Where fear or coercion prevented overt opposition, peasants and rural workers often showed their hostility through cultural symbols which were unintelligible to the colonial officials. The Chope, living in southern Mozambique, for example, developed an entire repertoire of songs denouncing the colonial regime in general and the hated tax official in particular. To the north, the Makua and Makonde artists ridiculed state officials – both African and European – in highly stylized carvings which distorted their features and eliminated their humanity.

Urban workers, like their rural counterparts, initially engaged in individual and sporadic actions, such as desertion or sabotaging of machinery or raw materials, to escape or minimize the new capitalist economic order. By the second decade of the twentieth century, urban wage-earners had begun to shift their tactics and organize within the new system in order to improve their conditions of employment. As early as 1911, a small group, headed by Francisco Domingos Campos, Alfredo de Oliveira Guimares and Agostinho José Mathias, attempted to organize the União Africano to include all African workers in Lourenço Marques. Despite their eloquence and the power of their critique, strong opposition from the colonial capitalist state and the white trade union movement, plus the apparent lack of unity among African workers, undercut União Africano even before it got started.

Despite this initial setback there were a number of sporadic attempts to organize African workers in Lourenço Marques. Strikes and work stoppages were reported by employees of the Merchants Association in 1913, tram workers in 1917, railway technicians in 1918, and employees at an engineering firm in 1919.

As in other parts of Africa, port workers were the most militant and relatively best organized sector in the labour force. There were seven major strikes between 1918 and 1921, precipitated by the refusal of the shipping and forwarding companies to increase African wages to keep up with the spiralling rate of inflation. Though these strikes were broken and despite the rise to power of a fascist government, strikes continued after 1926, though less frequently. Perhaps the most bitter port confrontation was the Quinhenta strike in 1933 in protest against the reduction of the already low wages of wharf workers by between 10 and 30%.

Several factors militated against the organized efforts of Mozambican workers during this period. First, their numbers were extremely small. Mozambique's limited capitalist sector employed relatively few full-time labourers. Moreover, the state explicitly pro-hibited the formation of African unions while the white labour movement, embracing the racial and cultural prejudices which were part of the official state ideology, with a few notable exceptions remained hostile. Thus, small in number, isolated from the larger working-class movement, and facing a hostile alliance of state and capital, African workers were clearly in an unenviable position.

As in other parts of Southern and Central Africa, independent churches offered another institutional framework for workers and peasants to vent their hostility against the new social order and the hypocrisy of the established Christian churches. As early as 1918 there were seventy-six separatist churches known to be operating in Mozambique. Twenty years later the number had jumped to more than 380. Membership ranged from a mere handful of adherents to more than 10 000 in the case of the Missão Christa Ethiopia, whose network extended throughout four provinces. Virtually all the independent churches were introduced into Mozambique by migrant labourers on their return home from South Africa and the Rhodesias. Most of these churches did not adopt an explicitly anti-colonial stance but rather limited their opposition to verbal criticism.

There is also some evidence of Islamic revisionist movements in northern Mozambique, whose Muslim population had historically opposed colonial rule. In the 1920s Islamic holy men protested against the abuses of forced labour, low wages and land appropriation in the area of Quilemane. A number of Muslim chiefs and their followers were also involved in uprisings in the early 1930s but the exact cause of the revolts remains unknown.

Urban intellectual protest, although not as deeply rooted in Mozambique as in Angola, nevertheless became important. The first, somewhat tentative, call for change came in 1908 with the publication of the Lourenço Marques newspaper, *O Africano*, the official organ of Gremio Africano (African Union) – a social and civil group founded by the *grandes familias* of colour two years earlier. Despite their relatively privileged position and their self-conscious sense of importance, the leading families of Gremio Africano took as their mandate the responsibility to speak for the oppressed Africans. Its successor, *O Brado Africano* (The African Voice), pursued a similar objective as the self-appointed guardian of African peasants and workers.

In their news stories and editorials both journals highlighted four recurring abuses – *chibalo* (forced labour), the poor working conditions of free African labour, the preferential treatment given to white immigrants, and the lack of educational opportunities – which to the editors symbolized the very essence of colonial oppression.

Although the tone of the editorials in both newspapers was cautious and reformist, appealing to the goodwill and sense of justice of the colonial government, mounting frustrations produced outbursts of anger and even implicit threats to the system. This somewhat more defiant tone surfaced with greater regularity in the period immediately after the Salazar regime imposed its authoritarian rule, smashing any illusion of reform and generating a sense of despair even among the most privileged members of the African and mulatto community. However, intense rivalries between mulatto and African segments of the colonial elite enabled the local state officials to drive a wedge between the two, and they encouraged several of the Africans to organize the Institutio Negrophilio in 1932. Four years later the Salazer regime imposed extremely stringent censorship laws, which effectively silenced *O Brado Africano*.

During this period a small number of Mozambican intellectuals living in Portugal helped to form organizations which were linked to the pan-African movement. The most important were, the Liga Africana and the Partido Nacional Africano. Liga Africana maintained close ties with W. E. B. Du Bois's Pan-African Congress, while the latter expressed greater sympathy for Garveyism. Neither, however, had any substantial following in the colony and the actions were largely symbolic.

Conclusion

To sum up, the countries of Southern and Central Africa stood up to colonialism and made a substantial contribution to the preparation of the liberation movement on the African continent which followed after 1935. The most advanced forms of anti-colonial protest in that period were observed in the Union of South Africa, where industrial development and the accompanying process of urbanization involved Africans in the capitalist economy earlier than in the other African countries. Nationalist and political organizations set up in the Union of South Africa were used as models in many countries of Southern, Central and East Africa.

28

Ethiopia and Liberia, 1914–35: two independent African states in the colonial era

In Chapter 11 above, we examined the survival of Ethiopia and Liberia in the face of European aggressive imperialism between 1880 and 1914. In the ensuing inter-war period both countries again became victims of European aggression. This chapter discusses, in comparative terms, this aggression, the responses of Liberia and Ethiopia to it, and other political, economic and social developments that occurred in both countries during the period 1914–35.

Liberia and Ethiopia: socio-cultural developments

During this period, Liberia and Ethiopia faced grave problems of national integration and survival, resulting partly from their vast expansion during the previous century and the increased diversity of their peoples and cultures. What major cultural and social changes occurred in both countries during this period?

Of Liberia's population, the Americo-Liberians as a group remained politically and economically dominant. Since the late nineteenth century their number had reportedly declined owing to a higher death than birth rate, and the virtual cessation of immigration of blacks from America in spite, as will be seen in the following chapter, of efforts to promote it. The situation led to increased intermarriage and relationships, mostly between Americo-Liberian men and indigenous African women (many of whom were educated in the Liberian schools), and a corresponding increase of Liberians with mixed Americo-Liberian/indigenous African parentage. The decline in Americo-Liberian population probably also intensified their practice of in-group marriages, and correspondingly the extended family system that had developed among them since the late nineteenth century. Thus throughout our period, established families like the Shermans, the Barclays, the Greens, the Brewers, the Gibsons and the Tubmans continued to provide most of Liberia's political and economic leadership.

As for the indigenous Liberians, the gradual expansion of schools and Christian missionary work throughout Liberia somewhat increased literacy, modernization and assimilation of some aspects of the Americo-Liberian culture. Indigenous Liberians thus assimilated were regarded as 'civilized' (or 'semi-civilized') by the Americo-Liberians, who granted a comparatively few of them, such as Dr Benjamin Payne (Bassa),

301

Henry Too Wesley (Grebo) and Didwo Twe (Kru) (see 28.1), equal political and civil rights.

Nevertheless, even the favoured educated Africans – let alone the mass of unenfranchised and largely oppressed indigenous Liberians – were more or less dissatisfied with 'Americo-Liberian rule' – as they rightly termed the Liberian government. However, as a rule, the educated indigenous Liberians sought to reform Liberia's sociopolitical system to secure a better deal for the indigenous Liberians rather than to overthrow it.

It should be pointed out that assimilation of culture was not in one direction only. Over the years the Americo-Liberians had themselves adapted many aspects of indigenous Liberian culture which they had earlier on condemned as superstitious or heathenish, such as belief in the efficacy of magic, witchcraft, 'native medicine' and initiation into the *poro*. During the period of this study, however, the degree of such Africanization was too limited to blur the main social, economic, political and cultural distinctions between the Americo-Liberians as a group and the indigenous Liberians.

As was the case with Liberia, a major consequence of Ethiopia's vast expansion under Menelik was to intensify the ethnic diversity of Ethiopia's population. Prominent among the peoples incorporated into Ethiopia by 1914 through this expansion were the Oromo, who numbered almost as many as the Amhara–Tigreans, the Gurage, Sisama and Beni Shanguls.

The Amhara–Tigreans as a group, like the Americo-Liberian oligarchy in Liberia, retained their economic, political and military dominance over the rest of Ethiopia during our period. Although they constituted a privileged group, actual economic and political power and high status were concentrated in some Ethiopian noble families, from whom the holders of high public office or titles like *negus, betwoded, ras, dejazmach* and *fitawrari* were mostly recruited. It was largely through these noblemen (and the armies they commanded) that Menelik expanded Ethiopia by conquest. Thereafter he occupied the conquered territories with 'garrison settlements' in much the same manner as did colonialists from Europe in other parts of Africa. Hence many of these noblemen and their descendants, as well as descendants of the garrison settlements, government officials and even Christian clergy often adopted the worst possible type of 'colonial' approach or racial attitude towards other Ethiopians.

Among the non-Amhara–Tigreans (that is, the Oromo, Sidama, Gurage, and so on), a major social and cultural development in the twentieth century has been increased 'Amharization', such as the use of the Amhara language, dress and calendar and changes in religious beliefs, despite resistance by Muslim, traditional and other influences. However, as in Liberia, acculturation was a two-way process. Some of the Amhara–Tigrean settlers in the more isolated garrison settlements were eventually assimilated by the local population.

Furthermore, Ethiopian society segmented into various classes and groups. These included slaves; peasants; the rising intellectuals and commercial bourgeoisie, who supported the Regent, Tafari Makonnen (later Emperor Haile Sellassie), and favoured reforms and a strong central government; and a conservative group comprising most of the great nobles and high clergy of Ethiopia's Coptic Church. This latter group, which

28.1 *Didwo Twe, Kru Senator, Liberia, one of the few indigenous Liberians to attain high public office* (I. K. Sundiata, *Black Scandal*, 1980. Not acknowledged to original source)

supported Empress Zawditu and favoured regional autonomy, constituted the bulwark of Ethiopia's socio-cultural system.

Thus, in both Liberia and Ethiopia, ethnic and cultural diversity and social inequality posed serious threats to social stability and harmony, or, as will be seen below, produced actual conflicts, during our period.

Political developments

Liberia

In both Liberia and Ethiopia during our period, strains and stresses occurred in the political system and processes in three main spheres: within the core, on the periphery, and between the core and periphery.

As regards Liberia's core, throughout the 1910s the True Whig Party firmly held the reins of power with minimum challenge from a formal opposition party. This situation changed somewhat in the 1920s when the People's Party, organized in 1922 under the leadership of ex-President Daniel B. Howard, seriously challenged the ruling True Whig Party. However, because of the weak and sporadic nature of the opposition, gross corruption and electoral malpractices, lack of any ideological or policy differences and the enormous patronage wielded by the government, there was no question of the True Whig Party being unseated. Indeed, Liberia had gradually evolved during the twentieth century into a virtual one-party state – one of the earliest African countries to do so. Nor was the political base in Liberia broadened to bring in the indigenous Liberians. Apart from Too Wesley and a few others already referred to, no such political developments took place. Liberia's political system therefore remained basically conservative, serving mainly the interests of the Americo-Liberian elite and perpetuating its political ascendancy.

Ethiopia

The political situation in Ethiopia during our period contrasted with that of Liberia in certain important respects, notably the nature and range of political institutions and the functioning and the extent of diffusion of political power and privilege. However, regarding the more fundamental issues of the structure of the political system, the extent of political change, and class structure and interests, Ethiopia had much in common with Liberia.

Menelik's last years were difficult times for Ethiopia. Following his protracted illness and up to his death in December 1913, the Emperor appointed his grandson, Lij Iyasu – a boy of twelve – as his successor in mid-1908. Later in that year, when he became paralysed and lost the power of speech, he appointed his former general, Ras Tasamma, as Regent. On the death of Tasamma in 1911, the Ethiopian Council of State declared that Iyasu was old enough to act for himself with their guidance.

Lij Iyasu, son of Ras Mikael, the ruler of Wallo, was impetuous by nature. Besides possessing little of his grandfather's statescraft, he lacked a power base outside Wallo.

Some aspects of his domestic policies, such as his friendship which the Muslim population, and his foreign policies, which centred on support for Germany, Austria–Hungary and Turkey on the outbreak of the First World War in 1914, alienated the nobles, the Church dignitaries and the Allied delegations in Addis Ababa. All of them therefore colluded to depose him in September 1916 and to keep him a prisoner from 1921 till his death in 1935. Menelik's daughter, Zawditu, was thereupon proclaimed Empress, and Tafari, son of the deceased Emperor's cousin Ras Makonnen, Regent and heir to the throne. Empress Zawditu's coronation, on 11 February 1917, was followed by a regime of dual authority in which power was shared between the Empress and the Regent, each with a palace, a distinct group of followers and often conflicting policies.

The advent of Tafari as Regent was an event of importance in that he was a resolute leader desirous of resuming Menelik's policies of modernization and of maintaining Ethiopia's independence. His personal style of administration partly enabled him to gradually extend his power during his regency over several crucial areas of the public sector and, in 1928, he was crowned Negus, and assumed complete control of the government. On the death of Empress Zawditu in March 1930, Tafari mounted the imperial throne and was crowned as Emperor Haile Sellassie I on 2 November 1930 (see 28.2).

As in Liberia's case, some political changes did take place during the reign of Haile Selassie. These included increased centralization, public appointments according to individual ability rather than birth, the elimination of the most conservative of the Ethiopian nobility, and the formal promulgation of a Constitution. But these changes were neither fundamental nor structural. Rather, in spite of increased political centralization, social separatism and cultural differences remained the dominant characteristics of Ethiopia and serious hindrances to national integration.

The Constitution that was promulgated in 1931 which provided for a bicameral parliament with a nominated Senate and a Chamber of Deputies, was far from being radical and had little immediate impact on Ethiopia's political culture. The Constitution left the Emperor's absolutist powers intact and largely retained the privileged position of the nobility. Given hardly any initiative in legislation or policy-making, and convened and dissolved at will by the Emperor, the Parliament merely rubber-stamped matters placed before it by the Emperor.

In all this Ethiopia differed markedly from Liberia. For, although the Liberian Constitution granted the Liberian president wide constitutional powers, these were far from absolute. The Liberian Parliament was politically active while the Ethiopian was docile and complacent. The most striking contrast was perhaps the absence of political parties in Ethiopia, owing mainly to the historically dominant position of the emperor in Ethiopian affairs, and lack of a westernized elite that could significantly modify Ethiopia's conservatism.

Thus, during our period, Liberia and Ethiopia had more common features than differences in the fundamental determinants of political culture, features such as their conservatism, inegalitarian and ascriptive social norms, and lack of national integration, economic development, or firm commitment to radical social change.

28.2   *Haile Sellassie I, Emperor of Ethiopia, 1930–74 (Harlingue-Viollet)*

Economic and social change

Liberia

In many respects, the years 1915–35 were trying times economically for most Liberians and the Liberian government. The decline as from the late nineteenth century of Liberian trade and agriculture, Liberia's leading sectors, drastically curtailed government revenue, which was derived mostly from customs duties. This deprived many Liberians of their principal means of livelihood.

Partly to repay Liberia's mounting debts, including the English loan of 1870, and partly to carry out internal development, the Liberian government secured a loan of $500 000 in 1906 at 6% interest from some English financiers and another one of $1 700 000 in 1912 from certain European banks at 5% interest. To pay the interest and the sinking fund on the latter loan, the collection and management of part of Liberia's revenues, termed 'assigned revenue' and made up of the customs duties, were entrusted to an 'International Receivership', consisting of an American as a 'General Receiver of Customs', assisted by French, German and British Receivers.

In actual fact, the proceeds from the 'assigned revenue' fell after the outbreak of the First World War, largely as a result of the decline of trade which followed the withdrawal of the Germans, who had controlled about three-quarters of Liberian trade, and the drastic fall in the prices of Liberia's exports such as coffee, cocoa and palm oil on the world market. Thus, as from 1916, the annual interest and sinking fund on the loan of 1912 could not be met regularly or in full. Arrears of payment therefore accumulated, amounting to $178 657 by 30 September 1918. At the same time, the remaining revenue, termed 'internal revenue', largely owing to corrupt practices by Liberian officials, hardly sufficed to meet the Liberian government's essential services, such as payment of the already severely cut salaries of government employees.

Thus, faced with bankruptcy, the Liberian Government first borrowed constantly and extensively from the Bank of British West Africa during 1917–18. The failure of an attempt to raise a loan from the United States government between 1918 and 1921 forced the Liberian government to introduce several measures designed to stimulate trade and increase revenue from it. These included an upward revision of the tariff, the reopening of the Liberia hinterland to foreign traders (closed to foreigners since the outbreak of the First World War) and the raising of port and harbour dues. Simultaneously, as will be seen in the next chapter, the Liberian government initially welcomed plans by Garvey's Universal Negro Improvement Association to bring capital and black immigrants to Liberia to develop her resources. These plans fell through, however.

Fortunately for Liberia, as from late 1923, partly as a result of the above changes, partly because of the sale of German property confiscated during the First World War, and partly because of the re-entry of Germans into her foreign trade in 1922, the performance of the Liberian economy gradually improved and the balance of trade began to shift in her favour. However, as the prices of Liberia's major products, such as palm oil, piassava and coffee, fell in the world market from the outset of the depression, the volume of Liberia's trade declined as well. Nor did the establishment of two large plantations in 1926 by Firestone coupled with the loan of $5 000 000 from the Financial

Corporation of America significantly affect the economy of Liberia until after 1935 when substantial exports of rubber commenced. Throughout the 1930s, therefore, the balance of trade was against Liberia.

In these more or less bleak economic circumstances throughout our period (1915–35), the Liberian Government was left with perennially meagre funds after continuous debt payments. However, some effort at economic and social development of Liberia was made. Its road-building programme, begun by President Arthur Barclay, was intensified, but mostly with forced and unpaid indigenous Liberian labour. During the 1920s, the Liberian government – for the first time in Liberia's history – established several elementary schools in the remote Liberian hinterland. Late in 1930, the government also started the Booker T. Washington Agricultural and Industrial Institution to train junior and middle-level technical and agricultural manpower. In 1934, it commenced a much-needed Teachers' Training College in Monrovia in addition to the existing institutions like the Liberia College and the College of West Africa. In 1924 the government built a hospital in Monrovia and in 1927 erected an electric power plant also in Monrovia. American missionary bodies, as they had done since Liberia's foundation, contributed by establishing schools and hospitals as well as churches. However, any significant expansion of education was inhibited as much by inadequate government revenue as by the Liberian government's traditional caution in opening the Liberian hinterland to missionaries, traders and other foreigners.

Ethiopia

Ethiopia, like Liberia, did not undergo any significant economic development during our period. Such economic and social changes as did occur were too limited to alter significantly Ethiopia's essentially feudal economy and conservative socio-economic fabric.

The principal initiator of economic and social change was the Regent, Tafari Makonnen. One of his first reforms was the extension of Menelik's ministerial system by the establishment in 1922 of a Ministry of Commerce and a Department of Public Works. In 1923, he set up the Berhanena Salam ('Light and Peace') printing press, which printed a newspaper of the same name, as well as religious and educational books. Tafari, much preoccupied with international relations, was quick to appreciate the advantages which the League of Nations and its system of collective security seemed to offer. He therefore applied for Ethiopia to join the organization at its founding in 1919 and, after opposition on the part of some of the European countries such as Britain, Ethiopia was admitted on 23 September 1923, when the Regent signed a declaration adhering to the principal international conventions for the suppression of slavery.

After his European tour of 1924 and his coronation in 1930, Haile Sellassie continued his modernization work, though this was seriously affected by the world economic depression, which led to a fall in exports and a decline in foreign investment possibilities. A law was nevertheless proclaimed in 1930 for the survey and registration of land and, in the same year, a Ministry of Education was established. The year 1931 witnessed three significant developments, namely, the promulgation of the written Constitution, which has already been discussed, the replacement of the old Bank of

Abyssinia, a foreign-owned private company, by a national bank, the Bank of Ethiopia, and the passing of a supplementary law for the gradual eradication of slavery. Efforts were also made to improve communications. A Ministry of Public Works was set up in 1932, and road-building was started. A temporary radio station was put into operation in 1933, and replaced by a more powerful one in 1935. Several new schools were opened, particularly in the provinces, both by the government and by missionaries. By 1935, Addis Ababa had fourteen government schools, with thirty foreign teachers and some four thousand students. A military college was founded in 1934 at Holeta, near Addis Ababa. The number of students studying abroad rose to several hundred. Some missionaries, notably the United Presbyterian Church of North America, the Seventh Day Adventist Mission, and the Italian Catholic Mission, operated hospitals in Addis Ababa, while the Sudan Interior Mission ran a leprosarium at Akaki. Other developments included the creation of a small civil service, partly staffed with students returning from abroad, and the increasing replacement of tribute in kind by taxes in cash. Efforts at modernization, however, were by then overshadowed by the impending threat of Italian fascist invasion.

Thus the period 1915–35 witnessed a wider spread and a greater degree of economic and social change in Liberia and Ethiopia than before. However, this change did not amount to much and both countries therefore remained economically backward and socially undeveloped. Finally, investment by foreign nationals and firms in commercial and agricultural enterprises was greater in Liberia than in Ethiopia; and, while this aided the processes of modernization, it also led to greater foreign control of the Liberian economy than was the case in Ethiopia.

Foreign intervention

Liberia

Foreign intervention in Liberia and Ethiopia, already discussed in Chapter 11, persisted during the period 1915–35. As in the era of the Scramble and partition, the grounds for intervention were provided as much by events and circumstances within Liberia and Ethiopia as by those in Europe and the United States of America.

First, the Liberian government's penury and perennial indebtedness partly led to increased foreign control of Liberia's financial administration by the International Receivership, the Bank of British West Africa, and Firestone interests supported by the United States government. The Liberian economy was also dominated by European, American and Lebanese firms. Secondly, Liberia's unfavourable economic, social and administrative conditions became a major issue in the bitter political rivalry between the True Whig and People's parties and attracted a lot of international attention, especially after the tour of Europe and America by Faulkner, the opposition leader to gain international support and to discredit the True Whig administration of President King. More importantly, reports in both the American and the British press and other reports by foreign missionaries and visitors accused the Liberian government and certain influential Americo-Liberians of practising slavery, recruiting forced and indentured labour, and exporting or selling migrant labour to the Spanish island-colony of Fernando Po.

As a result of these attacks, the League of Nations sent a fact-finding Commission to Liberia under the chairmanship of a British dentist, Dr Cuthbert Christy. The Commission reported on 8 September 1930, that, while no form of organized slave trading existed, labour was wastefully and forcibly recruited for public works, for private use and for export with the collaboration of the Liberian Frontier Force and high government officials. It also found Americo-Liberian/indigenous Liberian relations and the general administration of the Liberian government unsatisfactory and hence recommended, rather dubiously, that Liberia should be placed under a 'capable and warmhearted white administration'.

Although the Report led to the resignation of President King and his Vice-President Allen Yancy, and although the new administration of Edwin J. Barclay decided to implement most of the recommendations of the League and between December 1930 and May 1931 passed several Acts which abolished the export of labour, pawning, domestic slavery and forced labour, Britain and the United States of America still insisted 'that the Government of Liberia should be committed for a time to an International Governing Commission'. Barclay and his Cabinet promptly and rightly rejected this since they considered it to 'be tantamount to a surrender of sovereignty and autonomy'. They did, however, express their readiness to seek and accept assistance from the League, particularly in the form of experts in such fields as economics and 'native' administration.

Accordingly, the League commissioned another fact-finding mission, this time consisting of representatives of eight nations – Britain, France, Germany, Italy, Spain, Venezuela, Poland and Liberia – charged with the responsibility to end slavery and forced labour, and to give technical assistance to Liberia. A small committee of three persons, headed by a French lawyer, Henri Brunot, was also appointed to advise the mission on the financial and administrative reforms necessary in Liberia to make the League's assistance successful.

Like its predecessor, this second commission drew up elaborate plans for the improvement of Liberia's internal administration, finances and public health. In January 1932 the Brunot Commission also presented its Report to the League. It recommended, *inter alia*, that traditional African communal labour was to replace forced labour for public works; the indigenous Liberians were to be granted undisputed ownership of their lands; and the education of indigenous Liberians and the means of communication with the Liberian hinterland were to be improved. The commission also suggested that, for Liberia's finances to improve reasonably, Firestone would have to modify the terms of the loan agreement of 1926.

On the receipt of the Brunot Report, the League's Liberia Committee drew up the 'General Principles of the Plan of Assistance' to Liberia, and, on the basis of these principles and the Lighthart Report on the financial negotiations with Firestone, the Committee also drew up a 'Protocol' embodying the proposed plan of assistance and reforms. These included the employment of foreign 'specialists' as provincial and deputy commissioners and the appointment of a 'Chief Adviser' to the Liberian government by the Council of the League with the agreement of the Liberian President, who would serve as liaison between the Liberian government and the League. When the Liberian government refused to accept the Plan in its entirety, the League Committee withdrew it.

The Liberian government then drew up a 'Three Year Development Plan' of internal reforms in Liberia, including modifications to the Loan Agreement of 1926. This plan won the support of the American government under President Franklin D. Roosevelt and formed the basis of the negotiations between Firestone, the United States of America and the Liberian government in 1935, during which the necessary modifications to the loan were made. The interest on the loan was reduced from 7 to 5%.

Not surprisingly, as Liberia's relations with Firestone thus improved, Liberian–United States relations correspondingly improved, culminating in United States recognition of the Barclay Administration on 11 June 1935. Britain followed suit on 16 December 1936, with which event the crisis of Liberia's independence could be said to be formally over.

Ethiopia

Even more persistent and far more serious in its consequences was foreign intervention in the internal affairs of Ethiopia during the period under review. The Tripartite Convention of 1906, which divided Ethiopia into British, French and Italian spheres of interest, was an indication that European imperialist intervention would sooner or later recur in Ethiopia. Menelik's death in 1913, the accession of Lij Iyasu and the events of the First World War spurred Italy in particular to revive her imperial designs against Ethiopia as from 1913. Thus between 1913 and 1919 the Italian Colonial Ministry vigorously sponsored the implementation of a programme of Italian colonization in Africa, which sought particularly to give Italy control of the Red Sea and to make Ethiopia 'the exclusive sphere of influence of Italy'. This plan was, however, opposed by Britain and France and was therefore abandoned in 1919 after the Versailles Peace Treaty.

In spite of Italy's colonial ambitions in Ethiopia and the painful memories of Adowa, which many Italians wished to avenge, actual relations between Ethiopia and Italy were remarkably good during the Tafari Makonnen regency. In 1930, however, the Fascist regime of Mussolini changed its policy of peaceful penetration to military intervention and began secret preparations for the invasion of Ethiopia. Only a pretext for invasion was now needed and this was provided when a clash occurred at the well of Wal Wal in November 1934 between an Italian occupation force and Ethiopian troops involved in the demarcation of the boundary between Ethiopia and British Somaliland. Rejecting arbitration, Italy demanded not only an apology but also Ethiopia's recognition of Italian sovereignty over Wal Wal and an indemnity of 200 000 Maria Theresa dollars. Though Britain and France, anxious to avoid a conflagration, urged Ethiopia to agree, Haile Sellassie refused, and took the matter to the League of Nations on 14 December. While the League was considering the matter, Italy, without a declaration of war, launched her invasion of Ethiopia on 3 October 1935 under the command of de Bono.

The invasion, despite its long preparation, provoked world consternation. The League Assembly met on 9 October and decided by fifty votes against one (Italy) with three abstentions (Albania, Austria and Hungary) that Italy was the aggressor and had violated the League Convenant. Despite this near-unanimous condemnation, the League, dominated by the colonial powers of France and Britain, was reluctant to offend Mussolini and therefore imposed only limited economic sanctions on Italy, which included an embargo on the export of arms and munitions and loans and credits to Italy. As was expected, these sanctions proved totally ineffective. The Italian army therefore pressed on and occupied Adowa. But the Ethiopians put up a spirited resistance which obliged the invaders to halt. De Bono was thereupon dismissed and replaced on 16 November by a career soldier, Marshall Badoglio, who, faced with a strong Ethiopian counter-offensive, also found it impossible to advance for many weeks. In the hope of breaking Ethiopian morale, Mussolini then ordered his troops to make the first use of poison gas. In spite of this, much fierce fighting lay ahead before the Italians occupied Addis Ababa on 6 May 1936.

The Italian invasion evoked instant reaction in and around Africa. In August 1935, a group of Africans and persons of African descent in London founded the International African Friends of Abyssinia, whose committee included C. L. R. James of the West Indies, Dr P. McD. Millard of British Guyana, Marcus Garvey's wife Amy Ashwood Garvey, Mohammed Said of Somaliland, and Dr J. B. Danquah of the Gold Coast. The Society's aim, as stated by its secretary, Jomo Kenyatta, was 'to assist by all means in their power in the maintenance of the territorial integrity and political independence of Abyssinia'.

The subsequent outbreak of fighting, which placed Ethiopia in the headlines of every newspaper, made a deep impact on African thinking. Kwame Nkrumah, then a student passing through England, recalled that when he saw posters declaring 'Mussolini invades Ethiopia' he was seized by emotion, and added:

> At that moment it was almost as if the whole of London had suddenly declared war on me personally. For the next few minutes I could do nothing but glare at each impassive face, wondering if these people could realize the wickedness of colonialism, and praying that the day might come when I could play my part in bringing about the downfall of such a system. My nationalism surged to the fore; I was ready to go through hell itself, if need be, in order to achieve my object.

Similar sentiments were aroused all over Africa. The Nigerian intellectual, Nnamdi Azikiwe, devoted much space to Ethiopia's struggle in his newspapers, the *West African Pilot* and the *Comet*.

The outcome for Liberia and Ethiopia
of the European imperialist intervention

Why then, finally, had Liberia survived foreign intervention with her sovereignty intact by the end of 1936, whereas Ethiopia had succumbed to it, albeit temporarily? The answer cannot be found in the internal situations in the two countries, since both were practically the same by 1935, as has been shown above. Nor can it be found in the relative strengths of their armies, since both countries were militarily very weak compared with the military might of their potential or actual foreign aggressors. The crucial difference in the survival of Liberia and the non-survival of Ethiopia was that Ethiopia had a mad bloodthirsty imperial power as a neighbour who was bent on territorial aggrandizement and above all on avenging Adowa, and therefore on attacking and occupying Ethiopia. On the other hand, Liberia's neighbours, Britain and France, already possessed expansive colonial territories in Africa and had no Adowa to avenge and therefore had no compelling motivation to attack and conquer Liberia in the same manner that Italy attacked and conquered Ethiopia. But, though defeated, because of the spirited defence she put up and the enormous sentiment she aroused among Africans in particular and the black peoples throughout the world, Ethiopia had at the end of 1935 become the burning symbol of Africa's awakening from colonial rule.

Africa
and the New World

In the earlier volumes of this series, the forcible transportation of millions of Africans, mostly from West and Central Africa, during the notorious trans-Atlantic slave trade in the seventeenth and eighteenth centuries, was dealt with. In this chapter, the interactions between Africans and the peoples of African descent in the Americas during the colonial period of African history, some aspects of which have been touched upon in the earlier chapters of this volume, will be closely examined.

African and American black interactions in the period 1880–1935 consisted essentially of five types of activities: (1) back-to-Africa movements or black emigration – mostly from North America, but also from the Caribbean and Brazil – into parts of Africa (mostly West Africa, but also South Africa and the Horn); (2) American evangelism featuring Afro-American missionaries as 'gospel conductors' in Africa; (3) a renewed Middle Passage in the form of a stream of African students matriculating at American black schools and universities; (4) several varieties of pan-Africanist activities, including conferences, organizations and educational activities, which put Africans in touch with the black world of the Americas and which helped to influence events in colonial Africa; and (5) persistence and transformation of African cultural values in Latin America and the Caribbean. These five themes will be discussed in turn in the five divisions of this chapter.

Back-to-Africa movements

Despite a noticeable shift in black sentiment away from Liberian emigration apparent among North American blacks during the first half of the nineteenth century, Afro-Americans continued to display an interest in African emigration in the late nineteenth and early twentieth centuries. In 1878, for example, the South Carolina–Liberian Exodus Joint Stock Steamship Company brought some 206 black immigrants to Liberia, and, in 1889, Dr Edward W. Blyden, the St Thomas-born West Indian pan-Africanist, visited the United States of America to help generate black support for emigration. Moreover, between 1880 and 1900, Bishop Henry NcNeal Turner laboured to combine the two traditions long dominant in the modern history of Africa/Afro-American interaction: African emigration and Christian evangelism. Through Turner's efforts, over 300 Afro-Americans emigrated to Liberia in March

1896. Turner also later served as an adviser to the International Migration Society (IMS) of Alabama, which sent about 500 emigrants to Africa before it became defunct in 1900. Some of the 500 remained in Liberia while others returned to the United States.

After the turn of the twentieth century, the back-to-Africa baton was picked up by others. For example, one Captain Dean, early in the twentieth century, hoped to engineer the settlement of American blacks in South Africa to fashion a powerful black state there. After the briefest stay meant to arrange for this settlement, however, Dean was expelled by the white authorities for what were termed 'provocative activities'. In 1914, Chief Alfred C. Sam, a Gold Coast African, turned up in Oklahoma, persuaded about sixty black farmers that Africa offered them greater opportunities and sailed with them to Saltpond in the Gold Coast. Sam's scheme also failed, mainly because of the restrictions imposed by the Gold Coast officials which inhibited the entry of American immigrants. But no one made so deep an impression as an advocate of emigration on Africans and American blacks alike as did Marcus Garvey.

Because of his general appeal to black pride, Garvey focused the attention of millions of American blacks on Africa in the period following the First World War. In 1914, after extensive travels in the Caribbean, Central and South America and a two-year residence in Britain, Garvey launched in Jamaica his project designed to advance African emigration and related programmes, which he called the Universal Negro Improvement and Conservation Association and African Communities League (later simply UNIA). This project, which he transferred to the United States, included the establishment of industrial and agricultural schools for blacks in Jamaica, a Black Star fleet of ships for commerce between blacks in Africa and the Americas, and, most of all, a 'central nation for the race'.

Garvey, like the earlier advocates of emigration, chose Liberia as the African country for his scheme and sent an emissary there in May 1920 who laid out the aims of the Association: transfer of UNIA headquarters to Liberia, financial aid to Liberia for constructing schools and hospitals, liquidation of Liberia's debts, and the settlement of American blacks in Liberia who would help to develop agriculture and natural resources. The Liberian Government enthusiastically granted UNIA's initial request for land outside Monrovia and Garvey in turn sent a group of technicians to survey the site and erect buildings for between 20 000 and 30 000 families whom he hoped to send over in the course of two years beginning about 1924. But when Garvey's technicians arrived in Maryland in May 1924 they were arrested, detained and, in July 1924, deported. It was not long before the Liberian government proscribed UNIA altogether, which ended Garvey's colonization scheme in Liberia. Another move by Garvey to establish a similar scheme in Ethiopia in the late 1920s also failed.

The Afro-Brazilians

There was also an emigration of thousands of Brazilian blacks to West Africa until the time of the official abolition of slavery in Brazil in 1882. These bands of emigrants settled particularly in the coastal cities of Nigeria and Dahomey (now Benin) and, to a lesser extent, in Togo and the Gold Coast (see 29.1). They formed communities in these coastal areas, though a few of them settled in inland towns such as Abeokuta. A large

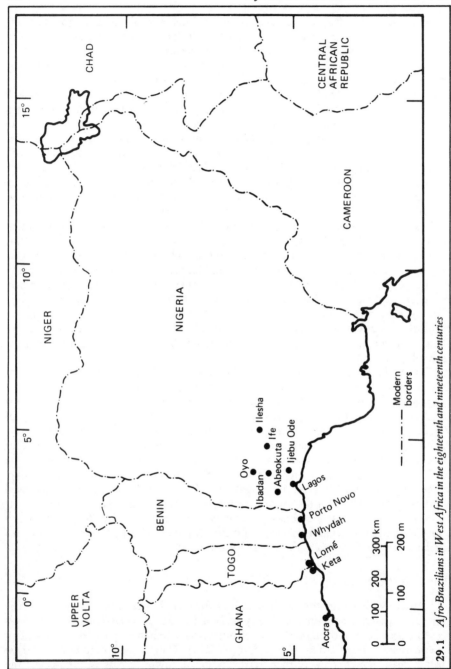

29.1 *Afro-Brazilians in West Africa in the eighteenth and nineteenth centuries*

number of emigrants had been *negros de ganho* in Brazil, in other words, slaves living in the cities who plied their trade (as masons, carpenters, caulkers, and so on) quite freely and shared their earnings with their masters. Bringing with them their technical know-how, a few outstanding builders created residential districts in Porto Novo, Whydah and in particular Lagos, where the Brazilian Quarter was built.

In Dahomey some of the children who attended the schools of the English and French missionaries were used as assistants by the colonial administration on account of their educational attainments. Although this group acquired a special status, they were not wholly accepted by European society and were not always on good terms with the indigenous African population owing to their habits and life styles.

In Lagos, the community maintained its identity, taking to the streets, for instance, on feast days to perform folk dances. With time, however, these groups in Lagos and Dahomey lost their distinguishing features. Portuguese, once considered a commercial language, was supplanted by English in Nigeria and French in Dahomey.

In the Gold Coast, the Afro-Brazilians, although established as a separate group on account of their more or less westernized habits and known for that reason as the Tabon, gradually forsook their specifically Brazilian traditions, while retaining other cultural traits such as the beating of drums on the occasion of such festivities as the two-day-long annual procession through the old streets of Accra. When the Tabon settled in the country, they had to sign a pact of vassalage with a Ga chief of Accra. They abandoned the use of the Portuguese language very early on. The rapid integration of the Tabon in the Gold Coast contrasts with the rather slow one of the Afro-Brazilians of Lagos, Abeokuta, Porto Novo, Whydah and other less important coastal towns in Nigeria, Dahomey and Togo.

In Lagos, alongside the Brazilian community, an Afro-Cuban community came into being, composed of the smaller number of individuals who had returned from Cuba.

Black American evangelism in Africa

One of the means by which African–American black interchanges were nurtured in the colonial period, short of mass migrations, was the coming of black missionaries to 'elevate' Africa by Christian evangelism. In the main, evangelization took the form of American black missionaries working, first, in the service of mainstream, predominantly white, denominations. For example, the Presbyterian Church sponsored black missionaries in French Cameroon as early as 1896. But black church organizations of their own volition and in their own right soon became the most effective missionary enterprises in Africa. Indeed, Afro-Americans in the nineteenth century were exhorted to assume a special stance toward the 'redemption' of African societies. Bishop Turner, for one, boldly argued that 'God brought the Negro to America and Christianized him so that he might go back to Africa and redeem that land'.

The African Methodist Episcopal (AME) and African Methodist Episcopal Zion (AME Zion) churches and the National Baptist Convention (NBC) all deployed black missionaries in Africa throughout the colonial period. Early stations of the NBC were set up in Liberia in 1883, building on the still earlier work of Lott Carey. The AME Zion Church also put down roots in Liberia in 1878 and in the Gold Coast in 1896.

Bishop John Bryan Small, of the Caribbean, subsequently organized two annual AME Zion conferences in the Gold Coast and consequently lured J. E. K. Aggrey and Franck Osam-Pinanko into Afro-American churches and ultimately into the service of the AME Zion Church. In 1930, AME Zion missionaries went to work in Nigeria, responding to a request from African churches there to affiliate with Zion. Meanwhile, the AME Church sponsored missions in several African venues, including Sierra Leone in 1886, Liberia in the 1890s and South Africa in 1896.

Many American blacks who responded to the call of their churches in the later nineteenth century went to Southern Africa as missionaries and with profound effect. An alliance between the schismatic independent African or 'Ethiopian' Church and the AME Church was formed in 1896. Though the AME – Ethiopianist Union broke up only a year later, when the Reverend James Mata Dwane seceded, the AME Church continued and even expanded its mission activities, with the assistance of Levi Coppin, who was appointed its first Resident Bishop, and Charlotte Manye, who returned from her American studies in 1901. For the next fifty years, the AME Church remained strong in South Africa.

Equally active, mainly in Nyasaland, was the National Baptist Convention, which was introduced by John Chilembwe, the young Yao who travelled to the United States in 1897, studied at the all-black Virginia Theological Seminary, trained as a minister and returned to his country around 1900. As pointed out already, before he led the ill-fated rebellion in 1915, he worked to set up an industrial mission 'in which Africans were trained in the arts and crafts as well as taught Christianity', that is, along the lines which he had observed among American blacks.

In spite of the resistance by white South African political and church authorities, the AME connections sown by Turner produced a large number of African students matriculating at American schools. Similarly, in British Central Africa and in West Africa, African students were encouraged and often subsidized by American black Churches. These missionary activities set the stage for a major new phase in African and Afro-American interaction in the colonial period, one which had great consequences for subsequent African nationalist movements in the mid-twentieth century.

Religious interactions between Brazil and the African coast

In matters of religion, and with regard more specifically to evangelism, there is no comparison between the influence of the North American blacks and that of the Afro-Brazilians. While the former were directly or indirectly involved in the work of spreading the Gospel, the latter were never committed to proselytizing work. Several of them, after arriving in Lagos, succeeded in making their way to their countries of origin. Reference is made in a few historical documents to Muslim Afro-Brazilians passing through Lagos on their way to Hausa country. In Lagos, on the edge of the Brazilian Quarter, a central mosque was erected by craftsmen from Brazil. Furthermore, the Catholics built their first Church, the Holy Cross Church, started in 1879, in Lagos, and sent their children to the schools of the French and English missionaries. The sons of Afro-Brazilians living in the Brazilian Quarter who had attended the missionary schools began to work as schoolteachers and catechists in the schools and missions that the priests of the African Mission Society were establishing in the region. These catechists were working for the missions, which were of European origin, and not for any educational missionary ventures originating in Brazil or resulting from an initiative of the Afro-Brazilian community of Lagos. In fact, the language of instruction was English and sometimes French.

In contrast with what occurred in the United States, where conversions took place at a deeper level with several North American blacks becoming propagators of the Christian faith, the Afro-Brazilians stood by their African religious beliefs. Thus, Afro-Brazilians living in the Brazilian Quarter and forming a middle-class nucleus which remained a cohesive and distinct social group, thanks partly to the Catholic religion, subscribed to the cult of the household *orixás* and consulted *babalaos ifa* (diviners). What is more, African religions still exerted their influence on Brazil from across the Atlantic. African cult objects and articles used in Afro-Brazilian religious ceremonies, such as cowrie shells and kola nuts, never ceased to be imported into Brazil and gradually came to be much sought after, consequently acquiring great value as the numbers of those practising Afro-Brazilian syncretism increased.

The educational impact of the Americas

When African students lived in America during the colonial period, they created the context for a different relationship between Africans and Afro-Americans and between African students themselves, drawn as they were from all over the African continent. On their return home, they also inspired thousands of their compatriots to enrol in American schools between 1880 and the Second World War. The number of African students in the United States was thereby increased and the time during which Africans as a group were in contact with American blacks was prolonged. The names of such American-educated colonial African students are legion and include recent heads of state (Nnamdi Azikiwe, Kwame Nkrumah and Kamuzu Banda) as well as earlier nationalist or community leaders (A. B. Xuma, John Dube, Marshall and Charlotte Maxeke, J. E. K. Aggrey, Pixley Ka Izaka Seme, D. S. Malekebu, F. Osam-Pinanko, Peter Koinange, Ndabaningi Sithole, Eduardo Mondlane and John Chilembwe). In time, the number of Africans booking passages to America surpassed substantially the flow of black missionaries in the opposite direction. What began as an American evangelistic crusade in Africa for spiritual redemption, in other words, eventually helped build springboards for an educational, technical and political revolution.

It may be possible to deduce the impact of American educational experience on colonial Africans and anti-colonial processes by examining brief biographies of some of the individual African students. J. E. K. Aggrey, for example, went to the United States under the direct influence of an American-educated AME Zion bishop from Barbados. Aggrey was steered to Livingstone College in Salisbury, North Carolina, the chief educational institution of the AME Zion Church, with the apparent understanding that he would return directly to Africa in the service of the Church. Upon taking a baccalaureate and a divinity degree, however, Aggrey accepted employment in the AME Zion publishing house in Charlotte, became correspondent for one or two black newspapers, conducted free classes for black teachers in the vicinity, was ordained a Church elder and was offered a pastorate by two black churches. His connections with black America had already been deepened when he married, in 1904, a young Afro-American woman, possibly a descendant of Frederick Douglass. After twenty-two years' work in black America, Aggrey returned to Africa on two separate occasions as a member of the Phelps-Stokes Commission, but died shortly after accepting the post of assistant vice-principal of the newly created Achimota College in the Gold Coast (now Ghana). Among the scores of young Africans on whom his impact was felt were Nnamdi Azikiwe, Kwame Nkrumah and Kamuzu Banda, all of whom later matriculated at American black schools.

The activities and impact of John Chilembwe of Malawi, who was educated in America and returned home, have already been dealt with. Another Malawian not so far treated was the Reverend D. S. Malekebu, who studied at the National Training School in Durham, North Carolina, and at the Moody Bible Institute in Chicago, and then took a medical degree at Meharry Medical School in 1917. Upon his return to Nyasaland in 1926, he reopened Chilembwe's Providence Industrial Mission, which the Nyasaland protectorate government razed to the ground after the abortive rebellion of 1915. Moreover, Malekebu founded the Chiradzulu Native Association, got appointed to the local district council, and emerged as a great community leader during the colonial period.

The last example to be cited is Nnamdi Azikiwe, who, like Banda, was prompted to journey to America by the ubiquitous James Aggrey and by the mood in the United States associated with Marcus Garvey. He enrolled first at a black preparatory school in West Virginia in 1925. When he attended Howard University a few years later, Azikiwe studied and worked closely with such black scholars as Ralph Bunche and, particularly, Alain Locke and William Leo Hansberry on such subjects as Afro-American and pre-colonial African history.

When he transferred to Lincoln University in 1930, Azikiwe continued his interest in black history and race relations. He also campaigned for the appointment of blacks to the all-white faculty, thinking it 'an enormity that a college for Negroes should have persisted for 86 years before a Negro was appointed to the faculty'. The university authorities were so enraged by Azikiwe's protest activities that they refused to recommend him for a renewal of his student visa, and therefore Azikiwe had to depart for Africa in 1934. He did not return to his native Nigeria but to the Gold Coast, where he settled temporarily after being refused positions in Nigeria as a teacher at Kings College, Lagos, and in the Liberian diplomatic service. In the Gold Coast, he became one of the leading anti-colonial journalists until he left for his own country, where he has been playing a very active role in politics ever since, once becoming its Governor-General.

Pan-Africanism: political and cultural aspects

Besides these educational exchanges, a series of pan-Africanist organizations and conferences, as well as commercial and literary or cultural activities put Africans in touch with American blacks and helped to influence events in colonial Africa. The activities of three persons dominated the development of formal, organized pan-Africanism during the colonial period. They were Booker T. Washington, founder and principal of Tuskegee Institute, Dr W. E. B Du Bois and Marcus Garvey.

The impact of Washington and Tuskegee on Africa and on enrolled and aspiring African students was considerable. The reputation and resources of Tuskegee were brought to Africa by African and American alumni, by numerous African visitors to the Institute or correspondents with Washington who had never been matriculated students, and through the media of numerous international conferences and technical missions.

In his keynote address to the pan-Africanist 'International Conference on the Negro', convened at Tuskegee in the spring of 1912, Washington stressed the theme of an exchange of techniques and resources between blacks in Africa and America. Among those attending the 1912 Conference were delegates from the Gold Coast, British East Africa, Liberia, Nigeria, Ruanda, Portuguese East Africa, and South Africa.

Related Tuskegee/Washington pan-Africanist activities included meetings of the Negro Business League in 1908, at which Washington showed his appreciation of pan-Africanism for African/Afro-American interchange. As he introduced five Liberian envoys who were seeking American financial assistance, Washington emphasized that 'they are here in the United States on an official visit, not merely as envoys of their land, but as representatives of the entire Negro race'.

The meeting of African and American blacks at Tuskegee as well as Tuskegee projects caused the spreading of the 'Tuskegee Spirit' in Africa. John Dube and D. D. T. Jabavu were two of the long list of African notables who passed over common ground provided in Tuskegee. Dube, during his years in the United States as a student at Oberlin and in New York, became associated with both Atlanta educator John Hope and Booker T. Washington at Tuskegee. Dube returned to South Africa in 1899, and established Ohlange Institute openly patterned after Tuskegee. Jabavu, then a student at the University of London, spent about six weeks in 1913 at Tuskegee, observing agricultural techniques, *en route* to other black institutions in the South.

In addition, a series of annual graduation exercises, called 'African Rhetoricals', were organized at Tuskegee also to respond to specific African urgent needs. In the exercises of 1916, speeches ranged from 'The Development of the Cocoa Industry on the Gold Coast', and the 'Possibilities of the Development of Agriculture in South Africa' by A. B. Xuma, to 'Religion and Social Life in Madagascar'.

The second person who contributed a lot to the development of pan-Africanism during the period was Dr W. E. B. Du Bois, and he did so mainly through the three pan-African congresses which he convened in various European capitals. He convened the first while in France to cover the Paris Peace Conference for *The Crisis*, to collect information for a proposed 'History of the American Negro in the Great War', and to lobby for the political rights of 'the Darker races living within the United States as well as throughout the rest of the world'. Among the resolutions adopted at the Paris Congress in 1919 was one calling for self-determination for Africans.

Du Bois attended the second Pan-African Congress convened in 1921, in company with Walter White, the Afro-American artist Henry O. Tanner, Jessie R. Fauset, who was a black editorial writer for *The Crisis* and the most prolific of the Harlem Renaissance novelists, the Afro-American concert singer Roland Hayes, and Blaise Diagne from Senegal. The 1923 Congress drew attendance from America, the Caribbean and

Africa. Besides Du Bois, Rayford Logan and AME Bishop Vernon of the United States, Chief Amoah III of the Gold Coast and Kamba Simango of Portuguese East Africa attended and helped to formulate several substantive resolutions, plus a general call for 'the development of Africa for the benefit of Africans'. The Congress also called for representation on the League of Nations Mandates Commission, 'an institute to study the Negro problem', the restoration or improvement of black rights throughout the black world, and the freeing of Abyssinia, Haiti and Liberia from 'the grip of economic monopoly and usury at the hands of money-masters of the world'. Du Bois personally took the resolutions to Geneva to place them before the League.

Possibly because of the statement of concern for Liberia, President Coolidge asked Du Bois to represent the United States at the inauguration of the Liberian president in 1923. While in Liberia, on what was his first visit to Africa, Du Bois may have spoken out against Garvey's brand of emigrationist pan-Africanism, for not long afterwards the Liberians rejected the UNIA plan.

The last example of those who made a profound pan-Africanist impact on Africa was Marcus Garvey. His activities were not confined to the field of emigration, which has already been discussed. Indeed, he became the focus of much pan-Africanist interest in the United States, the Caribbean, West Africa, East Africa, Central Africa, and, most of all, Southern Africa between 1916 and the mid-1930s. Garvey's message to all was: organize, buy black, support the Black Star Steamship Line (which could take black emigrants to Africa and bring back raw materials), and help drive whites out of Africa. Whereas Du Bois was a greater pan-African force among black intellectuals outside Africa and Washington was better known among rural artisan classes, Garvey's influence fell equally upon the submerged black masses of all strata both outside and inside Africa. Garvey received much of his own pan-Africanist inspiration from the Egyptian intellectual, Duse Muḥammad 'Alī, in England in 1912, and from reading, also in London, Washington's autobiography, *Up From Slavery*.

Initially organized around the idea of setting up a Tuskegee-type school in Jamaica, Garvey's UNIA became the organizational link between large numbers of Africans and American blacks outside Africa, and, through his militant newspaper, *The Negro World*, Garvey achieved substantial pan-African effect within Africa. Between 1920 and 1938, eight UNIA conventions were held. The first five, with Garvey in charge, were held in New York City in August of each year from 1920 to 1924, the next two, following Garvey's deportation from the United States, took place in Jamaica in 1929 and 1934, and the eighth, and last, in Canada in 1938.

Beginning with the first convention, Garvey advocated the creation of special schools to teach technical education to blacks in Africa and the Americas, the development of 'economic opportunities in agriculture, industry, and commerce' in order to promote commerce between blacks, the launching of the Black Star Steamship Line to facilitate that commerce, and the establishment of a daily newspaper 'in several large cities of the world to shape sentiment in favour of the entire Negro race', especially in London, Paris, Berlin, Cape Town, New York, Washington, the Gold Coast, and the Caribbean. Garvey believed that the implementation of this programme could unify 'every unit of the Negro race throughout the world into one organized body'. Contemporaries felt that Garvey's message literally 'reverberated inside Africa' and he certainly influenced African nationalist leaders and intellectuals such as Casely Hayford, Jomo Kenyatta, Kwame Nkrumah, Kamuzu Banda and Nnamdi Azikiwe.

While Garvey and Du Bois were stirring the black world politically during the first three decades of the twentieth century, a broadly influential Africa-oriented cultural revival was taking place. The reaffirmation of black culture took hold in Europe, the Caribbean, and West Africa, led by the French-speaking African and Caribbean students in Paris who were drawn into the pan-African Congress movement and the general excitement of the Harlem Renaissance.

In short, the interaction between Francophone Caribbean blacks (such as Aimé Césaire of Martinique, whose famous poem *Cahier d'un Retour au Pays Natal* was published in 1939) and West African intellectuals (such as Senegalese poet-politician Leopold Senghor) forged the *négritude* movement which has already been briefly discussed. Based on a belief in a common cultural heritage among all African and African-descended peoples, the *négritude* writers tried to re-link the spheres of the black world. The concept of *négritude* was strongly influenced by the black experience overseas, and by the writings and intellectual vigour of the Harlem Renaissance. In turn, the Renaissance movement was fuelled by a rising cultural identification with Africa. Countee Cullen wondered poetically 'What is Africa to Me?' in his poem called 'Heritage', while Langston Hughes in his poem 'The Negro Speaks of Rivers' mentions how he built his hut near the Congo and the river lulled him to sleep. Both greatly influenced Senghor and the *négritude* writers.

But it was another Jamaican, Claude McKay, whose poetry helped to unify cultural and political pan-Africanism, when he insisted through the vehicle of his poetry that blacks should acknowledge and protest against their common suffering and assert their dignity. In Brazil, the works of Solano Trinidade (1908–73) brought the concept of pan-Africanism and *négritude* into poetry.

The persistence and transformation of African cultural values in Latin America and the Caribbean

Several authors draw attention to the African presence in American and the Caribbean countries, which they assess in terms of the percentage of descendants of Africans in the total population of each country. Three main groups can be identified on the basis of this criterion.

The first group consists of countries where the majority of the population is black. This is true of Haiti, Jamaica, Trinidad and Tobago, and Barbados, for example. The second group comprises countries where the proportion of the population of African origin is insignificant in demographic terms. This is the case in Argentina, Chile, Uruguay, Paraguay and Bolivia, among others. The third group includes Brazil and Cuba, where blacks have played a key role in the economy and exercised considerable cultural influence and where the ethnic configuration is largely the result of cross-breeding.

Finally, mention should be made of two other groups of countries. The first consists of countries such as Colombia, Panama, Nicaragua, etc., which contain small, somewhat tightly knit population groups of African origin. The second group consists of those countries which have groups of African origin which have not undergone an integration process in the New World, such as Surinam where the Bonis, the Djukas, the Saramacas and the Akwas are found, and Jamaica, Santo Domingo and even Haiti and Cuba, the home of the maroons. Living in the forest, these groups in Surinam and in French Guiana have retained more or less intact their fundamental cultural values and a certain social organization.

The parallel between North America and South America and the Caribbean in terms of the African presence and particularly of African cultural values is not conclusive, for the situations were very different in view of the different ways in which the former slaves became 'integrated' in those regions, even from one country to another.

From the cultural standpoint, whereas in the United States conversion to the Protestant religion led to the forsaking of cultural traditions and to the emergence of a new outlook, in Latin America and the Caribbean African cultural values persisted to varying degrees or underwent a process of transformation. In Haiti, for example, where the black population is in the majority, a characteristically African religion was influenced by the structural realities of Haitian society and the role of the half-castes, and underwent a series of changes set in motion by new 'gods' that met the requirements of the new situation. In the neighbouring islands, as a result of Protestant mission work, a 'black culture' had already taken shape in various movements, such as that of the Rastafarians, a Messianic wave of reaction against the white overlord in which African imagery was thinly veiled, Haile Sellassie being cast as Messiah. On the other hand, in Jamaica, with the Sasabonsan cult, of Asante origin, elements of 'African culture' persisted during that historical period, subsequently vanishing to give way to spirit-based cults involving a large dose of magic, as was the case in 1894 of the 'Jamaica Baptist Free Church', a sect founded by Bedward. A feature of this syncretism was observance of Catholic feast days and saints' days, together with recourse to the *orixás* and to voodoo. Thus, the feast days of the gods coincided with the dates of the Catholic saints' days.

Examples of syncretism involving Amerindian culture can be seen in the West Indies, particularly in Honduras, where a mestizo people has emerged as the result of inter-breeding between Amerindian women and Africans, referred to as black Caribs. These Africans were the descendants of the Ibo and Efik and, subsequently, of the Fante, Asante, Fon and Congo.

The integration of blacks into rural society varied according to the requirements of agriculture, the shortage or availability of labour and the size of the contingents of migrants from Europe, some of these contingents arriving for the express purpose of finding work within the labour system, as in Brazil in the coffee plantations. This integration is revealed in a variety of ways, encompassing the songs of African religious groups in Cuba and Brazil (see 29.2), the rhythm of African instruments which were effectively incorporated in the musical culture, the art of African cooking, the utilization of certain African techniques as, for example, in Haiti, the use of agricultural implements such as the hoe among others, and the transmission of religious values and philosophies of life. Despite the break imposed by the practice of slavery, African culture survived and, what is more, created a new culture.

29.2 *Examples of the influence of Yoruba religion on the peoples of African descent of Bahia in Brazil (Pierre Verger)*

Conclusion

It should be obvious from the above that interactions between Africa and the New World during our period were varied and had important and far-reaching impact on the blacks in both continents in general and on those in Africa in particular. In the religious, educational, literary and political fields, there is no doubt that the activities of New World black evangelists, educational institutions and political leaders and activists such as Garvey and Du Bois very much influenced the emerging nationalist and pan-African ideas and activities in Africa and prepared the stage for the next and final phase of the onslaught on the colonial system in Africa.

30

Colonialism in Africa: its impact and significance

By 1935, as is evident from the earlier chapters of this volume, colonialism had been firmly established in Africa, and it looked as if it was going to remain there for ever. However, colonialism proved just as unenduring as any other institution created and maintained by force. Within a matter of only some forty-five years from 1935, the colonial system had been uprooted from over 90% of Africa and confined only to that part of the continent south of the Limpopo river. That is to say, colonialism lasted in most parts of Africa for under a hundred years, indeed from the 1880s to the 1960s. In the history of a people and a whole continent, this is a very brief span indeed. In the concluding chapter of this volume, we would like to address ourselves to two main questions. First, what legacies did colonialism bequeath to Africa, or what impact did it make on Africa? The second question is, in view of this impact, what is the significance of colonialism for Africa?

The colonial impact

Probably nothing has become as controversial a subject as the impact of colonialism on Africa. To some historians such as Gann, Duignan, Perham and Lloyd, its impact was on balance either a blessing or at worst not harmful for Africa. Others, mainly African, black and Marxist scholars and especially the development and underdevelopment theorists, have contended that the beneficial effect of colonialism in Africa was virtually nil. The black Guyanese historian, Walter Rodney, has taken a particularly extreme position. As he contends:

> The argument suggests that, on the one hand, there was exploitation and oppression, but, on the other hand, colonial governments did much for the benefit of Africans and they developed Africa. It is our contention that this is completely false. Colonialism had only one hand – it was a one-armed bandit.

Such are the two main opposing assessments of colonialism in Africa. From the available evidence, however, it would appear that a much more balanced assessment is necessary and this is what is attempted here. Let us begin, then, by drawing up the balance sheet in the political field, beginning first with the positive and then the negative aspects.

The impact in the political field

The first positive political impact was the establishment of a greater degree of continuous peace and stability following the consolidation of colonialism in Africa than before. The nineteenth century in Africa, as in Europe, was a period of political instability and insecurity, what with the *Mfecane*, the Fulbe *djihāds*, the rise of the Tukuloor and Mande empires in the Western Sudan, and the disintegration of the Oyo and Asante empires in West Africa – a situation comparable to the Napoleonic wars, the 'intellectual' revolutions, the German and Italian wars of unification, the Polish and Hungarian uprisings and the imperial rivalries culminating in the First World War in Europe. In Africa, while it should be admitted that the first two or three decades of the colonial era, that is from 1880 to the 1910s, even intensified this state of instability, violence and disorder and, as Caldwell has shown, caused wholesale and unpardonable destruction and loss of population, not even the anti-colonial and Marxist schools would deny the fact that, after the colonial occupation and the establishment of various administrative machineries, such wars of expansion and liberation came to an end, and most parts of Africa, especially from the end of the First World War onwards, enjoyed a great degree of continuous peace and security.

The second positive political impact is the very geopolitical appearance of the modern independent states of Africa. The colonial partition and conquest definitely resulted, as A. E. Afigbo has pointed out above (Chapter 19), in a revolutionary reshaping of the political face of Africa. In place of the hundreds of independent clan and lineage groups, city-states, kingdoms and empires, without any clearly marked boundaries, were now established fifty new states with, in most cases, fixed boundaries, and it is rather significant that the boundaries of the states as laid down during the colonial era have not been changed since independence.

Thirdly, the colonial system also introduced into most parts of Africa two new institutions which, again rather significantly, have been maintained since independence, namely, a new judicial system and a new bureaucracy or civil service. There is no doubt that, in practically all the independent states except the Muslim ones, the higher courts of judicature introduced by the colonial rulers have been retained. The machineries introduced for the administration of the colonies also steadily led, though in many areas rather belatedly, to the emergence of a civil service whose membership and influence increased with the years. There is no doubt that the British bequeathed a better trained, numerically larger and more experienced bureaucracy to her colonies than the French, while the record of the Belgians and the Portuguese is the worst in this respect.

The final positive impact of colonialism was the birth not only of a new type of African nationalism, as Sithole and Oliver have pointed out, but also of pan-Africanism. The former, as we have seen, was the fostering of a sense of identity and consciousness among the various classes or ethnic groups inhabiting each of the new states, or, as in the French West African colonies, a cluster of them; while the latter was a sense of identity of black men the world over.

But if there were positive effects, even greater were the negative ones. In the first place, important as the development of nationalism was, not only was it an accidental by-product, but it was not the result of a positive feeling of identity with or commitment or loyalty to the new nation-state but a negative one generated by a sense of anger, frustration and humiliation caused by some of the oppressive, discriminatory, humiliating and exploitative measures introduced by the colonial rulers. With the overthrow of colonialism, then, that feeling was bound to lose, and indeed has lost, its momentum. The problem that has faced the rulers of independent African states therefore, has been how to replace this negative response with a positive and enduring feeling of nationalism.

Secondly, while admitting that the new geopolitical set-up that emerged from the partition was an asset, it has nevertheless created far more problems than it solved. The first of these is the fact that some of the boundaries of these new states cut across pre-existing ethnic groups, states and kingdoms. The Bakongo, for instance, are divided by the boundaries of Angola, Belgian Congo (now Zaire), French Congo (now Congo) and Gabon. Today, some of the Ewe live in Ghana, some in Togo and some in Benin; the Somali are shared among Ethiopia, Kenya, Somalia and Djibuti; the Senufo are found in Mali, Côte d'Ivoire and Burkina Faso. The examples can be multiplied. Not only did this situation cause widespread social disruption but it has also generated serious border disputes between some independent African states – such as those between Sudan and Uganda, between Somalia and Ethiopia, between Kenya and Somalia and between Ghana and Togo. Moreover, because of the arbitrary nature of these boundaries, each African nation-state is made up of a medley of peoples with different cultures, traditions of origin and language. The problems of nation-building posed by such a medley of peoples have not proved to be easily soluble.

Another outcome of the artificiality and arbitrariness of the colonial divisions was that the states that emerged were of different sizes with unequal natural resources and economic potentialities. While some of these states are giants such as Sudan, Nigeria and Algeria, others are midgets like The Gambia, Lesotho, Togo and Burundi. Secondly, and worse still, while some states have very long stretches of sea coast, others such as Mali, Burkina Faso, Niger, Chad, Zambia, Uganda and Malawi are landlocked. Thirdly, while some states have very rich natural resources such as Ghana, Zambia, Zaire, Côte d'Ivoire and Nigeria, others such as Chad, Niger and Burkina Faso are not so fortunate. Finally, while some such as The Gambia, have single borders to police, others have four or more and Zaire as many as ten, which poses serious problems of ensuring national security and checking smuggling. The problems of development posed by lack of or limited natural resources and lack of access to the sea for those independent African states which inherited these unfortunate legacies can be readily imagined.

Another important negative political impact of colonialism was the weakening of the indigenous systems of government. In the first place, most of the African states were acquired as a result of the conquest and deposition or exile of the then rulers, which 'certainly brought into disrepute the whole business of chieftaincy, especially during the period before the First World War'. The way in which the colonial administrators used the traditional rulers to enforce measures hated by their subjects, such as forced labour, further deepened this disrepute. Besides, the colonial system of administering justice, in which subjects could appeal to the colonial courts, further weakened not only the authority but also the financial resources of the traditional rulers, while the spread of the Christian religion undermined their spiritual basis. In all these ways, then, the colonial system, certainly diminished the authority and standing of the traditional systems of government.

Another negative impact of colonialism in the political field was the mentality that it created among Africans that government and all public property belonged not to the people but rather to the white colonial rulers and could and should therefore be taken advantage of at the least opportunity. This mentality was the direct product of the remote and esoteric nature of the colonial administration and the elimination of an overwhelming majority of Africans, both educated and uneducated, from the decision-making process. It is important to note that this mentality is still with most Africans even after decades of independence and is part of the explanation for the reckless way in which government property is handled in many independent African countries.

A product of colonialism and one which is often ignored by most historians, but which has turned out to be of crucial and fundamental importance, was, as is evident from R. F. Betts's contribution (Chapter 13), a full-time or standing army, which was unknown in many parts of Africa, where all adult males, including even members of the ruling aristocracy, became soldiers in times of war and civilians in times of peace. These armies were originally created, most of them in the 1880s and 1890s, first for the conquest and occupation of Africa, then for the maintenance of colonial control, and, finally, for the prosecution of global wars and the suppression of independence movements in Africa. After the overthrow of the colonial rulers, these armies were not disbanded but were taken over by the new independent African rulers and, as will be seen in the next volume, as a result of their repeated and often unnecessary and unjustifiable interventions in politics, have become very serious impediments for the peoples of Africa.

The final and probably the most important negative impact of colonialism was the loss of African sovereignty and independence and with them the right of Africans to shape their own destiny, plan their own development, determine their own strategies and priorities and borrow freely from the outside world at large the latest and most appropriate technology. In short, colonialism deprived Africans of one of the most fundamental and inalienable rights of a people, the right of liberty.

Moreover, as Rodney has shown, the seventy-year period of colonialism in Africa was the very period which witnessed tremendous and decisive developments and changes in both the capitalist and socialist countries. It was that period, for instance, that saw the entry of Europe into the age of the motor vehicle, the aeroplane and the nuclear bomb. Had Africa been in control of her own destiny, she could have benefited from or even been part of these phenomenal changes. But colonialism completely isolated and insulated her from these changes and kept her in a position of dependency.

The impact in the economic field

The impact in the political field, then, was important, though a mixed blessing. Even more so was the impact in the economic field. The first and most obvious and profound of the positive impacts here, as is evident from many of the chapters above, was the provision of an infrastructure of motor roads, railways, the telegraph, the telephone and in some cases even airports. These did not exist in pre-colonial Africa where, as

J. C. Caldwell has shown (Chapter 18), until the colonial era, 'nearly all land transport was by human porterage'. This basic infrastructure had been completed in Africa by the 1930s and not many new kilometres of, say, railways have been built since then.

Equally important and significant was the impact of colonialism on the primary sector of the economy. As is obvious from the chapters above, every effort was made to develop or exploit some of the rich natural resources of the continent, and this was attended by some significant successes. It was during the colonial period that the full mineral potential of Africa was realized and the mining industry definitely boomed, while the cultivation of cash crops such as cocoa, coffee, tobacco, groundnuts, sisal and rubber spread. It was certainly during the colonial period that Ghana became the world's leading producer of cocoa while by 1950 farm crops were accounting for 50% of the gross domestic product of French West Africa.

This economic revolution had some far-reaching consequences. The first one was commercialization of land, which made it a real asset. Secondly, the economic revolution led to an increase in the purchasing power of some Africans and with it an increase in their demand for consumer goods and a higher standard of living. Thirdly, the growing of cash crops by Africans enabled individuals of whatever social status, especially in the rural areas, to acquire wealth.

Another significant revolutionary impact of colonialism in many parts of the continent was the introduction of the money economy, which in turn had some interesting effects. In the first place, even by the 1930s, a new standard of wealth had been introduced which was based not only on the number of sheep or cows or yams one possessed but on actual cash. Secondly, people were engaged in activities not for subsistence alone but also to earn money and this led, as will be seen later, to the emergence of a new class of wage-earners and salaried groups. Thirdly, the introduction of the money economy led to the commencement of banking activities in Africa, which have become another significant feature of the economy of independent African states.

The introduction of currency and with it banking activities and the tremendous expansion in the volume of trade between colonial Africa and Europe in turn led to the total integration of the economy of Africa into that of the world in general and into that of the capitalist economy of the colonial powers in particular. The years after 1935 merely deepened this link and not even independence has fundamentally altered this relationship.

Was the colonial impact on Africa in the economic field, then, such a very enviable one? Far from it, and most of the present-day developmental problems facing African countries can be traced to this.

In the first place, as M. H. Y. Kaniki has pointed out above (Chapter 16), the infrastructure that was provided by colonialism was not as adequate or as useful as it could have been. Most of the roads and railways were constructed not to open up the country or facilitate inter-African contacts or promote the overall economic development of Africa but merely to connect the areas having mineral deposits and potentialities for the production of cash crops with the sea. In the second place, such economic growth as occurred in the colonies was based on the natural resources of the area and this meant therefore that areas not naturally endowed were totally neglected. Thirdly, a typical feature of the colonial economy was the total and deliberate negligence or discouragement of industrialization and the processing of locally produced raw materials and agricultural products in most of the colonies. As D. K. Fieldhouse has pointed out, 'Probably no colonial government had a department of industry before 1945.' Simple and basic items such as matches, candles, edible oil and even lime and orange juice, all of which could easily have been produced in Africa, were imported. African states were therefore, in accordance with the workings of the colonial capitalist economy, turned into markets for the consumption of manufactured goods from the metropolitan countries and producers of raw materials for export.

Fourthly, not only was industrialization neglected but such industries and crafts as had existed in Africa in pre-colonial times were almost destroyed. It should be emphasized that Africa's pre-colonial industries produced all that Africans needed, including building materials, soap, beads, iron tools, pottery and above all cloth. Had these manufacturers been encouraged and promoted through the modernization of productive techniques, as was done in India between 1920 and 1945, Africa not only could have increased her output but could have steadily improved her technology. But these crafts and industries were all virtually killed as a result of the importation of cheap commodities produced on a mass basis into Africa. African technological development was thereby halted and was never resumed until after independence.

Fifthly, even though agricultural crops came to constitute the main source of income for most African states, no attempts were made to diversify the agricultural economy of the colonies. On the contrary, as has been shown in some of the earlier chapters, by 1935, the production of single or at best two cash crops had become the rule – cocoa in the Gold Coast, groundnuts in Senegal and The Gambia, cotton in Sudan, coffee and cotton in Uganda, coffee and sisal in Tanganyika, etc. Moreover, because of the concentration on the production of cash crops during the colonial era, Africans were in fact compelled to ignore the production of food for their own consumption. Food therefore had to be imported which the ordinary people had to buy, usually at high prices, to feed themselves. Thus, under the colonial system, Africans were in most cases made to produce what they did not consume and to consume what they did not produce, clear evidence of the lopsided and exploitative nature of the colonial economy.

Sixthly, the commercialization of land already referred to led to the illegal sale of communal lands by unscrupulous family-heads and to increasing litigation over land, which caused widespread poverty, especially among the ruling houses. In East, Central and Southern Africa, as has been shown in many of the earlier chapters, it also led to large-scale appropriation of land by Europeans, which generated much bitterness, anger and frustration and constituted the fundamental cause of the serious explosion that occurred in Kenya known as Mau Mau.

The colonial presence also led, as has been pointed out above, to the appearance on the African scene of an increasing number of expatriate banking, shipping and trading firms and companies, and from the 1910s onwards their amalgamation and consolidation into fewer and fewer oligopolies. Since it was these trading companies that controlled the export as well as the import trade and fixed the prices not only of imported commodities but also of the exports produced by the Africans, the huge profits that accrued from these activities went to them and not to the Africans. The other consequence of this development was of course the elimination of Africans from the most profitable and important sectors of the economy altogether. The African merchant princes of the second half of the nineteenth century therefore virtually disappeared from the scene during the period under review, while their descendants had to become the employees of the expatriate firms and companies in order to survive.

Colonialism, as Rodney has pointed out, also virtually put a stop to inter-African trade. Before the colonial era, a great deal of trading went on between African states, and long-distance and caravan trading activities were a very common feature of the economies of Africa. But, with the establishment of colonialism, such inter-African short- and long-distance trade was discouraged if not banned altogether. This prevented the strengthening of old links and the development of new ones that could have proved of benefit to Africans.

Finally, whatever economic growth was achieved during the colonial period was done at a phenomenal and unjustifiable cost to the African – what with forced labour, compulsory cultivation of certain crops, compulsory seizure of land, forced movements of populations with a consequential dislocation of family life, the pass system, the high mortality rate in the mines and on the plantations, etc. Above all, the monetary policies pursued by the colonial powers towards their colonies – tying their currencies to those of the colonial powers and keeping all foreign exchange earnings in the metropolitan capitals – while ensuring stable and fully convertible currencies, led to the freezing of colonial assets in the metropolitan capitals instead of their being realized and invested in the colonies. The repatriation of savings and deposits of Africans by the banks and the discrimination practised against Africans in the granting of loans further impeded African development.

From the above, it can be safely concluded, in spite of the protestations of Gann and Duignan, that the colonial period was a period of ruthless economic exploitation rather than of economic development in Africa.

The impact in the social field

Finally, what is the record of colonialism in the social field? The first important beneficial social effect was the overall increase of the population of Africa during the colonial period by about 37.5%, as J. C. Caldwell has shown (Chapter 18), after its decline during the first two or three decades of colonialism. Closely connected with this, and the second social impact of colonialism, was urbanization. As A. E. Afigbo has emphasized (Chapter 19), urbanization was of course not unknown in pre-colonial Africa. But there is no doubt that, as a result of colonialism, the pace of urbanization was greatly accelerated. Completely new towns, such as Abidjan in Côte-d'Ivoire, Takoradi in the Gold Coast, Port Harcourt and Enugu in Nigeria, Nairobi in Kenya, Salisbury (now Harare) in Southern Rhodesia and Luluaburg in the Belgian Congo, came into existence.

Moreover, as Caldwell has shown above (Chapter 18), the population of both the already existing towns and those of the new ones grew by leaps and bounds during the colonial era. The population of Nairobi, founded in 1896 as a transit depot for the construction of the Uganda Railway, increased from a mere handful to 13 145 in 1927 and to over 25 000 by 1940. The population of Casablanca rose from 2026 in 1910 to

250 000 in 1936 and that of Accra in the Gold Coast from 17 892 in 1901 to 135 926 in 1948. These towns grew so rapidly during this period simply because they were either the new capitals or administrative centres of the colonial regimes or the new harbours and railway stations.

There was undoubtedly also an improvement in the quality of life, particularly for those living in the urban centres. This, as Caldwell has shown (Chapter 18), was the product of the provision of hospitals, dispensaries, pipe-borne water and sanitary facilities, and the increase in employment opportunities.

The spread of Christianity and Islam was another important impact of colonialism. There is no doubt that, taking advantage of the peace and order as well as the patronage and in some areas the positive encouragement provided by colonialism, Christian missionaries and Muslim clerics pushed their activities further and further inland. As K. Asare Opoku has shown (Chapter 20), Christianity and Islam gained far more ground during the colonial period than had been the case during the previous three or four centuries put together.

Closely associated with the spread of Christianity was that of western education. As has been shown in many of the chapters above, the Christian missions were mainly responsible for this. It should, however, be borne in mind that they could operate mainly because of the grants they received from the colonial administrations. The spread of western education had far-reaching social effects, among which was an increase in the number of the westernized educated African elite, an elite which now dominates the civil service of African states.

Another important colonial impact, a mixed blessing as will be shown later, was of course the provision of a lingua franca for each colony or set of colonies. In all the colonies, the mother tongue of the colonial power, either in its pure or pidgin form, became the official and business language and in many cases the main means of communication between the numerous linguistic groups that constitute the population of each colony. It is significant that, except in North Africa, Tanzania, Kenya and Madagascar, these foreign languages have remained the official languages even to this very day.

The final beneficial social impact was the new social structure that colonialism introduced into some parts of Africa or whose development it accelerated in other parts. The new colonial order's emphasis on individual merit and achievement rather than birth, together with the socio-economic changes analysed already, such as the abolition of slavery, the introduction of western education, the expansion of cash-crop agriculture and urbanization, radically altered the traditional social structure. Thus, by the 1930s, in place of the pre-colonial social classes of the traditional ruling aristocracy, the ordinary people, domestic slaves and a relatively small educated elite, there had emerged a new society that had become more sharply divided than before into urban and rural dwellers, each of which was differently stratified. The urban dwellers had become divided into three main sub-groups: the elite or bourgeoisie consisting of lawyers, doctors, civil servants, etc., the non-elite or the sub-elite consisting of clerks, teachers, nurses, etc., and the urban proletariat consisting of wage-earners, drivers, mechanics, tailors, etc. In the rural areas there emerged for the first time in many parts of Africa new classes, namely, a rural proletariat, or landless Africans, and peasants. The former consisted of those Africans, especially in East and Southern Africa, whose lands had been alienated by the Europeans and were therefore compelled to spend their lives shunting between the urban and rural areas, mainly as migrant labourers. The peasants were those who lived in small communities and cultivated the land they owned or controlled, relying chiefly on family labour. It should be emphasized that, since mobility within this new structure was based more on individual effort and attainment than on birth, it was a considerable improvement on the traditional social structure.

But, if colonialism did have some positive social impact, it had some negative, indeed some seriously negative, ones too. The first of these was the creation and widening of the gap between the urban centres and rural areas. The phenomenal growth of the population of the urban centres that we noted above was not the result of the natural increase of the urban population but rather of the continuous pull of young men and women to the urban centres by the need for education, employment and better social facilities and the push from the rural areas, as C. Coquery-Vidrovitch has shown above (Chapter 15), by famine, epidemic, poverty, taxation and lack of amenities. It should be noted that this gap has still not been bridged. Nor did the migrants find the urban centres the safe and rich haven that they had expected. Most of them found themselves crowded into the suburbs and the shanty towns, in which unemployment, juvenile delinquency, drunkenness, prostitution and crime became their lot.

A second serious social legacy has been the European and Asian settler problem. Although there were European settlers in the North African states and in South Africa before the colonial era, not only did the number of these people increase but European and Asian settlers were also introduced into East and Central Africa and parts of West Africa during the colonial days. As M. H. Y. Kaniki has shown above (Chapter 16), the number of Europeans in Kenya rose from only 596 in 1903 to 954 in 1905, 5438 in 1914 and 16 663 in 1929; that in Southern Rhodesia increased from 11 000 in 1901 to over 35 000 by 1926, and that in Algeria from 344 000 in 1876 to 946 000 by 1936. But, in many areas in East, Central and North Africa, what made their presence so inimical to Africans was that the Europeans came to occupy most of the fertile lands, while in these areas as well as in West Africa the Asians monopolized the retail and wholesale trade. By 1935, this European and Asian problem had assumed very serious proportions for Africa and it has not been entirely resolved to this day.

Furthermore, although colonialism did introduce some social services, as has been pointed out already, it must be emphasized that these services were grossly inadequate and unevenly distributed in each colony. They were also by and large meant primarily for the benefit of the few white settlers and administrators, hence their concentration in the towns.

In the field of education, what was provided during the colonial days was grossly inadequate, unevenly distributed and badly orientated, and therefore not as beneficial as it could have been for Africa. While many primary schools had been established in many countries in Africa by the 1930s, there were relatively very few secondary and technical schools and teacher training colleges and hardly any universities. It was not until after the Second World War that technical schools and university colleges were established in most parts of Africa. Moreover, not only were these inadequate educational facilities unevenly distributed but the curricula provided by all these institutions were irrelevant to African needs and closely modelled on, if not carbon copies of, those of the metropolitan countries.

The impact of this colonial education on African societies has been profound and almost permanent. First, it left Africa with a huge illiteracy problem, a problem whose solution will take a long time. Secondly, the educated elite that was produced was by and large an alienated elite, an elite that adored European culture and civilization and looked down on African culture. Another gap thereby came to exist between this elite and the rest of the masses, which has still not been bridged. Furthermore, the explanation of phenomena such as death, rainfall and sickness in natural and scientific terms also struck at the very roots of African religious beliefs, sanctions and taboos and thereby shook the foundations of African societies, bringing in its trail a sense of uncertainty, frustration and insecurity.

The neglect of technical and industrial education and the emphasis on liberal and clerical training and the consequent love for white-collar jobs also created among the educated folk a contempt for manual labour and agricultural work which is still with us.

Beneficial as the lingua franca promoted through the educational system may have been, it had the regrettable consequence of preventing the development of some of the indigenous languages into national languages or lingua franca. Twi, Hausa and Swahili could easily have been developed as the national languages of the Gold Coast, Nigeria and the three British East African colonies respectively, but the colonial rulers discouraged and even, in countries like Uganda, prevented it.

Another highly regrettable social impact of colonialism was the deterioration that it caused in the status of the women in Africa. This is a new theme which needs further research, but there does not appear to be any doubt that women were inhibited from joining most of the activities introduced or intensified by colonialism such as western education, cash-crop farming in some parts of Africa, and many of the professions such as law and medicine. The colonial world, as J. Iliffe has pointed out, was indeed a man's world, and women were not encouraged to play any meaningful role in it.

Moreover, as a result of colonialism, the African himself was looked down upon, humiliated, and discriminated against both overtly and covertly. This racial discrimination, which grew in intensity during the colonial period, also created in some Africans a deep sense of inferiority, which has not entirely disappeared even after two decades of independence.

Even worse was the impact of colonialism in the cultural field. The Europeans who moved into Africa during this period, especially between 1900 and 1945 – missionaries, traders, administrators, settlers, engineers and miners alike – were generally filled with the spirit of cultural and racial superiority of the day. They therefore condemned everything African – African music, art, dance, names, religion, marriage, systems of inheritance, etc. To be admitted into a church, an African had not only to be baptized but had to change his name and renounce all the above. Colonialism therefore caused cultural stagnation if not degeneration in Africa.

It should be quite obvious from the above analysis that those scholars who are of the opinion that colonialism was an unmitigated disaster for Africa and that it caused nothing but underdevelopment and backwardness have overstated their case. Equally guilty of overstatement are those colonial apologists, the Ganns, Duignans and Lloyds who see colonialism as an unqualified blessing for Africa. A more accurate judgement in this writer's opinion is not that colonialism did not do anything positive for Africa, but that, given its opportunities and its resources and the power and influence it wielded in Africa at the time, it could and should have done far more than it did. Furthermore, the element of economic exploitation during the whole period of colonialism was very far in excess of that of economic development. It is for these two reasons that the colonial era will go down in history, on balance, as a period of growth without development, a period of lost opportunities and of the humiliation of the peoples of Africa.

The significance of colonialism for Africa

This leads us on, then, to the second question posed at the beginning of the chapter, namely, the real significance of colonialism for Africa. Does it constitute a break with Africa's past or was it just a mere episode in its history which is of limited importance and which did not affect the course of African development? Here, again, conflicting answers have been given to this question. To some historians, indeed a very large number, including the Marxists and the development and anti-development theorists but for very different reasons, though colonialism was a short interlude, it nevertheless was of great significance for Africa and left an indelible impression on Africa. As R. Oliver and N. Atmore contend: 'Measured on the time-scale of history, the colonial period was but an interlude of comparatively short duration. But it was an interlude that radically changed the direction and momentum of African history.' Gann and Duignan also regard the colonial era 'as most decisive for the future of Africa'. The answer of the Marxists and the underdevelopment theorists is neatly summed up in the title of Rodney's book, namely, *How Europe Underdeveloped Africa*. On the other hand, there are others who regard the colonial impact as skin-deep and maintain that colonialism did not constitute any break with the African past. In a series of articles, J. F. A. Ajayi has consistently maintained that colonialism 'represents only an episode in a long and eventful history' and did not cause any break in continuity.

To this author, there is really no simple yes or no answer to this question since the impact of colonialism varied from area to area and from theme to theme. There is no doubt that, in the economic field, the colonial impact was by and large decisive and fundamental and affected both the rural and urban areas. In virtually all parts of Africa, the money economy had become the rule rather than the exception by the end of the colonial period and status, even in the rural areas, was being assessed not only in terms of birth but also in terms of cash and the quantity of cash crops that one was producing per season. Furthermore, with the introduction of cash crops, land assumed a value that it had not had in pre-colonial days, while individual effort and achievement came to be regarded far more highly than the communalism of the traditional order. The African economy also became integrated deeper into the world economy in general and the capitalist economy in particular than before and this had effects that can probably never be undone.

Fundamental and destined to be lasting and felt by all members of the society, also, was the impact of colonialism in the political field. As we have already seen, the very physical appearance of the present independent states of Africa is the creation of colonialism. With the adoption of the principle of the sanctity of national boundaries by the Organization of African Unity (OAU), this appearance is not likely to be altered.

Secondly, even though independence has been regained, there is no doubt that there has been a fundamental and permanent shift in the source of political power and authority from the traditional elite of kings, queens, family, clan and religious heads to the new elite or members of the upper and lower middle classes, the creation of the colonial system, and this situation is never going to be reversed. Thirdly, it was colonialism that gave birth to African nationalism. Fourthly, one important colonial legacy, the full-time army, is not likely to be abolished and, as will be seen in the next volume, it has already changed the course of the history of many an African country, and it seems as if it has not completed its political innings yet. Finally, it appears that the judicial and political institutions – the courts, parliaments, regional and district commissioners, etc. – are going to be retained even though some modifications and adaptations have been and will continue to be made. Probably more than in the economic field, then, the impact of colonialism in the political field was really fundamental and in many respects has proved of lasting consequence.

On the other hand, in the cultural and social field, the impact of colonialism was relatively neither profound nor permanent. Such changes as were introduced in the cultural field, such racial discrimination as was practised, and such condemnation of African culture as was preached, even in the heyday of colonialism, were all confined primarily to the coastal areas and the urban centres, and never penetrated into the rural areas. African dance, art, music and traditional religious systems held their own and such borrowings and adaptations as were made by Africans were not only selective but also, to borrow M. J. Herskovits's terminology, 'additive' and not necessarily 'substitutive'. Thus, in the rural areas and even to some extent in the urban ones, new beliefs, new gods, new utensils, new artefacts and new objects were added to the old ones. What is even more important, the ground that was lost even in the urban centres in the field of culture has virtually been regained. Today, African art, music and dance not only are taught in educational institutions of all kinds but are now booming in Africa and gaining recognition in Europe. Thus, as far as the cultural field is concerned, colonialism was certainly a mere episode and its impact skin-deep.

Finally, in the social field, the significance of colonialism here is clearly a mixed one. On the one hand, the foreign or colonial lingua francas are going to be retained for a very long time if not for ever. Secondly, the new classes created by colonialism are bound to remain and in fact increase in complexity. Already, two new groups have been added since independence. One is the political elite made up of the leading members of the political parties that have been mushrooming in Africa and who have become the prime ministers, presidents, ministers, ambassadors, etc. The other is the military elite made up of present and ex-officers of the armed forces of each independent state. The members of these elite groups are definitely different from the people of the rural areas in terms of dress, life style, tastes and status. Now, had these elite groups constituted a good percentage of the population of Africa, one would have accepted their formation as yet another crucial and fundamental change introduced by colonialism. But the urban or elitist groups constituted by the end of the colonial era only a small fraction of the population, at most about 20%. Since the rural dwellers, who remained predominantly illiterate and maintained their traditional beliefs, values and standards, constitute the overwhelming majority of the population of every African state, it may be reasonably concluded that the colonial impact here, interesting as it is, was extremely limited.

In conclusion, then, though colonialism was a mere episode or interlude in the history of Africa, lasting as it did no more than eighty years anywhere, it is none the less an extremely important episode politically, economically and even socially. It marks a clear watershed in the history of Africa and the subsequent development of Africa, and therefore its history has been and will continue to be very much influenced by the colonial impact on Africa, and destined to take a course different from what it would have taken had there not been any colonial interlude.

Bibliography

'Abd al-Rahīm, M. (1986) *Imperialism and Nationalism in the Sudan: a Study in Constitutional and Political Development, 1899–1956* (Khartoum: Khartoum University Press)

Abraham, A. (1978) *Mende Government and Politics under Colonial Rule: a Historical Study of Political Change in Sierra Leone 1890–1937* (Freetown: Sierra Leone University Press)

Adamu, F. (1978) *The Kano Civil War and British Over-rule 1882–1940* (Oxford: Oxford University Press)

Adeleye, R. A. (1971) *Power and Diplomacy in Northern Nigeria, 1804–1906: the Sokoto Caliphate and its Enemies* (London: Longman)

Afigbo, A. E. (1972) *The Warrant Chiefs: Indirect Rule in South eastern Nigeria, 1891–1929* (London: Longman)

Ageron, C. R. (1978) *Politiques coloniales au Maghreb* (Paris: Presses Universitaires Françaises)

Ahmed, J. M. (1960) *The Intellectual Origins of Egyptian Nationalism* (London: Oxford University Press)

Ajayi, J. F. A. (1965) *Christian Missions in Nigeria, 1841–1891: the Making of a New Elite* (London: Longman)

Ajayi, J. F. A. and Crowder, M. (eds.) (1974) *History of West Africa*, Vol. II (London: Longman)

Ajayi, J. F. A. and Crowder, M. (eds.) (1985) *Historical Atlas of Africa* (Harlow and Nigeria: Longman)

Amin, S. (1970) *The Maghreb in the Modern World: Algeria, Tunisia, Morocco* (Harmondsworth: Penguin)

Arhin, K. (ed.) (1985) *West African Colonial Civil Servants in the Nineteenth Century: African Participation in British Colonial Expansion in West Africa* (Leiden: African Studies Centre)

Asante, S. K. B. (1977) *Pan-African Protest: West Africa and the Italo-Ethiopian Crisis, 1939–1941* (London: Longman)

Asiwaju, A. I. (1976) *Western Yorubaland under European Rule, 1889–1945: a Comparative Analysis of French and British Colonialism* (London: Longman)

Austen, R. (1987) *African Economic History: Internal Development and External Dependency* (London: James Currey)

Ayache, A. (1956) *Le Maroc: bilan d'une colonisation* (Paris: Ed. Sociales)

Ayandele, E. A. (1966) *The Missionary Impact on Modern Nigeria, 1842–1914: a Political and Social Analysis* (London: Longman)

Azikiwe, B. N. (1934) *Liberia in World Politics* (London: A. H. Stockwell)

Baer, G. (1962) *A History of Land Ownership in Modern Egypt, 1800–1950* (London: Oxford University Press)

Baeta, C. G. (1962) *Prophetism in Ghana: a Study of some 'Spiritual' Churches* (London: SCM Press)

Baldwin, R. E. (1966) *Economic Development and Export Growth: a Study of Northern Rhodesia, 1920–1960* (Berkeley, Calif.: University of California Press)

Barbour, K. M. and Prothero, R. M. (eds.) (1961) *Essays on African Population* (London: Routledge and Kegan Paul)

Barbour, N. (ed.) (1959) *A Survey of North West Africa (The Maghreb)* (London: Oxford University Press)

Bassett, T. J. (1988) 'The development of cotton in Northern Ivory Coast' *Journal of African History*, XXIX, pp. 267–84

Bauer, P. T. (1954) *West African Trade: a Study of Competition, Oligopoly and Monopoly in a Changing Society* (Cambridge: Cambridge University Press)

Beidelman, T. O. (1982) *Colonial Evangelism: a Socio-historical Study of an East African Mission at the Grassroots* (Bloomington, Ind.: Indiana University Press)

Beinart, W. (1982) *The Political Economy of Pondoland, 1860–1930* (Cambridge: Cambridge University Press)

Beinart, W. and Bundy, C. (1987) *Hidden Struggles in Rural South Africa: Politics and Popular Movements in the Transkei and Eastern Cape 1890–1930* (London: James Currey)

Bennett, G. (1963) *Kenya, a Political History: the Colonial Period* (London: Oxford University Press)

Bennett, N. R. (1986) *Arab versus European: Diplomacy and War in Nineteenth Century East-Central Africa* (New York: Africana)

Benson, M. (1966) *South Africa: the Struggle for a Birthright* (Harmondsworth: Penguin)

Berque, J. (1970) *Le Maghreb entre deux guerres*, 2nd edn (Paris: Ed. du Seuil)

Betts, R. F. (ed.) (1972) *The Scramble for Africa: Causes and Dimensions of Empire*, 2nd edn (London: D. C. Heath)

Bidwell, R. (1973) *Morocco under Colonial Rule: French Administration of Tribal Areas, 1912-1956* (London: Frank Cass)

Bley, H. (1971) *South West Africa under German Rule, 1894-1914* (London: Heinemann)

Blyden, E. W. (1887) *Christianity, Islam and the Negro Race* (London: W. B. Whittingham)

Boahen, A. A. (1966) *Topics in West African History* (London: Longman)

Boahen, A. A. (1985) *African Perspectives on Colonialism* (Baltimore; Md. Johns Hopkins University Press)

Bozzoli, B. (1981) *The Political Nature of a Ruling Class: Capital and Ideology in South Africa 1890-1933* (London: Routledge and Kegan Paul)

Bradford, H. (1984) 'Mass movements and the petty bourgeoisie: the social origins of ICU leadership, 1924-9', *Journal of African History, XXV*, pp. 295-310

Bret, R. J. (1987) *Vie du Sultan Mohamed Bakhit, 1856-1916: la pénétration française au Dar Sila, Tchad* (Paris: Éditions du Centre National de la Recherche Scientifique)

Brett, E. A. (1973) *Colonialism and Underdevelopment in East Africa* (New York: Nok Publishers)

Brooke-Smith, R. (1987) *The Scramble for Africa* (London: Macmillan)

Brunschwig, H. (1966) *French Colonialism, 1871-1914: Myths and Realities* (New York: Praeger)

Brunschwig, H. (1982) *Imperialism: the Idea and Reality of British and French Colonial Expansion, 1880-1914* (New York: Oxford University Press)

Brunschwig, H. (1983) *Noirs et blancs dans 'Afrique noire française ou comment le colonisé devient colonisateur (1870-1914)* (Paris: Flammarion)

Caldwell, J. C. (ed.) (1975) *Population Growth and Socio-Economic Change in West Africa* (New York: Columbia University Press)

Caldwell, J. C. and Okonjo, J. (eds.) (1968) *The Population of Tropical Africa* (London: Longman)

Carland, J. M. (1985) *The Colonial Office and Nigeria, 1898-1914* (London and Basingstoke: Macmillan)

Chinweizu (1975) *The West and the Rest of Us: White Predators, Black Slavers and the African Elite* (New York: Vintage Books)

Christopher, A. J. (1988) *The British Empire at its Zenith* (London: Croom Helm)

Clarence-Smith, W. G. (1979) *Slaves, Peasants and Capitalists in Southern Angola, 1840-1926* (Cambridge: Cambridge University Press)

Clarence-Smith, W. G. (1985) *The Third Portuguese Empire (1825-1975)* (Manchester: Manchester University Press)

Clayton, A. (1986) *The British Empire as Superpower, 1919-1939* (Basingstoke: Macmillan)

Coleman, J. S. (1958) *Nigeria: Background to Nationalism* (Berkeley and Los Angeles, Calif.: University of California Press)

Coleman, J. S. and Rosberg, C. G. (eds.) (1970) *Political Parties and National Integration in Tropical Africa* (Berkeley and Los Angeles, Calif.: University of California Press)

Collins, R. O. (1983) *Shadows in the Grass: Britain in the Southern Sudan, 1918-1956* (New Haven, Conn.: Yale University Press)

Colo, B. C. and Anignikin, S. C. (1982) 'Pouvoir colonial et tentatives d'intégration africaines dans le système capitaliste: le cas du Dahomey entre les deux guerres', *Canadian Journal of African Studies*, XVI, p. 2

Cooke, D. *et al.* (1985) *Teaching Development Issues, Section 2, Colonialism* (Manchester Development Education Project)

Cooper, F. (1980) *From Slaves to Squatters: Plantation Labour and Agriculture in Zanzibar and Coastal Kenya, 1890-1925* (New Haven, Conn. and London: Yale University Press)

Coquery-Vidrovitch, C. (1972) *Le Congo français au temps des grandes compagnies concessionnaires, 1898-1930* (Paris and the Hague: Mouton)

Coquery-Vidrovitch, C. and Moniot, H. (1974) *L'Afrique noire de 1800 à nos jours* (Paris: Presses Universitaires Française)

Crowder, M. (1968) *West Africa under Colonial Rule* (London: Hutchinson)

Crowder, M. (ed.) (1971) *West African Resistance* (London: Hutchinson)

Crowder, M. and Ikime, O. (eds.) (1970) *West African Chiefs: Their Changing Status under Colonial Rule and Independence* (New York: Africana Publishing)

Curtin, P. D., Feierman, S., Thompson, L. and Vansina, J. (1978) *African History* (London: Longman)

Dally, M. W. (1986) *Empire on the Nile: the Anglo-Egyptian Sudan 1898-1934* (Cambridge: Cambridge University Press)

Darby, P. (1987) *Three Faces of Imperialism: British and American Approaches to Asia and Africa 1870–1970* (New Haven, Conn.: Yale University Press)
Davidson, A. B. (1972) *South Africa, the Birth of a Protest* (Moscow: African Institute)
Davidson, B. (1978) *Africa in Modern History* (London: Allen Lane)
Davidson, B. (1983) *Modern Africa* (London: Longman)
Deng, F. M. (1978) *The Dinka in Afro-Arab Sudan* (New Haven, Conn. and London: Yale University Press)
Denoon, D. (1972) *Southern Africa since 1800* (London: Longman)
Deschamps, H. (1960) *Histoire de Madagascar* (Paris: Berger-Levrault)
Domergue-Cloarec, D. (1986) *Politique coloniale française et réalités coloniales: la santé en Côte d'Ivoire, 1905–1958* (Paris: Académie des Sciences d'Outre-Mer)
Duffy, J. (1962) *Portugal in Africa* (Harmondsworth: Penguin)
Ekechi, F. K. (1987) 'The British assault on Ogbunorie Oracle in Eastern Nigeria', *Journal of African Studies*, XIV, 2, pp. 69–77
Engel, L. (1976) *Kolonialismus und Nationalismus in Deutschen Protestantismus in Namibia 1907 bis 1945* (Frankfurt-on-Main: Peter Lang)
Erlich, H. (1982) *Ethiopia and Eritrea during the Scramble for Africa: a Political Biography of Ras Alula, 1875–1897* (East Lansing, Mich.: African Studies Centre, Michigan State University)
Esoavelomandroso, M. (1979) *La Province maritime orientale du Royaume de Madagascar à la fin du XIXe siècle (1882–1895)* (Antananarivo: FT)
Fabb, J. (1987) *The British Empire from Photographs: Africa* (London: Batsford)
Fabian, J. (1986) *Language and Colonial Power: the Appropriation of Swahili in the Former Belgian Congo, 1880–1938* (Cambridge: Cambridge University Press)
Fanon, F. (1967) *The Wretched of the Earth* (Harmondsworth: Penguin)
Fashole-Luke, E., Gray, R., Hastings, A. and Tasie, G. (eds.) (1978) *Christianity in Independent Africa* (London: Rex Collings)
Feltz, G. (1985) 'Histoire des mentalités et histoire des missions au Burundi, *ca.* 1880–1960', *History in Africa*, XII, pp. 51–63
Fetter, B. (1983) *Colonial Rule and Regional Imbalance in Central Africa* (Boulder, Colo.: Westview Press)
Fieldhouse, D. K. (1981) *Colonialism 1870–1945: an Introduction* (London: Weidenfield and Nicolson)
Finer, S. F. (1962) *The Man on Horseback* (London: Pall Mall)
First, R. (1963) *South West Africa* (Harmondsworth: Penguin)
Gahama, J. (1984) *Le Burundi sous administration Belge* (Paris: Karthala)
Gailey, H. A. (1982) *Lugard and the Abeokuta Uprising: the Demise of Egba Independence* (London: Frank Cass)
Gallaway, H. (1987) *Gender, Culture and Empire: European Women in Colonial Nigeria* (Basingstoke: Macmillan)
Gann, L. H. and Duignan, P. (1967) *Burden of Empire* (London: Pall Mall)
Gann, L. H. and Duignan, P. (eds.) (1969) *Colonialism in Africa, 1870–1960*, Vol. 1, *The History and Politics of Colonialism 1870–1914* (Cambridge: Cambridge University Press)
Gann, L. H. and Duignan, P. (eds.) (1970) *Colonialism in Africa 1870–1960*, Vol. II, *The History and Politics of Colonialism 1914–1960* (Cambridge: Cambridge University Press)
Garvey, A. J. (ed.) (1923–5) *Philosophy and Opinions of Marcus Garvey* (London: Frank Cass, 1967 edn)
Garvey, A. J. (1963) *Garvey and Garveyism* (Kingston: United Printers)
Geiss, I. (1974) *The Pan-African Movement* (London: Methuen)
Gershoni, I. and Jankowski, J. P. (1987) *Egypt, Islam and the Arabs: the Search for Egyptian Nationhood 1900–1930* (New York: Oxford University Press)
Gifford, P. and Louis, W. R. (eds.) (1967) *Britain and Germany in Africa: Imperial Rivalry and Colonial Rule* (New Haven, Conn. and London: Yale University Press)
Gifford, P. and Louis, W. R. (eds.) (1971) *France and Britain in Africa* (New Haven, Conn. and London: Yale University Press)
Gilkes, P. (1975) *The Dying Lion: Feudalism and Modernization in Ethiopia* (London: Julian Friedmann)
Goglia, L. (1985) *Storia fotografica dell 'imperofacista 1935–41* (Bari: Editori Laterza)
Grassi, F. and Goglia, L. (eds.) (1981) *Il colonialismo italiano da Adua all 'impero* (Rome and Bari)
Greenhalgh, P. (1985) *West African Diamonds 1919–1983; an Economic History* (Manchester: Manchester University Press)
Gulgelberger, G. M. (1984) *Nama/Namibia: Diary and Letters of Nama Chief Hendrik Witbooi, 1884–1894* (Boston, Mass.: Boston University African Studies Centre)

Hallett, R. (1970) *Africa to 1875: a Modern History* (Ann Arbor, Mich.: Michigan University Press)

Hansen, H. B. (1984) *Mission, Church and State in a Colonial Setting: Uganda 1890-1925* (London: Heinemann)

Hargreaves, J. D. (1963) *Prelude to the Partition of West Africa* (London: Macmillan)

Herskovits, M. (1941) *The Myth of the Negro Past* (New York: Harper)

Hess, R. L. (1966) *Italian Colonialism in Somalia* (Chicago: Chicago University Press)

Hill, A. C. and Kilson, M. (eds.) (1971) *Apropos of Africa: Sentiments of Negro American Leaders on Africa from the 1800s to the 1950s* (New York: Anchor)

Hodges, G. (1987) *The Carrier Corps: Military Labor in the East African Campaign, 1914-1918* (Westport, Conn.: Greenwood Press Inc.)

Hodgkin, T. (1956) *Nationalism in Colonial Africa* (London: F. Muller)

Holt, P. M. (ed.) (1968) *Political and Social Change in Modern Egypt* (London: Oxford University Press)

Holt, P. M. (1970) *The Mahdist State in the Sudan, 1881-1898*, 2nd edn (Oxford: Clarendon Press)

Home, R. (1982) *City of Blood Revisited: a New Look at the Benin Expedition of 1897* (London: Rex Collings)

Hopkins, A. G. (1973) *An Economic History of West Africa* (London: Longman)

Hull, R. W. (1980) *Modern Africa: Change and Continuity* (Englewood Cliffs, NJ: Prentice Hall)

Ikime, O. (ed.) (1980) *Groundwork of Nigerian History* (Ibadan: Heinemann)

Iliffe, J. (1969) *Tanganyika under German Rule, 1905-1912* (Cambridge: Cambridge University Press)

Iliffe, J. (1979) *A Modern History of Tanganyika* (Cambridge: Cambridge University Press)

Isaacman, A. (1972) *Mozambique: the Africanization of a European Institution: the Zambesi Prazos, 1750-1902* (Madison Wis.: University of Wisconsin Press)

Isaacman, A. (1976) *The Tradition of Resistance in Mozambique: Anti-Colonial Activity in the Zambesi Valley, 1850-1921* (Berkeley, Calif.: University of California Press)

Isaacman, A. and Isaacman, B. (1983) *Mozambique: from Colonialism to Revolution* (Boulder, Colo.: Westview Press)

Issawi, C. P. (1963) *Egypt in Revolution: an Economic Analysis* (London: Oxford University Press)

Joseph, R. A. (1978) *Radical Nationalism in Cameroun: Social Origins of the UPC Rebellion* (Oxford: Oxford University Press)

July, R. W. (1968) *The Origins of Modern African Thought* (London: Faber)

Kabwegyere, T. B. (1974) *The Politics of State Formation* (Nairobi: East African Publishing House)

Kadalie, C. (1970) *My Life and the ICU: the Autobiography of a Black Trade Unionist in South Africa* (London: Frank Cass)

Kaddache, M. (1970) *La Vie politique à Alger de 1919 à 1939* (Algiers: Société national d'édition et de diffusion [SNED])

al-Kaddāl, M. S. (1973) *Al-Mahdiyya wal Habasha* (Khartoum)

Kaniki, M. H. Y. (ed.) (1980) *Tanzania under Colonial Rule* (London: Longman)

Kay, G. B. (ed.) (1972) *The Political Economy of Colonialism in Ghana: Documents 1900-1960* (Cambridge: Cambridge University Press)

Kelly, R. C. (1985) *The Nuer Conquest: the Structure and Development of an Expansionist System* (Ann Arbor, Mich.: University of Michigan Press)

Kent, R. K. (ed.) (1979) *Madagascar in History: Essays from the 1970s* (Berkeley, Calif.: Foundation for Malagasy Studies)

Keppel-Jones, A. (1983) *Rhodes and Rhodesia: the White Conquest of Zimbabwe, 1884-1902* (Kingston and Montreal: McGill-Queen's Unversity Press)

Killingray, D. (1984) 'A swift agent of government: airpower in British colonial Africa, 1916-1939', *Journal of African History*, XXV, pp. 429-44

Kimble, D. (1963) *A Political History of Ghana: the Rise of Gold Coast Nationalism 1850-1928* (Oxford: Clarendon Press)

Kopytoff, J. H. (1965) *A Preface to Modern Nigeria: the 'Sierra-Leoneans' in Yoruba 1830-1890* (Madison, Wis.: University of Wisconsin Press)

Lacheraf, M. (1965) *L 'Algérie: nation et société* (Paris: Maspero)

Langley, J. A. (1973) *Pan-Africanism and Nationalism in West Africa 1900-1945: A Study in Ideology and Social Classes* (Oxford: Clarendon Press)

Last, M. (1967) *The Sokoto Caliphate* (London: Longman)

Lee, E. (1985) *To the Bitter End: a Photographic History of the Boer War 1899-1902* (New York: Viking)

Leith-Ross, S. (1983) *Stepping-stones: Memoirs of Colonial Nigeria 1907-1960*, edited by M. Crowder (London and Boston: Peter Owen)

Levy, N. (1982) *The Foundations of the South African Cheap Labour System* (London: Routledge and Kegan Paul)

Lewis, I. M. (1965) _The Modern History of Somaliland: from Nation to State_ (London: Longman)
Leys, C. (1975) _Underdevelopment in Kenya: the Political Economy of Neo-colonialism, 1964–1971_ (London: James Currey)
Liebenow, J. G. (1969) _Liberia: the Evolution of Privilege_ (Ithaca, NY: Cornell University Press)
Liesegany, G., Pasch, H. and Jones, A. (1986) _Figuring African Trade: Proceedings of the Symposium on the Quantification and Structure of the Import and Export and Long Distance Trade in Africa, 1800–1913_ (Berlin: Dietrich Reimer Verlag)
Lloyd, P. C. (1972) _Africa in Social Change_, rev. edn (Harmondsworth: Penguin)
Louis, W. R. (1963) _Ruanda-Urundi, 1884–1919_ (Oxford: Clarendon Press)
Louis, W. R. (ed.) (1976) _Imperialism: the Robinson and Gallagher Controversy_ (New York: Franklin Watts)
Lovejoy, P. E. (1988) 'Concubinage and the status of women slaves in early colonial Northern Nigeria', _Journal of African History_, XXIX, pp. 245–66
Lubeck, P. M. (ed.) (1987) _The African Bourgeoisie: Capitalist Development in Nigeria, Kenya and the Ivory Coast_ (Boulder, Colo.: Lynne Reinner Publishers)
Lynch, H. R. (1967) _Edward Wilmot Blyden: Pan-Negro Patriot_ (London: Oxford University Press)
McCarthy, D. M. P. (1982) _Colonial Bureaucracy and Creating Underdevelopment: Tanganyika 1919–1940_ (Ames, Iowa: Iowa State University Press)
McCracken, J. (1978) _Politics and Christianity in Malawi 1875–1940: the Impact of the Livingstonia Mission in the Northern Province_ (Cambridge: Cambridge Commonwealth Series)
Mackenzie, J. M. (1984) _Propaganda and Empire: the Manipulation of British Public Opinion, 1880–1960_ (Manchester: Manchester University Press)
Macpherson, F. (1981) _Anatomy of a Conquest: the British Occupation of Zambia, 1884–1924_ (Harlow: Longman)
Makonnen, R. (1973) _Pan-Africanism from Within_ (Nairobi: Oxford University Press)
Manning, P. (1982) _Slavery, Colonialism and Economic Growth in Dahomey, 1640–1960_ (Cambridge: Cambridge University Press)
Marcum, J. (1969) _The Angolan Revolution_ (Cambridge, Mass.: Massachusetts Institute of Technology Press)
Marcus, H. G. (1975) _The Life and Times of Menelik II: Ethiopia 1844–1913_ (Oxford: Clarendon Press)
Marks, S. (1970) _Reluctant Rebellion: the 1906–1908 Disturbances in Natal_ (Oxford: Clarendon Press)
Marks, S. and Rathbone, R. (eds.) (1982) _Industrialization and Social Change in South Africa: African Class Formation, Culture and Consciousness 1870–1930_ (Harlow: Longman)
Maunier, R. (1949) _The Sociology of Colonies_, 2 vols (London: Routledge and Kegan Paul)
Mazrui, A. A. (1980) _The African Condition_ (London: Heinemann)
Mba, N. E. (1982) _Nigerian Women Mobilized: Women's Political Activity in Southern Nigeria 1900–1965_ (Berkeley, Calif.: Institute of International Studies)
Mbiti, J. S. (1969) _African Religions and Philosophy_ (London: Heinemann)
Meebelo, H. S. (1971) _Reaction to Colonialism: a Prelude to the Politics of Independence in Northern Zambia, 1893–1939_ (Manchester: Manchester University Press)
Meredith, D. (1984) 'Government and the decline of the Nigerian oil-palm export industry, 1919–1939', _Journal of African History_, XXV, pp. 311–29
Monti, N. (ed.) (1987) _Africa Then: Photographs 1840–1918_ (New York: Knopf)
Morikawa, J. (1985) 'The myth and reality of Japan's relations with colonial Africa – 1885–1960', _Journal of African Studies_, XII, 1, pp. 39–46
Mosley, L. (1964) _Haile Selassie: the Conquering Lion_ (London: Weidenfeld and Nicolson)
Mosley, P. C. (1983) _The Settler Economies: Studies in the Economic History of Kenya and Southern Rhodesia (1900–1963)_ (Cambridge: Cambridge University Press)
Mourão, F. A. A. (1977) _La Présence de la culture Africaine et la dynamique du processus social brésilien_ (Lagos: Colloquium)
Mugomba, A. and Nyaggah, M. (eds.) (1980) _Independence without Freedom: the Political Economy of Colonial Education in Southern Africa_ (Santa Barbara and Oxford: ABC–Clio Press)
Munro, J. F. (1975) _Colonial Rule and the Kamba_ (Oxford: Clarendon Press)
Munro, J. F. (1976) _Africa and the International Economy, 1800–1960_ (London: Dent)
Munro, J. F. (1984) _Britain in Tropical Africa, 1880–1960: Economic Relationships and Impact_ (London: Macmillan)
Muriuki, G. (1974) _A History of the Kikuyu, 1500–1900_ (Nairobi: Oxford University Press)
Mutibwa, P. M. (1974) _The Malagasy and the Europeans: Madagascar's Foreign Relations 1861–1895_ (London: Longman)
Newitt, M. D. D. (1981) _Portugal in Africa: the Last Hundred Years_ (London: C. Hurst)
Nkrumah, K. (1957) _Ghana: the Autobiography of Kwàme Nkrumah_ (London: Nelson)

Nzemeke, A. D. (1982) *British Imperialism and African Response: the Niger Valley, 1851-1905* (Paderborn: Schoningh)

Nzula, A. T., Potekhin, I. I. and Zusmanovich, A. Z. (1979) *Forced Labour in Colonial Africa* (London: Zed Press)

Obichere, B. I. (1971) *West African States and European Expansion: the Dahomey - Niger Hinterland, 1885-1898* (New Haven, Conn.: Yale University Press)

Ofcansky, T. P. (1986) 'The East African campaign in the *Rhodesian Herald*', *Journal of African Studies*, XIII, pp. 283-94

Ogot, B. A. (ed.) (1972) *War and Society in Africa* (London: Frank Cass)

Ogot, B. A. (ed.) (1974) *Zamani: a Survey of East African History* (Nairobi: East African Publishing House, 2nd edn)

Oliver, R. and Crowder, M. (1981) *The Cambridge Encyclopaedia of Africa* (Cambridge: Cambridge University Press)

Oliver, R. and Sanderson, G. N. (1985) *The Cambridge History of Africa: from 1870 to 1905*, Vol. VI (Cambridge: Cambridge University Press)

Olivier de Sardan, J. P. (1984) *Les Sociétés Songhay-Zarma (Niger-Mali): chefs, guerriers, esclaves, paysans* (Paris: Editions Karthala)

Olorunfemi, A. (1984) 'The contest for Salaga: Anglo-German conflict in the Gold Coast hinterland', *Journal of African Studies*, XI, 1, pp. 15-24.

Oloruntimehin, B. O. (1972) *The Segu Tukulor Empire* (London: Longman)

Omu, F. I. A. (1978) *Press and Politics in Nigeria, 1880-1957* (London: Longman)

Opoku, K. A. (1978) *West African Traditional Religion* (Singapore: FEP)

Osuntokun, J. (1978) *Nigeria in the First World War* (London: Longman)

O'Toole, T. (1984) 'The 1928-1931 Gbaya insurrection in Ubangui-Shari: messianic movement or village self-defense?' *Canadian Journal of African Studies*, XVIII, p. 2

Owen, R. and Sutcliffe, B. (eds.) (1972) *Studies in the Theory of Imperialism* (London: Longman)

Pachai, B. (ed.) (1972) *The Early History of Malawi* (London: Longman)

Pachai, B. (1978) *Land and Politics in Malawi, 1875-1975* (Kingston, Ont.: Limestone Press)

Packard, R. M. (1984) 'Maize, cattle and mosquitoes: the political economy of malaria epidemics in colonial Swaziland', *Journal of African History*, XXV, pp. 189-212

Padmore, G. (1956) *Pan-Africanism or Communism?* (London: Dobson)

Page, M. E. (ed.) (1987) *Africa and the First World War* (Basingstoke: Macmillan)

Pankhurst, R. (1968) *Economic History of Ethiopia, 1800-1935* (Addis Ababa: Haile Sellassie I University Press)

Parson, J. (1984) *Botswana: Liberal Democracy and the Labour Reserve in Southern Africa* (Boulder, Colo.: Westview Press)

Peel, J. D. Y. (1983) *Ijeshas and Nigerians: the Incorporation of a Yoruba Kingdom. 1890s-1970s* (Cambridge: Cambridge University Press)

Pélissier, R. (1977) *Les Guerres grises: résistance et révoltes en Angola (1845-1941)* (Orgeval: Éd. Pélissier)

Pélissier, R. (1984) *Naissance du Mozambique: résistance et révoltes anticoloniales (1854-1918)*, 2 vols (Orgeval: Pélissier)

Perham, M. (1960) *Lugard: the Years of Authority, 1898-1945* (London: Collins)

Perham, M. (1961) *The Colonial Reckoning* (London: Collins)

Perkins, K. J. (1981) *Qadis, Captains and Colons: French Military Administration in the Colonial Maghrib, 1844-1934* (New York: Africana Publishing Co.)

Perrings, C. (1979) *Black Mineworkers in Central Africa: Industrial Strategies and the Evolution of an African Proletariat in the Copperbelt, 1911-1941* (London: Heinemann)

Person, Y. (1968-75) *Samori: une révolution Dyula*, 3 vols (Paris:Mém. de l'Institut Fondamental de l'Afrique Noire)

Phimister, I. R. (1984) 'Accommodating imperialism: the compromise of the settler state in Southern Rhodesia, 1923-1929', *Journal of African History*, XXV, pp. 279-94

Phimister, I. R. and van Onselen, C. (1978) *Studies in the History of African Mine Labour in Colonial Zimbabwe* (Gwelo: Mambo Press)

Porter, B. (1986) *Imperialism and Popular Culture* (Manchester: Manchester University Press)

Prouty, C. (1986) *Empress Taytu and Menelik II: Ethiopia 1883-1910* (London: Ravens Educational and Development Services)

Ragsdale, J. P. (1986) *Protestant Mission Education in Zambia, 1880-1954* (Selinsgrove: Susquehanna University Press)

Ranger, T. O. (1967) *Revolt in Southern Rhodesia, 1896–1897* (London: Heinemann)

Ranger, T. O. (ed.) (1968) *Aspects of Central African History* (London: Heinemann)

Ranger, T. O. (ed.) (1968) *Emerging Themes of African History* (Nairobi: East African Publishing House)

Ratcliffe, B. M. (1981) 'The economics of the partition of Africa: methods and recent research trends', *Canadian Journal of African Studies*, XV, 1, pp. 3–32

Reyntjens, F. (1985) *Pouvoir et droit au Rwanda: droit public et évolution politique 1916–1973* (Tervuren: Musée royal de l'Afrique centrale, Belgium)

Rich, P. B. (1986) *Race and Empire in British Politics* (Cambridge: Cambridge University Press)

Robinson, R. and Gallagher, J. (1961) *Africa and the Victorians: the Official Mind of Imperialism* (London: Macmillan)

Rodney, W. (1972) *How Europe Underdeveloped Africa* (Dar es Salaam: Tanzania Publishing House)

Rodrigues, J. H. (1964) *Brasil e Africa outro Horizonte* (Rio de Janeiro: Civilizacão Brasileira)

Rosberg, C. G. and Nottingham, J. (1966) *The Myth of Mau Mau: Nationalism in Kenya* (Nairobi: East African Publishing House)

Ross, R. (ed.) (1982) *Racism and Colonialism: Essays on Ideological and Social Structure* (The Hague: Martinus Nijhoff)

Rotberg, R. I. (1966) *The Rise of Nationalism in Central Africa: the Making of Malawi and Zambia, 1873–1964* (Cambridge, Mass: Harvard University Press)

Rotberg, R. I. and Mazrui, A. A. (eds.) (1970) *Protest and Power in Black Africa* (New York: Oxford University Press)

Rout, L. B. (1976) *The African Experience in Spanish America, 1502 – Present Day* (Cambridge: Cambridge University Press)

Rubenson, S. (1964) *Wichale XVII: the Attempt to Establish a Protectorate over Ethiopia* (Addis Ababa: Haile Sellassie I University Press)

Rweyemamu, J. (1974) *Underdevelopment and Industralization in Tanzania: a Study in Perverse Capitalist Industrial Development* (London and Nairobi: Oxford University Press)

Saint-Martin, Y. (1972) *L'Empire toucouleur et la France: un demi-siècle de relations diplomatiques (1846–1893)* (Dakar: Publications de la Faculté des lettres et sciences humaines, Université de Dakar)

Sanderson, L. P. and Sanderson, N. (1981) *Education, Religion and Politics in Southern Sudan, 1899–1964* (London and Khartoum: Ithaca Press and Khartoum University Press)

Schreuder, D. M. (1980) *The Scramble for Southern Africa, 1877–1895: the Politics of Partition Reappraised* (Cambridge: Cambridge University Press)

Schneider, W. H. (1982) *An Empire for the Masses: the French Popular Image of Africa, 1870–1900* (Westport, Conn.: Greenwood Press)

Segal, R. and First, R. (1967) *South West Africa: Travesty of Trust* (London: André Deutsch)

Serman, W. (1982) *Les Officiers français dans la nation, 1848–1914* (Paris: Aubier Montaigne)

Shenton, R. W. (1986) *The Development of Capitalism in Northern Nigeria* (Toronto: University of Toronto Press)

Shepperson, G. and Price, T. (1958) *Independent African: John Chilembwe and the Origins, Setting and Significance of the Nyasaland Native Uprising of 1915* (Edinburgh: Edinburgh University Press)

Shibayka, M. (1978) *Al-Sudan wal Thawra al-Mahdiyya*, Vol. I (Khartoum)

Shibeika, M. (1952) *British Policy in the Sudan, 1882–1902* (London: Oxford University Press)

Shipley, D. (1980) *Black Africa and de Gaulle: from the French Empire to Independence* (London: Pennsylvania State University Press)

Sik, E. (1964) *The History of Black Africa*, Vol. II (Budapest: Akadémiai Kiadó)

Silberman, L. (n.d.) *The Mad Mullah: Hero of Somali Nationalism* (London)

Simons, H. J. and Simons, R. E. (1969) *Class and Colour in South Africa, 1850–1950* (Harmondsworth: Penguin)

Spacensky, A. (1970) *Madagascar, cinquante ans de vie politique: de Ralaimongo à Tsiranana* (Paris: Nouvelles Éditions Latines)

Spittler, G. (1981) *Verwaltung in einem afrikischen Bauernstaat: das Koloniale Französisch – Westafrika (1919–1939)* (Wiesbaden: Steiner)

Steinhart, E. I. (1978) *The Kingdoms of Western Uganda, 1890–1907* (Princeton: Princeton University Press)

Stevens, R. P. (1967) *Lesotho, Botswana and Swaziland* (New York: Praeger)

Stokes, E. and Brown, R. (eds.) (1966) *The Zambezian Past: Studies in Central African History* (Manchester: Manchester University Press)

Sundkler, B. G. M. (1961) *Bantu Prophets in South Africa*, 2nd edn (London: Oxford University Press)

Suret-Canale, J. (1964) *L'Afrique noire, l'ère coloniale, 1900–1945* (Paris: Éd. Sociales)

Suret-Canale, J. (1971) *French Colonialism in Tropical Africa, 1900–1945* (London: C. Hurst)

Symonds, R. (1986) *Oxford and Empire: the Last Lost Cause?* (Basingstoke: Macmillan)

Thompson, V. and Adloff, R. (1960) *The Emerging States of Equatorial Africa* (Stanford, Calif.: Stanford University Press)

Thompson, V. and Adloff, R. (1968) *Djibouti and the Horn of Africa* (Stanford, Calif.: Stanford University Press)

Tosh, J. (1978) *Clan Leaders and Colonial Chiefs in Lango: the Political History of an East African Stateless Society, c. 1800–1939* (Oxford: Clarendon Press)

Touval, S. (1963) *Somali Nationalism* (Cambridge, Mass.: Harvard University Press)

Turner, V. (ed.) (1971) *Colonialism in Africa 1870–1960* Vol. III, *Profiles of Change: African Society and Colonial Rule* (Cambridge: Cambridge University Press)

Turrell, R. V. (1987) *Capital and Labour and the Kimberley Diamond Fields 1871–1890* (Cambridge: Cambridge University Press)

Ukpabi, S. C. (1987) *Mercantile Soldiers in Nigerian History: a History of the Royal Niger Company Army, 1886–1900* (Zaria: Gaskiya Corporation)

Uzoigwe, G. N. (1974) *Britain and the Conquest of Africa: the Age of Salisbury* (Ann Arbor, Mich.: Michigan University Press)

Vail, L. and White, L. (1980) *Capitalism and Colonialism in Mozambique: a Study of Quelimane District* (London: Heinemann)

Van der Ross, R. E. (1986) *The Rise and Decline of Apartheid: a Study of Political Movements among the Coloured People of South Africa, 1880–1985* (Cape Town: Tafelberg)

Van Onselen, C. (1982) *Studies in the Social and Economic History of the Witwatersrand, 1886–1914*, 2 vols (Harlow: Longman)

Vansina, J. (1966) *Kingdoms of the Savanna* (Madison, Wis.: University of Wisconsin Press)

Vatikiotis, P. J. (1969) *The Modern History of Egypt* (London: Weidenfeld and Nicolson)

Verrier, A. (1986) *The Road to Zimbabwe* (London: Jonathan Cape)

Vickery, K. P. (1986) *Black and White in Southern Zambia: the Tonga Plateau Economy and British Imperialism, 1890–1939* (New York: Greenwood Press)

Webster, J. B. (1964) *The African Churches among the Yoruba, 1888–1922* (Oxford: Clarendon Press)

Webster, J. B. and Boahen, A. A. (1967) *The Revolutionary Years: West Africa since 1800* (London: Longman)

Weiskel, T. C. (1980) *French Colonial Rule and the Baule Peoples, 1889–1911* (Oxford: Clarendon Press)

Weiss, H. (1967) *Political Protest in the Congo* (Princeton, NJ: Princeton University Press)

Welch, C. E. (1966) *Dream of Unity: Pan-Africanism and Political Unification in West Africa* (Ithaca, NY: Cornell University Press)

Wickins, P. (1986) *Africa 1880–1980: an Economic History* (Cape Town: Oxford University Press)

Williams, W. L. (1982) *Black Americans and the Evangelization of Africa, 1877–1900* (Madison, Wis.: University of Wisconsin Press)

Wilson, H. S. (1978) *The Imperial Experience in Sub-Saharan Africa since 1870* (Oxford: Oxford University Press)

Wolff, R. D. (1974) *The Economics of Colonialism: Britain and Kenya, 1870–1930* (New Haven, Conn. and London: Yale University Press)

Worger, W. H. (1987) *South Africa's City of Diamonds: Mine Workers and Monopoly Capitalism in Kimberley, 1867–1895* (New Haven, Conn.: and London: Yale University Press)

Yoshida, M. (1984) *Agricultural Marketing Intervention in East Africa: a Study in the Colonial Origins of Marketing Policies, 1900–1965* (Tokyo: Institute of Developing Economics)

Young, C. (1965) *Politics in the Congo: Decolonization and Independence* (Princeton, NJ: Princeton University Press)

Yudelman, D. (1983) *The Emergence of Modern South Africa: State, Capital and the Incorporation of Organized Labour in the South African Gold Fields, 1902–1939* (Westport, Conn.: Greenwood Press)

Zayid, M. Y. (1965) *Egypt's Struggle for Independence* (Beirut: Khayats)

Zulfu, I. H. (1976) *Shikān Ta'rīkh Askarī Liḥamlat Al-Ganarāl Hicks* (Abu Dhabi)

Index